Flying Buccaneers

Flying Buccaneers

The Illustrated Story
of Kenney's Fifth Air Force

Steve Birdsall

WITH A FOREWORD BY GENERAL GEORGE C. KENNEY

COLOR ILLUSTRATIONS BY JOHN PRESTON
MAPS BY GRAHAM BIRDSALL

DOUBLEDAY & COMPANY, INC.
GARDEN CITY, NEW YORK
1977

Unless credited otherwise, all photographs in this book
are from the files of the United States Air Force.

Library of Congress Cataloging in Publication Data

Birdsall, Steve.
Flying buccaneers.

Bibliography: p. 303
Includes index.
1. World War, 1939–1945—Aerial operations,
American.   2. United States. Army Air Forces.
5th Air Force.   3. World War, 1939–1945—Pacific
Ocean.   I. Title.
D790.B473   940.54'26
ISBN: 0-385-03218-8
Library of Congress Catalog Card Number 77–74293

DESIGN BY M FRANKLIN-PLYMPTON

Contents

About eleven o'clock that night I called General MacArthur, who was quite concerned about this latest Jap expedition, and told him I hated to wake him up but it was "one down, four to go." He said, "Don't apologize for news like that. Call me any time you can tell me that you're making some more Japs walk the plank."

At midnight I called again. "Two down, three to go," I reported. "Nice work, buccaneer," he laughed.

—General George C. Kenney, remembering the night of November 24, 1942, when five enemy destroyers made the run from Rabaul to Buna.

Foreword

Flying Buccaneers should be in the library of everyone interested in the war in the Pacific. Steve Birdsall has done a thorough job of research from available American, Australian, and Japanese records and reports, but this is not a dry recitation of dates, casualty lists, victories and defeats. Of course such things have to be included in a history, but here they are enlivened by frequent quotations from participants in the air action which was so vital to the success of General MacArthur's strategy of bypassing strongly held positions and leaving them to "die on the vine."

This is a most interesting story of spectacular individual achievements by colorful air heroes and real flying leaders whose ground crews refused to leave their airplanes until they were ready for another mission and whose air crews would follow their leaders without question. The morale of the Fifth Air Force from the date of its organization in September 1942 to the end of hostilities was higher than anything I have seen in any of the three wars in which I have been involved.

The graphic descriptions of some of the major air actions, like the Battle of the Bismarck Sea, the wiping out of a whole Japanese air force at Wewak and Hollandia, the November 2, 1943, attack on Rabaul, and the defeat of repeated enemy attempts to bring supplies and reinforcements to their troops on the west coast of Leyte in the fall of 1944, are so vivid that one can almost hear the stutter of machine gun fire and the crash of bombs. The author makes it easy to visualize and understand the intensity and persistence of the Fifth Air Force attacks, which never slackened until the target was destroyed or neutralized.

There are the Medal of Honor winners—Bong, McGuire, Walker, Pease, Zeamer, Sarnoski, Kearby, Cheli, Wilkins, and Shomo—and there are others whose names are recalled whenever Fifth Air Force veterans get together. Besides Bong and McGuire you hear about other great fighter pilots like MacDonald, Robbins, and Lynch, bomber leaders McCullar, Benn, and Rogers, and the low-altitude "skip bombers," Larner, Henebry, Ellis, and Howe. There was that colorful, uninhibited improvising genius "Pappy" Gunn and, finally, a couple of Air Force commanders —tough, efficient operators who always looked after both their officers and enlisted men—named Whitehead and Wurtsmith.

As happens in every war, controversies arise. In the Pacific, enemy vessels, both naval and merchant marine, were the prime targets of surface naval vessels, submarines, and aircraft who vied with each other for credit for the destruction of Japanese shipping. The Battle of the Bismarck Sea invoked one of these controversies, but regardless of the fruitless arguments that took place as to the number of enemy ships destroyed and damaged, certain facts remain. First, the Japanese took heavy losses in personnel, naval and merchant marine shipping, aircraft, and supplies and failed in their mission of reinforcing Lae. Second, following this disaster, the Japanese abandoned all further attempts to supply or reinforce Lae with surface vessels.

A similar controversy sprang up over the results of the Fifth Air Force attack of November 2, 1943, on the shipping in Rabaul harbor. Once again, regardless of claims and counterclaims, the fact remains that, after the heavy attacks of October and early November 1943, the Japanese abandoned all attempts to supply or reinforce the Rabaul garrison and notified them to get along the best they could without reliance on outside sources.

This enormously readable and unmistakably authentic book is going to be hard to put down once you have started reading it.

General George C. Kenney,
USAF, Retired

I

The Turning Point

THE two American generals stood in an office on the eighth floor of an insurance building in the city of Brisbane, Australia. One was the majestic Douglas MacArthur, who had come to Australia with the taste of defeat still particularly bitter in his mouth. In the morning of March 17, 1942, the Flying Fortress carrying the general and his family had reached Batchelor Field, near Darwin. A few hours later he had written a brief release to the press on the back of an envelope:

"The President of the United States ordered me to break through the Japanese lines and proceed from Corregidor to Australia for the purpose, as I understand it, of organizing the American offensive against Japan, a primary objective of which is the relief of the Philippines. I came through and I shall return."

When he had been instructed to leave the Philippines, MacArthur had believed he was coming to take command of a great avenging army. Now it was the end of July, and still much of the news was bad.

The other man in the office that day was Major General George C. Kenney, who had been sent from the United States to pick up the pieces of MacArthur's Allied Air Forces.

Five feet six inches tall, George Churchill Kenney was born in Nova Scotia on August 6, 1889, the son of an old Massachusetts family. He attended school in Brookline, then went on to the Massachusetts Institute of Technology until 1911. His interest in airplanes began when he saw a Blériot flying over Boston Harbor, and he and two friends proceeded to build an airplane which, although it taxied extremely well, rarely flew more than a few hundred yards. When the United States entered World War I Kenney naturally joined the Air Corps, and went to war for the first time with seventeen hours of flying experience. In seventy-five missions he shot down two German planes, and ended that war as a captain.

For the next twenty years he was involved in aeronautical development as he worked his way up to the rank of lieutenant colonel. He served as commanding officer of the Air Corps Experimental Division and Engineering School at Wright Field in 1939, and the next year he went to France as a military observer.

In January 1941 Kenney went straight to the rank of brigadier general, and to major general thirteen months later. He was given command of the Fourth Air Force, a training organization on the West Coast, until early in July 1942, when he was called to Washington by General Henry H. Arnold. There he learned he was going to Australia. It seemed General MacArthur was not happy with the performance of his air forces, commanded by Lieutenant General George H. Brett, and Kenney's name had been selected from a list of possible replacements.

The general with the close-cropped gray hair and dark blue eyes was a confident, able man who knew his aircraft and had his own ideas about how they should be used. Particularly close to his heart was the tactical concept broadly described as "attack aviation." Kenney had mounted the first Browning machine guns in the wing of an airplane back in 1922 and he thought up the parachute bomb for use in low-level attack in 1928, and as the Fifth's "parafrags," this particular idea was to prove invaluable. He also had the ability to get the best from his men, coupled with a genius for selecting the right people for the right job. The kind of people he valued most were those he called "operators"—officers able to carry out his plans with an independence and reliability based on mutual respect and understanding.

General Kenney reached Australia at sundown on July 28. It was now July 29, and for thirty minutes he had listened to General MacArthur criticize the air force until "finally there was nothing left but an inefficient rabble of boulevard shock troops." Pacing the office, MacArthur even hinted that there could be an element of disloyalty in his air officers. Kenney listened patiently until he felt the time was right to say a few words himself. When the opportunity came, he reminded MacArthur that he knew how to run an air force as well as or better than anybody else, and that he intended to correct whatever was wrong with this one. As far as loyalty went, he had always been loyal to his commanders and if he felt he could no longer offer that he would ask to be sent somewhere else. Kenney was brief and to the point and the initial stage of the meeting ended with a more amiable MacArthur saying, "George, I think we are going to get along together all right."

The two generals then got down to the hard facts of the situation facing them as the rest of the discussion took a completely different turn. MacArthur briefed Kenney on the current situation and the plans for the immediate future.

MacArthur explained that while there were many people talking about the possibility of surrendering the top half of Australia to the Japanese and falling back to fight for the more populous and valuable southern areas, he felt that New Guinea could be held. Keeping open the line of communications between Australia and the United States was absolutely vital, and if the Japanese were allowed to capture the islands still in Allied hands, this line would be cut.

Over to the southeast of Rabaul, New Britain, the Solomon Islands lay scattered over six hundred miles, from Buka in the north to San Cristobal in the south—the stepping stones to the New Hebrides and Fiji Islands. The Japanese realized the Solomons were essential in their defense of New Britain, and almost immediately after they had captured Rabaul in January 1942 and Kavieng on nearby New Ireland, they had begun to reach down into the Solomons.

By early April they had occupied Buka, Bougainville, and other points in the Shortland Islands area. They moved to Tulagi, off Florida Island, where they were

Star Dust, the 9th Fighter Squadron P-40 flown by Captain Andrew Reynolds. The 49th Group shot down fifteen Zeros and bombers on August 23, 1942, and between April and August had destroyed over sixty enemy aircraft as they won control of the daylight skies over Darwin. Reynolds was the leading ace in Kenney's new air force, with ten victories. (Australian War Memorial)

attacked by USS *Yorktown*'s aircraft in the first engagement of the Battle of the Coral Sea, on May 4. Tactically a draw, that battle was a major strategic victory, thwarting a seaborne invasion of Port Moresby. However, it seemed the Japanese plan favored a different route south—the island of New Britain curved down toward the Huon Peninsula of New Guinea, separated from it by the Vitiaz Strait, and from there the enemy had moved southeast along the northern coast of New Guinea. Enemy airfields on New Britain were located well within the range of Australian outposts, particularly Lae and Salamaua, on the Huon Gulf. Both had fallen in March, and by May 1942, enemy forces had been one hundred and seventy miles from Port Moresby, the last major Allied position in New Guinea.

Port Moresby, the main harbor of eastern New Guinea, lies in the shadow of the towering Owen Stanley mountains and was the key to stopping the Japanese. From Moresby tracks led back into the jungle and the mountains, which form a rugged spine, rising to a height of over two miles, along primitive New Guinea. Of most importance was the Kokoda Trail, which wound through thick jungle up to a pass known as The Gap, and coursed through the rugged mountains at heights between five and eight thousand feet, ending just short of Kokoda, site of an Australian outpost halfway between Moresby and the former government station at Buna, on the north coast. On the northern side of the Owen Stanleys, the mountain rivers drained into swamps streaked by sluggish, muddy rivers, and wild jungle or tall green kunai grass cloaked the land. There were no railways in New Guinea, and the villages were linked by tracks which quickly degenerated to slippery ruts after heavy rain. The island relied upon transport and communication by sea and air and the principal villages such as Lae, Salamaua, Buna, and Wau all had serviceable airstrips.

MacArthur went on to explain to Kenney the threefold nature of the task he had been given. Washington had decided that the Pacific would be an American strategic responsibility, and in April the Joint Chiefs of Staff had agreed to create the Southwest Pacific Area under MacArthur, while dividing the huge Pacific Ocean Area, which was commanded by Admiral Chester W. Nimitz, into the North, Central, and South Pacific. They doubtless knew the Navy did not like MacArthur but felt there could be benefits from any competition arising between MacArthur and Nimitz—as long as Japan suffered by it. It had been decided that Germany was to be beaten first, and although MacArthur sincerely believed this policy was incorrect, it would never change throughout the sometimes bitter arguments that followed.

The South Pacific Theater met the Southwest Pacific Area east of the Solomons and was charged with defending the island links between Australia and Hawaii. It was a complicated situation. MacArthur had originally wanted to assault Rabaul by way of the northeast coast of New Guinea, and Rabaul was certainly the hub of the threat to both Australia and the South Pacific islands, but the Navy was not ready to commit its forces in supporting action between New Guinea and the Japanese-held Solomon Islands. They had suggested instead the capture of the lower Solomons by South Pacific forces, with the Southwest Pacific in support. That way the approach to Rabaul would be up through the Solomons with the main responsibility going to the naval command in the South Pacific. Even so, command had been complicated because parts of the lower Solomons were actually in the Southwest Pacific Area. The Navy obviously anticipated that the opera-

An out-of-gas Martin Marauder slides to a stop at Seven Mile strip. In late July and August the missions to Lae, Salamaua, and closer to Port Moresby were almost the sole responsibility of the 22nd Group's Marauders and the 3rd Attack's B-25s, although during August there were never more than twenty-seven B-26s and a dozen Mitchells in commission. (Australian War Memorial)

tion would be launched from the South Pacific and that Vice-Admiral Robert Ghormley, the theater commander, would run it. By late June the Navy in Washington had proposed this, and Ghormley was to command until the capture of Santa Cruz and Tulagi had been achieved. Then MacArthur would take over leadership of a major effort against Rabaul.

A compromise had been found and the immediate plan had been divided into three phases. First, the lower Solomons were to be occupied by South Pacific forces with help from MacArthur. Then the northeastern coast of New Guinea was to be reoccupied, and the upper Solomons were to be captured. The final phase would be the invasion of New Britain, and that was to be MacArthur's main responsibility.

General MacArthur had realized he had to beat the enemy to northern coastal positions on New Guinea if the second phase was to be successfully accomplished. His ground forces needed training, and his air and naval forces were considered inadequate. However, the Joint Chiefs did not want to postpone the tentative schedule, which they had built around the beginning of August, because requirements in other areas could delay the provision of forces to complete the second and third phases of the plan. MacArthur was forced to prepare as best he could for the second, while assisting in the first. That deprived him of badly needed naval support, but his air involvement in the first phase was less of a problem. Reconnaissance and attacks on Rabaul were the main requirement and extremely important to both commands. If there was to be a battle for the northeastern coast of New Guinea, airfield sites were also vitally important, and Major Karl Polifka's 8th Photo Squadron had carried out surveys which showed there was an excellent location for an airstrip near Buna, at the mouth of the Giriwu River. On July 15 Major General Richard K. Sutherland, MacArthur's Chief of Staff, had announced plans for the occupation of Buna by way of the Kokoda Trail, and engineers were sent to Milne Bay on the southeastern tip of New Guinea to develop airfields there to enable Allied control of the approaches around New Guinea to the Coral Sea. Four days after Sutherland's announcement, the Australians were halfway across the mountains, moving toward Buna.

On July 21 at about the same time as Kenney was leaving Hamilton Field, California, the Japanese landed in force just north of Buna and won the race against time. Though the Battle of the Coral Sea had stopped the seaborne invasion of Port Moresby, the Japanese army had made its own plans to take the town by an overland route which would bring them swarming in from the rear. They believed their only real opposition would be the natural barriers, and expected the crossing to be made relatively easily.

There had been indications that the enemy landing was imminent—captured documents had revealed that a convoy had sailed from Truk on July 10, bound for eastern New Guinea. A 19th Group B-17 had reported shipping around Rabaul on July 19, and the Japanese bombed Port Moresby the following day. By July 21 it was reported that a cruiser, four destroyers, a transport, and other smaller craft were heading for Buna. During that afternoon a floatplane shot up the shore, and then the warships blasted the almost undefended beaches. The Australian advance party, coming along the Kokoda Trail, was still at least three days away. Only the Allied Air Forces were within striking distance, and any real opposition had to come from them.

But the Japanese had already succeeded—four or five thousand men had been put ashore. Allied air attacks had killed some troops and damaged some shipping, but the development of airstrips in the Buna area would strengthen the Japanese hold on New Guinea, and Port Moresby was seriously threatened. The enemy immediately began moving along the track toward Kokoda and they were twelve to fifteen miles inland by the afternoon of July 22, and pressing the Australian defenders of Kokoda four days later.

The campaign began with a Japanese thrust which brought them uncomfortably close to Port Moresby.

It seemed General Kenney had joined this particular battle at the turning point . . .

MacArthur then outlined the forthcoming Marine Corps invasion of Tulagi and Guadalcanal in the Solomons, due to take place on August 7. MacArthur was required to provide air and naval support, and asked Kenney what help he thought the Allied Air Forces could provide. Kenney first wanted to see what he really had to offer, and left the office to find out.

When Kenney went over to Charters Towers to see the 3rd Attack Group he found they were a "snappy, good looking outfit." With Colonel "Big Jim" Davies (hand on hip, at back) looking on, B-25 crews receive last-minute instructions before an early August mission. Originally equipped with a mixture of A-20s, A-24s, and B-25s, the 3rd Attack became the spearhead of the Fifth's minimum-altitude operations.

"The Goddamest Mess You Ever Saw"

General Brett introduced Kenney to his staff, and to the Allied Air Forces' way of doing things. To Kenney it was "the goddamest mess you ever saw," with numerous people issuing orders in the commander's name. Kenney never admitted to fully understanding this complex "directorate" system, and its days were numbered. The liberal mixture of Australian and American staff, while underlining the Allied nature of the effort, also seemed a questionable idea.

Kenney found that Brett had not had much luck, and he was certainly unpopular with MacArthur's staff. Although only three floors away from MacArthur's office in Brisbane, Brett had only seen him eight times in four months. Sutherland and Brett simply did not get along, and it was Sutherland with whom Brett was usually forced to deal. An antagonism toward MacArthur's headquarters extended down through Allied Air Forces and as far as the combat units. A bitterly disappointed man, MacArthur had surrounded himself with officers who had served with him in the Philippines. His Chief of Staff, the devoted and autocratic Richard Sutherland, was generally disliked, and this tended to increase the isolation of MacArthur's supreme headquarters from his three subordinate commands: Vice-Admiral Herbert Leary's Allied Naval Forces, General Sir Thomas Blamey's Allied Land Forces, and Brett's Allied Air Forces. As time passed, the ebullient Kenney would build a close and warm relationship with MacArthur, radically altering this situation, but these were early days.

After looking over the situation, Kenney decided his top priority would be to get rid of the "deadwood" and replace it with operators. With this in mind he inquired about two brigadier generals, Kenneth N. Walker and Ennis C. Whitehead, who had been sent to Australia before him. Kenney had plans for them.

Borrowing George Brett's old B-17D, *The Swoose,* Kenney took off to look over his domain. At the northern Australian bomber bases he found the same complex Allied structure, but decided to see how it was working before changing it. Picking up General Whitehead in Townsville, *The Swoose* took to the air again and droned toward New Guinea . . .

In the very early morning the B-17 touched down at Seven Mile strip, just north of Port Moresby township. The airstrip was defended by a couple of squadrons of Bell Airacobras, the 80th Squadron of the 8th Fighter Group and the 41st Squadron of the 35th Fighter Group. The P-39s had been meeting the Japanese with mixed success: although the pilots were openly critical of the performance of their aircraft compared to the nimble, fast Japanese fighters, they were rugged. The 39th Squadron, which had just left after almost two months in New Guinea, had scored a dozen victories and had nine of their own planes shot down, but all the pilots managed to survive and only one had been seriously injured after a high-speed bail-out.

Kenney found another complicated situation at Port Moresby. The Director of Bombardment back at Townsville in Australia assigned the missions, then the instructions were passed on to the 19th Bomb Group, flying B-17s from Mareeba, an airstrip a couple of hundred miles north of Townsville, and the 19th sent whatever Fortresses were operational up to New Guinea, where they were refueled and the crews briefed for their mission. Although the continuing raids on Port Moresby more than justified the caution of basing the bombers in Australia, it also meant that a mission took the B-17s away from their home bases at Townsville for thirty-six to forty-eight hours, including about eighteen hours in the air, which was hard on the crews.

The fighters at Port Moresby waited until the Japanese were coming over, and were rarely able to reach the altitude of their attackers in the available time. In the nine raids during July the Airacobras had been able to engage the enemy bombers only four times. After watching a midday air raid, in which only ten of the forty fighters got into the air before the Japanese arrived, Kenney was convinced the situation, overall, just could not get much worse.

The following afternoon he flew to Mareeba to look over his heavy bomber group, the 19th, commanded by Lieutenant Colonel Richard Carmichael. Some of

Lieutenant Norb Ruff leans against a shark-mouthed P-400 Airacobra of the 80th Fighter Squadron at Port Moresby. Originally the 8th Group was equipped with P-39s, while the 35th Group had P-400s, the export version of the Airacobra, but after a few months of operations in New Guinea the types were liberally mixed and pilots flew what was available. The squadrons of these two groups provided the Port Moresby fighter defense, rotating between New Guinea and Australia; when the 80th and 41st moved up in July 1942, they took over some aircraft which were already there, so this Airacobra actually carried a 35th Squadron number and yellow tip on the tail. (Norbert Ruff)

the 19th crews, who had been fighting a grudging retreat since December 1941, had a little too much combat experience, and more than half of their B-17s were out of commission because they lacked engines or tail wheels. The officers complained that when they requested the equipment they needed, the requisition generally came back about a month later with a notation that what they wanted was not available, or that the form was not correctly filled out. This sounded like an alibi to Kenney until he was shown a stack of requisition forms which had been returned. He grabbed a handful as evidence that some people were "playing on the wrong team" and told Carmichael to cancel all flying and get to work on the B-17s because a big mission was coming up in about a week.

Back in Brisbane, the second meeting with MacArthur lasted for two hours as

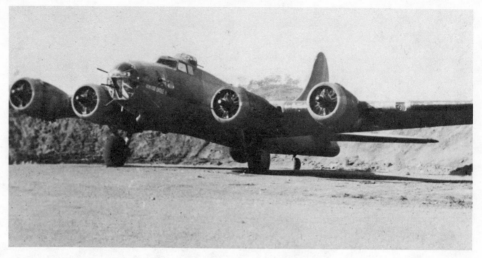

The early B-17Es of the 19th Group were the backbone of Kenney's bomber strength and provided his long-range reconnaissance. When the 19th went home in November surviving Forts were handed down to the 43rd if they were not too war-weary. This one, *Honikuu Okole,* served with distinction in the 64th Squadron until she finally went down over Rabaul on May 21, 1943. One man survived the crash and was rescued after living with New Britain natives for nearly nine months. (E. P. Stevens)

Kenney explained his feelings about how things could be improved. As his first job, he wanted to knock out the Japanese air force in New Guinea, because after seeing the Port Moresby operation he knew "there was no use talking about playing across the street until we got the Nips off our front lawn."

Kenney said that he had grounded all his bombers so they could be spruced up for a big mission, and that on about August 6 he would support the Solomons invasion by sending the Fortresses against Vunakanau airdrome, just southeast of the town of Rabaul. At the same time his B-25s and B-26s, escorted by fighters, would strike the enemy airfields at Buna, Salamaua, and Lae, the beginning of an effort which would not cease until the Japanese no longer had air power in New Guinea. Everything else Kenney had would be thrown into support of the Australians fighting on the Kokoda Trail.

MacArthur liked the optimism of the plans, and approved. When Kenney talked of sixteen or eighteen B-17s over Rabaul he was impressed, and remarked that it would be the biggest heavy bomber strike yet flown in the theater.

* * *

On August 4 General Kenney officially took command of the Allied Air Forces and that morning reconnaissance showed about one hundred and fifty Japanese aircraft, most of them bombers, at Vunakanau. The marked increase in strength there led Kenney to believe the Japanese might be expecting the American move in the Solomons and he told MacArthur that he would send the maximum B-17 force over there on the morning of August 7 to keep them away from Guadalcanal. The next day he flew up to Mareeba to talk with Carmichael and the 19th Group about the mission. The sheer magnitude of the strike impressed them, and Kenney shud-

The 22nd was the first Marauder group in the Army Air Forces, and one of their planes was the third B-26 to roll off Martin's production line. In the early days they had ranged as far as Rabaul, and they were in the forefront of attempts to stop the Japanese at Buna. (Australian War Memorial)

dered when somebody said something about not being used to flying "in such large numbers together." Kenney had already seen six B-17s take sixty minutes to get into the air at Moresby and he reminded the 19th that those days were now over.

In the afternoon of August 5 he went to Charters Towers, south of Townsville, to look over Colonel John Davies' 3rd Attack Group. They were equipped with a grab bag of planes which included A-24 Dauntlesses, A-20s, and some B-25 Mitchells. The A-24, simply an Army version of the Navy's Douglas Dauntless, was lightly armed and the pilots never liked flying it without fighter cover. However, it was slow to the point that fighters could not meander around it and give it continuous protection, even on average missions to targets in northeast New Guinea. The crews had suffered heavy losses in the vulnerable A-24, and when seven of them had taken off a week before to hit a convoy, only one, piloted by Lieutenant Raymond H. Wilkins, got back to Moresby. After this shattering mission the A-24s were withdrawn from combat, and the 8th Squadron would not be ready to fight again for more than five months.

Kenney found the 3rd was a "snappy, good looking outfit," but they had

The 3rd Attack's *Algonquin* at Port Moresby in the fall of 1942. These early B-25Cs, equipped with a single nose gun, were vulnerable to Japanese fighter attack, but soon became the most potent weapon in Kenney's arsenal.

problems—their A-20s had arrived in Australia without guns or bomb racks, and the B-25s, defended by only one nose gun, were not popular with the crews, who had to face the head-on attacks of the Zeros. Kenney added this to his mental notes.

* * *

The decision to move into Guadalcanal on August 7 was a fortunate one for the Allies. The Japanese had been speeding up work on their airfield there and aircraft were scheduled to move in that very day. Shortly after nine o'clock the 1st Marine Division began to go ashore, after landings had been made at Tulagi an hour earlier.

That morning sixteen B-17s of the 19th Group, led by Lieutenant Colonel Richard H. Carmichael, took off from Moresby. One Fortress crashed on takeoff and two turned back with mechanical troubles, but thirteen got through to attack Vunakanau airstrip. Japanese fighters attacked forty or fifty miles from the target, loosening the formation, but the B-17s held together and went over the target at twenty-two thousand feet. The harbor below was full of ships and the antiaircraft fire was heavy. In Carmichael's plane a crewman was wounded and the oxygen system was shot out, forcing him to take his plane down to a lower level. The rest of the B-17s followed into thickening cloud.

In the Fortress piloted by Captain Harl Pease, a bad engine had cut out near the target. Pease kept on going but after the bombing the B-17 with a feathered engine was singled out quickly by the fighters. The bomb bay tank in Pease's plane was set afire and seen dropping into the sea and then the B-17 burst into flame and fell. One tail gunner had seen Pease jettison the burning tank, another gunner thought he had seen a B-17 wing fall, another thought he saw a Fortress hit the water, but nothing more was ever heard of Pease or his crew. The previous day Pease had returned to Mareeba from a recon mission with an engine out on his aircraft, and to get in on the big Rabaul strike he and his crew had worked for hours on another unserviceable plane. They had not arrived at Moresby until after midnight. There was still a bad engine on their plane and no electric fuel pump, but Pease had borrowed a hand pump from the crew of Major Felix Hardison's *Suzy-Q* and gone along.

After an hour the weather cleared again and nine planes reached Moresby. The 19th was in high spirits and by the time the first crews had passed through the intelligence officers' questioning three more B-17s had landed. But there was still one missing, and Captain Harl Pease became the first of Kenney's airmen to receive the Congressional Medal of Honor.

It was difficult to judge the effect of the mission but the B-17s claimed good bombing and the destruction of seven of the intercepting fighters. Kenney concluded from enemy radio reports intercepted over the following days that a considerable number of the bombers had been put out of action. The Marines had landed at Guadalcanal with little opposition, although their hold would be tenuous for a considerable time.

The Fifth Air Force

Within a week Kenney had seen enough to convince him he should form an American air force, and separate the Australians and Americans. He asked Washington for permission to authorize this on August 7, and two days later approval came through.

At the outset the Fifth was a normal American air force, as Kenney began building his team of "operators." Brigadier General Kenneth N. Walker, an intense, stubborn expert in bomber aviation, took over Fifth Bomber Command at Townsville, and there was a Services Command, under Major General Rush B. Lincoln. When Lieutenant Colonel Paul Wurtsmith called in at Brisbane to see Kenney, he was promised Fifth Fighter Command—Wurtsmith's best recommendation was the performance of his 49th Fighter Group, and in fact theirs was a very bright page in the early record. The Curtiss P-40s they flew lacked the performance and agility of the Japanese fighters, particularly at high altitude, and at first this had affected morale, although they knew that their aircraft could absorb more punishment, did not catch fire as easily, and could dive away from a Zero. In fact, if they were able

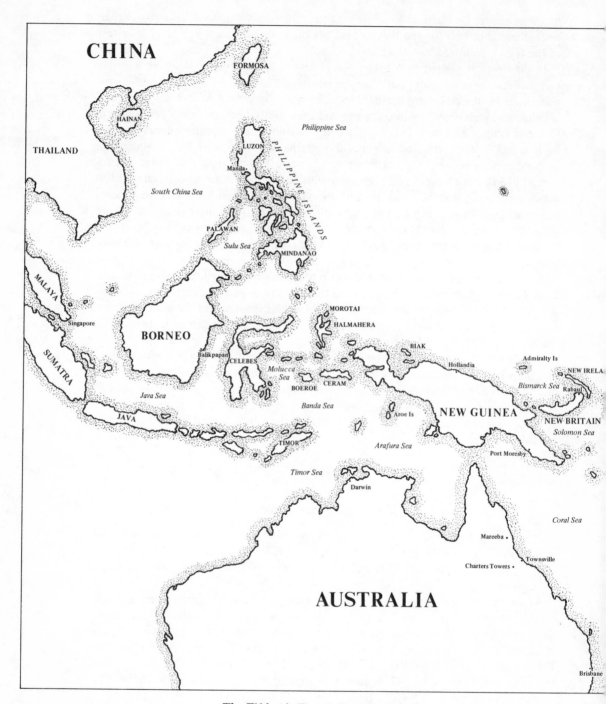

The Fifth Air Force's huge battlefield.

Lieutenant Robert McCompsey's P-40E, from the 9th Fighter Squadron. The 49th Group pilots used the sturdy fighter to advantage, never attacking Zeros unless they were as high or higher, and had speed. Clay Tice says, "Unless we had lots of altitude we didn't stick around in circle combat too long, in fact no more than a half turn or so. The Zero could outclimb us, outturn us, and outrun us at altitude. We could outdive and outrun on the deck only. We could take punishment; he couldn't." (Australian War Memorial)

to get sufficient warning to enable them to reach the Japanese fighters, they could do well, as they did in the afternoon of July 30 over Darwin when twenty-seven P-40s destroyed six Zeros and three bombers for one loss. Their P-40s had scored their first four victories back on March 14, and the 49th Group had destroyed over sixty enemy planes. One of their pilots, Captain Andrew Reynolds, was the leading ace in the theater, with ten victories.

To Kenney, Wurtsmith looked like a "partially reformed bad boy," but he decided to send him up to Port Moresby with the 49th, and if he made good, he would become a general and run Fifth Fighter Command. That promise would be made good on November 11.

Although better than the intricate "directorate" organization, the standard air force setup was just not flexible enough for the demands of the theater. Kenney's responsibility, as commander of both the Fifth and Allied Air Forces, made it necessary for him to operate from Brisbane, a thousand miles south of the New Guinea battle front. All the heavy and medium bombers were still necessarily based in Australia and staging through Moresby, and there appeared little hope of avoiding the "horrible handicap" of operations from advanced bases for some time, at least until the Japanese air forces were beaten down.

General Ennis Whitehead, commander of Advon, Fifth Air Force. (Roger Beaty)

Kenney's answer to the problem was Brigadier General Ennis C. Whitehead, an experienced fighter commander who was inexhaustible, demanding, and tough. He had the coldest blue eyes Kenney had ever seen, and he was the kind of person who only liked to have to say things once. He got things moving, kept them moving, and was always in touch with the details—if somebody was not giving his all, Whitehead soon found out about it. He believed the way to win was to never ease up the pressure. So Whitehead was made deputy commander and placed in command of the Fifth Air Force, Advanced Echelon, at Port Moresby. Abbreviated to Advon, this was a small advanced headquarters free of most of the administrative details in favor of the immediate direction of operations. Operating with "a minimum of attention to personal amenities for himself," as one history records, Whitehead would receive general directives from Brisbane but he had complete control over the aircraft implementing them from New Guinea. The Fifth Air Force itself and its various commands would take care of the rest.

Kenney had been curious regarding how many aircraft his Allied Air Forces had and when the report arrived on the desk it looked good. There were 245 American fighters, 53 light bombers, 70 medium bombers, 62 heavy bombers, 36 transports, and 51 miscellaneous types—517 aircraft in all.

The bad news was that 170 of the fighters were ready for salvage or being overhauled. None of the light bombers were ready to fight, and only 37 mediums were fitted with guns and bomb racks. Of the 62 heavies, 19 were being overhauled or rebuilt. There were nineteen different types of aircraft under the transport heading, less than half were flying, and they were already heavily com-

General Paul Wurtsmith, new leader of the Fifth's fighters, sits down to talk with Colonel Richard Legg of the 35th Fighter Group. (Charles King)

mitted to compensating for a lack of transportation in the theater. The Australians had twenty-two squadrons, but most were not equipped with first-line aircraft. Kenney found he really had about 150 American and 70 Australian aircraft, scattered all over his map.

The new Fifth Air Force still had only the partly equipped 3rd Attack Group, the 8th, 35th, and 49th Fighter Groups, the 19th, 22nd, 38th, and 43rd Bomb Groups, and the 21st and 22nd Troop Carrier Squadrons. Colonel Dwight Divine's 22nd Group had gone into action with Martin Marauders in April, and difficulties in maintenance were becoming more and more aggravating. The 38th Group did not have its planes and two of its squadrons were actually assigned to the neighboring South Pacific Theater, and Kenney did not even learn he had a 43rd Bomb Group until he had been in Australia nearly two weeks—it had no aircraft at all.

After Guadalcanal deliveries of new aircraft became even more uncertain. Although MacArthur had been given a "general schedule" of deliveries promising fifty-six heavy bombers over the three months from June to August, only forty-six arrived, and that was the best result. Of sixty-two mediums, fifty arrived. None of the forty promised A-20s turned up. The South Pacific's authority to divert aircraft on the way to Kenney caused more problems. This was only to be done in extreme emergency, but these emergencies were costly to the Fifth, and Kenney felt he should have a part in evaluating what was an emergency in the neighboring theater. The shipment of thirty P-39s from Australia to New Caledonia was the largest "diversion," but Kenney also lost B-17s, P-38s, and the invaluable C-47s.

Looking at those numbers in August, Kenney had more aircraft than the Japanese, but as he wrote to Arnold later, "the Jap is two days from the factory to the combat zone and he may swarm all over me." In essence, it was Kenney's lot to keep what he had flying. Battle damage was only one of the reasons why aircraft were struck off the list—crude airfields, battering storms, shortage of parts . . . the Fifth had problems. In August Kenney told Washington how they kept the B-17s flying in his new air force: "we are salvaging even the skin for patchwork from twenty-millimeter explosive fire; to patch up smaller holes we are flattening out tin cans . . ."

Struggle for Buna

As the battle for Buna began in earnest, the air forces served in a number of roles. The Fortresses were searching for convoys supporting the Japanese, and on July 28 transports had been seen moving south from St. George's Channel. They were sighted again the following day, and B-17s, A-24s, and RAAF Catalinas and Hudsons went out to oppose the landing. A formation of Fortresses reported direct hits on a transport but again the enemy landed and on August 13 still more troops got through, although the B-17s and B-26s tried to stop them.

The Australians lost the Kokoda airstrip on August 16, and the enemy air force continued to break through, raiding Port Moresby for the seventy-eighth time on August 17, when strings of bombs demolished buildings and parked aircraft. Three 22nd Group Marauders were destroyed as well as a transport, and eight more planes were damaged. There was a terrible feeling of frustration and impotence as precious airplanes burned to ashes on the ground. The 22nd Group B-26 *So Sorry II* was fully loaded with bombs that morning and the crew was standing around the aircraft when the white flag was raised, signaling an incoming raid. The pilot, Captain Gerald Crosson, told his men to get aboard, and taxied the plane down the strip. He was halfway along the runway when a bomb hit twenty feet in front of *So Sorry II* . . .

Crosson felt "the heavens bounce down and the world turned black. I didn't know whether I had been hit. I turned around and saw tongues of flame licking along the inside of the fuselage toward the bomb bay. I tried to get up from my seat, but I was too weak to make it. I rolled over and fell on my hands and knees. I crawled to the escape hatch and dropped to the ground. The rest of the crew

Bombing up a 19th Bomb Group B-17E at Port Moresby in August 1942. The ball turret on this aircraft has been removed and replaced with hand-held fifties. In Java the 19th had operated from sod fields which were often so wet that the ball turrets would be covered with mud on takeoff, and unless the aircraft could find a rainstorm to fly through the turrets were rendered useless.

were scattering for cover. I looked down and saw blood. The sight made something click in my mind. My co-pilot had been sitting next to me when the blast went off. I remembered as I rolled off my seat that I had seen a lot of red spattered about. It registered that he was trapped in the plane, too badly hit to get himself out.

"I crawled back into the ship. The fire was raging in the bomb bay. Flames were already eating into the cockpit where he was sitting, his head slumped on his chest. I crawled through the fire to his side. He had been terribly wounded about the stomach and one thigh. I reached my left arm around his waist and grabbed a handful of flying jacket. I jerked, and he rolled over on me. I held him slung over my shoulder as I went back to the escape hatch.

"The whole ship was on fire and the flames had completely engulfed the bomb bay where the bombs were still hanging. I don't know how I ever got away. Somehow I dropped to the ground and crawled to the crater made by the exploding Jap bomb. I pushed my co-pilot over the lip and tumbled in myself just as the bombs in the plane went off. Again the sky seemed to bounce down on the earth. Hot flame filled the hole where we lay. I hugged the ground and every part of me tried to sink deeper into its protection.

"The minute the raid was over the ambulance raced to our hole and loaded us on stretchers. We lay alongside each other in the bouncing wagon. I had my head tilted to one side and I watched as he died."

*   *   *

Before leaving the United States, Kenney had arranged to have three thousand of his "parafrag" bombs, the forgotten balance of the five thousand made up in 1928, shipped to Australia. Equipped with highly sensitive instant fuses, and with a tiny parachute attached, these little twenty-three-pound fragmentation bombs fluttered down until they touched something, then exploded into around sixteen hundred small pieces, which Kenney believed would literally tear aircraft apart. He was keen to try them on Japanese aircraft on the New Guinea airfields. They duly arrived, but the A-20s had no bomb racks that were suitable for them. He called in a rather fabulous character, Major Paul I. Gunn, who would gain an incredible reputation for the things he did to airplanes. Kept more or less honest by the skilled engineers of the 81st Depot Repair Squadron at Townsville, Pappy Gunn took the A-20s and turned them into potent weapons.

Kenney had first met Gunn on August 5, 1942, at Charters Towers, where he had settled down with the 3rd Attack Group as a sort of engineering and maintenance officer. Several of the people in the group had seen P-40s test fire their six .50-caliber machine guns, and watched holes ten to fifteen feet across torn into the targets. When the A-20s turned up without guns, quick minds recalled a lot of wrecked P-40s lying around, each capable of yielding six machine guns.

No structural changes were necessary to put four .50-caliber guns in the nose of an A-20, and although its short range had originally been enough to make even a flight over the Owen Stanleys dangerous, two bomb bay tanks increased the fuel capacity. Although all the work on the A-20 delayed its entry into combat until August 21, it was a far more effective weapon and became a key aircraft in the Fifth. Kenney told Gunn that he wanted some A-20s ready to carry parafrag bombs in two weeks.

Milne Bay: Taste of Victory

Kenney felt they were due for some more trouble in New Guinea, and he was sure it would come at Milne Bay. On the vital southeastern tip of New Guinea, this was the one place where the Allies held the initiative. Back in May of 1942 the location had been chosen for the development of airfields to command the approaches from the Solomons to the Coral Sea and to provide a base for the capture of the coastal areas above it. An Australian militia force and a squadron of RAAF P-40s were there by the middle of July, and the landing by the enemy at Buna had placed new importance on Milne Bay. A month later, another Australian P-40 squadron and a few Hudson bombers were operating from the airstrips, and Australian Middle East veterans had been brought in, building the forces there to a total of over eight thousand men.

It was obvious there would have to be a fight soon. The enemy capture of Buna had to be followed by an effort to take Milne Bay, which would possibly lead to another seaborne attempt to take Port Moresby, supplementing the overland attack which was already under way. Intelligence estimates on August 17 had indicated the Japanese would make a strong bid within ten days, and the Allied Air Forces were ordered to get ready. The Japanese might consider forcing the Marines off Guadalcanal as their first priority, but there was no reason why they would not try to win both New Guinea and the Solomons at the same time.

Enemy reconnaissance planes were prowling over Milne Bay daily. On August 24 the Australian P-40s intercepted a dozen Zekes and shot down two of them, then on the next day coastwatchers reported Japanese shipping activity. Flying Fortresses sighted a convoy and shadowed it far enough to confirm Milne Bay was its objective. Major General Cyril Clowes, commanding at Milne Bay, was warned that morning. Every aircraft in the Townsville area that could be spared was readied, the Fortresses were alerted at Mareeba, and every possible Mitchell and Marauder was sent up to Moresby to attack the convoy the following day.

The weather of the previous two weeks got worse, and the Fortresses could not find their target and brought their bombs back. Then a Hudson successfully took twenty-three P-40s from Milne Bay to the convoy, where they strafed and dive-bombed, claiming a sinking, but the invading Japanese were not delayed. An Australian patrol boat found the convoy just before midnight and reported that the landing was in progress.

All day long on August 26, in the face of appalling weather, the planes kept taking off to attack. Most had to return, but some got through. Eight 19th Group B-17s, led by Major Felix Hardison, commander of the 93rd Squadron, left Moresby an hour before dawn. Flying by dead reckoning, they let down through the gloom, and the convoy was below them.

The ships sent up a torrent of fire as the B-17s made their runs. The Fortresses were rocked by the bursts of the big navy guns as the decks of the ships lit up in the gray murk, and the gunners on the B-17s returned the fire. The ceiling was down to less than two thousand feet, and the smoke was thick, but Hardison's bombardier finally made out his target. The bombs hung up and would not move, so Hardison turned to make another run. The other B-17s had already bombed, when there was a tremendous burst of flame, and Captain Clyde Webb's plane dropped down. The Fortress struck the sea smoothly and shot ahead, leaving a slick of orange fire on the water before it sank.

Hardison's bombs still refused to go, and the B-17 was taking heavy damage as they made a third and fourth run, with another bomber covering them. After four more runs Hardison finally agreed to let his bombardier salvo the load, and four bombs struck close to the stern of a destroyer. On the final run the rest of the bombs went down, but missed by a hundred feet or more. The last exploded immediately under them, evidently set off by antiaircraft fire, blowing the door off the radio compartment and tearing a hole through the top of the plane.

Eight B-17s had gone out, and seven came back, one carrying a dead bombardier. Several planes had wounded aboard, all were badly shot up. One ground-looped into a tree—there was a terrific crash and smoke billowed from the B-17, but the crew was saved. That evening the officers in the 93rd did some purposeful drinking.

Feelings ran high at General Headquarters in Brisbane. Whether or not much more could have been done under the circumstances, more effective use of the air force was a necessity. Probably the main contribution of the air force during the Milne Bay crisis was a series of attacks against the Buna airfield, begun on August 25. The Allies were aware of the improvements made there and it was likely the enemy was going to base fighters there to support their Milne Bay operation. Plowing through a rainstorm to shoot up the airstrip on August 26, the Airacobras caught ten Japanese fighters taking off in flights of three. Lieutenant Danny Roberts blasted one Zero, which tumbled in flames among the treetops at the end of the runway. Roberts made a tight turn and came back head on at another Zero. Both pilots fired and the Japanese fighter crashed into the water just off the beach near Buna. The other pilots accounted for four more, and Roberts finished the work by setting fire to a fuel dump. Once a divinity student, he came as close to profanity as anyone in the 80th Squadron remembers when he quietly told his crew chief, "I got two of the devils." One Airacobra was lost.

While the B-26s and the fighters blew holes in the Buna runway and fought the fighters, the battle for Milne Bay was joined in the steaming rain and mud. The Japanese were actually outnumbered, but they took advantage of the terrain and they also had the support of destroyers which crept in close during the night and shelled the area. Although the enemy was gradually pushed back it was a hard and vicious struggle. Allied aircraft strafed everything from enemy barges to treetops concealing snipers, and although the fighting went on for weeks the Japanese did not reinforce the area and gained little after September. The figures indicated that about seven hundred were killed, nine were captured, and the rest evacuated, except for a few hundred still on nearby Goodenough Island.

* * *

The Milne Bay victory, which stopped the Japanese pincer movement on Port Moresby, was encouraging to the Allies and there were developments elsewhere. On August 29 the enemy had broken through the Kokoda Gap and within a few days they had forced a further retreat until the fight was less than thirty miles from Port Moresby.

Kenney had visited New Guinea during the early days of September and reported to MacArthur that he had little faith the Australians could hold the Japanese. The undergrowth where they were fighting was sparse, and the Japanese were able to work around and envelop the Australians. Allied aircraft were bombing the trail, but could not even see parts of it, and Kenney would have preferred to sink ships and destroy aircraft, because there was no food along the Kokoda Trail. The fierce, miniature nature of the clashes on the ground added to the difficulties facing the aircrews.

Then on September 8 the news came through that the Japanese had worked around the defenders in the Kokoda Gap and the Australians were falling back. MacArthur had looked over his American 32nd Division a couple of days before and decided to send them in. With Major General George Vasey's experienced 7th Division moving into New Guinea, MacArthur was determined to hold Moresby, and with the fresh American and Australian troops, he felt he would.

There was some good news. Pappy Gunn had made a "sort of honeycomb" rack

Kentucky Red from the 3rd Attack Group. Fitted out with a cluster of four machine guns in the nose, and modified to carry parafrag bombs, the A-20As proved their worth in the Buna campaign. (Adrian Bottge)

which enabled the A-20 to carry forty parafrags, and by September 12 Captain Donald P. Hall of the 3rd Attack Group was ready to lead nine A-20s in the first attack using the bombs. The day before, the Japanese had repaired Buna airstrip enough to bring in twenty-two planes just before dark, and they were on the ground when the A-20s roared in over the trees and hit the field in waves. As they strafed they each dropped their parafrags, scattering them over the airdrome, and seventeen of the Japanese planes were destroyed. The lead wave of four planes received ground fire, but the following wave reported none. When the first parachutes popped open some of the Japanese evidently thought it was a paratroop landing because they rushed out with their rifles and began to shoot.

After the attack by the A-20s, five Marauders and seven Fortresses went over Buna to complete the job. They dug large holes in the runway and it looked as if Buna would be out of action for a while. Kenney wired Arnold requesting 125,000 more parafrag bombs, and went back to watch the situation at Port Moresby. There he found preparations under way for a last-ditch defense, with Whitehead's house encircled by barbed wire and trenches. Kenney hoped his aircraft could cut off the Japanese supplies and finally stop them, but more troops were urgently needed and Kenney decided to suggest to MacArthur that he be allowed to fly some of the American troops in.

September 13 was a big day for Kenney. When MacArthur revealed he was ordering the 32nd Division to New Guinea, Kenney asked to be allowed to fly the first regiment in—it would be two weeks before they could get there if they went by sea, and time was running out. MacArthur's staff opposed the idea, but Kenney pressed the point about the time factor. MacArthur asked him what losses could be expected flying them in, and when Kenney answered that they had not lost a pound of freight yet, he agreed to sending some troops up by air to see what happened. It was decided to begin moving a company of the 126th Infantry at daybreak on September 15, and Kenney was sure he would have them all in Moresby that evening.

At dawn on September 15 the infantrymen began boarding a mixed batch of Douglas and Lockheed transports at Amberley Field. At six o'clock that evening Whitehead confirmed that they had all been landed safely at Moresby, and Kenney bounded upstairs to give MacArthur the news and ask permission to take in the rest of the regiment. MacArthur was delighted, but the rest of the 126th was already being loaded for sea movement. Hardly missing a beat, Kenney asked if he could have the next to go, the 128th Regiment, promising to have them in New Guinea ahead of the troops already going in by sea.

MacArthur's staff opposed again, but much more strongly, advocating a more "orderly" movement. General MacArthur asked when the 126th was leaving Brisbane Harbor, and when Sutherland told him the morning of September 18, he said to inform Lieutenant General Robert L. Eichelberger, the newly arrived American Army commander, that "George is flying the 128th Infantry to Port Moresby," beginning the same morning. Kenney promptly called the Australian Minister for Air and got twelve civil airliners on loan, and instructed that every bomber overhauled anywhere in Australia was to help move the troops to New Guinea. All aircraft delivered from the United States would be commandeered, along with their civilian crews, to help out. As the fighters and bombers flew back and forth strafing and bombing the whole length of the trail, Kenney delivered the 128th Infantry on schedule at the rate of about six hundred men every twenty-four hours. By September 24 the entire regiment had been airlifted to Moresby, where the remainder of the 126th Infantry arrived by ship two days later.

The reinforced Australians launched an attack on September 28, broke through the enemy defenses, and in the face of tough resistance fought their way back toward Kokoda. It would take another month to reach Kokoda and its airfield, but the turning point in the Japanese attempt to take Port Moresby overland had come. There was a long, bitter fight ahead—a fight for Buna, not Port Moresby.

Target: Rabaul

Veteran pilots claimed you could find Rabaul at night by the sulphurous fumes which drifted up from the volcanoes, and it was becoming an old target for Allied aircraft. Usually one or two planes would go out ahead to send back weather information, and because the attacks were usually made at night, they would illuminate

Miss Carriage from the 65th Squadron roars down the strip at Seven Mile. The Fortresses served Kenney well.

the target with incendiary bombs or drop flares every few minutes to guide the rest of the bombers on their runs. The B-17s usually bombed from between four and ten thousand feet and often made individual strafing runs over the searchlight and antiaircraft positions.

An aerial assault on Rabaul was part of the plans for Buna to "give the Japs something to look at" besides Kenney's troop carriers and on October 5 a daylight mission ushered in a three-week sustained effort. The Japanese were also beginning a new offensive on Guadalcanal, and record attacks were made on Rabaul by thirty B-17s on October 9, followed by twenty-one the next night. Three days later fifteen Fortresses dropped thirty tons of bombs on Lakunai and Vunakanau airstrips, but there were no spectacular claims until the attack of October 23. As usual, there was a large amount of shipping in Rabaul Harbor, and the very heavy concentrations found there on October 20 provided a tempting opportunity for the B-17s to test a new low-level bombing method. Kenney had "fired" Major William G. Benn, the aide he had brought with him to Australia, on August 24, giving him command of the 63rd Squadron of the 43rd Bomb Group. Throughout August and September Benn had devoted hours to tests in a B-17, skipping bombs or aiming them directly at the old wreck in Port Moresby Harbor. Air operations against shipping had been less successful than desirable; the established methods of bombing were just not suitable for the small heavy bomber force or the conditions in the Southwest Pacific. The British had used heavy bombers at mast height with success, and both Kenney and Benn had been intrigued by "skip bombing" from the beginning.

Major William Benn came to Australia as Kenn[ey's] aide, and both were fascinated by "skip bombi[ng]." Benn was given the 63rd Squadron and its B-17[s to] introduce the tactic to the Japanese. By Novem[ber] 1942, after painstaking experiments, Benn was [able] to define skip bombing this way: "The sight use[d is] an X on the co-pilot's window six and three qua[rter] inches from the top. The forward point of refere[nce] is the outline of the nose. Under these condition[s of] level flight at two hundred and fifty feet indica[ted] approximately two hundred and twenty miles [an] hour a bomb will fall from sixty to one hundred [feet] short of the vessel, skip into the air and hit sixt[y to] one hundred feet beyond. If perfect, the bomb [will] hit the side of the vessel and sink. During peri[ods] when the moon is twenty degrees or less above [the] horizon and at dawn, the slick on the water [is] given a perfect path on which to operate. By fly[ing] north or south at five hundred feet the slick of [the] moon follows the airplane so that when a vessel [ap]pears in the slick a ninety degree turn is execu[ted,] two hundred and fifty feet are lost, and power is [ap]plied. The results have been hits and sinkings. It [has] been found that enemy vessels turn their g[uns] directly upwards and shoot. So far they have [only] caused minor damage to a few airplanes." Bill B[enn] was lost on January 18, 1943. (General George [C.] Kenney)

Benn knew that the 63rd was ready, and while two of the three flights of B-17s bombed normally, selected planes of the 63rd Squadron, led by their commander, eased down through the moonlight. From less than 250 feet they dropped their bombs. Captain Ken McCullar in the B-17 *Black Jack* hit a destroyer and it was believed sunk, and other pilots claimed hits.

Fires and explosions threw smoke and debris high into the air and the experiment was judged a great success. Later assessment failed to prove any vessels were actually sunk, but the 63rd always called it "jackpot night."

In fact, the three-week maximum effort was only definitely credited with the sinking of one small vessel, but the fact that thirty B-17s could be put over Rabaul at all was an indication that fortunes were changing. Perhaps nineteen ships were damaged to varying degrees, and the town and its supply stores were hit hard.

*   *   *

As far back as August Kenney had flown along the northern coast of New Guinea to have a firsthand look at Wanigela Mission, about halfway between

The 63rd Squadron was equipped with new Boeing B-17Fs in August, and was attached to the 19th Group for training and combat indoctrination. (Roger Vargas)

Milne Bay and Buna, where there was a natural landing strip. Kenney also thought it was a "natural" for occupation and continuing supply by air, any time the Allies were ready. Although the coast between Wanigela Mission and Buna was not promising, there was flat country about ten miles west of Buna which looked as though it might be relatively dry and hard under the carpet of kunai grass.

Three days later, Kenney began talking about Wanigela Mission with Mac-Arthur, but was interrupted for ten minutes when he revealed that he had inspected the place himself from one hundred feet altitude, a risk General Mac-Arthur did not think it had been wise to take. Kenney prudently decided to wait a while longer before suggesting the airborne seizure of Wanigela. His opportunity came a few weeks later, when he suggested occupying Wanigela Mission by air and then moving northwest along the coastal trail to Buna, with the troops supplied by air. As soon as Buna was captured, Lae could be taken the same way by landing troops on the flat grass plains at Nadzab on the Markham River about twenty miles west of Lae. MacArthur simply said, "We'll see."

While the last defensive battles were still being fought in the ridges above Port Moresby, Kenney, representing MacArthur, had met with General Blamey and his Australian staff to discuss a three-pronged offensive to drive the Japanese from Buna. This involved an advance by the Australian 7th Division along the Kokoda

Trail, a flanking movement by a battalion of American troops which would intercept the Japanese on the trail halfway between Kokoda and Buna, and Kenney's
coveted project, the airborne occupation of Wanigela Mission, which would begin
the coastal drive toward Buna by the rest of the 32nd Division. Kenney promised
Blamey that he would provide the necessary air transport required by all three
forces, and Blamey agreed to provide an Australian battalion as the occupation
force for Wanigela Mission. However, Blamey was not so sure about the overland
flanking movement, which would mean relatively inexperienced troops moving
through some of the most primitive and rugged country in the world.

All the details were hammered out, and the final plan required nearly eleven
thousand men to be mainly supplied by air. Maximum requirements were estimated to be 102,000 pounds per day, but assuming some sea transport from
Milne Bay to Wanigela could be used, the maximum was fixed at 61,900 pounds.

On October 5 the troop carriers had begun moving an Australian battalion to
Wanigela. Australian officers had already landed there; using native labor, they
burned away the grass for a landing field and engineers hacked out a runway.
Twelve C-47s made seventy-one flights from Moresby, and the job was completed
in two days.

Inspired by this success, it was decided to look for fields even closer to Buna,
and a series of strips were cleared down the coast as far as Pongani, about twenty
miles below Buna.

On October 14 the C-47s began moving Australian and American troops to
Wanigela, and these flights continued for two days, but then it started raining. The
weather not only stopped the air movement but also bogged down ninety
Australians trying to reach Pongani overland from Wanigela. They got through the
fifty-mile trek, but with only twenty men fit for duty. An American detachment
had been heading for the same point in two luggers, but they were bombed by a
B-25. Because of the difficulty in getting from Wanigela to Pongani without an
airlift, General Forrest Harding, the 32nd Division commander, suspended the
movement of his troops to Wanigela, in the hope that one of the more advanced
landing fields in preparation might soon be available. After some debate, the troop
carriers were instructed to fly the remainder of the 128th Regiment to Wanigela, a
move completed on November 8. The same day the 126th Regiment, less the elements moving overland, began its movement by air to Pongani, where a strip had
been cleared a few days before.

Additional protection for this movement had been provided on October 23 by
the reoccupation of Goodenough Island. A battalion of Australian troops landing
that day soon cleaned out a few hundred Japanese who had been in possession
since their Milne Bay operation in August. This island held a prominent place in a
plan looking to future air operations, which was submitted to MacArthur on November 2. This plan proposed the development of strong fighter bases on
Goodenough, at Milne Bay, and at Buna, which would be staging fields for bomber
missions to the north, as well as defending New Guinea. Milne Bay already had
three airfields and Kenney had been able to bring most of his aircraft up to New
Guinea.

Kenney was telling the Fifth Air Force's future when he expressed this theory in
a letter to "Hap" Arnold: "In the Pacific Theater we have a number of islands gar-
risoned by small forces. These islands are nothing more or less than aerodromes or

aerodrome areas from which modern firepower is launched. Sometimes they are true islands . . . sometimes they are localities on large land masses. Port Moresby, Lae and Buna are all on the island of New Guinea, but the only practicable way to get from one to the other is by air or water: they are all islands as far as warfare is concerned."

Missions supporting the Australians as they fought their way toward Kokoda were successful. Aerial drops supplemented their supplies until recapture of Kokoda opened the airstrip there to the transports, and repeated attacks were made on the Japanese supply line. After passing Kokoda on the way out it had been the enemy's turn to face a problem which had previously hindered the Allies. All types of aircraft took part in the bombing of the track leading back to Buna, from the Airacobras to the big Flying Fortresses, and Japanese communications were unceasingly pounded. The Wairopi bridge, crossing the swift Kumusi River (suspended on the wire ropes which gave it its name), was the target of daily bombardment. The Japanese rebuilt and repaired it several times, but finally gave up and crossed the river on rafts, which became fine strafing targets.

Buna, particularly the airstrip, was also being attacked. The dense jungle in the battle area made close air support hard, but techniques were being improved. The A-20s, covered by Airacobras which added their weight to the strafing, performed most of these missions, and although it is always difficult in this type of operation to say exactly how effective air power is, they were dropping bombs and firing bullets into the Japanese. The starved condition of the enemy dead proved that Kenney's aircraft were denying supplies to the enemy.

The Allied Air Forces controlled the air over Papua. The Japanese were heavily involved in the Solomons, but even so, intelligence indicated there were never fewer than one hundred aircraft, and usually more, at Rabaul. The Japanese were not committing them to the New Guinea airfields, and there were only two big attacks on Allied bases in New Guinea during September and October. These were not effective and Allied planes were intercepted only twice.

There were obvious advantages stemming from Japan's operations in the Solomons, mainly the breathing space it allowed for the MacArthur forces, but with this went the continuing threat that the enemy might choose to throw his entire force against New Guinea. With this in mind, MacArthur again asked for a review of strategic decisions with regard to the Pacific. He felt that all the resources of the United States should be used to meet the emergency in the Pacific, but the only tangible result he achieved was a small reinforcement of heavy bombers—the 90th Bomb Group would be sent from Hawaii to the Southwest Pacific to replace the old 19th Group. The generosity of this move was dampened by the fact that a decision had been made to replace all the Fifth's B-17s with Liberators, and Kenney had doubts that the B-24 could serve him as well as the B-17. However, he was delighted at the prospect of getting some new aircraft and fresh crews.

The heavy bomber changeover could not be made until November, and the planes and crews of the 19th Group continued to support the Guadalcanal campaign by hitting Rabaul. The Fortresses also kept a constant watch over the enemy in New Britain and the upper Solomons, and throughout October and November most of the heavy bomber missions were flown in support of the South Pacific forces. In fact between September 18 and November 30 the B-17s flew one hundred and eighty sorties against Rabaul.

In the meantime the troop carriers were wrestling with the task of supplying the Advanced New Guinea Force. One problem had arisen because Whitehead was unable to give fighter cover to the supply boats which were to support the forward elements. Failure of the boats to stay hidden from patrolling enemy aircraft during the day was causing serious losses, and the troop carrier aircraft were given the job.

Transport planes were scarce and the Directorate of Air Transport was badly below its assigned strength. Of the seventy-eight planes allocated to American units, only forty-one had been available in mid-September, and fifteen of them were best used as sources for spare parts. MacArthur and Kenney managed to get two more troop carrier squadrons but the Fifth would not receive its full quota of C-47s and crews until late in November. One of the new squadrons got to Australia with thirteen C-47s in October, but the second was "sandbagged" by General Harmon in the South Pacific for over a month. While waiting for them, the Fifth activated the 374th Troop Carrier Group, to include the four C-47 squadrons which would soon be available. Kenney and other airmen believed that not only Buna, but Lae too, could be swiftly taken with the use of air transport, but he could not show that he had the capacity to land and then supply the necessary forces.

There were all kinds of other problems but gradually the techniques were improved. Mitchells were found to be excellent "transports" and almost any aircraft could help out in the airlift. The worst accident occurred on November 5, when a parachute on a package got caught up in the tail assembly of a C-47 and it

Kenney's "other" medium bomber group was the 38th, down to half its strength since two squadrons, the 69th and 70th, had taken part in the Battle of Midway and were eventually reassigned to the Thirteenth Air Force. These 71st Squadron Mitchells were flying out of Garbutt Field, near Townsville, on November 12, 1942. (Army)

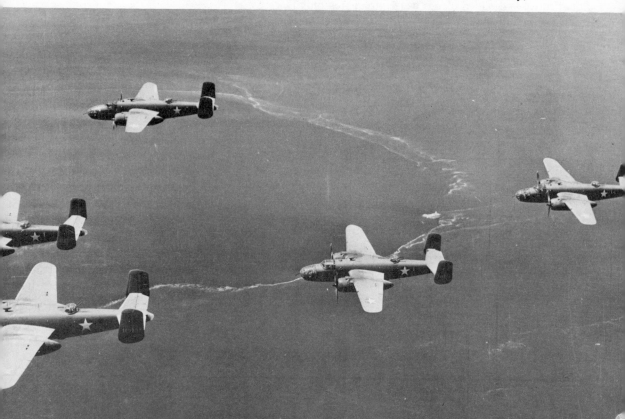

The 89th Squadron's *Little Hellion* bellied in at Port Moresby in November 1942.

crashed, killing the crew and the commander of the 126th Regiment. Between October and December, eleven C-47s crashed in New Guinea, but five were salvaged or rebuilt.

Early in November construction work on a landing field had begun at Dobodura, less than fifteen miles from Buna, and other strips had been prepared in the area. These advanced fields had to shoulder the load of transport operations during the struggle in Papua.

The Australians recaptured Kokoda on November 1, and on November 8 American troops began landing at Dobodura. Four days later the Australians and the battalion of American troops which had moved overland met at Wairopi on the Kumusi River.

MacArthur approved an attack on Buna, which began on November 19. Infantry which had been flown in below Buna was in position close to it on November 18, and the final drive began. Enemy positions were stretched along the coast from Buna north to Gona, and while a quick victory had been expected by some, the fight would be hard and long.

Air transport wrote a memorable record. Although about half the supplies brought in during the campaign for Buna came by sea, aircraft dropped or landed nearly five million pounds of rations, ammunition, vehicles, and supplies in the Buna area between November 13 and January 23, 1943. Four Flying Fortresses even carried four howitzers with their ammunition and gun crews from Brisbane to

This B-17E delivered a howitzer, its tractor, ammunition, and eight-man crew to Seven Mile airstrip; the following morning the five tons of equipment was stuffed into a couple of C-47s and the gun went into action on the other side of the Owen Stanleys.

Port Moresby and one of these artillery pieces, with its crew and one hundred shells, was carried into Dobodura in three DC-3s.

The evacuation of the sick and wounded by the transports saved many lives, and among Kenney's aircraft were ten DC-3s and ten C-60s fitted specifically for this role. In December and January these mercy aircraft were averaging more than a hundred evacuees daily. Every possible plane was used, and on December 8 the peak was reached, when two hundred and eighty men were taken out. The impressive air transport figures represented only a part of the Allied Air Forces' involvement in the Buna action, and not everything went as well.

Bad Beginning

Kenney's B-24 Liberators had begun arriving toward the end of October, but the anti-shimmy collars on the nosewheels showed cracks. Kenney had begun sending the 19th Bomb Group home, and he was left badly short of heavy bombers again. The replacement collars were also cracked and others had to be made in Brisbane. Finally, Kenney had enough nosewheel collars to equip the 90th Group's aircraft, and on November 16 they flew their first mission, when eight headed out to bomb the shipping at the Buin-Faisi anchorage at the south end of Bougainville Island. They got there but made no hits, and on the way back they became separated in a storm. Two landed in the water off New Guinea, both crews surviving, and the rest landed at four different airfields in northeast Australia.

That night they tried again; a Rabaul mission had been planned as a joint operation of three squadrons, to be led by the group commander, Colonel Art Meehan. It called for takeoffs at intervals from eleven o'clock onward during the night of November 16, and the airplanes would cruise at varying speeds designed to bring them over the target together at four o'clock in the morning.

Things went wrong quickly. The first B-24 got off on schedule, but the next was not airborne until fourteen minutes later. There was confusion because planes were not ready to take off in their assigned order, and there was no method of communication on the flight line. In the end, pilots were not sure whether to taxi out to the line or not. The first planes took off using landing lights, but those following did not, and lumbered dangerously close to aircraft parked along the taxi strip on the east side of the runway. The runway lights were placed too far apart, leaving inadequate space between the east string, which the pilots naturally followed from their left side of the cockpit, and the airplanes parked on the taxi strip. Ten B-24s got off, then the eleventh plane, from the 400th Squadron, swerved, hooked a wing on the trees at the edge of the runway, and caught fire, exploding the bombs. The entire crew was killed, and two other B-24s nearby were demolished.

Of the Liberators which made the mission, two got to Rabaul and set fire to a cargo vessel. Two others were missing, one of them carrying Meehan, and while the rest managed to get back, some of the crews were not sure exactly where they

Commanded first by Colonel Arthur Meehan, then Colonel Ralph Koon, the 90th Group brought Liberators to the Fifth Air Force in November. Their tragic entry into combat operations was hardly indicative of the eventual role the B-24 would play in the Southwest Pacific. (T/Sgt M. H. Clay)

Sally was an old 19th Group B-17E which had cracked up on landing at Mareeba. Stripped down and furnished with a table, a bunk, and a few chairs, she became Kenney's personal aircraft until a couple of spars were cracked in a thunderhead and she had to be retired. Captain Wilbur Beezley led the crew, also veterans of the 19th.

had been. Kenney ordered the 90th taken out of combat and given additional training, and he was back to his B-17s again.

* * *

At least six times during November and December the enemy attempted to reinforce Buna by sea and Kenney gave top priority to all-out attacks on these convoys. The weather and Japanese escort fighters from Rabaul made the task a tough one for the American bombers, but crews were now hitting the shipping from lower altitude and on the night of November 24 one B-17 pilot showed how it was done.

Seven B-17s from the 63rd Squadron found five Japanese destroyers in the Huon Gulf, after crossing the Owen Stanleys on instruments. Captain Ken McCullar, flying a B-17F named *Black Jack,* sighted the convoy and climbed to about thirty-five hundred feet. He chopped his throttles back to make his first skip-bombing run from two hundred feet at two hundred and fifty-five miles an hour. The B-17 roared through the darkness, dotted by bursts of flame. McCullar's bombs hit just off the end of the ship, but antiaircraft fire hit an ammunition can in the tail, exploding about seventy rounds and starting a fire. The tail gunner tried to

Captain Ken McCullar, pilot of *Black Jack*.
(E. P. Stevens)

smother the fire with a blanket and some heavy flying clothes until extinguishers
were rushed back to him and the fire was put out.

As *Black Jack* plowed through the bursting shells for a third run, the left outboard motor was hit and the controls were shot away. The feathering switch would
not work, so McCullar was forced to climb to fifteen hundred feet, and he made
another run from twelve hundred. This time the bombs hit close, but *Black Jack*
took more punishment. McCullar took the B-17 up to four thousand feet on the
three good engines and made yet another run, dropping his last bombs. The right
inboard engine cut out, hit somewhere in the fuel system. McCullar was able to
feather this engine, but found he could not maintain his altitude on the remaining
two. After a while he tried to bring the right engine in again, in the meantime sending his position, course, and condition, because things looked bad.

The shot-up left engine became red-hot from the windmilling of the propeller
and looked as though it would catch fire and blow up at any minute. Inside the
battered B-17 they placed the navigator and bombardier at the back of the aircraft
in case the prop spun off into the nose or they had to crash-land.

Evidently the propeller ground itself loose from the engine, because after a while
it cooled down. Still losing altitude, McCullar began working on his feathered right
engine again. They managed to get some power from it, threw all their ammunition
and loose equipment overboard, and *Black Jack* started to climb slowly. Two and

a half hours later they had struggled up to ten thousand feet. Luckily they found a pass to sneak through the mountains, and they were home. McCullar, in his report, summed up the night's work this way: "landed O.K. and forgot about it."

The seven B-17s had scored three near misses within thirty feet, one destroyer had been hit twice in the aft section, and large explosions were seen. This ship was burning fiercely and partly gutted an hour after the hits were scored. Another large destroyer was hit on the stern and apparently partly disabled. While the Japanese were not suffering heavy losses of major vessels, the increasing effectiveness of the shipping strikes was obvious. A Japanese report in the middle of November 1942 fixed the enemy force in the Buna area at about nine thousand men and reinforcement had been generally easy. After that, according to the same source, Allied aircraft stopped two efforts. Of two more attempts, in the first, three hundred out of eight hundred men were killed by bombing and strafing, and in the second, while most of the troops got ashore safely, they lost most of their weapons and equipment.

Four Japanese vessels landed about eight hundred troops during the night of December 1 without apparent loss, but on December 9 bombing drove off six destroyers evidently headed for Buna. Less than a week later the enemy tried again. A Liberator reported five warships heading for Vitiaz Strait on the morning of December 15, and Fortresses made an attack during the afternoon, through thunderstorms and thick cloud. Under cover of the weather the vessels managed to reach an anchorage and put their troops ashore. Out of the dawn on the day after, P-39s,

Usually flown by Lieutenant William Gowdy, this 403rd Squadron B-17F went down in Bootless Inlet, near Port Moresby, in December 1942. Pieces of it still lie there. (Army)

Lieutenant Charles Mayo of the 89th Squadron was one of the most daring A-20 pilots. Early in December he singled out an antiaircraft position surrounded by four machine gun nests at Buna. His plane was hit by a shell which came in through the bomb bay and holed the gas tank during the first pass. Mayo made a second run but misjudged it and hit the treetops, smashing the nose glass and twisting the control wheel. Furious, he made four more runs over the target, finishing the job. During the final pass the instruments were shot out and a bullet hit his radio headset, shearing off the wires, but Mayo got the battered A-20 home and it was flying again in a few days. (Adrian Bottge)

Beaufighters, A-20s, B-25s, and Marauders flew about a hundred sorties against the troops and supplies cluttering the shore, while other aircraft attacked the withdrawing warships. This was the last major enemy reinforcement of Papua.

However, if the Allies had gained this advantage, the enemy had taken advantage of the swampy and rough terrain. Their fortifications included bunkers built of heavy palm logs reinforced with sheet iron and layers of earth and rocks, and they fought for every inch of ground. The news was not good. The 32nd Division attacks were getting nowhere, and the Australians were only moving slowly. The American troops' morale was down, and transport crews reported flying food and ammunition to the fields around Dobodura, where they found that if everybody already had enough to eat there was nobody who would unload the planes. The crews would unload the supplies themselves, but they would just be left there on the side of the runway. The Allied advance had been all but stopped as November ended.

Lieutenant General Robert L. Eichelberger took personal command of the Allied forces early in December after being told by MacArthur to win "or don't come back alive." Kenney and Eichelberger had been friends for years, and air support for the troops in Buna received close attention. The favored Allied aircraft for close support was the Douglas A-20, and they had flown most of the missions, with an Australian Beaufighter squadron adding its weight. The Mitchells and Marauders operated behind the front lines. Both air and ground forces realized success hinged on effective liaison, and new procedures had been tried out late in November. When the infantry moved out to take Buna, the A-20s had zoomed in to shower the area with parafrags and B-25s bombed from medium altitude. Several machine gun nests were knocked out, but one A-20 had dropped its bombs in the water and a bomb from a B-25 dropped within the Allied bomb line and killed several men.

A new offensive was ordered on December 5, but despite the tons of explosives dumped on the Japanese, progress was measured in yards. Sickness and fighting drained the strength of the Allied forces. The next day fresh Australian troops replaced the men who had driven the Japanese across the mountains, and on December 11 troop carriers brought in two companies of American reinforcements. The new men succeeded quickly—in the wake of a strafing and bombing attack by A-20s, B-26s, and P-40s, the Australians took Gona on December 9 and Buna village was occupied by American troops five days later.

After these early gains the advance bogged down again, and it was January 2, 1943, before the Australians wiped out the Japanese between Cape Endaiadere and a corridor east of Buna Mission and the Americans took the mission itself.

The 374th Troop Carrier Group was activated in Australia on November 12, 1942, and was equipped with an assortment of aircraft including C-39s, C-49s, C-56s, C-60s, DC-3s, and DC-5s. When the 317th Group brought brand-new C-47s to Australia early in 1943 the two units simply traded aircraft. These troops from the 127th Infantry have just been flown into Dobodura on December 15. (Army)

A series of problems delayed the Lightning's entry into combat, but the 39th Fighter Squadron's first battle quickly proved their worth. (Jack Jones)

Liaison between air and ground forces was improving. Kenney was being asked to hit mortar pits and other positions blocking the Allied advance, and he was "straining at the leash to help."

The P-38s Draw Blood

Of all the delays and frustrations the worst had been in getting the P-38 Lightnings ready for combat. Finally enough of the Lockheed fighters had been produced to allow even the Fifth to have some, and they began arriving in September. Kenney possessed about sixty long-awaited Lightnings by October, but none had fired a shot in anger. The fuel tanks leaked, then the superchargers, water coolers, invertors, and armament all required attention.

The first P-38s went to the 39th Fighter Squadron under the command of Major George Prentice, a veteran of the 49th Fighter Group. During November eight had been loaned to the neighboring South Pacific Theater for a short period, but during their operations from Guadalcanal they had seen no action. It was the end of November when they scored their first kill, in a rather unusual way.

It had been planned to bring the P-38s into a dive-bombing attack on a convoy bringing reinforcements to Buna in late November, and eight five-hundred-pound

The day after Christmas, eleven Zekes came over Buna and were met by twelve 49th Group P-40s. Four Japanese were shot down, the third being the one hundredth victory for the group. Lieutenant John Landers, who scored the kill, was shot down and walked out of the jungle a week later. (Sid Woods)

Tom Lynch got his first two Zeros on May 20, 1942, while flying Airacobras, and became an ace on December 27. Lynch was a fine leader and destroyed twenty enemy aircraft before he was killed in March 1944. (Jack Jones)

bombs, to be hung on one wing pylon of each plane, were delivered to the 39th. Lieutenant Charles King thought the whole thing was "close to being insane," because they had no dive-bombing experience, the mission would be flown at night, and there were no radio aids to navigation. The strike was canceled because the ships had landed their cargoes and were already out of range of the fighters, leaving the 39th with some bombs to get rid of. So they were sent to blow holes in the runway at Lae with them.

On November 26, 1942, five P-38s took off and headed across the mountains to Lae. Captain Bob Faurot intended to plant his bomb on the ground installations, but he overshot and the bomb exploded in the water just off the end of the runway, which ran right down to the beach. There was a boiling explosion, and a solid tower of water rose into the air.

Simultaneously, a Zero was taking off to intercept the attacking Lightnings. The Japanese fighter flew straight across Faurot's bomb, and the blast caught the plane and simply flicked it over into the sea. Faurot had other pilots to supply eyewitness confirmation, the Zero was in the air, and he claimed credit for the kill.

But not without argument. General Kenney went to see Faurot and ask him if he had the nerve to call that the first P-38 kill in the Fifth Air Force. Faurot grinned and asked if he was going to get the Air Medal. Kenney said, "Hell no . . . I want you to shoot them down, not splash water on them!"

Then on December 27 the Lightnings got into their first big fight, along with the P-40s from the 49th Group. Near Dobodura they found a Japanese formation of seven dive bombers escorted by more than twenty fighters, and the twelve P-38s split into three flights and dived. The battle began about ten minutes after noon.

Captain Tom Lynch, leading the P-38s, swooped on three Japanese fighters sitting on the tail of another Lightning. He blasted one of them almost in two, and it was diving and burning when he last saw it. Lynch flew around for a while, snapping shots until he got a good, solid burst into another enemy plane which he followed down to the water and watched splash in. With empty guns, he headed for Port Moresby to get another aircraft, but by the time he got back the fight was over.

Lieutenant Richard Bong made his first couple of passes without results and then headed out across the coast at five hundred feet. He fired a dive bomber from three hundred yards, and it blew up. Bong snapped a short burst at a Zeke as it crossed in front of his P-38, and the Japanese fighter dived into the sea. Bong used up the rest of his ammunition on three more dive bombers, but did not get any results. He went home too.

Lieutenant Ken Sparks, leading his element, dived on a Japanese and poured fire into him. Smoke billowed from the engine, blanketing the cockpit, and the Japanese plane dived vertically into the water. Sparks fired at other planes without seeing any results, then glanced back to find five Japanese on his tail. He dived away desperately, but not before he had an engine shot out. Heading for Dobodura, he spotted two Vals, and got a shot into one that shredded pieces from the wing. Sparks's nosewheel would not come down as he landed, but he clambered out of the damaged plane, ran over to a C-47 that was about to return to Port Moresby, and got home almost as soon as the rest of his squadron.

Lieutenant Stanley Andrews latched onto three Zekes which peeled off in oppo-

George Kale's *Shittenengitten* was one of five Marauders attacking a Japanese convoy on January 6, 1943. During the bomb run the covering Zeros attacked, shooting out the B-26's hydraulic system, and despite the efforts of the crew they were forced to land at Milne Bay with the wheels up and the bomb bay doors open. Luck was with them and the plane screeched to a stop in the middle of the steel mat runway. (Marvin L. McCrory)

Lieutenant Richard Bong, a quiet farm boy from Poplar, Wisconsin, became an ace January 8, 1943. In all he shot down forty planes, creating a permanent record for American fighter pilot.

site directions. Andrews followed the one that went to the left—chasing him into the turn. He fired a long burst as he closed in to fifty yards. The whole tail of the Japanese fighter was sawed off by the concentrated fire and it spun crazily into the sea. Lieutenant Hoyt Eason had followed the one breaking to the right, and got solid bursts into the cockpit. The plane went straight down. Then he went after a fighter that was giving a 49th Group P-40 some trouble, and he and the P-40 ganged up on the enemy plane, which crashed into the water.

When the battle was over, the score was seven Zekes, two Vals, and two Oscars definitely destroyed, plus three probables. The cost to the 39th was the damage to Sparks's banged-up P-38.

Kenney visited the 39th to congratulate them and hear about the fight. He was amused to find that while Sparks was the "bubbling over type," and had a report "a mile long," Lieutenant Bong's really just answered the questions printed on the form: "Saw P-38 No. 36 on transport strip, Dobodura, on nose. Fired at range of 350 yds. at Val which blew up and crashed into water. Fired short burst at Zeke which passed in front of me. Zeke crashed into water."

As he listened to their description, Kenney learned that they had probably done nearly everything wrong. They had fired from too far away, they had tried to dogfight with the Zero . . . The general did his best to give them hell for it, then at the end of the session he slipped three bottles of scotch to George Prentice.

* * *

At the beginning of 1943 it was obvious that the Papuan campaign was nearly over, although three weeks of bitter fighting lay ahead before the last defiant Japa-

The fighters had curtailed Japanese attacks on Allied airstrips, but on January 17, 1943, about twenty bombers, escorted by fighters, hit Milne Bay. Although they destroyed six aircraft, including this 403rd Squadron B-17F, there were no casualties. (Norbert Ruff)

When Buna Mission was captured all that remained to be done was the cleaning out of the Sanananda Point area. These weary 32nd Division troops are about to be flown back to Port Moresby after turning the job over to the 41st Division. (Army)

nese waded out from the shore and were perfunctorily shot. Another regiment of American troops was ferried in from Port Moresby, but the Allied drive slowed down again on January 12. The next day Eichelberger assumed command of every Allied unit fighting north of the Owen Stanleys and began vigorous patrol actions which led to hand-to-hand fighting, precluding any close air support. From January 1 the Fifth had been bombing and shooting up areas around the Giriwu River and Sanananda Point, but on January 14 Advanced New Guinea Force directed that there should be no bombing or strafing without a specific request.

On January 12 the Japanese made their last effort, but it failed and all organized Japanese resistance would end in Papua by January 22.

The Allied Air Forces' contribution to this first major campaign is hard to assess. Colonel Frederic H. Smith, Jr., Kenney's deputy chief of staff, gave an airman's estimate when he later wrote: "In view of the bad weather and bad terrain the handling of the ground units was the key to the final outcome. It was in the transport of these units and their supplies that our air power was most useful."

Kenney just said, "We learned a lot and the next one will be better."

II

Sea of Blood

I F the Japanese had abandoned reinforcement of Buna, it was equally certain that they would strengthen Lae and Salamaua on the Huon Gulf. Regular patrols over Rabaul and the sea lanes indicated that at the end of 1942 an unprecedented amount of shipping was cluttering Rabaul Harbor.

There were signs that a convoy would attempt to make a run about January 6, and Kenney ordered a maximum effort against the more than ninety vessels at dawn on January 5. Brigadier General Ken Walker preferred to hit the Rabaul shipping at noon, although Kenney was adamant about a dawn strike. Walker's point was that the bombers would have to leave Moresby in darkness, and might have difficulty making their rendezvous, while Kenney knew the Japanese fighters were never up at dawn and he would rather risk a loose formation than the certain interception a midday strike would stir up.

A formation of six Fortresses and six B-24s attacked the shipping at noon on January 5, scoring hits on ten ships. The *Kurapaku Maru* was sunk and six more vessels were afire when the bombers left, but the antiaircraft fire was heavy and the fighters aggressive and eager. Two B-17s were shot out of the skies, and one of them carried Brigadier General Walker.

Walker had altered the takeoff time of the mission during the morning of January 5 and gone to Rabaul himself, both against Kenney's orders. Crews from other planes reported seeing the Fortress about twenty-five miles from the target, losing height, one engine afire, and under fighter attack. Kenney sent every available recon plane out to search for survivors, and in the evening a B-17 was reported on a coral reef in the Trobriand Islands. A relieved Kenney decided to reprimand Walker severely and send him on leave to Australia. MacArthur said, "All right, George, but if he doesn't come back I'm going to send his name in to Washington recommending him for a Congressional Medal of Honor."

A Catalina picked up the stranded B-17 crew, but it was not Walker's. He was awarded the Medal of Honor.

A 43rd Group Fortress on the long road to Rabaul . . . the view from Lucky Stevens' ball turret. (E. P. Stevens)

On the morning of January 6, a convoy was sighted fifty miles east of Gasmata heading for Lae, heavily protected by fighters. During that night an Australian Catalina bombed and strafed the *Nichiryu Maru,* and reconnaissance the next day proved the stricken ship had sunk. For the next two days the bombers and fighters attacked, but on January 8 the harassed shipping reached Lae and unloaded. The following morning the convoy pulled out, leaving a beached transport and perhaps four thousand fresh troops behind. Although two transports had been sunk and the P-40s and P-38s claimed over fifty of the protecting fighters shot down, Lae had been reinforced.

With their fresh troops, the Japanese moved inland toward Wau, where the Australians had a small, isolated force in the old gold fields area. The Australians fought a close, cruel fight for the trails around Wau, before a sudden attack near the airfield on January 29 was beaten off. The Japanese were back soon after, infiltrating the area. Wau had called for help, but bad weather was holding the C-47s at Port Moresby with the desperately needed reinforcements. Almost providentially, the weather changed over the mountains and the bloated transports moved out, taking to beleaguered Wau the first of the more than two thousand troops who would be delivered within the next two days.

The Japanese had already reached one end of the uphill strip and mortar fire was thumping into the vital field. The C-47s had only enough room to land, and as the doors opened the troops jumped to the ground and raced into battle, bullets and shrapnel whining around them. Some transports were even forced to wait above until the Australians grenaded the Japanese out of the way, but fifty-seven landed at Wau, unloaded with their engines running, then took off to make room for the next planes. The following morning the Japanese again tried to take the strip but by noon they had been driven back, and Wau would hold out.

For some reason the Japanese air forces were not used in the operations against Wau until the real struggle was over. Then on February 6 eight P-39s from the 40th Squadron were escorting transports to Wau when they spotted a formation of twenty-four Zekes and six Sallys over the area. They swooped on the neat formation, their nose cannon chugging, and shot down eleven Zekes and a Sally. Eight 49th Group P-40s attacked twelve Lilys, wrongly identified initially as Australian Beauforts, bombing the airfield with an escort of Hamps and Zekes, and seven more Japanese planes were shot down. Five other enemy planes fell to three squadrons of fighters Whitehead sent over from Port Moresby to help. The Japanese were the ones needing help that day—they lost at least twenty-four aircraft without inflicting a loss. It was such a stunning victory for the fighters, particularly the P-39s, that Kenney and MacArthur thought they should release the facts with a statement that "our losses were light," rather than strain their credibility.

While the Allied fighters ruled the sky over New Guinea, Kenney was anxious about the future. The Guadalcanal battle was winding down and he knew that the struggles in New Guinea would intensify proportionately. The Wau battle was in-

When the Japanese bombers arrived over Wau on February 6, 1943, there were four C-47s on the field and five more circling to land. One stick of bombs fell right along the center of the runway, but all except one transport escaped harm. This Australian Wirraway had just landed, and the pilot and observer were only a few yards from the aircraft. They dived to the ground as a bomb exploded alongside the plane and demolished it. (Australian War Memorial)

The 90th Group and their Liberators moved up to Port Moresby on February 10, 1943, and there was spirited competition with the Fortress fliers of the 43rd Bomb Group. General Kenney remembers the time when a B-24 crew mistook some rocks for a Japanese convoy, and the 43rd seemed unlikely to let the incident be forgotten. The 43rd Group officers were cordially invited to have dinner with the 90th's officers and they promptly accepted, as rumors had circulated that the 90th had flown in some Australian beer. That evening, as the 43rd's jeeps made the last turn in the winding road leading to the 90th's mess, they saw what was clearly an outhouse just off the road. A large billboard atop said "Headquarters, 43rd Bombardment Group." Nobody said anything about it all evening, as they ate and finished off the beer. Then early next morning, as the 90th was awakening, a lone B-17 roared over the treetops and opened fire on the structure with incendiary ammunition. The edifice blazed as the Fortress disappeared over the horizon. Kenney decided he knew nothing about this, but passed the word through to take it easy. The conflict continued on a lesser scale, with paint bombings, the dropping of insulting leaflets, and even the Jolly Roger flag was stolen and last seen over a Sydney bar. (T/Sgt M. H. Clay)

dicative and reported airfield development as far west as Babo and east to Lae added emphasis. Airstrips were being built and developed on Wakde Island, Hollandia, and at Wewak.

During January, Rabaul had been hit thirteen times, but never by more than a dozen bombers, because Kenney had no choice but to guard carefully the heavy bombers at his disposal. His Fortresses in the 43rd Bomb Group were well worn and of their fifty-five B-17Es and B-17Fs, twenty were usually being overhauled or repaired. With their heavy involvement in reconnaissance, this left the group with perhaps twelve or fourteen Fortresses available for strikes. The 90th Group's B-24s took over much of the work during January, but maintenance of the Liberators was difficult and there were modifications to carry out. So of the sixty B-24s in the group, only about fifteen were available for any combat mission.

The problem had been eased by movement of some of the heavy bombers to Port Moresby and Milne Bay rather than flying them up from Australia and staging them through forward bases. Development of the airfields at Port Moresby had been progressing rapidly and six of the seven fields within thirty miles of Moresby were in constant use. The three fields at Milne Bay were less efficient, but Dobodura had begun to take shape as a major base.

Kenney had based most of his twin-engine bombers at Port Moresby, where he had six squadrons of mediums. The 22nd Bomb Group, which had fought long and hard and taken plenty of punishment, had been sent back to Australia with their Marauders. Two squadrons of the 3rd Attack were equipped with B-25s,

The 63rd Squadron's *Black Jack,* with Captain Harry Staley and his crew. Staley, standing on the left, was Ken McCullar's co-pilot during the early days when the 63rd proved the value of skip bombing. The B-17F carries the fixed nose gun installation, sighted on a line of rivets on the top of the nose. (Anthony DeAngelis)

while the 8th and 89th Squadrons had suffered enough losses to force them to operate essentially as one A-20 squadron. Two squadrons of the 38th Group were virtually up to strength, with B-25s.

The 9th Squadron of the 49th Fighter Group had converted to P-38s early in January, while the other two squadrons kept their P-40s. There were five squadrons of Airacobras in the 8th and 35th Fighter Groups, and the 39th Squadron's P-38s.

It was toward the end of February when the Fifth received information that a large reinforcement convoy was going to run to Lae early in the following month, carrying the Japanese 51st Infantry Division. In detail, the Japanese plan revealed that seven merchant vessels and eight destroyers would leave Rabaul before midnight on February 28, reach Lae March 3, and be back at Rabaul five days later. One hundred army and navy planes would cover them along the way.

At Moresby, Whitehead was fully aware of the reports and tightened his reconnaissance net to make sure the convoy was sighted early, and kept in sight.

The B-25s and P-38s were concentrated at Dobodura and other missions were eased off so that every airplane could be thrown against the convoy around the clock. Kenney correctly believed that this was a golden opportunity to really punish the Japanese and stall new offensives in New Guinea. If the shipping could be located early the heavies would begin the attack, and when the convoy came within range of the B-25s and A-20s, they would be unleashed in co-ordinated attacks on a scale never attempted before. Meanwhile, the shorter-range aircraft could keep hitting Lae airdrome to limit the Japanese fighters' operations. He also had a surprise for the Japanese navy. Back in November he had sent word to Pappy Gunn to pull the bombardier and everything else out of the nose of a B-25 and fill the space with .50-caliber machine guns. For good measure, more guns were to be strapped around the nose to give as much forward firepower as the plane could carry. If it still flew, the Fifth would have a low-level bomber which could clear the decks of a Japanese ship as it made its run. With this "commerce destroyer," the aerial blockade could be enforced anywhere within their range. It was the morning of November 29 when Kenney first went to look over the job. A package of four guns, similar to those on the A-20, fitted neatly in the nose, and two more were being mounted in packages on each side of the fuselage just under the cabin. Three more were going underneath the fuselage, but the ammunition feed was causing difficulties, and it seemed they would have to be discarded. Pappy Gunn reported that firing the guns had popped some rivets, but that could be cured with longer blast tubes and stiffer mounts. Kenney thought the plane looked nose-heavy, and asked Gunn about the center of gravity. Pappy's lined face was impassive: "Oh, the C.G. Hell, we threw that away to lighten the ship."

Kenney returned about ten days later, and since the aircraft was still nose-heavy, it was decided to move the gun packages on each side of the fuselage back about three feet. They were still popping rivets even though the fuselage had been stiffened with steel plates, so felt was put between the plates and the skin to soak up the shock. However, the felt dried hard after it was wet and the vibration was tremendous. Sponge rubber was the answer. Every time the troublesome bottom guns were fired the door that folded up behind the nosewheel fell off, so Kenney settled for the four nose guns, the two on each side, and wanted the top turret guns fixed so they could be locked to fire forward. He told Gunn to fire twenty thousand rounds through the installation and if the plane was still holding together he would put together a squadron.

It worked, and Kenney told Captain Ed Larner, a daring pilot from the 3rd Attack, to help with the testing and learn to like the new B-25. It was December 29 when Larner flew the modified B-25 to Moresby, and Kenney promoted him and gave him the 90th Squadron. His first job was to train his squadron on the old wreck on the reef outside Port Moresby until they learned to like the aircraft too. Twice during February the 90th had gone out to try their modified B-25s against real targets, but had not been able to locate the shipping. As February ended they were ready.

Kenney flew up to Port Moresby to watch a full dress rehearsal of the forthcoming mission, to perfect the timing, on February 28. With Whitehead he went over and over the available intelligence trying to foresee what would happen, trying to put himself in the minds of the Japanese commanders. Studying the routes of every convoy for months previously, they found there was a consistent enough pattern. Over-all bad weather was predicted for the first few days of March, promising additional cover to the Japanese, but it would be worst along the north coast of New Britain, so the Japanese would probably use that northern route, which meant the job would belong to the B-17s and B-24s until the convoy passed through the Vitiaz Strait between New Britain and New Guinea.

The Battle of the Bismarck Sea

Stormy weather cloaked the convoy until the afternoon of March 1, when a B-24 sighted fourteen ships escorted by fighters. A couple of hours later another Liberator took off to shadow the convoy into the worsening weather. The bomber crew found increasing difficulty in keeping the convoy in sight and lost it altogether about an hour before midnight.

That afternoon the Fifth stood poised to strike . . . six Australian Bostons had hit Lae airdrome to keep it out of the coming action . . . seven Fortresses were sent out to attack the convoy and they searched the whole north coast of New Britain, dropping flares and flying fifty feet above the water with their lights on to attract fire, but to no avail; they returned to Moresby at midnight.

At four-fifteen in the morning of March 2, Lieutenant Archie Browning, flying the 90th Group's *The Butcher Boy,* took off from Moresby. Four hours later, as the big plane temporarily broke through the cloud, one of the waist gunners excitedly called in on the interphone that he had seen the convoy off to the left. Radioing the position of the sighting, Browning circled toward the ships and eased down from two thousand feet. When *The Butcher Boy* next popped out of the clouds she was almost on top of the convoy and the whole crew tried to count. Their figures averaged out at fourteen. They took the larger destroyers to be cruisers, a very common error, but the count seemed to be seven warships and seven cargo or transport vessels. By this time the weather which had sheltered the Japanese was beginning to break up.

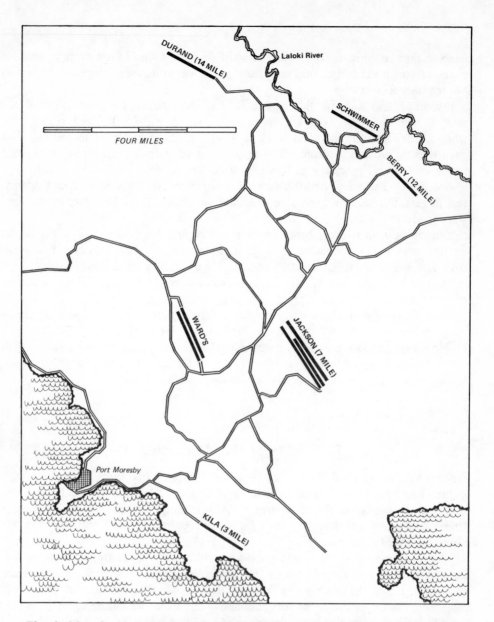

The six Moresby air bases in spring 1943. The B-25s of the 90th, 71st, and 405th Bomb Squadrons were at Durand with the 7th Fighter Squadron's P-40s. The Lightnings of the 9th and 39th Fighter Squadrons were at Schwimmer with the 13th Bomb Squadron's Mitchells. The 40th Fighter Squadron's Airacobras were at Berry, while the C-47s of the 6th and 33rd Troop Carrier Squadrons were at Ward's. Down at Kila were the A-20s of the 8th and 89th Bomb Squadrons with the 8th Fighter Squadron's P-40s. Jackson's three runways carried the weight of the 41st Fighter Squadron's P-39s, the Fortresses of the 63rd, 64th, and 65th Bomb Squadrons, the 22nd Troop Carrier Squadron's C-47s, and the Liberators of the 320th and 321st Bomb Squadrons.

Pappy Gunn and his masterpiece, the B-25 "commerce destroyer."

At 9:50 A.M. *The Butcher Boy* was still hugging the edge of the storm when the first B-17s arrived. Browning put them on the right track, waited a little while longer, then headed back to his base, dropping four bombs on Finschhafen on the way past.

Eight Fortresses from Major Ed Scott's 63rd Squadron made the first effective attack on the convoy. Flying in loose formation they reached the target area and the first three planes stayed together while the others split up for individual attacks. Scott was flying a B-17 named *Talisman,* with Captain Harry Staley on his right wing, and Lieutenant Francis Denault in *Lulu Belle* on his left. They made their bombing run from sixty-five hundred feet at ten o'clock on a large transport, one of the seven ships sighted at the time. Scott said that "suddenly the cloud cleared slightly, and though it was still raining like hell, we could see the ships below us. There were four lines, with the biggest baby in each category in the middle of each line. We turned and started our run with Staley and Denault on our wings, then the Zeros hit us. There were eight and they made a double co-ordinated attack, both high and low. The gunners in the waist, tail, ball turret and forward threw everything they had at the Zeros. The ship was a full-sized transport. We were bumping about as ack-ack from the destroyers went off in the clouds around us. Then the signal went on that the bombs were gone."

Crossing the ships diagonally the three Fortresses dropped their bombs, and Scott's string of four neatly caught his target, three striking amidship near the funnel and the fourth falling in the water. Staley's first three hit the water, but the fourth landed on the deck near the bow. Denault's first hit the stern and the other three exploded in a row less than forty feet away. The big transport was lost in a vast puff of smoke and boiling spray, followed by a series of internal explosions.

While the longer-range bombers stood poised to destroy the convoy, the A-20s kept the Japanese fighters at Lae out of the battle.

Lieutenant Jim Murphy, flying *Panama Hattie,* could hardly see through the rain lashing the windows of his cabin as he picked a destroyer for his target. The warship made a sharp turn and Murphy's bombs fell where it had just been. The destroyer pumped up shells as Murphy angled the B-17 for another run, and *Panama Hattie* was bucking and lurching as the explosions bracketed her. Murphy decided it would be wiser to try for a freighter, and chose one. His bombardier dropped one bomb which blew out the side of the ship—three members of his crew reported seeing it break cleanly in two, turning over with the bow and stern sinking separately within a couple of minutes.

The visibility was very bad, and one fighter squadron could not link up with the bombers and the other lost contact before the mission was over. The 39th Squadron was trying to find a break in the clouds when they saw three Oscars tailing the heavy bombers, and they struck quickly. Tom Lynch and his wingman went after one, which turned back into another flight and was shot down. Captain Charles King closed on a climbing Oscar and gave it three long bursts—the fighter rolled drunkenly and burst into flame before the pilot even had a chance to drop his belly tank. The Oscar trailed smoke as it went straight down. The third got away. The 9th Fighter Squadron met twenty fighters and destroyed at least five.

The P-38 fighter cover had failed to link up with the first B-17s and the second flight of twenty which had followed them also arrived without its fighter escort. These twenty B-17s claimed two hits and four near misses. The convoy had been spread over a wide area and broken cloud and heavy, opaque thundershowers confused the crews of the bombers, forcing them to split up and seek out targets on the gray water. It seemed that some of the ships were finding cover for themselves under local rain squalls.

In the evening eleven Fortresses made the final attack of March 2, and this last attack of the day left one vessel sinking according to the reports. A B-17 clung to the contact until nightfall, and an RAAF Catalina stayed with the convoy during the night, turning the job over to another B-17 early the following morning, March 3. Seven Australian Beauforts were sent to make an early morning torpedo attack, but only two were able to reach the target. One attacked a destroyer but missed and the other could not release his torpedo. It was a small beginning to a big day.

At 9:30 A.M. on Wednesday, March 3, the Allied Air Forces planes were assembled over Cape Ward Hunt. When the keyed-up airmen first glimpsed the convoy it was in perfect order again. Two rows of freighters flanked by destroyers, leaving parallel wakes behind them—clean, stark lines on the brilliant blue water. Upon sighting the first Allied planes they immediately broke, the destroyers speeding forward and swinging out in front as a screen, and the freighters turning every way to spread themselves out.

The aircraft began getting into position. The B-17s droned on, opening their doors, as the Japanese opened fire from five miles away. Thirteen Australian Beaufighters from Wing Commander "Black Jack" Walker's 30th Squadron began a shallow dive from six thousand feet. They came within range of the destroyers at

The Butcher Boy, one of the 90th Group B-24s which found and shadowed the Bismarck Sea convoy. (T/Sgt M. H. Clay)

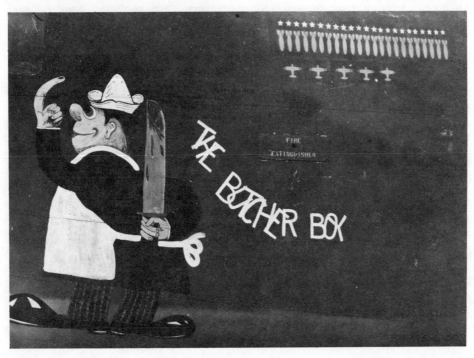

Lieutenant Woodrow Moore's B-17, seconds before it went down. Fire is faintly visible in the radio room area. Japanese fighters followed the plane down, strafing the crew as they bailed out. (Roger Vargas)

five hundred feet, where they formed in line abreast, dropping rapidly and picking up speed. Veering right around four destroyers, then switching back on their course, they attacked the merchant shipping.

As the Beaufighters strafed, thirteen Fortresses were making their bombing runs. The enemy fighters chose to concentrate their attacks on the B-17s. Twenty-eight P-38s, sixteen of them from the 39th Squadron flying high cover, and the rest from the 9th as close cover, were providing the fighter protection. Major George Prentice was leading the 39th and decided the best thing to do was find the largest pack of enemy fighters and just tear into them; they ran into a loose formation of twenty or thirty fighters flying in scattered flights of eight, including Zekes, Oscars, and Hamps. The P-38s followed the Japanese in a large climbing turn to the left, and in less than one full turn the fight started. Captain Bob Faurot dived his flight after three or four below the main bunch, and the P-38s shot down ten in the wild twenty-five minutes that followed. Lieutenant Jack Jones was out of ammunition and down on the deck after doing a simulated spin-out when he saw another P-38 with a smoking right engine pancake into the sea, bounce a couple of times, and nose in, with the tail sticking straight up. He saw the pilot, Lieutenant Hoyt Eason, get out in his Mae West about twenty miles from Cape Ward Hunt, but although Eason was sighted by several other aircraft during the morning, he was never found. Captain Faurot and another pilot were also lost, and it was the 39th's worst day of the war.

Four 63rd Squadron B-17Fs were making their runs, three in formation and the fourth about a thousand feet higher and behind. The wedge of three made a run on a small cargo vessel and dropped a couple of bombs without observing results, then continued on and dropped six more on a large merchant vessel, scoring some very near misses. The fourth Fortress also bombed this ship and placed three bombs just short of it and one just over it, bringing the total of near misses to six at least. Lieutenant William Thompson, flying *Panama Hattie,* was savagely attacked by ten to fifteen fighters—as one Zero slipped in from the left the tail gunner fired a burst which blew it apart in the air. The gunner in the ball turret got another and it crashed into the sea. A waist gunner shot the wing of another to shreds and saw it hit the water.

Lieutenant Francis Denault, in *Lulu Belle,* was flying "buddy" with Lieutenant Woodrow Moore's B-17. They too were attacked by fighters from every direction. Lieutenant Roger Vargas, the navigator, manning the flexible nose gun, knocked one out of the air. A waist gunner got another. Moore's plane, the third in the formation of three, was attacked by a Hamp from ten o'clock below. The Japanese fighter came up under the broad wing, rolled on its back, and dived out under. A fire started in the wing or radio compartment of the Fortress, and Moore pulled up and away from the formation and salvoed his bombs. Then the B-17 went down, disintegrating before it reached the water. Seven men were seen bailing out, but one was thrown from his chute when the harness slipped, and Japanese fighters strafed the others as they floated helplessly down.

So far the Battle of the Bismarck Sea had cost one bomber and three fighters.

Thirteen Mitchells followed the Beaufighters to make a medium-altitude attack. Following them were the twelve modified B-25C1s of the 90th Squadron, Major Ed Larner leading them in *Spook II.* Directly ahead of the speeding B-25s big splashes on the water showed that the P-38s had dropped their wing tanks as they prepared to fight high above.

After a fast descent the 90th Squadron broke out of some puffy cloud with the convoy directly ahead of them. Captain Jock Henebry, leading the second element of four planes, recalls seeing all those ships and feeling "scared as hell" at the thought of flying right up to their sides at water level. Then Larner peeled off. When three B-25s went with him he radioed, "Dammit, get the hell off my wing and get your own boat." That broke the spell, and the B-25s streaked toward the ships.

Each Mitchell strafer carried three or four bombs, and their eight forward-firing guns were feeding on belts of ammunition made up of one tracer, two armor-piercing, then two incendiary. Larner's four-plane element attacked from the front, Henebry's from the side, and the third immediately followed Henebry's planes, although it had to fly parallel to the convoy for some distance to find ships not already under attack by the first two.

Some B-25s began their one- or two-mile runs in shallow dives, pulling up just in time to clear the masts at an air speed of around two hundred and sixty miles an hour. Others made the entire run at wavetop level, sacrificing that final burst of speed which the dive made possible. Ed Larner attacked the biggest destroyer and scored a near miss and a direct hit, rolling the ship on its side. He then hit a transport, setting it on fire. His last bomb exploded off the stern of a destroyer.

Captain Robert Chatt in *Chatterbox* got two direct hits and near misses on a

Major Ed Larner, commander of the 90th Squadron. On November 7, 1942, Larner was attacking Japanese artillery and machine gun positions at Soputa when an antiaircraft burst under the tail tipped the nose of his plane, causing it to hit the trees at the end of the strafing run. Larner tore through the tree tops for a hundred yards and brought the plane back to Moresby with the wings dented, an engine full of leaves and branches, and the bottom of the fuselage grooved by a tree. He reported that "following this accident I was able to make only two more strafing passes before the plane became so unmanageable that I thought it best to return to base." Larner was killed in a landing accident at Dobodura on April 30, 1943. (General George C. Kenney)

large destroyer, blasting the superstructure entirely away. The burning warship lurched and stopped.

Henebry strafed his way up to a transport and dropped a bomb right on its waterline. On a second run he missed by fifteen feet, but the ship was burning violently as he came in to strafe it.

Lieutenant Gordon McCoun angled *Mortimer* toward an eight-thousand-ton transport loaded with soldiers. One bomb hit the waterline and another the middle of the ship, while the third passed right over, but the target was blazing.

Lieutenant Ray Moore selected a five-thousand-ton transport. He made a gentle turn away from a destroyer screening it and then began a power glide from four thousand feet to gather speed. At a thousand feet he turned parallel to his target and flew a descending course which put the B-25 at right angles to the ship. Moore swung sharply to the left and made a direct run in. Pouring on all the power he corkscrewed his B-25, skidding from one side to the other and jinking up and down. In range he opened fire, and the bullets sprayed over the ship. The decks of the transport were covered with enemy troops, lined up with their rifles in their hands. As the machine guns blazed from between the teeth of the leering shark mouth painted on the Mitchell's nose they slumped in heaps on the decks or tumbled over the side.

Moore stopped firing as the target drew close and he could no longer hold his B-25 in a firing position and make an effective bomb run too. His co-pilot opened the bomb bay and Moore made a gradual pull-up to avoid the mast of the ship as he released his bombs. They slammed into the water, skipped at the side of the ship, and exploded, rocking the vessel violently and leaving a huge hole at the waterline. Moore made a steep climbing turn to the left to sidestep a nearby destroyer, at the same time veering away from the target. His crew saw the ship was sinking as he pulled away.

The 90th had dropped thirty-seven bombs, and claimed seventeen direct hits on the eleven ships they attacked.

A dozen A-20s from the 89th Squadron were in the battle. Flying an A-20 named *Adam LaZonga,* Captain Ed Chudoba got his first glimpse of the carnage when a ship ahead and to his left blew up, throwing flames a half mile into the air. Chudoba first thought it was a destroyer, but the destroyer he had mentally noted in that position slowly pulled away, revealing another ship beyond it wrapped in flame and smoke from stem to stern. The destroyer, looking like a battleship to Chudoba, opened fire.

The A-20s were almost opposite the middle of the convoy on its left side, in two vees of six planes each. Then *Adam LaZonga* was sliding down from two thousand feet at an angle which would bring it out just over the masts of the ship.

The chatter in the earphones was terrific. The time was exactly three minutes after ten o'clock and the ships ahead were rapidly growing larger. Lieutenant Charles Mayo, in *Rebel Rocket,* was flying on Chudoba's right wing, on the right side of the six-plane formation. There was one ship ahead and two to the left. Chudoba dived and turned to the left under Captain Glen Clark, the flight leader, with Mayo following, but the two planes on the left side were also going after the nearest ship on the left. In spite of the briefings not to pile up on the same ship, things were getting confusing. Chudoba wrenched the A-20 back toward the big ship right ahead.

He remembers looking over his right shoulder and seeing Clark's aircraft behind him. Mayo, on his right, said, "I'm going off and get me a fat one," and made a mast-height run on a transport. Strafing all the way, he attacked it broadside—both his bombs hit, and *Rebel Rocket* passed over the ship at deck level.

The ship was near as Chudoba pulled the trigger on the wheel, and there was the smell of smoke as the guns roared. He could see tracers and heavier fire coming from the ship. As he pulled the bomb switch a small-caliber bullet smacked through the Plexiglas canopy, but Chudoba couldn't see anyone on the deck and the gun crews were well hidden. He let his two bombs go then, "Wham! I got it just as I passed over the ship. Old *Adam LaZonga* shuddered with the blow. There was something wrong with the right wing and the plane wasn't flying right. I thought I had been hit with ack-ack, but Captain Clark told me later that I had clipped the top of the ship's radio mast. There was a dent in the front surface of my wing six inches deep. In the same second I got a kick in the pants from the explosion of Captain Clark's bomb. Some of our planes were equipped with cameras and Captain Clark got a picture of my ship taken just as my bombs exploded; it

Captain Ed Chudoba's target, the *Taimei Maru*.

also showed that one of his bombs had skipped right over the ship. We got the name of the ship as we passed over and checked it. It was the *Taimei Maru,* an eight-thousand-ton cargo ship. The *Taimei Maru* was a familiar caller at the port of San Francisco before the war. There was a warship off to my left throwing up a lot of stuff. I executed a violent series of zooms, diving and soaring to keep the gunners from holding a bead on me. Nothing hit me."

Chudoba strafed a transport from bow to stern and then there was a lot of chatter on the radio as they tried to check each other in. Some Zeros were chasing an A-20, but broke off when a couple of others turned toward them. Chudoba could hear Clark calling to the squadron that they would rendezvous again at Cape Ward Hunt. On his way out, he looked back and watched eight tall columns of smoke rising starkly into the sky. *Adam LaZonga* was not flying quite right, and Chudoba could not get much speed, but he made it home.

The A-20s claimed eleven direct hits and six more Mitchells later reported four additional hits. These B-25s also reported two cargo ships burning as a result of a collision while attempting to get out of the way of bombs.

As the morning ended the battered Japanese convoy received a brief rest, and shortly after noon a B-17 on reconnaissance saw five ships burning and four standing by. Visibility was clear, and all of the remaining ships were probably observed. If so, the difference between this sighting and the morning sighting of fourteen suggests four merchant vessels had been sunk as well as either a destroyer or another merchant vessel.

The afternoon strikes were necessarily lighter, but using the same mixture of aircraft. As usual the weather was worsening over the Owen Stanleys, and this upset the planning and timing. The Beaufighters and A-20s could not cross New Guinea, and of twenty-nine B-25s, six could not locate the target. The B-17s made the first attack midway through the afternoon, and Major Ed Scott of the 63rd Squadron found himself alone in *Tuffy* when his wingman had to return with engine trouble. Scott decided to continue and tagged onto the B-17s from the other squadrons. Approaching a large destroyer in a diving turn and leveling off at seven thousand feet, Scott dropped two bombs which stopped the warship and set it afire. Dropping *Tuffy* down to fifty feet, Scott beat over the waves, his gunners shooting every survivor in sight. The crew, bitter about the fate of Woodrow Moore's aircraft that morning, relished the job. One gunner fired eleven hundred rounds of ammunition and burned out two guns.

Then eight strafer B-25s of the 90th Squadron came in low. They left a destroyer sinking after four direct hits and another probably sinking. Fifteen other B-25s claimed another ten hits. At about the same time five RAAF Bostons singled out a destroyer while more B-17s bombed through both the Mitchells and the Bostons. The battle had been won before the last bombs erupted—it was a tremendous victory for Allied air power. Reconnaissance planes strafed survivors until dark, and then during the night Navy torpedo boats finished off a crippled vessel.

Kenney left for Washington to fight for more airplanes and men at six o'clock in the morning of March 4, but before he went he sent a message to Whitehead: *Congratulations on that stupendous success. Air power has written some important history in the past three days. Tell the whole gang that I am so proud of them I am about to blow a fuze. Kenney.*

During the morning and afternoon of Thursday, March 4, the last ship of the Lae convoy afloat in the area, a destroyer, was attacked several times and finally sunk. The weather continued to be good, with visibility clear. Fittingly, the final attack on the convoy was made by B-25Cls from the 90th Squadron, split into three flights of three planes each. Major Ed Larner, Lieutenant Charles Howe, and Lieu-

Stopped in a heavy oil slick, its superstructure shattered, this *Asashio* class destroyer is rocked by bombs from a lone B-17 in the morning of March 4, 1943. That afternoon the B-25s finished it off.

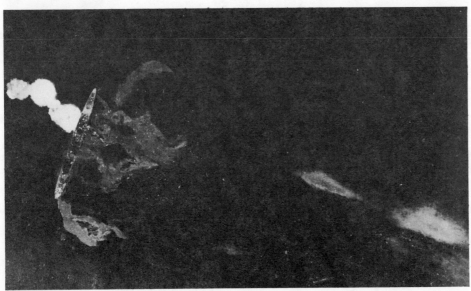

During the last bloody hours of the Bismarck Sea battle, the survivors bobbing in the water saw this before they died—shark-mouthed strafer B-25s like *Fat Cat*. (T/Sgt M. H. Clay)

tenant Edward Solomon came upon the crippled destroyer about fifty miles east of Cape Ward Hunt. It was scuttled and Japanese in full jungle uniform were clinging to lifeboats and wreckage for two miles around. Bread, tin drums, and life vests were bobbing in the water. The warship was alone and stationary. Larner peeled off with Howe and Solomon.

From a hundred feet the B-25s released six bombs, scoring two hits and three near misses. Solomon, in *Fat Cat*, made the best run of the day, coming in from the stern and catching the tail end of the ship and lifting it out of the water. From then on it sank rapidly. Larner called Jock Henebry to leave his search area and bring his flight over to join in, and they arrived to find the P-40 cover playing a round-robin strafing game on the sinking destroyer.

The remaining survivors in the sea were killed, and gigantic sharks which hovered around the floating bodies made crisscross patterns through the water as they darted in and out of the wreckage. *Spook II* zoomed down on a piece of debris with about fifteen Japanese troops on it—they had hardly jumped into the water when numerous fins flashed toward them and they all climbed aboard again. One threw his helmet at *Spook II* as Larner strafed his way toward them. The gunfire from the B-25 blew them to bloody rags.

The strafing went on for about twenty-five minutes, taking on an impersonal quality, like practice off Port Moresby. A gliding approach, a touch on the trigger to get the guns right, then a long burst. Larner's co-pilot, Lieutenant Ross Miller, had blistered hands from charging and trying to clear the hot nose guns.

At four-fifteen Larner gave the order to go home. The bloody but necessary business would continue because survivors still amounted to a large enough force to represent a danger if they could reach land. Also, the Japanese had showed no signs of surrender, futilely firing their rifles at passing planes. Some fliers were sickened by the blood and sharks but the gory work went on for three days, until by March 7 a hundred thousand rounds of ammunition had ensured nothing lived in the coastal waters of the Huon Gulf.

Unfortunately, the brilliance and success of the Bismarck Sea action has at times been almost overshadowed by an often bitter argument over the exact number of ships in the convoy. General Kenney believes that there were at least twenty-two, eight of them destroyers. Jock Henebry mentions the figure eighteen. Reports of combat crews vary to such an extent that no definite conclusion could be based on them. Japanese records often disagree with Allied reports, and appear very incomplete; basically they state that there were eight troop transports, escorted by eight destroyers, and that the convoy set out from Rabaul during the night of February 28, 1943. The destroyers were the *Tokitsukaze, Arashio, Yukikaze, Asashio, Uranami, Shikinami, Skirayuki,* and *Asagumo.* On March 2 a direct bomb hit set fire to the *Kyokusei Maru,* carrying fifteen hundred troops. The stricken ship was abandoned and sank later northeast of Cape Gloucester. The destroyers *Yukikaze* and *Asagumo* safely collected about eight hundred of the troops and raced for Lae, ahead of the rest of the convoy. They were able to unload the troops and rejoin the convoy early in the morning of March 3.

The naval transport *Nojima* had been damaged, but according to Japanese records there were fifteen ships off the Huon Peninsula when the major attacks be-

At six in the morning on March 4, 1943, three B-17s, *The Mustang, Talisman,* and this one, *Fightin Swede,* went out looking for targets. Finding about six landing barges near Lae, they strafed them unmercifully, and one capsized trying to escape the gunfire. Two Zeros continually attacked the B-17s, slightly wounding the pilot and two crewmen on *Fightin Swede.* (Roger Vargas)

gan. The Japanese expected a torpedo attack when the 90th's B-25s roared in, and their evasive action played into the hands of the strafers. After about an hour, all seven transports were either sunk or burning, as were three of the destroyers, including the *Tokitsukaze*. Four of the other five destroyers found as many survivors as they could before racing north to escape further punishment. After losing contact with one of these ships the Japanese presumed it had dropped back and been sunk by the Allies. With darkness, three of the destroyers headed back to the battle area to try to rescue more troops before sailing to Rabaul and Kavieng just before dawn on March 4.

Out of nearly 7,000 troops, the Japanese acknowledge the loss of 3,664. All that reached Lae were the 800 or so rushed in by the destroyers, and 2,427 survivors were taken to Rabaul.

One fact has never been challenged—the important fact that the convoy was annihilated by Allied air power.

* * *

The Fifth Air Force had won a stunning victory, but it was still a small force fighting on an immense front. The men were under a continual strain in the poor conditions and although the food was all that was required medically, most of the men could expect to lose up to twenty pounds in New Guinea. The climate made them particularly susceptible to the local illnesses and at Milne Bay malaria was so great a problem that it led to the withdrawal to Australia of the 80th Fighter Squadron. Kenney moved his units between Australia and New Guinea as often as he could because while in Australia they were provided with plenty of fresh food. Visits to the capital cities of Australia also played an important part in the morale of combat crews. Sydney was more than two thousand miles away from the war, and it was a city where most of the male population was somewhere else. For the crews, usually with plenty of money, there were apartments to rent, swimming and surf riding at Bondi and Manly beaches, horse racing at Randwick . . . there were movies and night spots, and tossing pennies into the chandelier at the Australia Hotel was a long, long way from the sweat and flies at Port Moresby.

When he asked for reinforcements in Washington Kenney only received the assurance of getting an additional heavy, medium, and light bomber group by September 1943, plus two fighter groups and an observation group and some other increases in strength—estimates of what would be needed to carry out the plans involving the Fifth were put aside. Yet although Kenney got less than he wanted he had actually talked them into giving more than had been intended.

March was the sixth month in which losses in the Fifth exceeded the replacements received, and this caused Kenney only a little less worry. Some of the 8th Fighter Squadron's P-40s had over four hundred flight hours and one medium group and an A-20 squadron were out of combat between March and May simply because they had nothing to fly. A B-17 squadron never had more than five aircraft on hand during this time and another medium squadron which had seven B-25s operational at the end of March had only three at the end of May. So the official count of groups and squadrons was still words, and numbers on paper. Real combat strength until May was really one light, three medium, and seven heavy bomber squadrons, and the nine fighter squadrons.

The 65th Squadron's *The Old Man,* at Dobodura after tangling with Zeros over Gasmata on March 8, 1943. This B-17F was one of the most tenacious—after the battles she became Whitehead's personal transport, with the radio compartment specially modified for passengers. (Army)

It seemed that everybody had priority over the Fifth. When Kenney wanted A-20s the Twelfth Air Force had priority, and they also had the P-38 market cornered. Eight Lightnings of a scheduled fifteen per month had arrived in January, but Kenney was advised in February that things were bad in North Africa and there would be no more P-38s until summer. He managed to secure the 348th Fighter Group, a P-47 Thunderbolt unit originally earmarked for Europe, for the Fifth and the activation of the 475th Fighter Group in June was authorized, and P-38s would be available for it if Kenney provided the men.

While there was hope for the future, reinforcements in April and May were just six P-70s of the 418th Night Fighter Squadron, fulfilling a request made back in October 1942. Converted A-20s, the P-70s had to be reworked to improve their speed, ceiling, and maneuverability before they could be used and other modifications to aircraft had to be carried out in the theater. When they first arrived the 90th Group's B-24s had insufficient forward firepower and the Japanese quickly exploited the weakness. While training in Louisiana Lieutenant Colonel Art Rogers, commander of the 400th Squadron, had walked by a B-24 tail and thought it was a pity the nose was not as well protected. He wondered why not and got a steel tape and began measuring. Within a couple of hours he had been sure his idea would work, but he was still "negotiating" to get the pieces from a cracked-up

Liberator when the 90th was ordered elsewhere. When the group again moved it was to Willow Run, Michigan, where the Ford plant was building Liberators, and Rogers discussed the idea with the technical experts and a mock-up was built. But a few days later the 90th was on its way to Hawaii, Rogers taking pictures and drawings of the mock-up with him. In Hawaii Colonel Marion Unruh and a crew at the Hawaiian Air Depot began working on the installation of the tail turret in the nose of a B-24, but before the job was completed the 90th was moving again, this time to the Southwest Pacific. In combat the Japanese tactics quickly convinced Rogers of the worth of a nose turret, so he got permission to go to Brisbane to see if it was possible to install a tail turret from a wrecked 90th B-24 in the nose of his aircraft. In Brisbane he found his onetime commander Brigadier General Carl Connell running the Air Service Command, and he was eager to help. He arranged for Rogers to talk it over with General Kenney, who agreed it was well worth trying.

With the pictures and drawings as models the turret was installed after a lot of trial and error, and Rogers took the aircraft up. He was delighted to find that the aircraft had picked up over eight miles an hour in speed, and during the first week of March the B-24, named *Connell's Special,* landed at Port Moresby. A lone mission to Wewak by the modified B-24 quickly proved the effectiveness of the installation, and the Fifth had already asked for thirty-five of the turrets, requesting also that they be installed in Hawaii on all aircraft bound for the Southwest Pacific. The

The modified *Connell's Special* draws a crowd at Port Moresby. The 90th Group had some of the finest gunners in the Fifth Air Force—Art Rogers reasoned that lack of education or minor physical deficiencies were secondary factors to the killer instinct, and sought out good natural marksmen in the group, men who had been hunters back home. A power turret was fitted with twin shotguns and set up on a skeet range, and sixteen "kills" out of twenty-five shots were required for a gunner to qualify. (T/Sgt M. H. Clay)

turrets arrived during March and two months later Kenney asked for thirty-six more for new B-24s he had received. He also wanted to substitute manually operated twin belly guns for the Sperry ball turret, but if planes were to be sent out with this modification it meant a production line problem, since the other theaters wanted the ball turret. Finally it would be agreed that Kenney's Liberators would be sent without the turrets, but it is not surprising that about this time the general noted that he hoped for the day when the Fifth's groups could be entirely equipped with four types of aircraft—the B-25, B-24, P-38, and C-47.

* * *

On the northern coast of New Guinea, Dobodura had been invaluable during the Buna battle. The road to Dobodura from Oro Bay, a small port about fifteen miles southeast of Buna, would not be open until May, so in the meantime plans for the development of the field were implemented in every possible way. At Oro Bay wharves were built for receiving supplies coming in by small boat and these were carried on to Dobodura by jeep and native carriers over improved tracks. The C-47s continued delivering men and matériel to the airstrips, and the 49th Fighter Group's ground crews had been sent to Dobodura in February so that their planes could fly in every morning, stand alert all day, then return to Moresby in the evening. By April the whole group was stationed there but the forward movement brought the usual difficulties—shortly after arriving, the 9th Squadron reported that P-38s which were out of commission were being scavenged to keep the sixteen needed for the daily alert flying. One of the main disadvantages at Dobodura was a lack of reliable communications with Port Moresby. The high

The 49th Fighter Group faced problems at dusty Dobodura—refueling facilities were inadequate, transportation was inadequate, spare parts were hard to come by—but the advantages easily justified the hardships.

Closely covered by 35th Group Airacobras, the 374th Group C-47 *Swamp Rat II* heads for Wau. The Douglas transports enabled Kenney to fight the air war on his terms, and allowed isolated Allied outposts to exist.

mountains and the New Guinea weather disrupted radio reception and it was decided to run a telephone line right across the one hundred and fifty miles between
Port Moresby and Dobodura. It seemed an impossible job but by May the work
had begun and in just over a month it was completed. This did not entirely solve
the problem because the constant dampness rotted the poles and corroded the
wires, and violent storms grounded the lines. However, Kenney's headquarters had
to be kept in Brisbane where he could work closely with MacArthur, and
Moresby was the obvious location for Whitehead's Advon. Yet if every move had
to be cleared by Moresby or Brisbane, operations from the north of New Guinea
would be delayed, and Kenney considered a new headquarters was necessary for
operational control over the planes at Dobodura. So in March 1943 he created the
First Air Task Force (briefly known as the Buna Air Task Force), which was basically a headquarters setup composed of whatever combat units were attached to it
for a specific operation. The theater demanded this kind of tactical flexibility.
Whitehead, commanding Advon, directed the operations of all the combat units in
northeastern New Guinea, but the task force commander had the authority to send
the planes on combat missions whenever necessary. Washington did not like the
plan because it was felt that the Southwest Pacific had requested too many headquarters personnel. Kenney knew the peculiar problems of the Fifth were not fully
appreciated, but the task force was never actually authorized by the War Department, and its people were drawn from other organizations. Colonel Frederic H.
Smith, Jr., the commander, was still officially deputy chief of staff of the Fifth Air
Force. His task force was just the 49th Fighter Group at first, but by the end of
June had grown to include the 9th Squadron's P-38s, the 7th and 8th Squadron's
P-40s, a Beaufighter squadron, an A-20 squadron, a B-25 squadron, and the 90th
Squadron and its shark-mouthed strafers.

Kenney had been promised fourteen troop carrier squadrons, and he certainly
had plenty of use for them. Dobodura had to be supplied, and Japanese attacks on
the base were causing the Navy to have second thoughts about sending shipping as
far north as Oro Bay. The Fifth's transports were still supplying the Australian
troops in the Wau area and Kenney felt this work was minor by comparison to
what the troop carriers would have to accomplish in the planned capture of Lae.
He wanted to organize his troop carriers into a command on the same level as his
fighters and bombers, and on May 20 eight officers under the command of Colonel
Paul H. Prentiss were assigned to the 54th Troop Carrier Wing. Washington had
approved the move in February but things moved slowly for the first few months
and the wing was only Prentiss' old group, the 374th, and most of the staff were
men from that group.

* * *

The growing number of air raids on forward Allied bases revealed that the Japanese were becoming concerned about the gains in the Huon Gulf. Heavy enemy
raids began on March 9 when Wau was bombed with little effect. Two days later
an estimated force of twenty-six bombers and twenty-one fighters hit Horanda airstrip at Dobodura, destroying three aircraft on the ground. The defending fighters
lost a P-40 but claimed destruction of at least nine of the enemy planes. During the
night of March 14 another raid damaged installations at Oro Bay. Eighteen

bombers escorted by fighters bombed Porlock Harbor on March 17 and the worst attack of the month was carried out by forty bombers against Oro Bay on March 28. American fighters shot down six Hamps, five Zekes, and two Vals but a P-40 and its pilot were lost, a new wharf was damaged, and a couple of small ships were sunk.

Enemy attention was diverted to the Solomons, meaning a short breathing space for New Guinea, but every field around Rabaul was crowded with aircraft. On April 11 forty-five Japanese bombers and fighters were intercepted off Oro Bay by fifty P-40s and P-38s. Seventeen Japanese planes were knocked down but the bombers scored direct hits on a merchant vessel and hit a corvette and a supply ship. The next day a larger enemy force attacked Moresby. The defenders were warned in time and the fighters claimed fifteen Japanese bombers and nine or ten fighters for the loss of two, but the Japanese bombing caused heavy damage—a Beaufighter and three B-25s were destroyed and fifteen other aircraft were damaged. Bombs cratered runways and began a raging fire in a precious fuel dump.

Two days later there was a heavy but unsuccessful raid against Milne Bay, and the series of attacks abruptly ended.

Kenney simply did not have the strength to smash the bases the Japanese were flying from, and his heavy bomber force was further depleted by the vital need for

Colonel Paul Prentiss' 374th Troop Carrier Group, equipped with new C-47s in February 1943, had been born to hard times. Built around the old 21st and 22nd Squadrons, it had been filled out with the 6th Squadron, which had arrived in October 1942, and the 33rd Squadron, which got through in December after being "borrowed" by Kenney's South Pacific neighbors. These are 6th Squadron aircraft at Wau in April 1943.

Captain Franklin A. Nichols' P-40 being refueled at Dobodura. The shark-mouthed planes were part of the 7th Squadron flight known as "Nick Nichols' Nip Nippers."

Lieutenant "Jump" O'Neill stood this 9th Squadron P-38G on its nose at Dobodura after the landing gear failed on April 5, 1943. *Elsie* was Clay Tice's plane, and when he got back from hospital after a bout of malaria, he picked out a new one. The 9th's P-38s were the first fighters to use the vital forward base, operating from the bare ground in clouds of dust. (Army)

The 90th Squadron's strafer B-25s, snugly in their bulldozed revetments at Dobodura in June 1943. About thirty-five minutes by air from Port Moresby, Dobodura was the headquarters of Colonel Frederic H. Smith's First Air Task Force. (Harold Newman)

By the spring of 1943 there were six Allied airfields around Port Moresby. These 43rd Group B-17Fs are at Seven Mile.

Lieutenant Dave Brennan's *Deliverer* over Lae. When the 380th Group arrived in Australia two squadrons were sent to learn the ropes from the 43rd and 90th Groups. They reached Moresby on April 27, 1943, and their initial missions were usually daylight strikes against the New Guinea and New Britain airfields, and night attacks on Rabaul. Fourteen B-24s and crews made the trip, accompanied by only eight ground crewmen. Briefed for a week's stay, they lived on in wretched conditions until late June.

reconnaissance. The 90th Group's 319th Squadron was at Darwin watching the enemy in the Netherlands East Indies and calling themselves the "Asterperious" squadron—nobody really knew what it meant until they arrived at the definition "a superior attitude in an inferior environment." The B-17s and B-24s in New Guinea were patrolling the sea lanes and the photo Lightnings were covering New Guinea and New Britain. Even the B-25s were flying non-combat missions, meaning most of the strikes had to be carried out by the 90th Squadron's strafers, the 89th Squadron A-20s, and as many heavies as could be spared. The B-17s and B-24s sometimes attacked Rabaul, but more often Cape Gloucester or Gasmata, and a constant watch was kept for Japanese convoys although few ventured within range. The heavies did have some success attacking ships at anchor and a series of attacks against a convoy which had been tracked into Kavieng Harbor, New Ireland, was the most spectacular. For four days beginning on April 1, B-17s and B-24s attacked the ships; the skip-bombing B-17s claimed the best results, and although only one ship was sunk without any chance of salvage, hits were scored on merchant vessels, "probable cruisers," and destroyers.

Sadly, April cost the 43rd Group one of its finest pilots. In the early morning of April 12 an old 64th Squadron B-17E named *Blues in the Nite* took its position at the end of the runway for the takeoff, with Major Ken McCullar at the controls. The Fortress started down the runway, but before it had covered half of it one wheel appeared to be on fire with the flames quickly streaming the length of the B-17. Stories of what happened next are conflicting. Behind McCullar's plane was Captain Bill Crawford in *Loose Goose;* as *Blues in the Nite* lifted Crawford

Ground crewmen swarm over *Scatter Brain,* 7th Fighter Squadron commander Captain George Manning's P-40.

pushed his throttles wide open and began to roll. He saw McCullar's plane rise about fifty feet and burst into flame, fall off on one wing, and nose-dive to the earth. There was a tremendous explosion as the bomb load detonated on impact and long tongues of flame from the burning gasoline danced into the sky. It was a horrifying sight. Crawford's plane was moving too fast for him to stop and *Loose Goose* was already halfway down the runway when the explosion erupted. As soon as Crawford was airborne he dragged the nose of his B-17 up as far as he could and bounded over the mass of burning wreckage, through the thick smoke and stabs of flame. He remembers, "We never did find out exactly what happened to the ill-fated Fortress. Some said that a kangaroo had darted across the runway just as McCullar took off and became caught in the number-two engine, causing the supercharger to blow up. It was never verified. There wasn't enough left."

Leaders like Ken McCullar were not replaceable, and when Ed Larner was killed less than three weeks later in an accident the victories of the preceding months became a little less sweet.

A new series of attacks on Allied bases in New Guinea began on May 13, and the next day more than twenty bombers and twenty-five fighters attacked Dobodura, destroying a bitumen dump and a barge, but forty-three fighters shot down at least seven of the bombers and nine of the fighters. One Lightning was lost, its pilot last seen swimming twenty miles out in the shark-infested waters. Wau was hit four times in a week but on May 18 a dozen P-38s shot down seven of fifteen fighters. So the "slugging match" continued, but by the end of May a major Allied offensive was ready to begin.

III

Leaps and Bounds in New Guinea

E VEN during the Buna campaign there had been discussion regarding the capture of Lae and Salamaua, two Japanese strongpoints on the upper coast of eastern New Guinea, and ever since then the Fifth had been searching for a site to build an airdrome close enough to Lae to provide the necessary fighter cover. Dobodura's location prevented the fighters' staying more than about thirty minutes over Lae, not enough time to give absolute cover to an airborne or seaborne operation. The Fifth had surveyed Kokoda, Wau, and many other areas without finding the right place; finally a flat spot was located along the Watut River about fifty miles west of Lae near a village named Marilinan. Aviation engineer Lieutenant Everette Frazier had trekked through the thick jungle and rain forest with an Australian officer and some natives and when he reached Marilinan he found an old airfield which could handle C-47s and could possibly be improved for use by the fighters.

Although Marilinan could only fill the need until the heavy rains began in September, it was anticipated that by then the Allied advance would have reached Nadzab, about twenty miles west of Lae, which had already been assessed as ideal for a permanent base. The timing was tight but it was estimated Nadzab could be made ready in time and Marilinan would be just a stopgap base. General Paul "Squeeze" Wurtsmith wanted to fly up to look the place over, and Kenney told him to have Lieutenant A. J. Beck follow him in an A-24 to bring him out if his P-40 cracked up or the field was too short for a takeoff. Kenney also thought it would be a good idea to fill the back seat of the A-24 with trade goods to establish sound labor relations with the natives in the area.

After seeing Marilinan, Wurtsmith judged it would only be satisfactory for planes like the C-47, but a few miles north there was an excellent site near a village called Tsili Tsili.

Captain Paul Gottke's *Moby Dick* flew over one hundred missions and inspired the whole 320th Squadron to adopt her name and emulate her shark-mouth design. The old B-24D learned the hard way—on one of the 90th's early missions she came back with over two hundred holes shot through her. (T/Sgt M. H. Clay)

Kenney also planned to deceive the Japanese. Whitehead had suggested building an airfield near Bena Bena at a place called Garoka, but transport was not available for the necessary effort there. Instead Kenney gave instructions to get the natives there clearing a strip immediately, thus giving the Fifth an emergency strip and also raising enough dust to attract the Japanese and perhaps fool them into believing that the main Allied interest was there. Some camouflage and devious flying by the troop carriers just might make it work, and with luck the Marilinan activities would go unnoticed. Australian troops would be flown to Marilinan to cover the trails in the area while the engineers went to work at Tsili Tsili. That name, pronounced "silly silly," did not appeal to Kenney, particularly if something went wrong there, and he ultimately decided to call it Marilinan instead.

To haul supplies from Marilinan to Tsili Tsili the Fifth flew in jeeps and trailers at first but needed something larger. Sawing the frames of a couple of two-and-a-half-ton trucks in two, they then stuffed the pieces into C-47s and flew them over the mountains to Marilinan, where the trucks were welded and bolted together again. It worked. They then started converting trucks ahead of time, cutting them in two and bolting them together again.

By June 20 the field at Marilinan proper had been enlarged enough to handle the troop carriers and the road had been built through to Tsili Tsili. The industrious activities at Garoka and Bena Bena had apparently had the desired effect, because after June 14 the enemy attacked there almost every day, bombing empty grass huts and the cleared strips. The C-47s were able to land at Tsili Tsili by July 1 and in less than ten days they had delivered a company of engineers equipped with miniature bulldozers, graders, and other equipment. The weather interfered but soon Tsili Tsili was bustling, receiving up to one hundred and fifty C-47s a day.

This forward airstrip development was only one part of plans which had been completed by the middle of 1943, plans aimed at the reduction of Rabaul. The dual offensives in New Guinea and the Solomons would begin with a landing on Rendova Island near New Georgia by South Pacific forces; Woodlark and Kiriwina islands, at the southeast tip of New Guinea, and Nassau Bay, about fifty miles up the New Guinea coast from Morobe, were to be seized. Then Lae would be taken while Salamaua was bypassed and isolated, with other steps to cement Allied control of the Huon Gulf and Peninsula, which commanded, with Cape Gloucester on New Britain, the important Vitiaz Strait. Admiral Halsey in the South Pacific would advance into the upper Solomons as opportunities arose, setting the stage for Rabaul's demise, while in New Guinea the Australians from Wau would seize

Air transport advanced again when Kenney started drilling teams which the Fifth called Air Freight Forwarding Units. They set up an old, wingless C-47 wreck at the edge of Seven Mile and practiced loading and unloading. The time studies quickly showed the result: at first it took forty-five minutes to load a jeep and about the same to unload it, but after a few days the time was down to two and a half minutes to load and two minutes to unload. The trucks bringing supplies from warehouses to aircraft were loaded in reverse so that the cargo fed automatically and balanced correctly. Before long, C-47s were landing, unloading, and clearing Marilinan at the rate of thirty to thirty-five per hour. (Australian War Memorial)

the ridge dominating the enemy supply line between Salamaua and Mubo and American troops would push inland from Nassau Bay to join with the Australians.

Woodlark and Kiriwina were the first objectives and, although the Japanese had not bothered to occupy them, both were considered good airfield locations by the Allies. Woodlark was to be invaded by South Pacific forces, Kiriwina was the responsibility of Southwest Pacific, and both were important experiments with amphibious landing techniques. As there was no enemy defense, the air forces only had to provide fighter cover.

Reconnaissance Mission

As the ambitious plans unfolded the day-to-day work went on. The heavy bombers hit the Rabaul airfields during the second week of June and continued carrying out their share of the vital surveillance of Japanese strongpoints. In the morning of June 16 a volunteer crew in a 65th Squadron B-17E named *Lucy* was flying toward Buka to take photographs. The pilot of the aircraft was Captain Jay Zeamer, and from twenty-eight thousand feet he could see the enemy fighters taking off to intercept his Fortress. *Lucy* cruised on, continuing her run, as the crew counted the tiny Japanese planes taking to the air and climbing toward them.

More than fifteen fighters assembled in front of the Fortress and made their first pass. Lieutenant Joseph Sarnoski, the bombardier, shot one down. The top turret gunner, Sergeant John Able, got another, but an enemy bullet had sliced through the main oxygen line, forcing Zeamer to dive down to eighteen thousand feet. As he leveled the bomber he spotted a fighter coming in from the left. *Lucy* carried a fixed .50-caliber machine gun in the nose, fired by the pilot, and Zeamer slammed the rudder and made a diving turn to the left to line her up on the fighter. Sighting

The 43rd Bomb Group began converting to the B-24 Liberator in May 1943, and the change-over was completed toward the end of September. The loss of their Flying Fortresses was not greeted warmly in the group, but Ken's Men soon adjusted. *Joltin' Janie* flew with the 403rd Squadron.

on a line of rivets on the nose Zeamer pressed the trigger on his control wheel and shot the Japanese fighter out of the sky.

Leveling out again *Lucy* was hit in the nose by cannon fire which blew Sarnoski off his feet. Mortally wounded, he groped his way back to his gun and managed to shoot down another of the fighters before he died. The same attack had badly damaged the B-17—the radio, compass, flaps, and brakes were shot out. Zeamer had been peppered in both legs by shrapnel, and as the fighters continued their attacks, he was wounded in both arms and four other crewmen were hit.

The Japanese attacked relentlessly for forty minutes as Zeamer, in agony, fought to control and save *Lucy*. Finally he passed out from loss of blood; co-pilot Lieutenant John Britton was also hurt, so John Able, the wounded but bandaged top turret gunner, took over the controls.

Zeamer regained consciousness occasionally during the long flight home and tried to encourage and instruct Able, who had never flown a B-17 before. As they neared their base Britton was able to take his controls again, and twenty-five miles from Dobodura Zeamer, although barely able to move, clutched at consciousness and helped as much as he could.

Lucy came straight in downwind without flaps or brakes and roared along the strip, stopping just a few feet from the end. She was ripped and torn by nearly two hundred cannon and bullet holes, one crewman was dead and five were wounded. Zeamer had lost half his blood but somehow he survived, after lingering on the edge of death for three days. Both he and Sarnoski were awarded the Medal of Honor.

* * *

The Kiriwina landing went off without real hitches on June 30 and at Woodlark a similar operation was successful the same day. The first plane landed on the strip at Woodlark on July 16 and an airstrip was ready on Kiriwina two days later. These new airfields brought Southwest Pacific air power appreciably closer to the Solomons and New Britain, but the Nassau Bay operation was not as easily completed. After landing in heavy surf the troops quickly made contact with the enemy but they hesitated to advance because of the lack of artillery and the loss of much equipment in the rough seas. The dangers of enemy air attack were emphasized because almost all their radio equipment had been lost.

During the week of the landings the Fifth's missions were plagued by bad weather, prevalent until June 30. That day it cleared enough for eleven B-17s and B-24s to hit Vunakanau, and the next night Liberators bombed Lakunai and Rapopo. Vunakanau and Rapopo were the targets for eighteen heavies on July 2 and all three Rabaul airfields were attacked by the B-24s a day later. One Fortress was lost in this four-day assault in which almost a hundred tons of bombs were dropped. Meanwhile B-25s and A-20s attacked airfields and supply points in the Lae and Salamaua area. The missions apparently had an effect on the enemy's capacity to interfere with the landings, although the Japanese chose to use most of their strength against Halsey's operations in the Solomons.

The U.S. troops gradually advanced toward Salamaua and by July 13 had joined the Australians, leading to the early capture of the enemy base at Mubo after it had been pounded by more than forty B-25s and a dozen heavy bombers. The

American troops moving up the coast reached Tambu Bay on July 20, joining an amphibious force landed the same day to gain a position around five miles from Salamaua. Within a week American artillery was pumping shells into Salamaua itself. The Allied planes worked closely with the troops as they moved forward. As well as the essential troop carrier missions, the fighters and bombers were carrying out intense offensive and defensive operations. As the Japanese stepped up attacks in the Bena Bena and Salamaua areas the fighters shot down fifty-eight enemy planes and after July 5 the bombers hit the Lae and Salamaua area almost daily. When intelligence indicated that supplies from Madang were being sent overland to enemy troops in the south, three heavy raids were made on that target, the B-25s penetrating deeper into enemy territory than ever before.

Enemy barges comprised most of the shipping targets in July but on July 28 the most successful attack on warships since the Bismarck Sea began. Major Jock Henebry was leading one element of the fifteen 3rd Attack strafers on a hunt along the New Britain coast. Making a turn around Cape Gloucester he found Japanese fighters circling above two destroyers. As he and his two wingmen prepared to make their runs Henebry glimpsed a Japanese transport plane turning in for final approach on the Cape Gloucester runway, and momentarily diverted from his run to spray a couple of bursts at the enemy plane. Its right engine began burning, but Henebry was already attacking the destroyers. Strafing and dropping delayed-action bombs at mast height the B-25s claimed fourteen hits.

In Colonel Don Hall's element there was a B-25 named *Li'l Fox,* the first B-25 in the theater to be fitted with a 75-mm. nose cannon. Pappy Gunn was piloting the flying artillery piece, and he had been waiting to try it out. Gunn also saw the Japanese transport plane turning toward the Cape Gloucester airstrip. Hall, not wanting to get in front of that cannon, was following *Li'l Fox* into the attack. The B-25s went in low just as the transport was about to touch down.

The big cannon boomed, the B-25 shuddered, and the Japanese plane burst into smoking wreckage. A second shell exploded among a group of about fifteen Japanese. Jock Henebry was pretty sure the transport would have crashed anyway, but lost his aerial victory when Pappy Gunn demolished it.

The destruction of both warships, the *Ariake* and *Mikatsuki,* was confirmed.

*   *   *

Although the Fifth's operations during July were rewarding they were just the beginning of the effort which would be needed to support the final conquest of Lae. Foremost in Kenney's mind was the task of smashing the Japanese air force until it was no longer a significant threat. Wewak, two hundred miles above Madang, had developed into the main Japanese air base in New Guinea, and while they were still directing their main effort against the Solomons they moved a couple of hundred army planes into Wewak during June and July and the headquarters of their Fourth Air Army was transferred from Rabaul in August. For the Fifth a hard fight lay ahead, but at last Kenney was getting some new men and planes. The 348th Fighter Group and its P-47s reached Australia in June and by the end of July had moved up to Moresby. The 475th Fighter Group was activated in Australia in May and would be Kenney's first totally P-38 group. Built around a core of experienced combat pilots like Danny Roberts and "Nick" Nichols, the

Captains Sid Woods and James Watkins, old hands in the 9th Fighter Squadron. Watkins, flying his P-38, *Charlcie Jean,* scored all but two of his twelve victories in one hectic week: on July 26, 1943, he got four, two days later another three, and three more on August 2. Woods's best day was long after he left the Fifth—on March 22, 1945, flying from England with the 4th Fighter Group, he shot down five Focke-Wulf 190s. (Bob Brooks)

475th was commanded by Lieutenant Colonel George Prentice, the man who had molded the Fifth's first Lightning squadron. More than a hundred P-38s arrived during June and July and they were pushed through the Eagle Farm assembly line at Brisbane. The 475th would be ready for combat in the middle of August.

In July another new unit, the 345th Bomb Group, entered combat flying B-25s from Port Moresby. The 38th Group was brought up to full strength when two new squadrons, the 822nd and 823rd, were added, and they would be ready for combat in October. Some of the delay was because of the disagreement over the type of Mitchell to be used by the Fifth; Kenney was not completely satisfied with the new B-25G with its 75-mm. cannon but in the end accepted sixty-three. For replacements he wanted the newer B-25H for his strafer squadrons and the B-25J for the others, and he was unhappy to hear that the early design, which had included eight forward-firing machine guns, was to be modified by eliminating the co-pilot's position and two guns so that a cabin heater could be installed. Kenney had no use for cabin heaters in planes which usually did their fighting at a thousand feet or lower, and this raised the old problem of meeting the Fifth's needs and everybody else's too. When the first B-25G, *Li'l Fox,* had arrived Pappy Gunn had

In January 1943 the 22nd Bomb Group had only thirty-two Marauders on hand, and they were taken out of combat. When it was decided that there were enough sound B-26s for one squadron, the 19th decided to stay with the veteran aircraft, while the other three converted to the B-25. Stripped of their paint, *Little Audrey* and the other shiny Marauders were back in New Guinea in June 1943, where they were joined by the Mitchell squadrons in October. Tokyo radio called the restored planes the "Silver Fleet," and the unique squadron designed a tail insignia to fit the name. In January 1944, when the Marauders were flown back to Australia for the last time, there were twenty-eight. (William K. Miller)

recommended the addition of four machine guns; the first attempt to do this was not successful—"the skin began to ripple and tear loose at the bomb bay, the leading edge of the wings cracked between nacelles and fuselage." The 4th Air Depot Group saved the project by strengthening the structure at the critical points and although they had to add ninety-seven new items, fifty-two of them fabricated at Townsville, they were able to modify thirty-eight planes in less than two weeks.

Delivery delays made it necessary to postpone the conversion of the 3rd Attack Group to A-20s, and they continued flying B-25s in three squadrons. Production difficulties and promises to Russia meant the Fifth could not have a full A-20 group until at least the end of the year. However, the C-47s were arriving approximately on schedule—in the first week of July the new 375th Troop Carrier Group reached Moresby, followed soon after by two more squadrons. So by September, when the 433rd Group joined the Fifth, the 54th Troop Carrier Wing totaled fourteen squadrons, four of them assigned to the First Air Task Force.

Replacements were still a problem. Kenney warned Washington that by September he would have less than a dozen B-17s and that they should be replaced by B-24s, an aircraft which he had been compromised into accepting due to the priority given to the European Theater and its desire for the Fortress. The promise that sufficient aircraft would be on the way to keep his heavy bomber strength at nearly two hundred had been subject to two postponements of the due date, which was currently September 15. He had received a new B-24 group, the 380th, in May, but it was attached to the Royal Australian Air Force.

Wurtsmith's five fighter groups had five hundred and sixty-five aircraft at the end of July and nearly six hundred at the end of August, amounting to full strength on paper. Included were over two hundred P-39s, P-40s, and P-400s, and more than half of these older aircraft were in depot, the rest were not dependable for combat, and in July the Airacobras already had an average of three hundred combat hours each. Kenney tried to get two combat crews per aircraft for his tactical units and 15 per cent a month replacement; he was promised the 15 per cent but was told additional crews would have to come from these. Also, replacements for troop carriers would be half that for combat crews.

Kenney was irate over this limit on "non-combat" troop carrier replacements and wrote to Arnold to remind him that "a man lives longer in a P-39 than he does in a C-47 flying the troop carrier supply runs in New Guinea. These kids get a hundred hours a month, so that if I replace them at the five hundred hour mark I will need twenty percent per month for that reason alone instead of the seven and one half percent your staff has promised me. The replacement rate for troop carriers should be twenty-five percent." The protest paid off and by August 17 it had been decided that it would be possible to furnish replacement crews in excess of the 15 per cent early in 1944 to give the Fifth Air Force a strength of two crews for each aircraft.

The Flying Circus at Balikpapan

In June a new heavy bomber group, Lieutenant Colonel William Miller's 380th, had begun operating B-24s from Darwin, relieving the 319th Squadron, which had been covering the Netherlands East Indies and attacking distant targets.

The 380th, calling themselves the Flying Circus, took over the long-range work with a vengeance. Six B-24s struck Soerabaja, a fourteen-hour mission involving a round trip of twenty-four hundred miles from northern Australia. Then on August 13 they made the first strike against Balikpapan, on the island of Borneo. A dozen B-24s struggled from the strip near Darwin in the hot afternoon, laden with six bombs each and thirty-five hundred gallons of fuel. Before them lay seventeen long hours. Weather was the first problem and they encountered three severe fronts; over Makassar Strait they ran into heavy thunderstorms and along the way four planes were forced to turn back for various reasons.

Naturally surprise was complete when they reached the target and the town was sprinkled with lights as Captain Forrest Brissey took the lead plane low over Balikpapan Harbor. He was after shipping and attacked at mast height, his bombs dropping squarely on the deck of a large merchant vessel, which later photos proved was sunk. Captain Zed Smith's bombs landed alongside the *Katuri Maru,* a large freighter.

The other Liberators were after the oil refineries, and as tanks exploded, huge

The 380th's *Golden Goose* taxies out at Fenton strip, a hundred miles south of Darwin. Colonel William Miller, a former airline pilot, was the group commander; after many turnbacks due to weather he took the whole group out looking for a thunderhead, then led them through it on automatic pilot. After that the Flying Circus was ready to fly anywhere, any time. (Joe Dally)

billowing fires swallowed up the installations. Blazing oil spilled down the hillsides and spread into the harbor—Colonel Miller, one of the last to come over the target, flew into heat so intense he had to bomb from seven thousand feet.

Lieutenant Doug Craig was flying *Shady Lady* over Timor early the next morning when Japanese fighters found him. They chased *Shady Lady* all the way back to the coast of Australia before they finally broke off, leaving her low on gas and a hundred miles off course. Craig had little choice but to pick a flat stretch of sand near the coast and land. *Shady Lady* rolled smoothly along the undulating sand until the nosewheel found a hole and snapped off. Curious aborigines surrounded the aircraft and were able to take care of the crew until they were rescued by boat, and *Shady Lady* was repaired in time to be flown off the beach before an expected high tide came in.

Three days later two Circus B-24s took off at two o'clock in the morning, staggering under their huge gasoline, ammunition, and bomb load. The night takeoff was to allow a daylight reconnaissance of Balikpapan and this time interception was a certainty. Captain Jack Banks was flying *Miss Giving* and Captain Howard Hahn was in *Five by Five*.

Banks arrived over the target to see fires still burning from the previous attack and he could see the sunken ship in the pale waters of the harbor below. *Miss Giving* made a photo run from eleven thousand feet, then began a bomb run on a transport through intense antiaircraft fire. The bombs blew a hole in the side of the ship, but as Balikpapan disappeared behind, the lone B-24 was attacked by eight Zekes. Lining up on each side of the bomber they began to come in, making co-ordinated passes at the nose. They flew in close, then dived out underneath and took their places at the rear of the line again. The gunners on *Miss Giving* were having trouble beating off these attacks until the Japanese decided to change their tactics and began making direct beam attacks which exposed them to the waist gunners. They shot down one each and the top turret got another. The nose gunner scored a fourth and final victory. Banks kept turning into the attacks and dived to stop the fighters hitting him from below. An hour dragged by before the remaining four gave up and by then *Miss Giving* was badly shot up. The right outboard engine was holed and running rough, and finally quit entirely a thousand miles from home. Over the Timor Sea the crew tensely sweated out the fuel supply, with poor visibility and battering turbulence adding to their anxiety. Finally Banks reached the Australian coast, off course and with almost empty tanks. The crew was lined up in the waist with their parachutes on as the navigator gave a course change, but soon Fenton strip was below them and Banks set the aircraft down with ten minutes of gasoline to spare.

The other Circus B-24, *Five by Five,* had fought its way into and out of Balikpapan, and the photographs the two B-24s brought back revealed two large transports and eight freighters in Balikpapan Harbor. Another strike was planned with shipping the target, and although surprise was now lost it would be another low-level attack.

In the late afternoon of August 18 eleven Liberators set out and all but two got through the weather to the target. There were the usual thundershowers in Makassar Strait and most of the bombers were not in clear weather until they were almost over the target. Captain Bob Horn was there first and his bombardier selected a target for a mast-height run. The harbor lit up with a lashing crossfire of light antiaircraft. Horn dropped his bombs and took the B-24 up. Lieutenant Jim Soderberg was thundering across the bay as tracers looped around his aircraft. His first three bombs scored a hit and a near miss on a freighter which began to burn. Soderberg planned another run on a second ship but then a fuel tank was hit and smoke filled the bomb bay. Crewmen clambered in with extinguishers as Soderberg pulled *Lady Jeanne* up and dumped his remaining three bombs south of the refinery. The smoke pouring into the bomb bay suddenly stopped and the relieved crew thought the extinguishers had done the job, but when they reached home, they found the fire had been in the rubberized wing tanks and a large, gaping hole had been closed over by a perilously thin rubber seal.

Lieutenant Bob Fleming in *Robbie L II* roared down as his bombardier picked out the dark shape of a ship. Incendiaries and explosive fire hit the B-24, wounding the bombardier, who pressed his toggle switches as fire started around him in the nose. Grabbing an extinguisher he smothered the fire and reported to Fleming that he was hurt. In the cockpit the pilots were having troubles too—the oil pressure was dropping in one engine and Fleming was trying to gain altitude before it had to be feathered. Gunners were giving the bombardier first aid but the engine was going and Fleming soon found himself thirteen hundred miles from home and flying on three engines. Somehow he made it.

Captain Bob Fleming's *Robbie L II*, one of the B-24s which flew the long and audacious Balikpapan missions in August 1943. (Frank Smith)

Grace, a P-39 of the 35th Group's 40th Squadron; the Airacobras shepherded the C[ ] from Post Moresby to the burgeoning Tsili Tsili base. On August 15, Japanese fig[ ] and bombers attacked as a formation of transports was arriving, but the valiant [ ] were able to destroy fourteen Japanese aircraft for a loss of four of their own. [ ] Hanna)

This Tess, the Japanese version of the C-47, wandered out of the clouds and into the path of the 380th's *Juarez Whistle,* flown by Captain Gus Connery, on August 21, 1943. Connery veered out of formation and chased the equally startled Japanese pilot. Moving alongside, he ordered his gunners to open fire. The top turret sprayed the transport and sent it down in flames.

Soderberg's aircraft was a calmer place after the smoke had cleared and they were on their way home—thirteen hundred miles at three miles a minute. *Dauntless Dottie* was on the way home too, with three wounded men lying in the waist, and it had been, to quote General MacArthur, "a magnificent performance."

* * *

In August it was time to begin the offensive that would lead up to the capture of Lae, and the first task was to crush the Japanese air force. Wewak became the prime target and the new advanced base at Tsili Tsili put the four Wewak airstrips within the range of the Fifth's fighters. By the end of July the C-47s had flown in an American antiaircraft battery and Australian infantry to defend the base, and on August 5 Lieutenant Colonel Malcolm Moore took command of the new Second Air Task Force. On August 14 Kenney moved a couple of squadrons of 35th Group P-39s into the base just before dark—at midday an enemy reconnaissance plane had circled overhead for several minutes before racing northwest toward Wewak, and Kenney knew the quiet days were over. The new base had a radar cover which would give perhaps a fifteen-minute warning, and the thirty-five P-39s were refueled and readied as soon as they arrived.

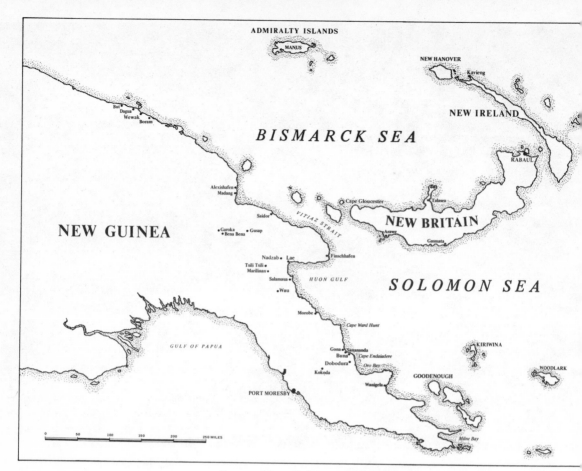

Eastern New Guinea and New Britain.

The first Japanese attack caught the troop carriers as they brought in the 35th Group's ground echelon on August 15. One flight had just touched down when twelve Sallys, escorted by a dozen fighters, came in through the mountain passes. One C-47 was caught in the air, shot to pieces, and crashed. Another disappeared into the mountains and was never found. The others in the second flight raced for Moresby at treetop level and escaped while the P-39s tangled with the Japanese fighters. Although four Airacobras were lost, three of the pilots were saved, and all but one of the Sallys were shot down as well as two or three of the fighters. Damage to the field was slight.

The Japanese struck again the next day, but P-38s and P-47s shot down about fifteen of the fighters. That day Captain Harry Brown of the 431st Fighter Squadron scored the first victories for the 475th Group. He made a run on a Zero from behind and kept firing until the enemy fighter burst into flames. Then he and another pilot caught another fighter in a crossfire—Brown scored with his burst and it caught fire. Another Zero flew across his line of fire and he exploded it. Harry Brown was an old hand. On December 7, 1941, he had been playing poker when the Japanese attacked. Still wearing a tuxedo, Brown drove to the field where his P-36 squadron was based, managed to take off, and shot down two Kates although he had only one .30-caliber machine gun firing.

According to Kenney, "everyone in the Fifth, from Whitehead and Wurtsmith down, decided that the P-47 was no good as a combat airplane," except of course the people in the 348th Fighter Group. The Thunderbolts built a fine record—in their first three months of combat they shot down fifty-one Japanese aircraft for two losses. These 342nd Squadron aircraft, led by Colonel Neel Kearby in *Fiery Ginger,* have the white markings introduced for Allied fighters in fall 1943, and blue tail tips to identify the squadron. (Bill Lybrand)

The unmistakable silhouette of the P-38 Lightning. When Colonel George Prentice's 475th Fighter Group went into combat in August, Kenney had the equivalent of two P-38 groups, although his other three squadrons were spread over three fighter groups. This aircraft is from Captain Franklin A. Nichols' 431st Fighter Squadron, which completed its first combat mission on August 13, 1943.

Wewak: "The Big Takeout"

From the end of July Japanese air power in Wewak had been building up until over one hundred bombers and fighters were counted at Boram and Wewak, and more than ninety at Dagua and But. To destroy them Whitehead had available two heavy groups with sixty-four B-17s and B-24s in commission and two medium groups with fifty-eight B-25s equipped with turret tanks to enable them to make the round trip.

During the hour before midnight on August 16 a dozen B-17s and thirty-eight B-24s took off from Moresby on the biggest mission since the Bismarck Sea. The weather was generally good and all got through to the Wewak area except for a couple of Liberators which aborted with mechanical failures. Soon after midnight the first bombs fell and for the next two hours the Jolly Rogers and Ken's Men blew holes in the four airstrips. The searchlights and heavy antiaircraft fire lit up the night sky around the bombers and there were Japanese night fighters out in the darkness. Three heavies were lost and the results were hard to assess. Photos taken the next morning of three of the airstrips showed at least eighteen unserviceable aircraft out of some two hundred counted. While these photos were being taken three squadrons of 3rd Attack were warming up at Dobodura and two squadrons of the 38th Group were ready at Moresby—about to make the deepest medium bomber penetration yet into Japanese-held New Guinea, the five hundred miles to Wewak. The Lightnings would cover them along the way.

Bad weather interfered, and of the twenty-six aircraft taking off from Moresby only three reached the target. The tiny formation scattered their parafrags over Dagua, destroying at least seventeen aircraft on the ground and knocking down one of fifteen intercepting fighters. However, the field at But was now not being attacked at all.

Eight strafers from Dobodura failed to reach the target, but twenty-nine parafraged Boram and Wewak. The 90th Squadron claimed about fifteen aircraft destroyed or damaged at Wewak, and Major Donald Hall led the 8th Squadron into Boram, followed by the 13th. Hall said, "It was too much to ask, after the heavy bombers had made their attack in the dark, that we would catch the Japs at Boram completely off guard. Yet that is exactly what happened. We crossed and recrossed a winding road leading to the airdrome. Several vehicles were moseying along. We let them have it and they stopped as if paralyzed. Jap soldiers were swimming in the surf. Many were lolling on the beach, some wearing brightly colored robes. Our fifties blazed away at them. Some ran, some fell.

"Before we were within effective range, we threw in a few shots to make them duck. We waited a few seconds, and then cut loose again. A Betty bomber blew up on the runway. From then on we held our gun switches down raking plane after plane. The Jap airplanes were lined wing tip to wing tip the whole length of the runway. Several fuel trucks were parked alongside airplanes. Crews were busy. In the revetment area, a few airplanes were being loaded with bombs.

"The surprise was complete. Not an AA gun was fired. Not a plane got off the ground to intercept us. A fellow dreams of a situation like that, but never expects to see it. We let go our parachute bombs, in clusters of three, one after another. They drifted lazily down like a cloud of snowballs. As we turned left toward

Colonel George Prentice warms up a 432nd Squadron Lightning at Moresby. A veteran of the old 49th, Prentice commanded the Fifth's first P-38 squadron and then took the 475th into combat. (Dennis Glen Cooper)

Wewak, it became apparent that the 90th Squadron had done a good job there. We had no bombs left but we blazed away with our fifties. The P-38s gave us beautiful cover, as always, enabling us to concentrate on our job. We turned and flew back behind a ridge, lifting now and then to look at the two dromes. Fires were blazing everywhere, and broken, twisted planes lined both sides of the runways. The Boram drome looked like two powder trains. We hadn't lost a plane."

Hall's squadron reported that at least fifteen aircraft at Boram had been completely destroyed, and perhaps another thirty were burning when they left. The 13th Squadron claimed that of seventy to eighty aircraft on the runway all had been destroyed or severely damaged. By the time they reached the target there was heavy antiaircraft fire, but only one fighter attack and the B-25s themselves broke it up. The heavy bombers had certainly done their job, but a combination of favorable factors led to the outstanding success of the strikes. Colonel Koji Tanaka, a staff officer from Rabaul who was at Wewak during the strikes, said that, "Wewak was the end of the plane ferry route. Its fields accordingly were loaded with planes which had been delivered but had not been assigned to any units. In addition, there were many unserviceable planes on the field which were awaiting repairs or could not be repaired. The fields at Wewak were too small at this time and there was no possibility of dispersal. The reason all the planes were assembled there is that we thought we were out of your fighter range."

Green Dragon B-25s from the 405th Squadron bare their fangs. The 38th went into combat with only two squadrons, the 71st Wolf Pack and 405th Green Dragons, and both decorated their strafers with nose designs fitting the names. As further identification the 71st painted their tail tips white, and the 405th used green. (James V. Wallace)

The next day, weather was a problem. Only twenty-six heavies made it through to the target, led by Colonel Art Rogers of the 90th. On the tail of *Connell's Special* was a ten-foot grinning skull and crossed bombs, stark and white and the new insignia of the Jolly Rogers. Rogers was determined to save something of the mission, and led his small force down into the black, forbidding blanket shielding the target. Rain lashed *Connell's Special* and the B-24s out on the wings were dimly visible. "Do what you can," Rogers told his bombardier.

Through the rain and cloud the bombs fell toward Wewak, now alive with spots of orange as the guns on the ground opened up. Rogers' first bombs burst white in the water, then others exploded in the green blur that lay below. Following the trail of these first bombs later aircraft were able to do better, and without the benefit of a proper bomb run it was a pretty good mission.

Immediately following the heavy bombers, the low-level B-25s were able to fare better—fifty-three strafers reached the target, flying under the weather and into heavy antiaircraft fire. Captain Verl Jett of the 431st Fighter Squadron, flying one of the escorting 475th Group P-38s, saw twelve fighters diving out of the overcast to hit the B-25s. He sawed the wing off a Zero, then sent a stream of tracers into

Captain Ralph Cheli survived the crash of his B-25 at Wewak and became a prisoner of war. He was killed in an Allied bombing raid on Rabaul in March 1944.

another until it burst into flames. Lieutenant Edward Czarnecki got two more, and in all the P-38s shot down fifteen and lost two of their own, but the Japanese fighters pressed their attacks vigorously.

Near Dagua between ten and fifteen Zekes and Oscars hit Major Ralph Cheli's flight. One Oscar shot up another 38th Group B-25 and then went after Cheli's plane. Fire streamed back from the right engine and wing as Cheli led the flight over the airstrip. The burning B-25 shot up a row of enemy planes before Cheli called his wingman and told him to take over the command of the flight, then crashed into the sea. Cheli survived to die as a prisoner in 1944.

The offensive continued for the rest of August. Liberators flew over one hundred more sorties, and the B-25s made twenty-one against targets in the area. As Wewak reeled other heavy strikes battered enemy supply centers at Hansa Bay and Alexishafen. The Fifth built an impressive record. Between August 17 and the end of the month the bomber gunners claimed fifty-seven enemy planes shot down, and the fighters accounted for another sixty-nine. The photos showed over two hundred aircraft destroyed on the ground at the Wewak strips, and even though the statisticians in the United States revised this downward to one hundred and seventy-five, August was still remarkable—the same statisticians had never previously come up with a monthly total higher than six. The actual combat losses had been two B-25s, three B-24s, and six P-38s. At this cost the Japanese stronghold at Wewak had been reduced to "a handful of planes."

Mangled Japanese aircraft dot this dispersal area at Wewak; surprise was the Fifth's best ally. (Larry Tanberg)

Hansa Bay, August 28, 1943. Twenty-six Mitchells from the 3rd Attack Group seeking shipping up the coast from Finschhafen to Hansa Bay and a miscalcul[a] placed this B-25 too close to the preceding aircraft. The explosion tore the bo[m] apart. (Tom Jones)

Preparations for the Lae assault continued. American and Australian forces were within sight of Salamaua and a determined effort was made to convince the enemy that it was the next objective. This worked, because intelligence later showed that most of the Japanese 51st Division was in position there by September 1943. A total of five thousand Japanese were waiting at Salamaua, while at Lae there were only half as many. In the Allied plan Salamaua would be bypassed, and an amphibious landing at Hopoi Beach, about ten miles east of Lae, would be complemented by the airborne invasion of Nadzab, perhaps twenty miles inland on the Markham River, a day later. After the Hopoi landing, the Australian 9th Division would move west along the coast to capture Lae. The flat, grassy plateau at Nadzab was capable of handling C-47s, and was admirably suited to the development of a major base. The 503rd Parachute Regiment would clear the old strip there and then move out to cover the trails while Major General George Vasey's 7th Division was flown in. Moving east, these troops would help the 9th Division in wiping out the Japanese at Lae. The weather could disrupt an operation which depended on paratroopers so General Blamey added an overland march by a force of Australians which would take up position across the Markham River from Nadzab before the air drop.

Kenney had worked out his overall plans for the air operations, but there was debate over his intention to protect the amphibious force by maintaining his fighters on ground alert. The Navy wanted continuous coverage, but Kenney argued that Wurtsmith's command had insufficient planes to provide this although he agreed to have as many aircraft continually in the Lae vicinity as he could. MacArthur leaned toward Kenney's way of thinking, but the Navy would not yield and another compromise called for continuous cover by thirty-two fighters during daylight, as well as the ground alert.

Radar cover of the seas through which the convoy would have to pass was incomplete and it was believed that Japanese aircraft from Wewak or Madang could fly behind the mountains to Lae, while others could cross the Vitiaz Strait from New Britain without being discovered until it was too late. It was suggested that posting a destroyer, equipped with radar and radio sets, between Lae and Finschhafen would solve this problem, and USS *Reid* was ordered to take up station forty-five miles southeast of Finschhafen.

While the forces for the attack gathered at the end of August, Allied planes paved the way with heavy attacks on airfields, shipping, and supply points in New Guinea and New Britain. Beaufighters, B-25s, and Marauders hit barges, fuel dumps, and other supply points along the southwestern coast of New Britain on September 1. Other B-25s and B-24s set fire to fuel dumps at Alexishafen the same day, and a large force of Liberators struck the Madang area while six old B-17s struck Labu, a strategic outpost near Lae. On September 2 the B-25s hit Wewak, the strafers sweeping low over the harbor, sinking at least two ships. The bombers kept up the pressure as the amphibious force gathered off Buna on September 3. The following morning the invasion convoy was moving toward Lae. The *Reid* took up position as aircraft control ship off Finschhafen, and as the landing craft made ready, Allied aircraft were coming from Moresby, Dobodura, and Tsili Tsili.

The fighters and bombers swept over the beaches, strafing and bombing, as five

Lieutenant Jay Robbins of the Headhunters had a remarkable record of multiple victories. In all he shot down twenty-two planes, half of them in three fights—three on July 21 near Bogadjim, four on September 4, 1943, covering the Lae landing, and four more escorting the B-25s to Rabaul on October 24. (Bob Brooks)

destroyers shelled the beach. By 6:30 A.M. the first Australian troops had landed, and except for an attack by three bombers, enemy interference was slight until the afternoon. As part of the attempt to deny the enemy the use of his airstrips, nine B-25s bombed the Hopoi landing ground near the beaches, and an hour later B-24s bombed gun emplacements and depots at Lae airdrome and hit Gasmata and Cape Gloucester.

About two o'clock in the afternoon, as the support ships were preparing to withdraw, their part of the invasion completed, the *Reid* picked up a formation approaching from southwest of Gasmata and less than a hundred miles away. As the destroyer flashed details to the fighter controllers at Dobodura and Tsili Tsili, fighters took off, the pilots carrying grid references which enabled them to trace the enemy course as it was plotted.

Sixteen Headhunter P-38s of the 80th Squadron were already on their assigned patrol over Lae, led by Major Ed Cragg. Lieutenant Jay Robbins' flight was the first to make the interception, racing toward about thirty Zekes.

Robbins dragged the nose of his P-38 up a little as the Zeros saw the Lightnings and changed course to meet them. The P-38s were still below the Japanese fighters, and one tried to turn and get on Robbins' tail, so he hit the rudder and climbed left; turning the other way to the Japanese, the P-38 was almost level with the enemy fighter as Robbins turned again to get behind. The Japanese also turned, but Robbins was gaining on him. He glimpsed more Zekes behind him but a long way away.

The Japanese pilot tried to dive away, but the P-38's fire chewed into his right wing, and smoke streamed back. Robbins kept firing as pieces flaked from the enemy fighter, until finally the whole wing tore off and tumbled back past the P-38.

Turning to escape the other Japanese behind him, Robbins pulled out of his dive and zoomed up. He saw another Lightning boxed in by Japanese fighters, and headed toward them. Seeing Robbins coming, several Zeros broke away and turned to meet him head on. Robbins saw the nearest open fire, but he was too far away. When the range was right Robbins fired a short burst—the Zero broke to the left and Robbins tried to slip the P-38 to the right and keep him in the gunsight ring. The planes whipped past each other.

A second enemy fighter was now headed for him, and almost in range by the time Robbins saw him and wrenched the Lightning into a firing position. This time the Zeke pilot didn't miss, and the green P-38 was being hit before Robbins could retaliate. He pressed the firing button, the two aircraft roared together, and the Zeke began to take hits. Robbins hunched in the cockpit as he heard the enemy fire smacking into his P-38. Then the Zeke pulled up and Robbins watched his shells ripping into the belly and wing. Black smoke jetted from the enemy fighter, and he spun down; not seriously shot up, Robbins watched his second victim turn into a fiery ball as it headed for the water—but he watched a moment too long. A pattern of holes suddenly appeared in his right wing, and he instinctively pushed the control wheel forward. The damaged P-38 dived, a Zeke following and shooting. The heavy Lightning plummeted down, slipping away from the Zero. Nearing the end of a ten-thousand-foot dive, Robbins had to pull out. He eased back on the throttles and pulled the yoke back, hoping the shells hadn't weakened the wing. As the P-38 strained out of the dive Robbins was crushed into the seat. His vision blurred and sweat rolled down his face. He tried to keep from blacking out entirely as the P-38 gradually leveled off. There was a lone Zeke a long way off, but the enemy fighters which had chased him into the dive were still following, moving up on each side. Robbins eased the Lightning down to close in on the Zeke ahead, keeping an eye on the others behind him to his left. As some of the enemy fighters moved out ahead on both sides, the lone Japanese pilot saw him and tried to turn in behind the Lightning. Robbins turned left, catching the Japanese by surprise, and without waiting to get on his tail, lined the Zeke up for a deflection shot. While the other Japanese watched, the gray Zeke began to collapse between the engine and the tail. It was perfect shooting. The fighter was out of control, trailing pieces of itself in a coil of smoke, but the Japanese pilot managed to straighten his plane long enough to jump over the side.

This time Robbins didn't watch. He turned toward the land, now about fifty miles away, with several fighters in his path, coming head on. He knew his ammunition must be low, and he had heard the telltale discordant sound which meant one of his guns must have jammed.

A Zeke was dead ahead. Robbins waited until he was within range. Some of his guns fired, some didn't, and his P-38 was hit again. The Zeke flashed past. Robbins pressed his mike button and called for help but got no answer. Another Zeke was straight ahead and opened fire first—Robbins squeezed off a short burst and, still heading for the coast, dived to three thousand feet. Robbins heard his starboard engine missing as a Zeke turned in ahead. He fired another short burst, but the Lightning was hit again. Robbins was now on the deck, with only a few guns firing and an engine running rough. One Japanese fighter turned and lined up behind to close in, and there was another ahead, coming down. Robbins pulled the nose up slightly, and when he fired, the tracers flying out from the P-38's nose told him that he was down to his last few rounds. His aim was good, the shells ripping into the Japanese plane as it turned away. Robbins turned after him and got a deflection shot at his wing. The wing broke away from the fuselage and the burning Zeke plunged down straight into the sea.

Robbins looked around. It was clear ahead, but he had to reach land before his engine went or he was caught from the rear. With a sinking heart he saw two Tonys and a Hamp closing in. He managed to get to six thousand feet and now he could only bluff. He angled the damaged P-38 for a head-on pass. When the wings of the Japanese plane trailed wisps of smoke, Robbins' one gun with ammunition answered. Then he was down at a thousand feet again, radioing for help.

The enemy were on both sides, and Robbins could either bail out or try to dogfight—he could not fly straight for shore and hope to survive. He turned into a Japanese fighter—it fired, missed, and whipped by. Another peeled off and Robbins drove toward him. The P-38 was hit again but Robbins straightened the crippled plane. A Tony peeled off to make a pass. Robbins tried to be facing each attack, skidding his P-38 to ruin their aim. The enemy shells smacked into the Lightning, knocking out the radio and whanging into the armor plate at the back of the seat. Robbins was thinking of ditching, but turned toward some ships of the U.S. invasion fleet off to his right. The Japanese fighters were nearly within range as Robbins went almost down to the water to get more speed.

As he raced across the waves toward the ships, bursts of fire exploded near him. Robbins stood the P-38 on one wing to show the silhouette to the Navy gunners, and hoped. The American ships realized what was happening, and their fire began building an explosive barrier between the Japanese fighters and their quarry, and the enemy fell back. Alone at last, Robbins decided to try for Moresby and crossed the Owen Stanleys at eleven thousand feet. He got the P-38 down safely and dragged himself from the cockpit, completely exhausted. He had destroyed four Japanese aircraft and his battered P-38 would fly again.

The rest of the Headhunters had a good day and the squadron, being in the right place at the right time, had dominated the action. "Porky" Cragg had shot down two and the other pilots got five more. In all, the enemy had been met by about forty P-38s and twenty P-47s, and for the loss of one P-38 twenty Japanese planes were shot down, but others got through to the shipping. Dive bombers damaged two destroyers and hit a landing craft, and torpedo planes hit another. Three hours later another attack set fire to an ammunition dump but by this time the congestion on the beach had been relieved, and the engineers had pushed a road through to Hopoi village, four hundred yards inland. The action was successfully completed. The next step was the paratroop invasion the following day.

Nadzab: Airborne Invasion

The capture of Nadzab would cut off the Japanese in the area and give the Allies control of the Markham River Valley. The Australian force which had come down the Watut River from Tsili Tsili was waiting almost within gunshot of the drop zone, while at Moresby, in the morning of September 5, the C-47s loaded the 503rd Parachute Regiment. At eight twenty-five the first transport took off, and in fifteen minutes the entire force was airborne in three flights. Over Thirty-Mile they met the first of the hundred fighters which would escort them, crossed the Owen Stanleys, and arranged themselves into six-plane elements over Marilinan.

Just before ten o'clock the paratroopers were alerted, and the first man tumbled out of *Honeymoon Express* at 10:22 A.M. General Kenney, watching from the old B-17F *Cap'n & The Kids,* later sent this description of the flight to Hap Arnold:

"You already know by this time the news of the preliminary move to take out Lae but I will tell you about the show on the 5th of September, when we took Nadzab with 1,700 paratroops and with General MacArthur in a B-17 over the area watching the show and jumping up and down like a kid. I was flying number two in the same flight with him and the operation was a magnificent spectacle. I truly don't believe that another air force in the world today could have put this over as perfectly as the 5th Air Force did. Three hundred and two airplanes in all, taking off from eight different fields in the Moresby and Dobodura areas, made a rendezvous right on the nose over Marilinan, flying through clouds, passes in the mountains and over the top. Not a single squadron did any circling or stalling around but all slid into place like clockwork and proceeded on the final flight down the Watut Valley, turned to the right down the Markham and went directly to the target. Going north down the valley of the Watut from Marilinan, this was the picture: heading the parade at one thousand feet were six squadrons of B-25 strafers with the eight .50 cal. guns in the nose and sixty frag bombs in each bomb bay; immediately behind and about five hundred feet above were six A-20s flying in pairs

Generals Kenney and MacArthur watch from the sidelines as the troop carriers prepare for the Nadzab drop. (James Watson)

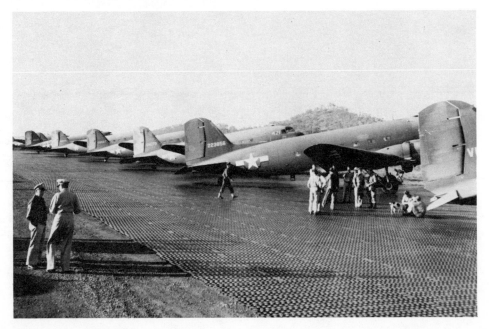

When Colonel Harry Hawthorne of the 43rd Group was told that Generals MacArthur, Sutherland, and Kenney wanted to see the Nadzab drop he arranged a flight of three B-17s. On the morning of the mission Hawthorne took off in *Talisman* with General Howard Ramey of Fifth Bomber Command in the ço-pilot's seat and General Douglas MacArthur as a very important passenger.

A battalion of paratroopers floats down from the C-47s. White parachutes were used troops, colored ones for supplies and ammunition.

General Kenney watched the Nadzab project go off like clockwork from the black-bellied *Cap'n & The Kids*. Obviously elated, the Allied Air Forces commander shakes hands with the crew of the B-17. (General George C. Kenney)

—three pairs abreast—to lay smoke as the last frag bomb exploded. At about two thousand feet and directly behind the A-20s came ninety-six C-47s carrying paratroops, supplies and some artillery. The C-47s flew in three columns of three plane elements, each column carrying a battalion set up for a particular battalion dropping ground. On each side along the column of transports and about one thousand feet above them were the close cover fighters. Another group of fighters sat at seven thousand feet and up in the sun, staggered from fifteen to twenty thousand, was another group of P-47s. Following the transports came five B-17s, racks loaded with three hundred pound packages with parachutes, to be dropped to the paratroopers on call by signal panels as they needed them. This mobile supply unit stayed over Nadzab practically all day serving the paratroops below, dropping a total of fifteen tons of supplies in this manner. Following the echelon to the right and just behind the five supply B-17s was a group of twenty-four B-24s and four B-17s which left the column just before the junction of the Watut and the Markham to take out the Jap defensive position at Heath's plantation, about half way between Nadzab and Lae. Five weather ships were used prior to and during the show along the route and over the passes to keep the units straight on weather to be encountered during their flights to the rendezvous. The brass hats flight of three B-17s above the centre of the transport column completed the set up."

The paratroopers met no resistance and had soon lined up with the Australians, and by midday the C-47s were safely back at Port Moresby.

The area was secured within twenty-four hours and the development of an air base began immediately. The grass was burned off, and early in the morning of September 6 the strip was ready to receive C-47s; the troop carriers made their

Nadzab was soon a bustling center of activity, as the C-47s brought in load after load of equipment. (Roger Beaty)

The when and why of this installation of B-17 tail guns in the nose is forgott The aircraft, *The Last Straw,* was a 43rd Group B-17E, one of the last to flown by the 63rd Squadron. On September 8, 1943, piloted by Lieuten Harry Park, she was one of a formation of B-17s and B-24s bombing Lae the ground troops closed in. (Boeing)

first landings that afternoon, bringing in the Australian infantry. A week after the paratroop drop, two parallel strips had been completed, and by September 14 Nadzab boasted two parallel runways and a dispersal area which could handle thirty-six C-47s at one time.

The ground campaign against Lae and Salamaua rapidly reached its climax. The Australian 7th Division moved down the Markham Valley toward Lae, quickly breaking through the enemy positions along the way, and it was soon a race between them and the 9th Division. In fact, Kenney had heard rumors that bets totaling twenty cases of whiskey hinged on the outcome.

About noon on September 16, while the planes were still bombing the defensive positions at Lae, a radio message came through from the 7th Division commander: *"Only the Fifth Air Force bombers are preventing me entering Lae. Vasey."*

* * *

The surprisingly rapid victories at Lae and Salamaua meant a change of plans. Finschhafen, on the Huon Gulf sixty-four miles beyond Lae and intended for future Allied use, had been marked for attack four weeks after Lae fell. The weakness of Japanese resistance led to an acceleration of the timetable, and the Finschhafen operation was brought forward to September 22. This barely gave time to get the landing barges and destroyers up from Milne Bay for loading at Lae, and as the bombers struck at Japanese airfields and supply dumps, the fighters shepherded the shipping movement to Lae and the loading there. In the night of September 21 the convoy moved out and around the tip of the Huon Peninsula.

Scarlet Beach was the carefully chosen landing point, and in the early morning the invasion was heralded by a naval bombardment. There was no strafing of the beach, but the Allied Air Forces had begun hitting other targets before dawn—the B-24s and B-25s put Cape Gloucester out of business, while RAAF P-40s hit Gasmata. Other B-25s and A-20s shot up Japanese troops in the Finschhafen area, where Australian troops consolidated the beachhead, broke through fortifications nearby, and made for the airstrip. The landing was almost unopposed and there was little need for air support.

Just before noon the shipping began to go back to Buna. An hour after they had left, the fighter controller aboard the destroyer *Reid* was plotting large formations coming from New Britain. Once again, the Japanese had chosen a bad time. Three fighter squadrons had been patrolling the area for several hours, and while they were due to be relieved in a few minutes, they still had enough gas to fight for about an hour. More fighters were preparing to take off and relieve them, so at least five squadrons could make the interception. The controllers on the *Reid* sent them all to positions over the convoy, and the Japanese force—twenty to thirty bombers and thirty or forty fighters—flew straight into the jaws of the trap.

The top honors went to the 432nd Squadron, which had been in combat for a little over a month. They had already taken off when they received the first radar plot, and circled between ten and twelve thousand feet until they were told that the enemy was in sight from six thousand on down. The P-38s dived and saw eight or ten bombers with four Zekes covering them and another twenty-five fighters diving

With Lae in Allied hands, the Fifth's aircraft had yet another forward base. This P-38 is Lieutenant Jim Farris's *Baldy*, from the 432nd Fighter Squadron, which destroyed eighteen enemy aircraft in the classic fighter interception near Finschhafen on September 22, 1943. Farris got one of the Bettys. (Australian War Memorial)

Major Dave Conley, commander of the 13th Squadron, crashed *P.I. Joe* on takeoff on September 29, 1943. Jagged pieces of propeller ripped through the cockpit, killing Brigadier R. B. Sutherland. (Australian War Memorial)

and swarming at five thousand feet. Two flights of Lightnings hit the Zeros while the others continued down to get the Bettys. The P-38s were flying through friendly fire from the ships as the battle raged for forty-five minutes between sea level and five thousand feet. Twelve 432nd Squadron pilots accounted for the eighteen Japanese which fell to the squadron, Captain Frederick Harris getting a Betty and two Zekes, and four other pilots scoring two each. In less than an hour the Japanese lost ten or more bombers and twenty-nine fighters to the American fighters and the ships' gunners had knocked down nine of ten torpedo bombers which came through at low altitude. The convoy was left intact, and the pilot of one of three lost P-38s was rescued.

Meanwhile Finschhafen had become the objective of a pincer operation. In addition to the troops landed on Scarlet Beach, others were working up from the earlier landing at Hopoi village. The main force had taken one of the Finschhafen airstrips by September 23, but the advance was still slow because the Japanese had been able to dig in. Enemy aircraft occasionally held up the advance, but their efforts were puny when compared to what the Fifth was doing. Routine operations continued against Gasmata and Cape Gloucester, and against communications targets in the Madang area, with the heaviest strikes sent against the airfields and shipping at Wewak. On September 27 seventeen B-24s followed by about one hundred B-25s swept over the airfields and harbor installations at Wewak. Three B-25s fell to antiaircraft fire but the others tore into the tankers and other shipping in the harbor. They sank at least one cargo vessel, and the one hundred and twenty-one fighters covering them shot down eight of the twenty Japanese fighters which attempted to intercept. The next day forty B-24s attacked the major fuel and ammunition dumps, and they were considered destroyed.

On October 2 Finschhafen town fell to the Australians, and Allied forces were now on the upper side of the Huon Peninsula. The Huon Gulf campaign was not over, because the Japanese garrison had retreated and would have to be wiped out, and reinforcements were on the way to Madang. The Japanese could still replace their lost aircraft, and Wewak was only temporarily knocked out.

Nadzab, the planned home of the Second Air Task Force, was being rapidly developed, and by the end of October two squadrons of P-39s were providing fighter defense, and four airdromes were in use by the middle of November.

Meanwhile the C-47s were moving the Australians forward in the drive to Kaiapit and Dumpu, selected as advance bases for the operations against Wewak. The Australians had planned to go overland, but Whitehead thought an airborne operation would be better. Captain Everette Frazier was called in again to explore the Ramu Valley, and he was able to land a light plane a few miles from Japanese-held Kaiapit. On September 16 Colonel David Hutchison of the Second Air Task Force approved the site for C-47s and the next day two hundred and fifty Australians were ferried in to attack Kaiapit. By September 20 they had finished the Japanese off and were helping Frazier to improve the old strip they had just captured, which was soon ready to handle C-47s.

The Australians continued advancing through the valley, depending upon air transport for their rations and supplies. Engineers went with them, marking out places where the C-47s could land, and by the end of the month they had reached the junction of the Gusap and Ramu rivers. The valley in this area was very promising for airfield construction and Colonel Murray Woodbury and Colonel Donald R. Hutchinson of the new Third Air Task Force decided to hold back construction at the swampy Kaiapit location and build the task force base at the place they decided to call Gusap. To secure the area more troops were flown in and by October 2 they were thirty-five miles farther up the valley at Dumpu. It had taken fifteen days to "steal" the entire valley.

An all-weather runway would not be completed until January, after months of hard work, but four usable strips were quickly laid out and a P-40 squadron was at Gusap by November. At Gusap and Nadzab materials had to be moved in entirely by air at first, at the daily rate of about two hundred plane loads. Transportation was a difficult problem and the C-47s alone could not enable the kind of development planned for the Nadzab area, so major airfield construction had to be delayed until heavy equipment could be brought in by road from Lae. The Allied successes had caught them by surprise, and although Kenney stated that nine engineer battalions were needed if adequate road and base facilities were to be constructed in 1943, only two were actually available.

Brigadier General Carl Connell was working to complete the road from Lae to Nadzab by December, but Kenney wanted it earlier. Torrential rain cut down the amount of work which could be done—it poured on better than two out of three days during the last two months of the project. As Connell later declared, they "literally floated that road into Nadzab." Finally it was opened on December 15 and the equipment began to roll.

The 49th Fighter Group moved to Gusap in November 1943, the vanguard of Colonel Donald R. Hutchinson's Third Air Task Force. This base, at the junction of the Gusap and Ramu rivers, was considered the "most pleasant" of all the Fifth's advanced outposts.

Neel Kearby looked like "money in the bank" to General Kenney. The Thunderbolt pilot shot down twenty-two enemy planes before his death in March 1944. (Joe Fetherston)

As the general movement of tactical units to Nadzab, Finschhafen, and Gusap went on, there were the usual problems. The two 49th Group P-40 squadrons were well established at Gusap, and within a month two medium squadrons moved to Nadzab from Dobodura, and another two fighter squadrons from Moresby, making a total of four fighter squadrons at Nadzab. By early December it was thought two fighter squadrons could operate from Finschhafen in an emergency, but Kenney and Connell pushed so hard that by December 17 the whole 348th Fighter Group was there, and the 35th Fighter Squadron and their P-40s moved in on Christmas Day. There was almost no aircraft warning system, and the lack of control meant numerous accidents on the runways, but the tactical gains were worth the risks. Four squadrons of fighters were two hundred miles closer to Cape Gloucester and one hundred and fifty miles closer to Wewak.

Neel Kearby: Thunderbolts over Wewak

Colonel Neel Kearby, commanding the 348th Group, had an idea about how to take advantage of the tremendous diving speed of the P-47 against Wewak—his scheme was simply to plunge down on any unsuspecting aircraft taking off or landing. On October 11, 1943, he decided to try it, and with him he took Captain William Dunham, Major Raymond Gallagher, and Captain John T. Moore. Kearby reported it this way:

"I was leading a flight of four P-47s on a fighter sweep. We arrived over Wewak at twenty-eight thousand feet, the weather was excellent with a few scattered clouds between two thousand and eight thousand feet. We saw a number of aircraft parked on Boram strip and one aircraft taxiing on the runway. He did not take off. The fuel in our belly tanks had been consumed so we dropped them to increase our speed and conserve fuel. One Zeke was sighted at eight o'clock below at twenty thousand feet. I came in on him from seven o'clock above and opened fire at fifteen hundred feet. He took no evasive action, caught fire and dived into the sea. We climbed back to twenty-six thousand feet and saw about thirty-six fighters; Zekes, Hamps and Tonys, at ten thousand to fifteen thousand feet and twelve bombers, type unidentified at five thousand feet, approaching from the east. Our P-47s came in from above on a Zeke, opened fire at fifteen hundred feet and closed as he burst into flame. He took no evasive action. I turned slightly and opened fire on a Hamp at fifteen hundred feet from seven o'clock. He burst into flame. No evasive action was taken. I looked up and another Hamp was turning slightly above and from about eight o'clock. He burst into flames after he had passed beyond my sights in the turn. The Nips realized we were there so I pulled up sharply to about twenty thousand feet and started for home.

"Immediately at two o'clock below at about twenty thousand feet I saw a P-47 with one Tony about three thousand feet to the rear and another about three thousand feet behind the first one. I turned and came in at four hundred mph on the tail of the rear Tony, opening fire at fifteen hundred feet. He took no evasive action and burst into flame. I closed for another Tony but he must have seen me as he turned and dove down in front of me. I opened fire from about two thousand feet closing in and saw tracers going into him and pieces of his wing and fuselage flying off. I did not see him catch fire nor did I see him crash. (This plane was confirmed by a member of the flight who saw him crash into the sea.) Tonys were all over the sky. I made another pass at a Tony from about ten o'clock but deflection was wrong. I looked and saw a Tony closing in on my tail so I dived for the nearby clouds. When coming out of the clouds I could no longer see the Tony. I climbed to fifteen thousand feet and called the flight. They all checked and proceeded to Lae, where we peeled off to land."

Major Raymond Gallagher chased a Zeke out to sea during the first seconds of the battle, but Dunham and Moore stayed with Kearby. In the early minutes of the fight Dunham and Moore shot down a Tony each, and by then Kearby was twenty miles away fighting six Tonys. Moore dived from sixteen thousand feet, blasted one of the six to pieces, and distracted two others. By then the P-47s were low on fuel and landed at the emergency base with less than seventy-five gallons left in their tanks. For destroying six of the nine planes, Kearby was awarded the Congressional Medal of Honor.

*   *   *

MacArthur's headquarters had issued a revised plan in October 1943, and it had been decided that Rabaul could be bypassed in favor of moves more directly aimed at the ultimate liberation of the Philippines. This change of plans stipulated early occupation of bases in the Bismarcks and along the northwest of Vitiaz Strait, and naturally the isolation and neutralization of Rabaul. Plans had already been prepared covering the seizure of Cape Gloucester on New Britain and these were to be carried through to assure Allied control of the Vitiaz Strait. The plan made it clear that the responsibility for keeping the pressure on the enemy was largely the role of the Fifth Air Force and Kenney assessed his forces. In October of 1943 he

They finally sent *The Mustang* home at the end of 1943, after she had flown one hundred and nine missions. The old B-17F had been flown by most of the 63rd Squadron's pilots, including the legendary Ken McCullar.

had the following tactical units: five fighter groups; one light, three medium and three heavy bomb groups; four and a half troop carrier groups; a photo squadron; and a night fighter detachment.* In September MacArthur had been informed that within two months he would get an additional light bomber group, a night fighter squadron, and another fighter group. A second light bomber group, another night fighter squadron, and the 20th Combat Mapping Squadron had also been allotted for early shipment to the Southwest Pacific.

What Kenney needed most was fighters—fighters with long range, firepower, and speed. He was losing the P-38s, which had these qualities, to the European Theater. In fact the number of P-38s in the Fifth would decline from two hundred and twelve in September to one hundred and fifty in February 1944. Instead of the P-38s originally scheduled, Arnold authorized three hundred and fifty Republic P-47s during November and December, but this number had to be reduced because of the limits of transportation. Between October and December only forty-five P-38s and a couple of hundred P-47s arrived in Australia, and Kenney was forced to be satisfied and comfort himself with the promise that he would get P-38s

* Kenney's strength was richly varied. His five fighter groups were the 8th (its 80th Squadron had P-38s, the 35th and 36th had P-39s), the 35th (P-38s in the 39th Squadron, P-39s in the 40th and 41st), the 49th (9th Squadron with P-38s, P-40s in 7th and 8th), the 348th with P-47s, and the 475th with P-38s. The light bomber group was the 3rd Attack, but actually only the 89th Squadron was equipped with A-20s—the 8th, 13th, and 90th Squadrons had B-25s. The medium groups were the 22nd, whose 19th Squadron was still flying the old B-26s while its 2nd, 33rd, and 408th flew B-25s, and the 38th and 345th Groups, with B-25s. The heavy groups were all equipped with B-24s—the 43rd, 90th, and 380th. The troop carrier groups all flew C-47s, with a sprinkling of old B-17s as armed transports—these were the 317th, 374th, 375th, and 433rd Troop Carrier Groups; the "half" group was part of the 433rd, which had six squadrons.

originally destined for the South Pacific; the priorities had been adjusted since the crisis days of Guadalcanal, and Kenney could be optimistic.

It was a shifting situation as 1943 drew to a close. The new 417th Bomb Group was in the theater, but without aircraft, and only two of the Fifth's light groups, the 3rd and 312th, would have their A-20s by February 1944. Kenney wanted B-25Js, but these might not be available until April 1944, and this caused complications. Most of the B-25s were modified as they arrived in the theater, meaning that although the Fifth had over two hundred and fifty B-25s, most new planes were in depots and the combat squadrons were below strength. The Townsville Air Depot had converted one hundred and seventy-five B-25Cs and B-25Ds into strafers by September 1943, then began working over the B-25Gs. Between November 1943 and April 1944 it added two .50-caliber machine guns in the nose, two more in the gun tunnel, and twin .30-caliber guns in the tail to eighty-two Mitchells. Fifth Bomber Command's over-all power was being increased by the effectiveness of the heavy bombers, and one of the most welcome reinforcements of 1943 came when Colonel Ed Scott and thirteen B-24Ds specially equipped for blind bombing arrived and went to the 63rd Squadron. Kenney had grown to like the B-24, because it had done everything asked of it, and in January would get the green light to convert the old 22nd Group to the Liberator. Range was of primary importance, and Kenney was hoping to get some of the new Superfortresses for the Fifth.

But in the meantime his B-24s, B-25s, and P-38s had another big job facing them.

IV

Knocking Out Rabaul

THE neutralization of Rabaul drew near. The Fifth Air Force, with advanced bases at Dobodura and in the Markham and Ramu valleys, was getting ready to cross the Vitiaz Strait to Arawe and Cape Gloucester on New Britain as soon as the ground forces captured them. Admiral Halsey's South Pacific forces were about to move into Bougainville from New Georgia. Along the road to Rabaul, both MacArthur and Halsey had been able to use their air power to smash Japanese strongpoints without costly landings, and it had been decided this could also work with Rabaul.

While Halsey's forces went into Bougainville, Rabaul would be pounded by the Fifth to keep the Japanese off balance, and then Halsey's South Pacific forces would return the favor by keeping Rabaul quiet during the Southwest Pacific forces' planned invasions at Arawe and Cape Gloucester.

The Japanese had been casual concerning improvements to Rabaul during the early days of victory, but by the fall of 1943 it was heavily defended. Lakunai and Vunakanau airfields had been improved despite the Allied bombing which had been carried out since early 1942. Lakunai was an all-weather strip of sand and volcanic ash, while Vunakanau was surfaced with concrete, and Rapopo, lying fourteen miles southeast of Rabaul, had been completed in late 1942 with concrete strips and other facilities. Tobera airfield, completed in August 1943, was inland between Vunakanau and Rapopo. These four airfields contained revetments for over four hundred planes. On New Ireland, just across the St. George's Channel, was Borpop, the fifth airfield protecting Rabaul.

The port facilities at Rabaul were seven wharves, supplemented by floating cranes and new piers in Simpson Harbor. The myriad inlets on the north shore of Blanche Bay, sheltered by heavy jungle, were used for dispersal of boats and barges, and there were also facilities for submarines. Rabaul was well supplied, and the depot for the whole area extending to the Solomons and eastern New Guinea. Most of these stores were in warehouses in the township or in dumps aboveground. The enemy had established strong beach and coastal defenses around Rabaul and naturally high priority had been given to antiaircraft defenses. An efficient joint army and navy organization had been effected to control the three hundred and sixty-seven weapons there. The Japanese radar web was extensive and Rabaul could expect thirty to sixty minutes' warning of an attack.

Kavieng on New Ireland, with its large airfield, was another potentially strong supporting position. Gasmata Island, just off the south coast of New Britain, had poor dispersal facilities and sustained attacks had made it non-operational, but to replace it the Japanese began developing a strip at Cape Hoskins, on the north coast of New Britain, in September 1943. This was a satellite airfield for the defense of Rabaul, and to protect convoys in the Bismarck Sea. The two strips at Cape Gloucester endangered Allied fields in New Guinea, and Talasea (also on New Britain) provided another emergency landing strip for the enemy. There were two airdromes in the Admiralty Islands to the northwest, Lorengau on Manus and Momote on Los Negros. In New Guinea, Madang was seldom used after the two Alexishafen strips were completed by August 1943. These were heavily bombed during September and were too far forward to be of much operational use to the enemy. Strips in the Hansa Bay area were also under Allied attack, and the airfields at Boram, Dagua, Wewak, But, and Tadji, though pounded since August, could still present a serious threat. Tadji and the strips at Hollandia were staging and dispersal areas for the Wewak and Madang fields.

Rabaul's commanders had problems keeping their air garrison at the desired strength. About sixty fighters and forty bombers of the Fourth Air Army had been sent to Wewak in August 1943, and the heavy losses sustained by Japanese naval air units in the Munda operations had necessitated the recommitment of the air units of Carrier Division 2 from Truk, and by November it would be necessary to send down the air group of Carrier Division 1. After moving to Wewak the Fourth Air Army not only faced the crushing Fifth Air Force attacks of August and September, but was further weakened by the need to return an air division to the Celebes in November 1943, to replace naval units drained by the continuing reinforcement of Rabaul. Losses along the ferry routes to Wewak were high, maintenance was poor, and Allied attacks on shipping forced many planes to be grounded due to lack of parts. So the enemy units in New Guinea were hardly in a condition to spring to the aid of the navy units at Rabaul. Japanese commanders had been forced to consider withdrawal of their outer ring of defenses to the Marianas and Carolines, but decided to hold Rabaul at all costs to shield the fleet base at Truk.

Target: Rabaul

Moresby, by this time, was almost a rear base—Advon, the bomber and fighter commands, and the 54th Troop Carrier Wing were based there, and the four active airfields based two heavy groups, the 8th Photo Squadron, and four fighter squadrons. The C-47s and a few additional units such as night fighter squadrons were also there, but the offensive had moved forward.

Australian engineers had finished two airstrips at Kiriwina, about three hundred and twenty-five miles from Rabaul, and from these the B-25s could reach Rabaul with worthwhile bomb loads. The P-38s, by staging or basing at Kiriwina, could provide cover for them. The heavies from Port Moresby could stage through Dobodura, headquarters of Colonel Freddy Smith's First Air Task Force, which at the end of September 1943 was composed of the 22nd Group with B-25s and a squadron of B-26s, the 3rd Attack Group with one squadron of A-20s and three of B-25 strafers, and the 475th Fighter Group and 9th Squadron of the 49th with P-38s.

In future the main base for New Guinea operations would be Nadzab, and since its capture it had become the headquarters of Colonel Jarred V. Crabb's Second Air Task Force. The advanced base of the Third Air Task Force at Gusap filled a vital role, because from there P-47s could reach Wewak while the shorter-range P-40s and P-39s could watch over the Alexishafen and Madang airfields. So Whitehead was able to throw his P-38s against Rabaul yet still keep a heavy foot planted on the enemy in New Guinea.

Rabaul had been under continual surveillance since January 1942, and the recon photos on October 1, 1943, showed a heavy cruiser, a light cruiser, ten destroyers, twenty-six merchant vessels, and five submarines in Simpson Harbor as well as two hundred aircraft on the airstrips, fifty-nine of them fighters. By October 11 the fighter count had reached one hundred and forty-five and plans for the first strike were finalized. Weather predictions pointed to October 12, and with the first monsoon nearly due, advantage had to be taken of any good weather.

On October 12, the largest attack yet made in the theater began. The crews had been carefully briefed on their approach routes, antiaircraft, and individual targets. As planned, the mission would be a one-two blow—the B-25s would go in low to neutralize the airfields, then the B-24s would destroy the shipping in the harbor.

The B-25 groups had gathered at Dobodura and the 3rd Attack was using its three squadrons with P-38 cover to hit Rapopo with parafrag bombs and strafing. The 345th and two squadrons of the 38th were to hit Vunakanau the same way. In all, one hundred and seven Mitchells, led by Colonel Clinton True, the 345th commander, made the attack.

Apparently achieving surprise, the B-25s flew at a thousand feet from Oro Bay to Kiriwina, dropped to minimum altitude as they went up the St. George's Channel, then veered sharply inland at the mouth of the Warangoi River. At treetop level they divided, with the 3rd Attack's forty planes streaking for Rapopo and the other sixty-seven to Vunakanau.

The 3rd Attack formed in shallow vees twelve to fifteen planes wide, following each other by about a mile. They opened fire on the antiaircraft positions from long range, and roared in to drop their parafrags over the bomber dispersals and revetments. The explosions and the churning dust and smoke made damage assessment difficult, but they claimed between fifteen and twenty-five planes destroyed on the ground and three in the air.

At Vunakanau Colonel True's groups went in the same way. There was light ground fire and fighters managed an attack as the fifth and sixth squadrons were

Parafrags drift lazily down on Vunakanau airstrip, Rabaul.

over the target. One Zeke was shot down, but the fighters set fire to the right engine of a B-25—the landing gear flopped down and a tire fell off as six Zekes ganged up on the crippled plane. The gunners got one of them before the pilot radioed, "I'm going in," and hit the water. The P-38s from the 49th and 475th Fighter groups, covering the B-25s, had little opposition, picking off a Betty and an Oscar over Vunakanau. In less than ten minutes the B-25s were on the way home. A squadron of RAAF Beaufighters from Kiriwina was scheduled to hit Tobera and Rapopo between the B-25 and B-24 attacks, and twelve made their strike as soon as the B-25s cleared the area.

The Liberator force leader was Colonel Art Rogers and the night before the mission he had little sleep; after midnight he had gone down to the line to check on the remaining airplanes to make sure everything would be loaded and ready to go. His alarm clock had woken him for breakfast at 3:30 A.M. and he picked up his little emergency kit, buckled on his pistol, and went out to his jeep. As the starter whirred, the motor backfired loudly, wakening Rogers' large white cockatoo. Thinking it was another enemy air raid, the bird screeched, "Damn the Japs." It seemed like a good omen to Rogers.

After briefing, the B-24 crews went down to their airplanes and were on alert until takeoff time, set as forty-five minutes after the last B-25 had left the ground. Rogers had been persuaded by his squadron commanders not to fly his gleaming, unpainted *Connell's Special* that day because they felt it was too tempting a target.

Colonel Art Rogers, flamboyant commander of the 90th Bomb Group. The grinning skull and bombs marking began appearing in September 1943, and soon the background color to it became squadron identification in the Jolly Rogers—red for the 319th, blue for the 320th, green for the 321st, and black for the 400th. (Rogers)

His crew was studying the target of their particular six-plane element. It was a large destroyer tender and in the past few days the recon photos had shown at least four destroyers tied alongside undergoing repairs.

After a delay caused by a takeoff accident, seven squadrons of B-24s from the Jolly Rogers and Ken's Men left Moresby and made the rendezvous—they had been briefed for selected targets in the harbor, and over Kiriwina the Liberators were met by forty-seven Headhunter and 39th Squadron Lightnings. As the mission progressed, twenty-five Liberators and nineteen P-38s were forced to turn back with mechanical troubles.

There was no chance of surprise after the B-25 attack, but it was hoped that the strafers had knocked out enough fighters and created enough chaos to make the small escort enough. The Japanese fighters which had survived the low-level attack would hopefully be tied down refueling.

The formation was at around eighteen thousand feet and still climbing when it reached the southern coast of New Britain. Twenty miles due west of Rabaul Rogers gave the signal, wobbling his wings, to break up the large formation into smaller formations of six planes. The B-24s were still far enough from the target to enable each element leader to maneuver his plane into the predetermined position from which he would begin his run. As the formation spread out it was almost impossible for the P-38s to cover all the Liberators.

At 12:05 P.M. Art Rogers led the 400th Squadron and the rest of the Jolly Rogers over Simpson Harbor, into a sky black with bursting shells from the guns on the land and aboard shipping in the harbor.

"Once I began my run," Rogers remembers, "I kept my eyes on the instruments, preventing me seeing the many large bursts in and around our formation. I could tell by the indication of my instruments that my bombardier, 'Ace' Dunmore, was making a good bombing run.

"As the little light flickered on the instrument panel, telling me the bombs were on their way, I glanced out to see which way to turn to avoid the flak so that my entire formation would not be blown out of the air. I was amazed and flabbergasted to see just ahead the biggest swarm of enemy fighters I had ever seen in the air at one time. About this time 'Ace's' words came clear over the interphone, 'We hit the target, Sir.' I had no time to congratulate him or anyone else as the Zeros prepared to attack. They had spotted us and apparently another of my elements that was off to the left of us. As we left the target, by actual count made from the window of General Kenney's aide, Major Kip Chase, who was riding as observer, there were eighty-seven individual attacks made by the Jap fighters. There were equally as many made on the other side, not counting attacks from underneath and above. The Japs would fly by us in formations of twenty-five to thirty airplanes on each side of our formation just out of reach of our guns until they were out ahead of us about five miles. Then they would simultaneously turn in from the right and the left and make their passes.

"I was on the radio calling for help from our fighters, but from their own conversations I decided they were having a problem looking after themselves. As a result I never saw one of our fighters after I commenced my bombing run.

"I knew now that something had gone wrong with the original plans and wondered if the Mitchells had been able to reach their target. I could not imagine how it would be possible for the Japs to throw this many fighters at us if they had a previous engagement.

"I could see Zeros flying to pieces in front of us as our good old nose turrets rotated. My plane had received a 20-mm. shell in the left wing tank and the hole had been so large that the self-sealing material of the tank was allowing the gasoline to seep out. With the exhaust flame not far from the escaping gasoline our plane became a fire hazard. I had to slow down as one of my wingmen's engines had been struck and was belching smoke. From radio conversations the other flight commanders were all having their difficulties and I began to wonder if any of us would get back. The Japs had followed us out seventy-five miles and were still attacking us fiercely as if the fight had just begun. I saw one of my elements off to the left, with one of his wingmen losing altitude rapidly. Apparently all but one engine had been shot out and he called his flight commander and said he would have to make a forced landing in the ocean. This he did and it was well done, since the airplane did not break up on landing. He had no sooner come to rest when at least twenty Zeros dove down on him, opening their guns up on the defenseless plane and crew, seventy-five miles from land. Before the last of the Zeros passed in attack the plane burst into flames and we were positive there would be no survivors of this crash as the men had not launched their lifeboats or were probably killed in the attempt. Another wingman in my element reported an engine out and the air was full of troubles for every flight commander. I kept wondering if these damned pests would ever run out of gas or ammunition since it looked like this would be the only cause for them to leave us alone. They were flying so close you could actually see the Jap pilots as they passed below or above you in the completion of the attacks.

"With all our airplanes in trouble I sent out a call to all flight commanders and airplane commanders notifying them to head for the Trobriand Islands, which was our nearest base. Other airplanes which thought they could make it as far as Buna were to proceed on there and land. I didn't want too many planes landing in the Trobriands because a crack-up on the runway, which was almost inevitable, might prevent the other planes from coming in.

"The Japs continued to dog us until we were one hundred and seventy-five miles out. All the planes in my flight had holes in them, but after conferring with the airplane commanders I decided that none of my six planes were damaged to the extent that we could not make it to Buna. My navigator was working furiously as I had used many evasive maneuvers during the running fight across the Bismarck Sea.

"He gave me a new course that would bring me into Buna and after following it for thirty minutes my engineer informed me that our gas loss from the damaged wing tank was far greater than I had expected. It was a question then of could I get to Buna or should I go back to the Trobriand Islands? I decided to try to make it to Buna, and we arrived there alright.

"A nice landing was made but as the plane slowed down to within five or ten miles an hour the nosewheel strut gave way and we stopped just off the edge of the runway on our nose."

The B-24s claimed the sinking of a destroyer and heavy damage to two tenders, as well as the setting of two large merchant vessels ablaze and the sinking or damaging of three other ships. The Japanese fighters, mostly Zekes, concentrated on the 400th and 321st Squadrons in the running fight after the attack, and shot down two B-24s, but the gunners claimed at least ten fighters. Trying to cover the B-24s, the P-38s were unable to get much action for themselves, although one Headhunter shot down a Hamp. The three squadrons of the 43rd Group, following the Jolly Rogers, reached the target as the last of the 90th's bombs were exploding. Heavy antiaircraft fire from all types of weapons burst around them and they saw large fires and great confusion in the harbor as ships circled or tried to get out to sea. The Jolly Rogers had dragged most of the Japanese fighters away with them, so the 43rd was relatively untroubled. Their claims were confused, and limited mainly to damage, although the 65th Squadron reported forty-eight hits with forty-eight bombs.

In all, the first raid was an outstanding success and the initial estimate was one hundred planes destroyed on the ground, twenty-six shot down, and heavy damage to the airfields and wharf areas. Three large merchant vessels, three destroyers, and forty-three smaller merchant vessels, as well as seventy harbor vessels, were thought sunk or destroyed. This was conservative regarding damage to aircraft, but

When weather closed off Rabaul there were other targets. *Red Wrath,* gaudily decorated with the yellow, green, and white nose of the 498th Squadron, the Falcons, taunts Boram's antiaircraft gunners on October 16, 1943.

optimistic regarding the damage done to shipping in the harbor, and the photo interpreters soon after revised the preliminary estimate downward. However, there were about two hundred destroyed or damaged aircraft at Vunakanau and some of the wrecks were later used to conceal fighters.

The next morning another large strike was sent out but weather turned it back. A few of the Liberators hit targets on western New Britain, but it was not until October 18 that the weather allowed an attack on Rabaul again. The Fifth not only lost flying days, but was losing the cumulative effect of sustained heavy raids.

Evidently assessing the big Rabaul attack as a prelude to invasion, the Japanese struck back at New Guinea ports. They hit Oro Bay on October 15 and the entire force of twenty-seven Vals and their escort was knocked down. On October 17 they attacked both Oro Bay and Finschhafen, and Finschhafen again two days later. At the cost of ten planes, the Allied fighters claimed over one hundred Japanese aircraft, and no shipping had been hit. The types of Japanese planes indicated the attacks had come from Rabaul.

There was another Rabaul strike on October 18, and two squadrons of B-24s from the Flying Circus at Darwin were borrowed to be added to the Jolly Rogers and Ken's Men. A strike force consisting of the 38th and 345th Groups' B-25 strafers and eight squadrons of Liberators took off early in the morning to hit Vunakanau, Lakunai, and Tobera. Over Kiriwina they picked up three squadrons of P-38s, but when the formations ran into a weather front the Lightnings were forced to turn back. The Liberators flew west along the coast of New Britain, searching for a break in the weather. Fifteen of them hit "targets of opportunity" on western New Britain and six hit New Guinea, while the rest dumped their bombs and returned home.

The B-25s faced the same weather, but by dropping down to the wavetops were able to slip under it. Fifty Mitchells got through and split up as they went inland over Cape Gazelle; the 38th achieved surprise at Tobera and claimed sixteen planes destroyed.

Three squadrons of the 345th were to attack Rapopo airstrip. Led by Colonel Clinton True in a B-25D strafer named *Red Wrath,* they had flown between twenty and fifty feet above the water as they sidestepped squalls. The nine planes of the 498th Squadron roared toward Rapopo. The first flight of three, loaded with parafrags and with True in front, attacked the runway and dispersal areas.

Red Wrath tore along the runway to catch anything that might be trying to take off. Nothing was there so True opened up on the guns at the end of the strip as his wingmen shot up both sides. The rest of the squadron followed through. Immediately after leaving the target they were intercepted by an estimated forty fighters, and in a fight lasting twenty-five minutes, ten fighters were claimed by the crews of the tightly packed B-25s. The 501st Squadron followed, and claimed another ten enemy aircraft in the running gunfight past the target. The 499th was next, flying through the smoke and dust of the previous waves. They claimed two as they passed through the fighters.

The Japanese fighters had apparently remained overhead, waiting for the expected P-38 escort, allowing the first three squadrons to finish their strike. The fourth squadron of the group, the 500th, had been assigned to attack shipping off Vunapope. One flight of their planes had turned back, but six B-25s got through and as they moved toward the coast at treetop level they sprayed a stream of bullets at everything that crossed their path. Over the coast the six planes divided into two flights and lined up on a freighter and transport at anchor. The freighter was straddled and overturned and the B-25s headed for a corvette which was trying to escape their attack. Lieutenant Thane Hecox dropped two bombs and the delay was just enough to catch the ship over them. The corvette simply disappeared in a pillar of spray and steam.

The second flight, led by Captain Lyle Anacker, strafed their way toward the transport and their bombs lifted the ship from the water. Then the enemy fighters came at them. *Tondelayo,* Lieutenant Ralph Wallace's aircraft, was hit in the right engine, which spewed smoke. Vibration threatened to tear it from the wing, so Wallace feathered the propeller and the other two B-25s dropped back to box him in.

Wallace saw the left engine on Lieutenant Harlan Peterson's aircraft throw smoke and then the left wheel dropped down. Peterson feathered the prop but was losing height fast, and hit the water tail down. Seven or eight fighters swooped to strafe the B-25 as it floated on the water. Anacker positioned his B-25 on Wallace's wing as the two Mitchells headed for home.

Three ships had been sunk, but avenging fighters were waiting for the attackers

Lieutenant Thane Hecox's bombs demolished this corvette in Vunapope Harbor on October 18, 1943.

at five thousand feet over Cape Gazelle and an estimated forty to fifty dived on the five B-25s. Some attacked the first flight but the crossfire from the three close-packed, speeding B-25s drove them to easier prey.

For seventy minutes, a few feet above the waves, Wallace and Anacker fought for their lives. The Japanese pressed right in, and one fighter even eased up and flew in formation between the two B-25s, blinding their guns. For fully a minute he was within fifty feet of each plane. One crewman said he was a "mean-looking bastard."

The gunners were busy, squeezing off short bursts as targets flashed across their sights. In all, *Tondelayo*'s crew claimed five of the fighters and Anacker's claimed two. The top turret on *Tondelayo* ran out of ammunition and two of the crew passed back belts from the nose. These two crewmen were also manning waist guns, operating the radio, and taking turns clamping their hands over a severed gas line which was filling *Tondelayo* with fuel and fumes. The aft end of the B-25 was ankle-deep in cartridge cases, the three men were becoming groggy from the gasoline fumes, and up front the co-pilot was wounded.

Racing along the coast of New Britain, Anacker's plane was so badly damaged that he finally had to head for the shoreline about twelve miles away. He ditched the burning B-25, two of the crew survived, and *Tondelayo* fought on alone. The

Japanese became furious and at least four crashed into the water as they made desperate attacks on the B-25 as it skidded across the waves at thirty feet. Wallace was an excellent pilot, and his handling of the crippled Mitchell saved all their lives—*Tondelayo* met head-on attacks by climbing into them, then turning into her dead engine to get down to the water again. Finally all but one of the fighters had turned back—he did a couple of slow rolls, waggled his wings, and left the battered B-25.

Tondelayo clanked into Kiriwina in need of a new right wing and engine, new radio equipment, a new propeller blade, and scores of patches.

* * *

Bad weather at Rabaul gave Whitehead a chance to get some strikes in against the New Guinea targets, but photographs taken on October 19 revealed that the Japanese had restored their fighter strength at Rabaul to over two hundred planes; forecasts of clearing weather on October 23 led to plans for another big strike. This time a fighter sweep by three squadrons was to lead in a B-24 attack on Lakunai and Vunakanau, but the Liberators and P-38s reached the target only to find it locked in by cloud cover. Rapopo was open, and the bombers made a damaging attack on the field while the P-38s shot down thirteen Japanese planes for the loss of one of their own; the Lightning pilot was eventually rescued after living with the natives on New Britain.

Next day the heavies stood down while the mediums hit Tobera, Rapopo, and Vunakanau. The mission was planned to reach Rabaul around ten o'clock, but slow takeoffs and scattered formations delayed the arrival by about two hours. The Japanese patrols were usually up at noon, and the leading squadron of the 3rd Attack was hit hard. They lost a B-25 before the fighters could come down to their aid and saw only four planes on the ground at Tobera, but destroyed twenty-one at Rapopo. The 345th got twenty-seven more at Vunakanau. In the hot fight the B-25s shot down eight fighters and lost two, while the P-38s got thirty-seven without loss.

The weathermen looked dubious, but Whitehead sent out a strike on October 25. Two squadrons of fighters were supposed to sweep in followed by two groups of Liberators, but again the force ran into bad weather. The fighters decided to return to Kiriwina, with seventy-three of their eighty-one P-38s, but the bomber leaders apparently did not hear the announcement over the command frequency and only eleven B-24s turned back. Fifty pressed on, flying on instruments, and Major Charles MacDonald and his flight of eight 475th Group Lightnings stayed with them. Battling through the storm the heavy bombers were met by fierce resistance at Rabaul. Warships joined with land batteries to put up a heavy barrage and about sixty fighters struck as the bombers began their run. MacDonald, with only eight P-38s over the leading squadron, hoped that "the Nips seeing us would be discouraged and perhaps figure that there were lots of us." These lonely Lightnings performed a weaving patrol over the target for forty-five minutes, MacDonald shooting down one of the few fighters which interfered with them.

Lieutenant Colonel Harry Bullis was leading the Jolly Rogers, and all the B-24s. Before the bomb run started, Lieutenant Charles Showalter's ship, *Tear-Ass* (*The Bull*) took a direct hit in the left outboard engine, which began to smoke and burn. The right outboard was also hit, stopped, but started again. The propeller was nicked in one of the good engines and started vibrating. Showalter's plane dropped out of formation as he radioed Bullis, asking him to reduce speed. The formation slowed down to shepherd the cripple.

Sergeant Harry Clay, photographer on *Tear-Ass,* will never forget what it was like in "a crippled plane over Rabaul by itself. Those Zeros actually lined up to get a shot at us. I estimate that there were thirty-five giving us their undivided attention but it may have just seemed that way. Every gun we had was going and as close as they pressed their attacks I don't know why they didn't shoot us all to pieces. They did a pretty good job of it anyway. The nose turret took a head on shot with a 20-mm. cannon but the shell exploded on contact and just blew glass in on the gunner. Cut him up some but he kept shooting. They came in on us from every angle."

Clay grabbed a walk-around oxygen bottle and began using the belly guns. He saw some of his tracer bouncing off the belly of a fighter but didn't know whether he got him or not.

"Showalter kept plugging away at it, feathering Number One, fire went out, trying to keep Number Four going, doing what he could for the engine with the nicked prop, trying to keep what speed and altitude he could and still heading for that damn target.

"What the hell else could we do? Those Zeros weren't going to go away, no matter which way we went. Colonel Rogers got us all a DFC for continuing on to the target but I really don't see that we had any option. The co-pilot kept calling off the incoming shots, and he certainly didn't lack for calls. The more that came in though, it seemed to me, the calmer he got until it sounded like a yawn would be next."

Between the stream of urgent fighter calls Harry Bullis' voice came over the radio: "Where's Showalter? Bullis to flight. Where's Showalter? Can anybody see Showalter?" Bullis' left wingman answered, "Bearskin to Bullis. Yes, yes, yes. Showalter's here. I am with Showalter on the wing."

The bombs tumbled down from the B-24s and the squadron leaders reported in. Bullis radioed Showalter to ask if he was still carrying his bomb load. "Salvoed bombs on target," was the answer, Showalter adding, "Thank you for slowing up." "That's all right, baby," answered Bullis. "That's fine."

The six B-24s of the 400th Squadron were credited with destroying eighteen of the thirty-eight enemy aircraft claimed by the bombers—Showalter's crew in *Tear-Ass* got four, and Lieutenant Sidney Webb's crew in one of the two aircraft closely protecting *Tear-Ass* got another four.

Although at long last there was nobody shooting at her, *Tear-Ass* was still in deep trouble, trudging along with only one engine operating perfectly.

They threw everything out of the plane that was not tied down. The camera, the guns, canteens, what little ammunition was left—anything to lighten the load as they slowly lost altitude. Harry Clay thinks it might have been his imagination, but some of them seemed to be eying their photographer and wondering what weight difference he might make. They made it to Kiriwina, shot to pieces, but Showalter landed the plane on the strip, although there wasn't twenty feet of it to spare when they stopped rolling.

Bloody Tuesday

Late in October, Admiral Mineichi Koga responded to pleas from the battered Rabaul bastion and sent three hundred fighters from the Combined Fleet at Truk. These aircraft began arriving at Rabaul's airfields on November 1.

A shipping strike was next on the Fifth's schedule, in support of the Bougainville landings on November 1. Kenney's combat crews had been ready since October 30, and on November 2 more poor weather reports seemed likely to cancel the mission until two 8th Photo Squadron Lightnings reported clearing skies at Rabaul.

The plan worked out between Colonel Freddy Smith of First Air Task Force and the attack leaders was uncomplicated and the mission was purely a B-25 and P-38 effort. Two fighter squadrons, the 39th and Headhunters, under over-all command of Major Ed Cragg, were to make a circular sweep of the harbor three minutes before the bombers came in. Escorted by two squadrons of P-38s from the 475th Group (the 431st and 432nd), Major Ben Fridge would lead the 345th Group in a gun and phosphorous bomb attack against the shore defenses and Lakunai airstrip. They would be followed ninety seconds later by two squadrons of strafers, the 90th and 13th, covered by Captain Jerry Johnson and the 9th Fighter Squadron. Four minutes later three more squadrons of B-25s, the 8th from the 3rd Attack and the 71st and 405th of the 38th Group, covered by Captain Danny Roberts' 433rd Squadron, would fly a devious course around the North Daughter

Headhunter Lightnings bracket a 345th B-25 on the way to Rabaul. The fighter pilots are Cy Homer, credited with a total of fifteen victories, and Ed Cragg. Although the Rabaul missions only cost sixteen P-38s in combat, attrition was so great that Kenney, unable to get the Lightnings he wanted, was forced to take the 9th and 39th Squadrons' aircraft and give them to the 475th as replacements. Neel Kearby was assigned the job of "selling" the P-47 to the two unhappy squadrons, and the argument over the relative merits of the fighters became so heated that at one stage Kearby challenged Jerry Johnson to settle it over Port Moresby.

volcano and cross Simpson Harbor. Then all the P-38s would form up to cover the
Mitchells as they retreated out to sea.

The 3rd Attack had been briefed at five o'clock in the morning and thirty minutes later they were by the fully loaded B-25s, ready to go at ten minutes' notice.
Dobodura was blanketed by a clinging ground fog, and to the north there were
rain and shafts of lightning. Time dragged by until the phone in operations rang.
Major Jock Henebry, commanding the B-25 force, was first there, and those clus-
tered around the phone knew the answer before he put the receiver down.

Ben Fridge's 345th Group B-25s were already taking off as the engines on the
3rd Attack's B-25s coughed into life. Henebry was leading in his *Notre Dame de
Victoire*—he had played ball for Notre Dame and the group chaplain had thought
the name appropriate, and the plane had been blessed. In his flight was Captain
Chuck Howe in *Here's Howe,* and Major Richard Ellis in *Seabiscuit*—least well
named as she was reputed to be the slowest B-25 in the Southwest Pacific. Henebry
was first off, his plane struggling with the weight of two and a half thousand pounds
of bombs, with *Seabiscuit* following.

At Rabaul the 39th Squadron found little opposition as Captain Ralph Bills led
the sweep across the harbor, but the following Headhunters met an estimated sixty
to one hundred interceptors. They lost two planes, but shot down eight in all, Lieutenant Allen Hill getting two Zekes.

Just before they reached the harbor, the P-38s of the 431st Squadron climbed to
seven thousand feet to begin a long, slanting dive across the target. Thirteen Lightnings belonging to the 432nd Squadron went to four thousand feet to meet the
Japanese fighters. It was just after one-thirty in the afternoon.

Simpson Harbor almost disappeared behind the wall of fire which met the B-25s
and P-38s. The nine planes of the 431st Squadron dipped in and out of the bowl
of flying steel to help the B-25s. Lieutenant Marion Kirby saw three enemy fighters
working over a crippled B-25 and took off after them alone. He got the first one
and then went after another. As he shot down the second, the third swung in
behind him and fired. Lieutenant Fred Champlin was already turning to help as the
Japanese fighter moved in, and before he could finish off Kirby, Champlin shot
him to pieces.

The Japanese were after the B-25s, which were calling for help. Lieutenant Low-
ell Lutton set one enemy fighter on fire, but two others clamped onto his tail.
Two other Lightnings forced them to break away and Lieutenant Ed Wenige shot
one of them down. When the P-38s moved back and forth above the bombers,
blocking enemy attacks, the frustrated Japanese turned on them. Two Zeros dived
on Lutton, but again Wenige and Lieutenant Franklin Monk met them, with the
same results. A third followed the first pair and Wenige was already out of ammunition. He ducked under the attack while Monk met the enemy fighter and shot
him down.

The thirteen planes of the 432nd Squadron were slithering in and out of the
clouds, trying to break up the diving attacks coming from above. The enemy
fighters swarmed overhead, ready to pick off any plane which became separated
from the rest in the overcast.

Lieutenant Grover Gholson saw an Oscar climbing out of its dive in front of
him, latched onto its tail, and squeezed off a short burst—the Japanese plane

ng *Hill's Angels*, Lieutenant Allen Hill got two of the Headhunters' victories on the
ember 2, 1943, Rabaul mission. In all he was credited with the destruction of nine
ny aircraft. (Howard Dean)

Dick Ellis, Jock Henebry, and war correspondent Lee Van Atta, beside *Seabiscuit*. Van
Atta flew the November 2, 1943, mission with Ellis and typed the story on the way
home. (Ellis)

caught fire. The flames went out momentarily as Gholson tried to keep the gunsight ring around the Oscar. After a few seconds the flames blossomed again and the fighter exploded. Gholson maneuvered himself onto the tail of a Zeke, followed him around in a turn, and fired several long bursts. As Gholson shot past, his wingman watched the enemy plane burn and head downward.

A Japanese fighter tried to ram two P-38s and as they dodged, Lieutenant Leo Mayo blasted a Tony. As it broke apart under the onslaught of the P-38's fire, pieces of it flew back and slammed into the Lightning, knocking the right wing completely off. Mayo managed to bail out of the crippled P-38 and landed in the water fifty feet from the shore, but he was never heard from again. As two other pilots dived down to circle Mayo and block Japanese trying to strafe him, Lieutenant Howard Hedrich stayed up alone to cover them. Four enemy fighters dived at him, shooting out one of his engines, then tried to finish him off. Hedrich dodged their fire, turning and sliding his plane; one of the Japanese passed in front and he shot him down. Finally the rest gave up the chase and left him alone.

The 345th had flown into the heavy ground fire and fierce fighter attacks. Two of the B-25s were hit in the bomb bays before they could unload their phosphorous bombs, one crashing and one making it back to base, smoldering all the way. Eight B-25s in the lead suffered hits, and two more were unable to get back. Between the 345th and their escort, thirty-four enemy fighters were claimed.

The attack with the "Kenney cocktails," standard one-hundred-pound bombs loaded with white phosphorus, was a success, and thick smoke rolled lazily between the harbor and the shore gun positions, as the seeping fire gutted large portions of the township. Sixteen aircraft were destroyed where they stood on Lakunai airstrip, and the effectiveness of this neutralization played a major part in the success of the strike. It allowed the strafers to attack from the east, over Crater Peninsula, passing over the town, then crossing the harbor, a route normally exposed to deadly fire. The only disadvantage was that the smoke from the fires and phosphorus made target selection in the harbor more difficult.

With *Seabiscuit* a few yards off his wing, Henebry was climbing to cross the pass between the Mother and North Daughter volcanoes. Two destroyers circling outside Rabaul Harbor had already livened things up for the 3rd Attack, but although the warships ran directly toward the B-25s firing their heavy guns, they were soon past.

Seabiscuit's speed was flagging as she made the steep climb, but suddenly Simpson Harbor was there. A bowl below them, full of shipping which was frantically trying to maneuver around the two-mile-wide anchorage. The township was choked with white smoke, spotted everywhere with black blobs as the gun positions beneath it fired at the attacking planes.

Henebry lined *Notre Dame de Victoire* up on three ships in a row—a freighter, a transport, and a cruiser. Ellis pointed *Seabiscuit* at a destroyer tender. *Here's Howe* broke sharply to the left and made for a transport.

The ships in the harbor were firing every kind of gun at the B-25s, and the heavy fire from the warships at water level threw up huge waterspouts in front of the attackers. The forward firepower of the B-25s again bewildered the Japanese, and some hid behind their armor plating and never attempted to return the fire. The maneuvering warships were the most dangerous.

Kenney cocktails about to engulf one of the eighty-three guns along Sulphur Creek at Rabaul. The Japanese called the phosphorous bombs "fiendish warfare," and they were dangerous concoctions. One 500th Squadron B-25 was hit in the bomb bay, slow-rolled in a huge swirling smoke cloud, and crashed. Captain Max Mortenson's plane was hit when he had four of his dozen bombs left—thick white smoke choked the plane but Mortenson was able to dump his bombs and clear most of the smoke from the plane. Back at Dobodura his B-25 smoldered and glowed for hours. (Joe Dally)

Henebry strafed the freighter, and thought he saw some fires before he bombed. He pulled up sharply directly amidships and dropped a thousand-pound bomb. He thought he got a hit as he sped on. Then the freighter was there, and a second bomb definitely hit, setting fire to the ship. But Henebry had made what he called the "arch mistake." When he pulled up over the second ship he found the cruiser was a lot closer than he had thought and he couldn't get *Notre Dame de Victoire*'s nose down to get his guns on the decks of the cruiser. He saw the Japanese pom-pom guns following him but could not retaliate. He could feel the hits and knew they were shot up "pretty good." The tail was badly damaged and both he and his co-pilot had to fly with both feet on the right rudder. There was no way to hold a formation in the confines of the harbor, and Henebry knew they were on their own. He had to get out as fast as possible.

Jock Henebry's *Notre Dame de Victoire* swooped down and raced across this line of three Japanese ships. He got a possible hit on the first, the *Hokuyo Maru,* and definitely hit the second, the ten-thousand-ton *Hakusan Maru.* The heavy cruiser spoiled his flight home.

Seabiscuit was low to the water, and her guns were sending a brilliant stream of fire before her as Ellis cut a path across the crowded harbor. His first bomb dropped as he was perhaps fifty feet from the tender. The ship filled the cockpit windscreen, then was gone from sight as Ellis zoomed up. He dived for the water again to line up a transport, but in between there was the heavy cruiser, getting under way, firing her guns. The eight-inch turrets were pointed at the onrushing B-25s. Ellis kept at fifty feet as his plane shuddered and rebelled against the concussion of the heavy shells. *Seabiscuit* crossed the cruiser ten feet above the forward turrets and the men in the B-25 could see the Japanese officers on the bridge.

Just past the huge ship, a parting blast from its guns whipped *Seabiscuit's* tail. Ellis fought with the controls as the aircraft's nose was irresistibly forced downward. Ten feet from the water he had the B-25 level again, and her nose guns were sending streams of bullets toward another transport. The tracers spattered over the ship. *Seabiscuit* was jinking and skidding as the ship came closer. Ellis held his finger on the trigger, his right hand holding the bomb release. Then the two bomb lights on the instrument panel went out and Ellis and his co-pilot heaved the B-25 up, up over the ship, then down to hug the water again.

His bombs gone, Ellis strafed a gunboat which had crossed his path and headed for home.

After breaking away, *Here's Howe* had started a two-hundred-and-thirty-miles-

Captain Danny Roberts led his 433rd Fighter Squadron on seven missions to Rabaul. Roberts did not smoke, drink, or swear and was a cool and calculating leader who meticulously planned his squadron's tactics, always urging the pilots to "stay together, like a pack of wolves." On November 9, 1943, he was killed when he and his wingman collided while chasing an Oscar over Madang. He had fifteen victories. (Dennis Glen Cooper)

per-hour run on a freighter. At eight hundred yards Howe opened fire with his eight fifties. He kept up the constant stream of bullets until he was forced to pull up to clear the masts. One of his thousand-pound bombs was dropped early and skipped into the side of the ship, the other banged off the decks. The ship sank immediately.

Captain Danny Roberts kept his twelve 433rd Squadron P-38s low, beating off Japanese fighter attacks and dodging the antiaircraft fire, staying with the bombers.

The final wave of B-25s was led by Major Raymond Wilkins of the 8th Bomb Squadron. Wilkins had flown the surviving A-24 Dauntless back from the dive bombers' deadly last mission in July 1942, and the retiring pilot had once confided over a few late-night beers that he thought there was some "magic" which would keep him alive.

Wilkins had to make a late change in tactics because of the smoke, thick over the harbor, and he was leading his B-25s through heavy fire. He was flying in the most vulnerable position, on the left flank, and his plane was hit almost immedi-

Major Raymond H. Wilkins, commanding the 8th Squadron of the 3rd Attack Group.

ately. The right wing was badly shot up and at mast height Wilkins was fighting desperately for the control he needed. Rather than pull up to safety, he kept going. His nose guns ripped into a cluster of small vessels, then he picked out a destroyer. His bomb hit amidships, but by then the enemy gunners had shredded the left stabilizer of his B-25. Wilkins still kept on. He dropped another bomb, setting fire to a transport. In his crippled aircraft he began leading the withdrawal, but there was a heavy cruiser between him and safety. Wilkins made a strafing attack, and the cruiser blasted off what remained of the left stabilizer. The B-25 pilot had to turn or collide with his wingman, but in turning he exposed the lower surface of his plane to the Japanese gunners. Shellfire disintegrated his left wing and the B-25 plunged into the harbor. Wilkins was awarded the Medal of Honor, posthumously.

Once clear of the harbor, the battered *Notre Dame de Victoire* became a target for the fighters. They shot the left engine to pieces so thoroughly that when Henebry hit the feathering button his oil pressure was so low that it was too late. Now there was a windmilling propeller, with its drag and fire danger to add to his problems. He managed to gain a little height as his crew threw out everything they could—gun barrels, ammunition, everything. Still he was unable to hold his altitude and *Notre Dame de Victoire* was going down, slowly but surely.

Seabiscuit was indicating one hundred and thirty-five miles per hour when she reached the top of the volcanic ridges and roared along the plateau where Vunakanau airstrip lay. The destroyer tender in the harbor had damaged the right engine and Ellis was watching it with some concern. At the top of the climb, *Seabiscuit*'s crew had found they were alone, the faster B-25s already a couple of miles ahead. Ellis poured on the power, but the right engine was throwing oil, and

Lieutenant Colonel Larry Tanberg led the 38th Group to Rabaul on November 2, 1943. He vividly remembers that "the firing from the ships looked as though there was no way to get through . . . the thing that sticks in my mind is the water spouts and the tremendous salvoes from the naval vessels . . . it was a miracle to get through all that firepower." *The Scoto Kid* carries the drooling wolf design painted on all the 71st Squadron's strafers. (Larry Tanberg)

A wolf-nosed 71st Squadron B-25 crosses the harbor as Japanese gunners cringe behind their armor plate.

Chuck Howe brings *Here's Howe* out of Simpson Harbor and dashes past the lava slopes of Vulcan Crater.

there were rips in the right wing. The B-25 splashed through a rain squall and ran into about nine Tonys and Zeros waiting at three thousand feet. Ellis desperately maneuvered his damaged plane even closer to the ground as the Zeros attacked from each side. In the top turret, Sergeant Emmor Mullenhour saw one come in from left to right, in the B-25's blind spot. Cannon fire thudded into *Seabiscuit*'s tail and then the Zero pulled out of its firing pass, exposing its belly to Mullenhour's guns. The tracers zipped into the fighter behind the cockpit and the whole tail section broke into flames. The Japanese pilot bailed out while the plane was in a ninety-degree bank.

Ellis had to ease back on the throttles because the number-one engine threatened to burst into flames at any minute, and anyway he had no hope of outrunning the fighters. His co-pilot was yelling for help from the P-38s as the Japanese kept up their passes. A fighter turned in toward *Seabiscuit,* so Ellis whipped up the nose and fired the eight machine guns at him, driving him off. Then he was off the plateau and Jerry Johnson's P-38s lent a hand. The fighters were no longer a problem, but Ellis had others. Far ahead he could see the rest of the squadron, but for some reason he was gaining on them. As he drew closer he could see why. The crippled *Notre Dame de Victoire* seemed to be falling apart as all kinds of equipment tumbled out and splashed into the water, which was a little too close. *Seabiscuit* coasted up alongside, long enough for Henebry to tell Ellis to get the others back home and that Howe would escort him to Kiriwina—or as near Kiriwina as he was going to get.

Seabiscuit and the rest reached Dobodura around five in the afternoon.

Notre Dame de Victoire, with *Here's Howe* close by, was just above the water, the cushioning effect helping keep the B-25 dry. Finally Kiriwina was in sight, but Henebry was not going to be able to get enough altitude to get over the palm trees to the airstrip and he decided to ditch as near to the beach as he could. Although a gunner sprained an ankle and Henebry banged his head getting out, it was a pretty good ditching. The crew got into a raft, watched their B-25 sink beneath the surface, and then a Navy torpedo boat came along to pick them up. When they reached the jetty, Howe and his crew were waiting. They all jumped into a jeep, drove back to Kiriwina strip, climbed into *Here's Howe,* and were back home at Dobodura before their clothes were dry.

While Simpson Harbor had been a confused battleground, the B-25s had been extremely accurate, nearly all scoring hits or near misses. Assessment of the damage was difficult but the official communiqué claimed three destroyers, eight large merchant vessels, and four coastal vessels sunk, a total of about fifty thousand tons. A later Fifth Air Force estimate reduced this to thirteen thousand tons sunk, but after the war the Strategic Bombing Survey found the Japanese willing only to admit damage to a ten-thousand-ton tanker and the loss of three small merchant vessels totaling eight thousand tons, a minesweeper, and two smaller boats.

*   *   *

November 2 was the most costly Rabaul attack for the Fifth—there were forty-five pilots killed or missing, nine P-38s and eight Mitchells lost, and others just made it home to be junked. The B-25s had shot down twenty-six enemy fighters and destroyed sixteen more on the ground at Lakunai, and they got ten flying boats or float planes in the harbor. The Lightnings claimed forty-two Japanese fighters, and noted in their combat reports that these were the best enemy pilots they had fought for a long while. Australian Beauforts attacked Rabaul during the night, and then the weather closed in again.

Reports from the reconnaissance planes caused concern to Whitehead and on November 4 he advised Kenney that for the past day he had been watching the movement southward of a task force. That morning he had ordered the 345th Bomb Group and 475th Fighter Group to Kiriwina, and the Ken's Men B-24s into Dobodura. At that time the first part of the task force, three heavy cruisers, two light cruisers, and nine destroyers, seemed likely to reach Rabaul between three o'clock and seven o'clock in the morning of November 5. Later reports indicated they had been delayed by a rendezvous and could not be there before eight o'clock.

Reports on this movement also reached Halsey, whose forces had landed at Empress Augusta Bay on November 1. Whitehead was ready to use everything he had against either Rabaul or the task force itself, if it should head for the American beachhead. Halsey, not intending to let this force steal his initiative, planned to stop at it Rabaul with a carrier strike and asked the Fifth to smash Rabaul township and the airdromes around it while his planes hit the shipping in the harbor. The mission was carried out on November 5, with Halsey's carriers catching the task force as it entered the harbor. The Fifth's part in the attack, limited to twenty-seven Liberators of the 43rd Group, covered by fifty-eight P-38s, was hitting the wharf area. Opposition was light, and only one P-38 was shot down, ironically the first and only Lightning the 39th Squadron lost during the Rabaul missions.

The heavy bombers were airborne on November 6 but were called back because of bad weather; next day they got through and ran into strong opposition during an attack on Rapopo airdrome, where sixteen planes were destroyed on the ground. Sixty Japanese fighters intercepted and the P-38s claimed twenty-three, and lost five.

On November 10 the heavies hit Rabaul again while another big mission was prepared to complement a carrier raid to be made on November 11. This time Halsey requested the Fifth Air Force mediums to attack shipping targets in the harbor, so it was planned that a heavy bomber force would take off at midnight and bomb Lakunai in the early morning hours. The B-25s, with P-38 cover, would hit the shipping while unescorted heavies again hit the airdromes. Twenty-three Liberators struck Lakunai early in the morning of November 11, and more B-24s took off at seven o'clock, but the weather planes out in front reported impassable conditions from sea level to thirty-five thousand feet, completely cutting off Rabaul. At nine o'clock there was no choice but to call the aircraft back, and there the all-out Fifth Air Force campaign against Rabaul ended quietly, except for continuing surveillance. There was plenty of work to do at other targets on the island of New Britain.

With Rabaul neutralized rather than occupied, Allied planes needed a foothold on western New Britain in order to control the Vitiaz Strait, and it was planned that a major landing would be made by the 1st Marine Division at Cape Gloucester and an Army force would seize the airfield at Gasmata. Whitehead had doubts about the entire operation—closer examination revealed that the south coast of New Britain offered little to the Fifth; at Gasmata the coral runway was good but the island was small and had an average annual rainfall of nearly two hundred and fifty inches. Even Cape Gloucester held little appeal because it was no closer to Rabaul than Kiriwina, and Whitehead felt that the Vitiaz Strait could be effectively controlled from New Guinea bases. Kenney had already indicated to headquarters that facilities at Cape Gloucester were no longer a requirement, but the Navy insisted on cover for their convoys from both sides of the strait.

The landings had originally been planned for November, but for a variety of reasons that was not possible and it was decided to schedule the Gasmata operation for December 2, with Cape Gloucester on December 26. Discussions between Kenney, the Army, and the Navy brought another change. The Navy wanted to locate a patrol boat base on the south coast of New Britain to guard the Vitiaz Strait, and it seemed that Arawe Island, west of Gasmata, was most suitable—the enemy force there was much smaller and agreement was quickly reached to substitute Arawe for Gasmata. If this landing was made no less than eight days before Cape Gloucester Kenney felt sure he could guarantee some air cover, and MacArthur readily approved of the revised plan. The change to Arawe released forces originally scheduled for Gasmata, and this made possible their use for an additional landing at Saidor on New Guinea, which would help accelerate the destruction of enemy forces along the coast above Finschhafen.

While Australian planes were filling the gap between the Fifth's reduction of Rabaul and the beginning of neutralizing attacks by the South Pacific air forces, the Fifth itself was supporting Australian troops in their struggle along the coast of the Huon Peninsula and in the Ramu Valley. They continued hammering Wewak and other airfields in New Guinea and these strikes, while protecting the Allies' own bases, also contributed to the neutralization of enemy air power in preparation for the imminent landings.

On November 13 nine B-25s escorted by eighteen RAAF P-40s began the pre-invasion bombing of western New Britain, shooting up the area from Gasmata to Lindenhafen. There was a P-40 strike four days later, and for four days from November 20 Liberators and Mitchells blanketed the defenses at Gasmata, and in early December the B-25s and A-20s attacked the Arawe Islands and Peninsula. None of these targets was strongly defended and the enemy fighters already had their hands full defending Wewak and Rabaul.

Four missions were flown against the north coast of New Britain during November and December, and then the aerial preparation for the invasion really began, with a campaign to eliminate barge and merchant traffic from Rabaul and knock out defenses in the invasion area. For over five weeks, beginning on November 19, the bombers and strafers swept New Britain on all but nine days, and fighter sweeps and night patrols attacked the area. The cannon-armed B-25Gs were thor-

Operating with First Air Task Force, the 22nd Group's B-25s and Silver Fleet B-26s hit supply dumps, installations, shipping, and airdromes on the north coast of New Britain throughout October and November of 1943 as the pressure was applied.

Jerry Johnson, one of the best shots in the Fifth Air Force. On November 15, 1943, near Nadzab, he shot down an Australian Boomerang by mistake. The aircraft was wrecked but the pilot was unhurt. Johnson eventually had to come out of hiding and mended Allied relations with a bottle of gin. Unabashed, he included an Australian flag among the rising suns painted below his cockpit. (Harry Brown)

oughly used, lobbing over twelve hundred and fifty rounds into the targets, particularly Cape Gloucester airdrome and its antiaircraft defenses. The beach defenses at Borgen Bay were hit, and Cape Hoskins airdrome was bombed by B-24s to put it out of action during the landing. This was saturation bombing as never before seen in the theater. Although the 1st Marines estimated there would be nine thousand troops in the area, five thousand more around Cape Hoskins, and potential reinforcements from Rabaul where there were perhaps eighty thousand, Kenney hoped the Marines would be able to walk ashore with their rifles on their backs.

On November 22 the target was changed from Gasmata, Ring Ring, and Lindenhafen to Arawe, but then it was decided best to keep the main attack on the other areas and hope to achieve surprise at Arawe. On December 13 two squadrons of B-24s from the Flying Circus, with two from the 43rd, were weathered out of Cape Hoskins and hit Lindenhafen. That afternoon twenty-six B-25s struck the same area from minimum altitude while the Jolly Rogers and 345th Group Mitchells went to Ring Ring plantation. On December 14, the 22nd Group, the Red Raiders, hit Gasmata airdrome with their B-25s and B-26s in a medium-altitude attack which fulfilled the requirement to protect the invasion force. The bombers then hit the invasion areas, Amalut plantation on the Arawe Peninsula and nearby Pilelo Island.

The operations planned for the day of the Arawe landing, December 15, included attacks in the Cape Gloucester area and direct support for the amphibious force, fighter cover for the shipping, and whatever aid the ground forces called for. The convoy was off the beaches at dawn on December 15 and after a sharp destroyer bombardment the troops went in. The main landing was made against little

Lieutenant Charles Howard steers the 500th Bomb Squadron's *Saturday Nite* across Boram airstrip on November 27, 1943.

The 348th Fighter Group, at Finschhafen, had to be supplied entirely by air. This 433rd Group C-47 moves up as two others clear the strip on December 13, 1943. (Roger Beaty)

opposition and only one strike was called in all day, but a small force landing at the base of Arawe Peninsula to cut off Japanese troops retreating from the Amalut plantation area ran into heavy opposition. When twelve of their fifteen boats were lost and a dozen men were killed the effort was abandoned and complete resupply was requested. The equipment was loaded into nineteen B-25s and a B-17 at Dobodura and dropped on Amalut plantation the next day.

The fighters-found more action than the bombers. One Japanese recon plane appeared over Arawe early in the morning, before the P-38s arrived, and evidently sighted the convoy and radioed the information. At nine o'clock between thirty and forty Vals and Zekes bombed and shot up the beach, racing away without loss. Throughout the rest of the day P-38s and P-47s guarded the Arawe area and the Japanese sent in seventy to eighty fighters and dive bombers. There were only two battles, one when the P-38s shot down a Zeke and the other when four P-38s drove off thirty Zekes and a force of twelve Betty and Sally bombers.

After December 15 the Japanese kept sending in strong attacks, but were usually unable to penetrate the fighter screen, and they lost heavily. By the end of the year they had sacrificed at least two dozen bombers and thirty-two fighters. After the New Year they made most of their attacks at night.

There was little demand for the Allied bombers during the Arawe operation, the A-20s getting most of the work, bombing and strafing their way through enemy build-ups between Gasmata and Arawe or clearing the way in front of Allied troops. It was apparent that some of the Japanese planes disrupting the Arawe beachhead were coming from Madang so on December 19 Red Raider B-25s hit that airdrome. Allied advances from Arawe met solid Japanese resistance on December 21 and reinforcements had to be called in; on January 16 an attack was begun to clear the area, and B-24s and B-25s added to the pressure on the enemy. Light tanks rumbled ahead of a drive which advanced for about a mile and after this attack patrols found that the enemy was withdrawing. They steadily moved on until February 10, when the Arawe patrols met the Marine patrols from Cape Gloucester. Gasmata airdrome was occupied by March 17 and after that there was little to do except routine patrolling.

Cape Gloucester

After the successful beginning of the Arawe operation on December 15, the attacks on Cape Gloucester were stepped up in preparation for the landing there ten days later. A couple of Japanese fighters had been spotted taking off from one of the Gloucester strips on December 17 and the next day the Jolly Rogers struck the field with eighty tons of bombs to stop any recurrence of that kind of thing. The Flying Circus and Ken's Men gave Cape Hoskins a dose of the same; the Flying Circus flew a double mission on December 19 and Ken's Men flew two missions daily from December 21 to Christmas Day. The bombing peaked on Christmas Eve, when seven groups flew two hundred and eighty sorties. While the daylight attacks went on, the 63rd Squadron's radar B-24s cruised over the area nightly, dropping bombs and tossing out grenades, beer bottles, and anything else that would make the Japanese miserable and sleepless.

A Jolly Roger over the pitted Cape Gloucester airstrip. The pounding received by this area of New Britain led to the coining of a new verb in the Fifth Air Force, "Gloucesterizing."

Every target was hit. The 345th, which would attack the beach on the day of the landing, sent their strafers over the course on December 24 to check their timing. The Second and Third Air Task Forces used their planes to ensure that no opposition to the landing could come from the New Guinea airfields, and Rabaul was harassed by Australian Beauforts and South Pacific Theater aircraft. The Japanese reeled under the storm of bombs and bullets.

There was a meticulous schedule for the fighter cover to make sure the Japanese planes could not interfere, and forty-five minutes before the landing five squadrons of Liberators were to suppress the defenses guarding the Cape Gloucester beaches. Then the fleet would bombard the entire area. A minute later three Mitchell squadrons were to bomb and strafe the shore while another blanketed rear positions with white phosphorus. The A-20 squadrons would be on air alert from the time of the landing, and four squadrons of B-24s and four squadrons of mediums were to bomb and strafe along the coast east of the beachhead to break up enemy troops attempting to regroup. Other strikes were organized to stop any real Japanese reaction.

The Fifth's fighters provided cover as the shipping moved along the New Guinea coast on Christmas Day; a Japanese plane was sighted and destroyed in the afternoon but there were no attacks, the weather was good, and the bombardment went off as scheduled. In the morning of December 26 the Marines landed without opposition, and although the beaches were not heavily fortified, they found abandoned guns and equipment as they moved toward the airdrome. The A-20s were

El Diablo IV, a 3rd Attack strafer, cruises over the barren Cape Gloucester landscape.

not needed for support so they began hitting previously assigned targets, and the mediums and heavies hit others.

In the morning there were no air attacks on the beachhead, but the expected strike came in the middle of the afternoon. About twenty-five Vals, evidently from Rabaul, escorted by more than thirty Zekes, Oscars, and Tojos, made up the attacking force. The radar lost the formation and two squadrons of fighters sent out to intercept were not in position when the attack came. Although there were more than seventy fighters patrolling the area the dive bombers reached the convoy and sank a destroyer and damaged three others. Then the air battle began, and in twenty-five minutes the Japanese lost twenty-two Vals and at least twenty-four of their fighters. The Vals made their attack just as the 345th was going in on a strafing mission, the Japanese dive bombers flying through the B-25 formation. The guns on the ships fired indiscriminately at the bunch of planes and unhappily scored best on the B-25s, shooting two down and badly damaging two more. They also got a Val. One of the Mitchells was being flown by the group commander, Colonel Clint True, who ditched his aircraft a few miles out and paddled ashore. Approaching the beach he was challenged and asked for a password. True shouted a few well-chosen words, none of them the correct one, but enough to convince the guard he was an American.

The Fifth suffered their most serious loss of the operation when Major Ed Cragg of the Headhunters was in one of the four fighters lost. In the battle the Headhunters had scored ten of the kills and Cragg had notched up his fifteenth victory. Porky Cragg had led the fighter sweep to Rabaul on November 2 and had flown scores of tough missions. He had helped build the 80th Squadron into the hottest fighter squadron in the Southwest Pacific and while he commanded they had shot down one hundred and sixty enemy aircraft in nine months. It was a short, sharp fight and apparently Cragg bailed out and landed in Japanese territory—the Head-hunters never knew for sure.

The second attack of the afternoon was made by fifteen torpedo-carrying Betty bombers. Two squadrons of 348th Group Thunderbolts intercepted and destroyed all but one of the Bettys, and claimed the other as a probable. The only loss was one P-47, again shot down by antiaircraft fire from the shipping they were protecting.

On the last day of the year P-40s and P-47s shot down eight Vals and four fighters, bringing the total destruction over Arawe and Cape Gloucester since December 15 to more than one hundred and sixty Japanese aircraft. It was a critical loss when their base, Rabaul, was being blown away by the South Pacific forces. The Japanese raids became smaller and were usually made in darkness.

The Marines steadily slogged through the mud and rain. A-20s of the 3rd Attack Group hit machine gun posts at Cape Gloucester airdrome on December 28, and the next day an air strike was called in to knock out defenses around the field. Liberators and mediums bombed and strafed and by noon on December 30 both airstrips were occupied. Whitehead was anxious to get the field ready to give fighter cover to strikes at Kavieng in support of Halsey's landing on Nissan, one of the Green Islands, and to have an emergency field for his own planes during attacks on the Admiralties, but the rain caused unavoidable delay. It was February 1 before a C-47 landed at Cape Gloucester, and the 35th Fighter Squadron's P-40s began moving in on February 13. The Headhunters and their P-38s arrived ten days later.

Cape Gloucester was a bad location. Mud oozed through the perforations in the steel mat and while this was little problem to the P-40s, the Lightnings found the strip too short. But luck was still with the Fifth because acceleration of the move into the Admiralties would give Whitehead another base for crushing Kavieng. He needed all his units at Nadzab so he decided to replace both 8th Fighter Group squadrons with Australian P-40s from Kiriwina.

The campaign to control the western tip of New Britain had been successfully completed when the patrols from Arawe and Cape Gloucester linked up, and an operation to extend the Allied holding to Talasea and Hoskins plantation on the northern coast was already under way. A landing at Iboki plantation on February 25 succeeded, and though the amphibious operation at Talasea on March 6 ran into a strong force of Japanese, they were not eager. The Headhunters covered the landing and the Marines occupied the Talasea strip two days later. The Cape Gloucester operation had been a real success and the Fifth had played a major part, adding the word "Gloucesterizing" to their vocabulary. There was unease about the fact that gunners on ships still shot at "anything that was not a P-38," but the P-47s had knocked down a Catalina and small Allied landing craft had been attacked. These mistakes would be less easily repeated.

* * *

To complement the New Britain operation a third landing, on the New Guinea coast opposite Cape Gloucester, was planned. The target was Saidor, midway between Blucher Point and Madang, which would yield a good harbor for small craft and yet another forward air base. Its capture would accelerate the destruction of the Japanese along the coast above Finschhafen and it was decided to go ahead with the operation on January 2. The capture of Lae, Salamaua, and Finschhafen back in September had led to constant fighting as the Allied troops attempted to consolidate and extend these areas. Along the Markham River and across into the Ramu River Valley the Australians were driving the enemy back and wiping out pockets, while other American and Australian troops were doing the same tough job along the coast. The extensive activity which surrounded the landing at Arawe had also helped pave the way for the Saidor operation—attacks on Wewak and increased pressure on Madang and Alexishafen at the end of 1943 had educed the risk of Japanese interference. As the landing force moved toward Saidor on New Year's Day over a hundred B-24s and B-25s plastered the surrounding coastline.

The convoy reached the three landing beaches on schedule the second of January, and seven thousand troops landed almost without opposition. The weather had closed out the planned air support, but later that morning three B-25s managed to get through the storm front and laid smoke over Saidor airstrip and elsewhere. Soon after, B-24s bombed targets behind the beachheads, and they were followed by the A-20s at treetop altitude. A strong fighter screen was established in expectation of heavy Japanese opposition but actual resistance was weak. The landing craft had been able to unload completely and were on the way back to Oro Bay before the first Japanese retaliation. Nine Helens escorted by about a score of Zekes and Tonys arrived late in the afternoon, but the enemy pilots were not eager and some of the bombers jettisoned their loads and turned back as soon as a dozen P-40s appeared. Although a 7th Fighter Squadron P-40 went down in flames, they shot down two Helens and three enemy fighters; during the night there were several small bombing attacks and other raids over the next few days.

In soaking rain a runway at Saidor was bulldozed and graded, and by January 11 a flight of C-47s was able to bring ammunition in to the restored airfield. Saidor was intended as a forward supply depot although it was estimated that it would be several months before the necessary facilities could be developed. There were problems in the wretched weather but in three weeks Saidor had become a key link in Whitehead's fighter network.

* * *

January 1944 was a big month for the P-40s, particularly the 35th Squadron of the 8th Fighter Group. On January 16 their sixteen P-40s met a force of Vals escorted by fighters which was attacking a Saidor supply convoy; the P-40s dived and scattered them, and the score for the day was eighteen for the 35th. Lieutenant Lynn Witt made a frontal attack and after firing a very long burst he saw his first victim, an Oscar, stagger and tumble in flames. While breaking away he intercepted another Oscar pursuing a P-40 and while he was shooting it began to burn. After climbing to get more altitude he closed in on a Val and slowly tore it apart with a long burst. The dive bomber trailed smoke and plunged into the sea.

Four Japanese fighters dived on Lieutenant William Gardner's flight but he damaged one during a head-on attack, turned, and scored with another burst— his fire severed both wingtips of a Hamp before it began to spin down into the sea.

An A-20 comes in to Dobodura, carrying the white tail tip of the 90th Squadron. When the 3rd Attack converted entirely to A-20s in January 1944, they began using formal markings—colored tail tips and white letters on the rudder. A note of informality crept in in the 8th Squadron, where one aircraft had a question mark instead of a letter, and one day group commander Jock Henebry went down to the flight line and found his A-20's rudder adorned with a freshly painted white wheel.

At the beginning of 1944 the old 8th Fighter Group was flying quite a collection of aircraft—the 35th Squadron had these P-40Ns at Cape Gloucester, the 36th had P-47 Thunderbolts, and the 80th was still flying P-38 Lightnings. It was the middle of the year before the group was entirely equipped with the P-38.

Gardner moved up behind another formation of four Japanese fighters and set upon the last Hamp; it rolled over and crashed. Gardner was in a few more sharp skirmishes before he scored his third Hamp with a deflection shot. There were explosions in the enemy's engine and cockpit as the shells hit him and the fuselage quickly became enveloped in flames. Four other P-40 pilots got two each, four more one each—it was cause for some celebration.

A week later P-40s from the 49th Group's 7th Squadron were taking the B-24s on a strike to Cape Moem, near Wewak, when they met a large force of Zekes, Oscars, and Tonys already fighting the P-38s. Seeing the P-40s the Japanese fighters broke off into pairs to attack them and the Liberators; while most of the P-40s stayed close to the bombers, one flight dived at the Japanese to scare them away whenever they came too close. The enemy attacks were not enthusiastic, and after the bombing run was over Lieutenant Bob DeHaven's flight dived after the fighters, using the hit-and-run tactics the 49th had learned so long ago. The 7th Squadron got two Zekes and three Oscars. Less than thirty minutes later, the 8th Squadron's P-40s, escorting B-24s to Boram, met thirty to forty Hamps, Zekes, and Oscars. While the rest shielded the bombers, six Warhawks tore into the enemy formation. In all they claimed nine enemy fighters without loss, and Lieutenant James Hagerstrom got four before lunch; leading his flight he saw ten to fifteen enemy fighters diving on a formation of P-38s. Hagerstrom's first burst turned one of them into a blazing torch. Turning, he pressed a frontal attack against another, which dived vertically to destruction. Hagerstrom closed on a third fighter and fired until it fell away in flames. He saw another circling in behind a P-38 and riddled its fuselage with a sustained burst. The Japanese plane flipped out of control, but Hagerstrom followed and kept firing until number four disappeared in a cloud of spray.

*   *   *

Allied forces were moving well along the coast: the Australians pushing forward from Finschhafen had broken through to easier terrain and the Americans at Saidor were moving out in all directions and meeting little more than Japanese patrols. However, the Ramu Valley continued to be a stalemate. Trying to reach the Bogadjim Road and the approaches to Madang, the Australians were confronted by the enemy defenses on Shaggy Ridge, about forty miles south of Madang. The Japanese held the north end of the ridge and controlled the path, which was only two or three feet wide with drops of up to five hundred feet on either side. Shaggy Ridge was pocked with enemy machine gun posts and foxholes and by late December the infantry had made several attempts to take it without success. It was time to try something new.

The Third Air Task Force worked out the details. Using a slow, stubby Australian Boomerang fighter as a guide, P-40s would dive-bomb the targets only one hundred and fifty yards away from the Australian troops. The preparations were precise and the attacks were very successful. The Boomerang pilots were thoroughly acquainted with the area and the P-40s, dropping five-hundred-pound bombs from a thousand feet, were accurate. The position was easily captured after a heavy attack by the 7th Fighter Squadron on December 27, but proved to be only one of a string of strongpoints the Japanese had prepared. Shaggy Ridge seemed to extend endlessly to the north and south and was riddled with foxholes and trenches along its crest and sides. The Third Air Task Force again came to help, and planned the "Cutthroat" operation. Beginning on January 18 and continuing over several days, the B-25s of the 22nd and 38th Groups plastered the ridge and other installations with high explosives. The P-40s worked over the area for two days more and by January 23 the Australians had taken the strongest positions.

While these aircraft were clearing the way for the infantry, other units were slamming the major enemy bases in New Guinea, from Madang to Hollandia. Alexishafen and Madang received the heaviest tonnage of bombs and by January 13 Allied intelligence had learned that the former had been abandoned as a major supply center, and the final attack of the month was made that day. From then until the end of January Hansa Bay and Wewak were targets—Kenney planned to make these the decisive attacks on Wewak. The Fifth hit Borma and Wewak itself, the nearest two of the four airdromes, for three successive missions to make the enemy feel safe at But and Dagua. About thirty-five planes were destroyed in these attacks, then on February 3 the Fifth put fifty-eight heavy bombers over Wewak and Boram to crater the strips with two-thousand-pound bombs. At treetop level behind the B-24s were sixty-two B-25s with fighter escort, and they continued on to But and Dagua. Kenney thought "the Nip behaved perfectly and had his planes lined up nicely, most of them with their engines turning over, crews in their seats

The Fifth sent three successive missions to Wewak and Boram, the nearest of the four Wewak airdromes, to deceive the Japanese into believing they would be safe at But and Dagua. Then on February 3, 1944, the heavy bombers and strafers struck. This 501st Squadron B-25 is one of forty-three 345th Group aircraft hitting Dagua.

and mechanics standing by." At But and Dagua sixty Japanese planes were destroyed on the ground, and the fighters shot down another sixteen. The Fifth had no losses.

The capture of Saidor and the Australian gains in the Ramu Valley ended the campaign for the Huon Peninsula. The surviving Japanese troops tried to fall back to Madang, disease and the constant harassment of the air forces killing nearly half of them along the way.

The Reduction of Kavieng

Admiral Halsey's South Pacific forces had been keeping the enemy at Rabaul under control, but Kavieng on New Ireland had to be knocked out before his operation to occupy the Green Islands, a little over a hundred miles from Rabaul, scheduled for February 15. It was a Fifth Air Force task, but until February 1944 attacks against the target had been limited.

Wewak would not be a problem for a while, so Kenney told Whitehead the target until February 15 would be Kavieng. These attacks would not only cover the right flank of MacArthur's Admiralties operation and support Halsey's landing, but also shield a planned carrier strike against Truk.

The weather spoiled the Kavieng missions for several days, but on February 11 the Jolly Rogers and Ken's Men got through and caught Japanese planes getting ready to take off. Two days later the B-24s struck again and wrecked the runway. There was clear weather the next day, enabling the Liberators to hit both Kavieng airdrome and Panapai, the other airfield on the tip of New Ireland.

Then as Halsey's forces landed on Nissan Island on February 15, the Fifth struck Kavieng. The 3rd Attack's A-20s were assigned shipping in the harbor and the floatplane base and wharf on Nusa Island, while seven squadrons of B-25s bombed the town and stores along the shore. The 38th Group led into the target, the 345th following. As the first flight passed the main wharf a huge explosion erupted hundreds of feet into the air, adding to the smoke, dust, and flame smothering the area. A B-25 was hit in the left engine and caught fire. The navigator in the Mitchell managed to get the fire extinguished but a blazing tire began it again and the flames quickly spread to the bomb bay. The aircraft was a torch by the time the pilot was able to ditch. Three of the crew got out, and the first B-25 was down.

Flying through the gunfire, smoke, and debris, the second squadron of 38th Group B-25s came in between fifty and a hundred feet and escaped with minor damage. The third squadron chose to attack at fifty feet, dropped its bombs, and set fire to a fuel dump. One of their Mitchells trailed flames, struggled for height, then tumbled.

The 38th Group had created a holocaust into which the 345th was racing. Lieutenant Edgar Cavin, pilot of a B-25 named *Gremlin's Holiday,* was forced to pull up to avoid exploding fuel drums flung up like medieval Greek fire. At one hundred and fifty feet the B-25 became a clear target for the Japanese gunners. The fuel tank in the fuselage was hit and set afire, then a wing tank. *Gremlin's Holiday*

Liberators lumber out prior to a mission, led by Colonel Art Rogers' *Connell's Special*, gleaming flagship of the 90th Bomb Group. (Art Rogers)

trailed smoke and flame. Cavin had to ditch and the B-25 skipped, plunged, then disappeared in a mountain of spray. The entire crew survived to scramble into life rafts dropped by other members of their group rushing overhead. They began paddling away from the erupting shore.

Lieutenant Thane Hecox's B-25 was shot down and smashed into a coconut grove as the toll mounted. Lieutenant William Cavoli, who led the fourth flight over the target, abreast of and to the right of Hecox's flight, was "strafing at tree-top level when I pulled up to about one hundred feet for bombing. Due to the thick black smoke over Chinatown I was forced to go on instrument flying while crossing the target. It was at this point that I felt my right engine had been hit. I glanced at the manifold pressure; it had dropped down to zero. I immediately tried to feather the right prop and when it was almost feathered it started up all over again. I gave the good engine full power. Slipping the plane in a vain attempt to put out the terrific fire that had started, I again attempted to feather the prop but to no avail. The plane was losing altitude all the time and the fire had already melted away half the right engine nacelle, the right flap and the whole right side of the fuselage. The right wheel had dropped out of the nacelle and caught fire and I was unable to close the bomb bay doors or drop any flaps because of hydraulic failure. The airspeed indicator went out also, probably due to the heat. A crash landing was inevitable so I prepared for it.

"At that time only the navigator, the engineer and my co-pilot were in the forward part of the airplane. Everything happened so fast I was unable to contact my gunner or the radioman, who were in the rear of the ship, to tell them to prepare for a crash landing. However, I'm sure they knew it was coming because pieces of the right engine and right flap were falling off and the heat inside the plane was terrific.

"I levelled off just a few feet above the water and kept holding it off in a tail-low manner until the tail hit the water. As it hit the right wheel snapped off and flew back and broke off the right vertical stabilizer and rudder. We hit again, only this time a little harder and with the whole underside of the fuselage. The plane skipped once more and then made the final plunge, nose first. The time was 11:30.

"The cockpit immediately filled with water. The engineer pulled the escape hatch and then the life raft release. The co-pilot, then I, the engineer and the navigator left in that order. We all climbed on the right wing and called for the gunner to get up there too; he was swimming on the left side of the plane. We heard the radioman yelling for help. He was pinned in near the rear escape hatch with his right arm broken and his chute still on. The engineer and I rowed the life raft to a small window and after removing his chute, we managed to pull the radioman through the small opening.

"We picked up a few supplies, all got in the raft and rowed away just as the plane sank. It had remained afloat, I believe, for about four and a half minutes. We noticed that we were about three fourths of a mile north of the tip of Kavieng. We managed to row perhaps another mile away from the shore and after approximately an hour and a half we were spotted by a B-25 of the 498th Squadron which was circling the area looking for survivors. Major Coltharp, the pilot of this plane, called for a Catalina and at 12:55 we were picked up."

That Navy PBY Catalina, piloted by Lieutenant Nathan Gordon and covered by four P-47s, carried out probably the most spectacular rescues of the war. Gordon landed three times to pick up nine men from *Gremlin's Holiday* and a 38th Group B-25, while the 345th's Major Chester Coltharp and Captain Anthony Chiappe suppressed Japanese gunfire. They were on their way home when Coltharp spotted Cavoli's crew. He called the PBY back, and Gordon landed his damaged plane under fire, made the pickup, and finally returned to Finschhafen with fifteen airmen. Coltharp and Chiappe, low on gas, barely made it to Cape Gloucester. The 345th had lost six planes, but not six crews. The strong P-38 escort had met no interception, but a total of eight B-25s had gone down.

After this devastating attack, Kavieng saw the writing on the wall, and there was feverish shipping activity. The very next day a fourteen-ship convoy was caught by the Mitchells off New Hanover, and revenge was sweet for the 345th. They attacked a Japanese corvette escorting a merchant vessel, leaving the corvette burning and listing badly and destroying the other ship.

As the 38th Group took over the attack on the convoy, Captain Keith Dougherty of the 500th Squadron left to search for Captain Michael Hochella, who had not returned from the mission the day before. At the debriefing nobody could really account for their loss, and Dougherty had pieced together the clues. During his search he found a freighter and sank it, but he got more satisfaction soon after—searching the string of small islands about ten miles from Kavieng he saw a man and a life raft. The next day a Catalina, with Dougherty aboard as guide, made the pickup of Hochella and his crew.

The 345th's *Stingeroo,* piloted by Lieutenant Carl Cessna, brackets a corvette with bombs off New Hanover on February 16, 1944. In the background a Japanese tanker is rocked by explosions.

Other convoys were scurrying from Rabaul and Kavieng. The strafer B-25s and A-20s struck again on February 17 and February 19, and the B-24s claimed two ships on February 20. The last attack was on February 21, when sixteen B-25s from the 345th found five ships and sank the *Kakai Maru* and *Kowa Maru.* These were the last large vessels to leave Rabaul Harbor and they had been evacuating members of air units which had already flown to Truk. The Fifth's job at Kavieng was done.

* * *

There was still a debate about the exact path to be followed in the Pacific, and only tentative plans had been made. In January 1944 Admiral Nimitz produced a basic plan of operations for the Central Pacific, and went into conference with representatives of both MacArthur and Halsey at Pearl Harbor. General Kenney was there with Sutherland, representing the Southwest Pacific. It was widely believed

Captain Carl Conant got this photo of the stricken corvette, its deck ablaze. The following day the 345th was back in the area and found the hulk aground.

that Japan could be defeated only with the aid of bases in China, so Nimitz wanted to get his fleet to Chinese bases as early as possible. He was concerned about Truk but expected his carriers to force the Japanese fleet out of the stronghold and back west of the Philippines. Nimitz thought it would be necessary to capture the Philippines before landing on the China coast; Sutherland, speaking for MacArthur, put his plans forward, and Nimitz's own Navy commander agreed that the Southwest Pacific forces were reaching a point where they could unhinge the Japanese defenses in the Central Pacific without a fight there.

Finally the general consensus seemed to indicate the following: completion of the Marshalls campaign and the capture of Eniwetok atoll in the Central Pacific, together with Kavieng and Admiralty operations to isolate Rabaul, then an advance by Central Pacific forces to the Palaus, bypassing Truk, and concentration on MacArthur's drive up the New Guinea coast.

MacArthur urged that all South Pacific forces be assigned to him, asking for Halsey as his naval commander. Even with the combination of forces the movement into Geelvink Bay and the Vogelkop, in northwest New Guinea, seemed impossible before October 1944, delaying any Philippines landing until perhaps

March 1945. MacArthur felt the B-29s should operate from Southwest Pacific bases and that the Mariana Islands possessed no real value. In fact, he thought Washington had planned two weak thrusts by divided forces which would delay his return to the Philippines by as much as six months. Sutherland went to Washington to put the viewpoint across and insisted that Nimitz and MacArthur could work together without friction and with neither in command of the other. The Navy considered MacArthur was overestimating his rate of advance up the New Guinea coast, and as for the Marianas, Truk would have to be seized, or at least part of the southern Marianas invaded to isolate Truk from the north. After reviewing all the arguments, it was decided the major effort should still be thrust across the Central Pacific, aimed at the eventual capture of Formosa. The importance of Mindanao to the Southwest Pacific was appreciated, but it seemed their advance would be through the area of heaviest opposition from Japanese ground troops. The Central Pacific scheme meant fewer and longer moves, took full advantage of American naval power, and would deliver the Marianas for B-29 bases. The seizure of the Admiralties was recommended, as well as capture of either the Marianas or the Carolines, according to later estimates of Japanese strength at Truk, capture of the Palaus, and an advance to Formosa, either direct or via Luzon. Mindanao would be seized as an intermediate objective in case a direct attack on Formosa or Luzon was impracticable. Southwest Pacific, relegated to a position of secondary importance, should move along the New Guinea-Mindanao axis. Sutherland considered that the final report and recommendations were "a biased argument to support a predetermined decision," and used stronger language in informal conversations.

The competing strategies posed a critical question regarding the disposal of forces, among them the little Thirteenth Air Force. MacArthur recognized that a major point in favor of the Central Pacific strategy was the promise of the time to be saved by thrusting directly into the inner defense of the Japanese Empire. On February 23, when General Kenney proposed an earlier move into the Admiralties, which might speed up the whole schedule, he was very receptive. Kenney summed it up this way: "There had been no washing on the lines for three days. In short, Los Negros was ripe for the picking."

The Admiralties had been originally scheduled for occupation on or about April 20, a month after the seizure of Kavieng, and to be followed up by a landing at Hollandia in June. Since moving into the Admiralties in 1942, the enemy had improved Lorengau airfield on Manus, the largest island, and had developed a second field at Momote on Los Negros; these two islands are separated by a narrow, shallow strait. Los Negros curves around to enclose Seeadler Harbor, which is also sheltered by small islets along the northern shore of Manus. The harbor, about six miles wide and twenty miles long, had been considered for use by the American fleet as an alternative to Rabaul. In January the schedule had been brought forward to April 1, and plans for massive air support proved unnecessary: February carrier attacks on Truk, the South Pacific raids on Rabaul, and Fifth Air Force missions against Kavieng shattered Japanese air power in those areas, and they chose not to use their aircraft in New Guinea.

Between the heavy and medium attacks during February and March, fighter sweeps kept the Japanese at Wewak down but this suppression claimed one of the

Fifth's leading fighter pilots. On March 5 Colonel Neel Kearby was leading his headquarters flight, Major Sam Blair and Captain Bill Dunham, and the three P-47s headed for the Wewak area, Kearby's hunting ground. Bill Dunham recalled, "We circled the target area and saw a Tony approaching the strip. A few minutes later we saw three bombers coming in from the sea. We dove on the bombers which were flying parallel to the strip at five hundred feet. Blair and I got one each on the first pass but Colonel Kearby had to make a three-sixty and make another pass. He finished his off that time and I turned and saw an Oscar on the Colonel's tail. I made a head-on pass and saw hits on the fuselage and wings. He broke his attack and turned into me. As he passed me his canopy flew off and he crashed into the hills. We got three Nells and one Oscar." The mission was a tragic one for the 348th Fighter Group. The Japanese pilot had evidently killed Kearby with a burst into the P-47's cockpit. *Fiery Ginger IV* went straight down and the search missions flown later never came up with an answer. Time had simply run out for Neel Kearby.

It was only four days later that the odds claimed another leading fighter pilot. Colonel Thomas J. Lynch and Captain Dick Bong were flying together as a team. Bong called it a "flying circus," and they could fly whenever and wherever they wanted to. They had come back from leave in the United States at the same time and "Squeeze" Wurtsmith made Lynch operations officer of Fifth Fighter Command with Bong as his assistant. Lynch at the time had eighteen victories, and Bong had twenty-one, tied with Kearby. Neither of them loved desk work and they asked Wurtsmith for permission to start flying again. He gave them a free hand as long as they could keep operations running smoothly.

Sometimes they tagged other squadrons taking the bombers to their targets, they went out on sweeps by themselves, they flew the early morning weather recon over Wewak—all the time looking for stray Japanese planes.

Bong recalled their "flying circus" on February 15. "Lynch and I had hooked on to a flight of P-38s taking Havoc and Mitchell bombers to Kavieng and, coming home after seeing nothing at all, we left the main flight at Makieng. Lynch and I had decided to alternate on passes. If we saw something one day, it was his turn to attack first. If either he or I saw something the next time we were out, it was my turn first. On this particular day it was mine. It was getting on toward dusk and we were just parallel to Cape Hoskins on the northwestern coast when I spotted a Jap fighter plane all by itself.

"I judged he was at about twelve thousand feet. I don't think the Jap pilot ever knew what hit him or if he did, he didn't have long to think about it. I made a one hundred and eighty degree turn and closed in to about seventy-five yards from his tail. I gave him one long burst and that was enough. He blew up right in front of me. It may sound a little far-fetched but I was so close to that Nip I had to fly right through a ball of fire which was all that was left of him."

That Tony had been Bong's twenty-second victory. He and Lynch continued shooting up anything they could find until March 9, 1944. Bong said: "It cost me one of my best friends and it cost the Air Force one of its best combat pilots. Tom and I were up on a routine sweep above Tadji when we came across three Nip 'luggers' flubbing around in the water off the coast. It looked perfect for a strafing pass and it appeared as if there were fuel barrels on the ships' decks. Tom led us down and must have been doing a good three hundred miles an hour.

Porky II was Major Ed Cragg's P-38, from his 80th Fighter Squadron, the Headhunters. Cragg shot down fifteen enemy aircraft before he was killed on December 26, 1943.

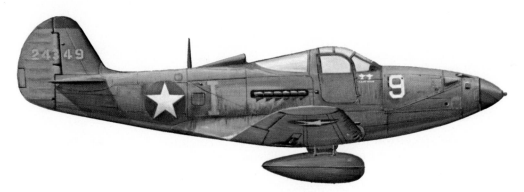

Captain Tom Winburn's P-39K from the 35th Fighter Group's 40th Squadron. Winburn's two victories were scored during the big battle over Wau on February 6, 1943, when the squadron destroyed a dozen enemy aircraft without loss.

This P-40N was flown by Captain Robert M. DeHaven of the 7th Fighter Squadron, 49th Fighter Group. In all, Bob DeHaven shot down fourteen Japanese aircraft, ten of them before his squadron converted to the Lockheed Lightning.

Lulu Belle, a veteran of the Bismarck Sea battle and a hundred other missions, flew with the 63rd Squadron, 43rd Bomb Group. The last time navigator Roger Vargas saw her was in November 1944 at Nadzab—stripped of paint and guns the old B-17F was serving as a staff transport.

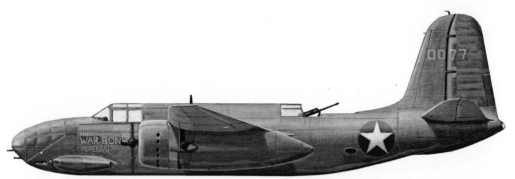

War Bond Special was Lieutenant Risden Lyon's A-20A from the 89th Squadron, 3rd Attack Group, modified to carry four additional machine guns in the nose. Work began on this "brain storm" as early as May 1942, but there were problems to be solved and crews to be trained. Finally, on August 30, eight of the strafers hit Lae hard and fast, and Kenney had a potent new weapon.

Dirty Dora, the grand old lady of the 499th Squadron of the Air Apaches. A B-25C strafer, she was handed down from the 38th Group in August 1943 and survived Rabaul, Wewak, Kavieng, and all the other hot targets. Her year of combat with the 345th and her previous experience all added up to around one hundred and eighty missions.

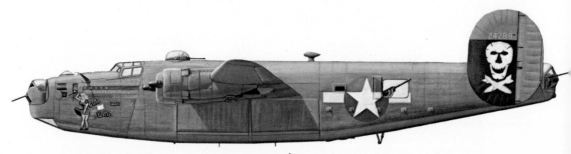

Gone with the Wind was a venerable B-24D from the 90th Group's 400th Squadron, the Black Pirates. Her one hundredth mission was the first daylight raid on Hollandia, in April 1944.

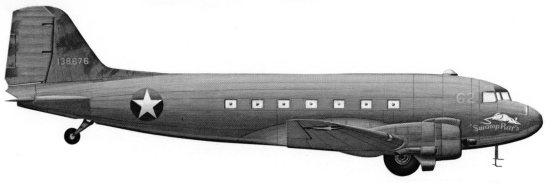

Swamp Rat II, Lieutenant Irwin Dial's C-47, from the 6th Troop Carrier Squadron of the 374th Group. She was one of thirteen C-47s which the squadron brought to Australia in October 1942.

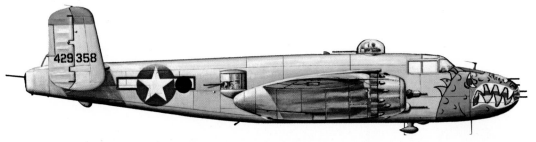

Lieutenant Jim Wallace bellied in this B-25J at Mangaldan, after the aircraft had been damaged by machine gun fire over Karenko, Formosa, on April 18, 1945. She flew with the 38th Group's 405th Squadron, the Green Dragons.

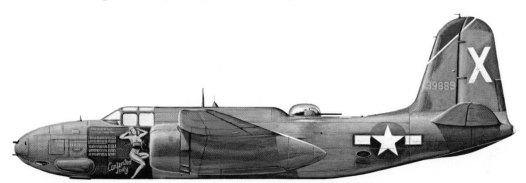

Contented Lady, an A-20G flying with the 672nd Squadron of the 417th Bomb Group. She went to war with her group at the end of March 1944, and flew well over one hundred missions.

St. Louis Blues was an F-7A from the 20th Combat Mapping Squadron, named by her pilot, Lieutenant Dave Ecoff, and decorated by Corporal Al Merkling. These original photo reconnaissance Liberators were painted blue until the crews were given buckets of solyent and told to remove the paint, and traces of the original scheme remained.

Bonnie, the P-47D flown by Major Bill Dunham, commander of the 460th Fighter Squadron, the Black Rams. Dunham was credited with sixteen Japanese aircraft, and ranked second only to Neel Kearby among Kenney's Thunderbolt pilots.

This F-6K was flown by Major Rubel V. Archuleta, commanding the 110th Tactical Reconnaissance Squadron, the Musketeers.

Putt Putt Maru, the P-38L flown by Colonel Charles MacDonald, commander of the 475th Fighter Group. MacDonald was a cool and daring leader who personally accounted for twenty-seven enemy aircraft.

"I didn't see any kind of ack-ack and the run was easy—we were only going to make one pass. I was following Tom and when we pulled up I suddenly noticed his right propeller fly off and his engine start smoking.

"Tom made for the nearest shore and just as he approached it he bailed out. Almost right away, his plane exploded. And that's the last I ever saw of him."

Danny Roberts on November 9, Ed Cragg on December 26, Neel Kearby and Tom Lynch within the space of a week—four of the finest pilots and leaders in the Fifth Air Force. It was a cruel turn of fate.

Reconnaissance in Force

On January 22 Lightnings had photographed Lorengau and Momote airstrips in the Admiralties and found plenty of activity. The same day, eleven 345th Group B-25s bombed and strafed shipping in the harbor to begin the onslaught leading up to the landing. They were back two days later in a bombing and strafing mission which resulted in claims for the last eight or nine Japanese fighters reported on the Admiralty airfields. On January 25 the 38th Group joined in but two B-25s were shot down by accurate antiaircraft fire while a third had to ditch south of Manus.

The Liberators from the Jolly Rogers and Ken's Men hit Momote on January 26, and Lorengau the next day. Both fields were knocked out, temporarily at least, and on January 29 recon revealed that they were still unserviceable and no attempt had been made to repair them. On February 6 weather forced the Jolly Rogers to divert to Madang, but Ken's Men's twenty-four planes and two dozen P-38s broke through the weather and found good conditions over Los Negros. There was no antiaircraft fire on this or later missions, and the Allies wondered about this. Later they would learn that the Japanese commander had stopped any shooting at Allied aircraft and prohibited all movement during the day in the open. He wanted to convince the Allies that the islands had been abandoned, and he was partially successful. Weather and other targets gave the Admiralties relief until February 13, when the B-25s were sent over Momote at medium altitude. This new role for the strafers delighted the pilots when they found how accurately they bombed, and the next day they continued the work. Weather kept the bombers away on February 22, only three B-24s got through on February 24, but the next day nine Mitchells from the Green Dragons squadron reached the target, and their attack brought the tonnage of bombs dropped on the Admiralties to six hundred and fifty.

There had been no Japanese reaction in the Admiralties since February 6, and on February 23 three B-25s of the 17th Reconnaissance Squadron cruised low over Manus and Los Negros for an hour and a half without a shot being fired at them and saw no signs at all of activity.

Whitehead had already suggested to Kenney that the even earlier target date of February 15 for both the Admiralties and Kavieng would allow more time to work over Wewak and Hollandia in advance of the next New Guinea landing, at Hansa Bay. When Kenney read the report of the recon mission, he suggested and "sold" the idea of a "reconnaissance in force" of the Momote area instead of the planned seizure of Seeadler Harbor. The details were worked out and approved by MacArthur on February 26.

John Wayne, visiting the Fifth in spring 1944, beside an early B-25H. Although equipped with an improved 75-mm. cannon, these Mitchells were soon modified to carry a nose armament of six machine guns, two replacing the cannon in its gaping tunnel. Cannon-armed B-25s were not only unpopular with aircrews, but also with the ground crewmen who had to swarm over them tightening up screws after the gun had been fired on missions. (Larry Tanberg)

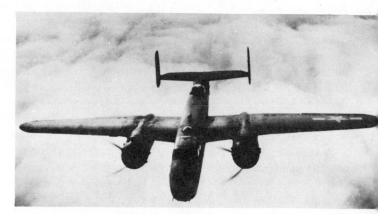

Its cannon removed, this 38th Group B-25 bares the most fearsom nose marking of the war, the lion motif of the 823rd Squadro (Larry Tanberg)

This B-25G carries the Black Panther marking of the 38th's 822nd Squadron. (Larry Tanberg)

Kenney had written to Whitehead two days earlier: "The plan is that about the 28th or 29th February six destroyers, accompanied by three APD's and carrying the equivalent of a battalion of 1st Cavalry with a battery of mountain artillery and a battery of fifty caliber ackack machine guns, will make a reconnaissance in force of the Momote airdrome area. The destroyers will open fire on possible shore installations and if they draw no return fire will land troops to take over the Momote area. Two minesweepers will leave Finschhafen in the afternoon before, timing their arrival at Hyane Harbour with that of the raiding force. As soon as they have swept the harbour entrance clear, the destroyers are to steam in and discharge their cargoes and probably remain there the day.

"You will have to provide a flight of fighters over the minesweepers during the afternoon preceding the landing, and I have told the Navy that the landing should not be made before 8:15 in order that we have a chance to deluge any possible opposition around Momote and Hyane Harbour by attacks with the heavies and strafers. I do not believe there is much possibility of any Jap air opposition to the show but you had better use P-38's to afford fighter cover for the landing operation and during at least the morning the raid takes place. To further insure the safety of the landing, I would clean out any gun positions that may be located in the Momote area, and in addition comb over the four Wewak dromes with strafers the afternoon and the morning of the landing operations.

"With their regular equipment the troops will carry some shovels to fill up enough holes on Momote strip so that our transports can land there. As soon as this is possible, we will fly up some airborne engineers to put the strip in shape for transport operations for the purpose of bringing in supplies of reinforcing troops in an emergency. This probably will not be necessary as the Navy seems willing to consider the Bismarck Sea our own private lake and Admiral Kinkaid is perfectly willing to send APD's or destroyers from Finschhafen at any time after the Hyane Harbour is cleared out by the minesweepers.

"Following the landing of this cavalry expedition a CB battalion has been ordered to get ready for movement into Momote about March 3rd. They will take over construction of the strip in order for us to base two or three squadrons of fighters there.

"Better get in touch with the RAAF and warn them that they may have to move in soon after that date."

There was little time for preparation, but the Fifth had already begun pre-invasion operations, and from February 29 Whitehead could devote his entire bomber force to the Admiralties as it was needed.

General Headquarters had recommended an initial assault force of eight hundred men, but the total force was slightly over one thousand; the landing area was White Beach, on the eastern side of Los Negros Island and about two hundred yards from the edge of Momote airstrip. The over-all mission of the air forces was crowded into a three-day bombardment building to a climax just before the landing. The 345th's B-25 squadrons would fly air alert for successive hours over the invasion area . . . three 17th Recon B-25s would be ready to smoke the landing area if necessary . . . the fighters would cover the convoy and the beachhead . . . three Australian fighter squadrons would be prepared to move to Momote as soon as possible. The Fifth was also ready to supply the invasion garrison by air dropping as required, and to close down enemy airfields in New Guinea before the landing. Whitehead even ordered eight aging B-17s, modified to drop supplies, into Finschhafen in case they were needed.

The B-24s and B-25s set out to attack Lorengau and Momote on February 26, but the weather turned bad and only two squadrons of B-24s got through. Next day, the 38th Group was over the two airfields and a party of scouts landed from a Catalina on the southeast coast of Los Negros under cover of the raid. They were picked up the next morning and reported that the area was "lousy with Nips." Although this caused concern, there was no turning back.

As February ended, the Liberators, B-25s, and A-20s hit the Wewak strips and the Tadji strip at Aitape, Hansa Bay, Hollandia, and the Admiralties themselves. Although the weather had not allowed the Fifth to pulverize the Admiralties, the bombs diverted to the New Guinea targets trimmed potential opposition.

On February 29, the day of the invasion, weather disrupted the preliminary bombing. Thirty-eight minutes before the landing seven B-24s made their bombing runs, and only three B-25s of the 38th Group got through to bomb and strafe. They attacked Japanese gun positions and as usual were fired on by the American landing craft. The 345th, scheduled to fly air alerts, had their 499th Squadron there a minute behind schedule, and circled until the command ship ordered them to attack. They made a couple of runs and headed home, as twelve P-38s and the 498th Squadron arrived. Rain and clouds were closing in the area, and neither the 498th nor the other two 345th squadrons could be used. The 475th Group sent fifty-seven P-38s and lost four in the appalling weather on their return flight; the 348th Group Thunderbolts did not manage to get through at all. The Fifth Air Force made its chief contribution to the operation by discovering the opportunity for it to take place.

The entire reconnaissance force was landed and had occupied Momote airstrip before ten o'clock. Patrols returned with warnings of a large Japanese force, and after dark the enemy attacked, luckily mistaking the outposts for the perimeter. They were disorganized by the time they reached the main area, but the usual infiltration tactics were used and by morning's light more than sixty Japanese lay dead within the perimeter. Next day it was decided to bring in more troops and take advantage of the initial success by seizing Seeadler Harbor.

The first day and night were critical on Los Negros, as reinforcements could not arrive until March 2, but the weather changed for the better and the Fifth was able to help. Three B-25s dropped supplies in the morning, then *Yankee Diddl'er,* an old B-17E from the 317th Troop Carrier Group, flew a couple more supply missions; four other B-17s from the 54th Troop Carrier Wing dropped twelve tons of blood plasma, ammunition, barbed wire, and weapons. The 38th Group hit several targets during the morning, and when there were indications that the Japanese were assembling around Lorengau for an attack, the Ken's Men Liberators blasted the area at noon. While the rest of the 345th attacked Hansa Bay, the 499th Squadron flew the last mission over the Admiralties that day, bombing the dispersals at Lorengau. A Japanese patrol was found within thirty-five yards of the command post that afternoon, and the troops looked forward to a sleepless night, but the perimeter held. The next morning a 38th Group mission was fouled up by bad communication; an afternoon mission by the 345th met the first interception, but

P-47s drove off the enemy fighters and shot down eight of the fifteen. This strike also went amiss, with two squadrons of the 345th dropping in an area which the ground troops had already moved into, killing two men before the bombing was stopped. A later attack by A-20s was more successful. Thunderbolts strafed the coast northeast of Momote and sixteen Lightnings shot up gun positions, bringing the day's strikes to an end.

Old *Yankee Diddl'er* was back that afternoon with a couple more B-17s, one of them a lumbering warhorse from the 69th Troop Carrier Squadron heading for Momote carrying critically needed ammunition. The pilots were Lieutenant Colonel A. J. Beck and Flight Officer Ralph Deardoff, and the aircraft was *Cap'n & The Kids,* once of the 43rd Group.

She reached Momote as Japanese fighters arrived high above; four dived down but the Fortress crew saw them coming and dashed toward the friendly destroyers off the beach. The Japanese had time for four passes—one Tony zipped by, but the fifty calibers from the B-17's guns found their mark and the fighter cartwheeled into the sea. The umbrella of gunfire from the ships forced the other three to break off the attack.

Cap'n & The Kids then headed back to Momote, where possession of the airstrip was still in dispute. The Japanese were on the western edge of the strip, the Americans in the jungle along the east. The B-17 dropped the ammunition and turned and flew back along the length of the strip, firing into the Japanese positions while the Americans on the ground raced to retrieve the precious boxes from the exposed runway. The old B-17, a veteran of the Bismarck Sea battle exactly a year before, stayed for fifty-five minutes, her gunners strafing anything that moved.

On March 3 the weather kept out a heavy bomber strike but B-25s and A-20s got through. One enemy fighter ventured over and late that night another dumped a few bombs in support of a major Japanese attack, but by dawn it was clear that the battle for Los Negros had been won. On March 7 a shot-up B-25 was able to make an emergency landing on the Momote strip and Australian P-40s moved in a couple of days later. The next step was the occupation of Manus Island, and to achieve this, control of Seeadler Harbor and the defended islets within it was necessary. The weather thwarted a seventeen-plane attack on them on March 7, only five planes hitting the target, but better results were obtained by B-24s and B-25s the next day. One B-24 from the 64th Squadron was credited with a direct hit on a gun emplacement, killing seventy-five Japanese, and on March 11 reconnaissance patrols were sent to occupy the islets of Hauwei and Butjo Luo. Butjo Luo was occupied without trouble, but at Hauwei there was bitter resistance. The next day another attack was mounted, supported by artillery and six RAAF P-40s. Hauwei was taken and artillery was moved in, ready for the Manus operation.

The pre-invasion attacks by the Fifth began on March 10, and by March 15, the day of the landing, the target had been hit with more than one hundred and forty tons of bombs. The B-24s even eased down to treetop level and strafed. The D-Day strikes by B-25s practically ended Fifth Air Force involvement in the Admiralties.

Although the fighting continued for several weeks the campaign had been little in doubt as early as March 4, and MacArthur was able to look forward to stepping up the whole schedule.

V

Finale in New Guinea

HOLLANDIA, between Humboldt Bay and Tanahmerah Bay, had become the major Japanese air base in New Guinea. In the shadow of the Cyclops Mountains the Japanese had built three airdromes on the north side of Lake Sentani, about fifteen miles in from the coast. A rough road connected these airfields with one another and with Pim, a small village on Humboldt Bay about five miles east of Hollandia. The Japanese obviously felt secure—their building air strength was again parked almost wingtip to wingtip, and fuel and ammunition dumps bordered the fields.

Aitape, one hundred and twenty-three miles southeast of Hollandia, with no natural defensive barriers and thirteen miles of exposed landing beaches, was overlooked by neither the Allies nor the Japanese. By December 1943 the enemy had begun working on two runways at Tadji, eight miles from Aitape town, and by March 1944 they had cleared a third strip, but only their bomber field was operational. These airdromes were believed to be lightly held, and they lay near the coast. They were of great interest to Allied planners looking for a place where airfields could be quickly taken and used to cover a landing at Hollandia.

With Hollandia in view, a series of smashing attacks finished off Wewak as an airdrome area and as a garrison to aid the defense of Aitape. From March 11 over sixteen hundred tons of bombs and a million rounds of ammunition were thrown at the four airstrips until on March 16 there was really no target left. The runways were full of craters fifty to seventy-five feet across and twenty to thirty feet deep. Wrecked and burned-out aircraft dotted the airdromes and dispersals like so many piles of silvery junk. Although the airstrips could be easily repaired, the Japanese did not try to fill in the holes and by March 21 the Liberators held the Japanese gunners in such contempt that they tried single four-minute runs over Wewak Mission. These 403rd Squadron planes drew only twelve "pitifully inaccurate" bursts of fire from the once heavily defended area.

The Japanese sent in one merchant ship convoy during the period, their 21st Wewak Resupply Convoy. Three transports and a sea truck, escorted by three subchasers, sailed from the Palaus for Wewak, via Hollandia. Two of the freighters were damaged before they reached Hollandia, one so badly that it was forced to remain there. The others got to Wewak and speedily landed their cargo, which included several hundred troops, and were on the way home in the early morning of March 19. They were quickly discovered.

Forty Liberators were diverted to this target but sank only one of the ships. The B-25s and A-20s finished the job: the 345th went in first, like a swarm of bees. In a few minutes the strafing and bombing left nothing but bobbing debris and alive and dead Japanese floating in huge slicks of oil. Two A-20s crashed, but the pilot of one was picked up by a Catalina after seventeen hours floating in a life vest.

One of the A-20s taking part was *Jew Louie* of the 89th Squadron, piloted by Lieutenant Rade Vukelic. When he landed and inspected his plane he found a scrap of paper jammed in the left engine cowling, blown there by an explosion as he roared over a merchant ship. It was a ragged page from the ship's records, which revealed that it was the *Taiei Maru,* a 3,221-ton freighter. The paper, dated November 30, 1936, was finally handed over to the intelligence officers, who had been slowly simmering as Vukelic smugly described his target right down to the tonnage. As he said, "It's proof, isn't it?" After this attack the Japanese chose to unload the 22nd Wewak Resupply Convoy at Hollandia.

During the fierce convoy attack on March 19, 1944, this 89th Squadron A-20 struck the mast of its victim and crashed into the sea. Coming off the target, Jock Henebry spotted a dye marker and yellow life jacket and the pilot was picked up by a Catalina the next morning, after seventeen hours in the water. (Henebry)

Japanese interference with the Wewak operations was never strong, although on March 11 about forty or fifty fighters had tried to disrupt the Boram strikes, and fewer and fewer fighters continued to intercept on the four days afterward. On March 16 the Japanese had pulled their fighters back to Hollandia to cover their doomed approaching convoy, and Wewak was almost undefended from that time. The Fifth's fighters claimed fifty-nine enemy planes destroyed during the sustained attack. Neutralizing Wewak cost the Fifth only nine fighters and five bombers.

*   *   *

April promised bad weather conditions at both Aitape and Hollandia, and the Japanese were apparently convinced that the next Allied move would be directed against the Hansa Bay and Wewak areas, allowing them enough time to reinforce Hollandia. In late March they built up Hansa Bay and Wewak while another force was moved to Aitape and But. Thus the Japanese almost entirely misplaced the seventy thousand combat troops at their disposal. The Imperial Japanese Navy had lost so many of its experienced pilots that defense of New Guinea had to be undertaken by the Fourth Air Army, which had established its headquarters at Wewak back in September 1943 and concentrated its forces there. The Fourth Air Army was forced to move its headquarters back to Hollandia toward the end of March.

Allied aircraft were generally out of place for maximum support of the Hollandia operation because previous strategy had been aimed at Hansa Bay and Kavieng. Finsehhafen had been developed to provide cover for New Britain operations, but would be relegated to an air depot; two Fifth Air Force squadrons had been placed at Cape Gloucester on New Britain. By March 1944 the aircraft at Dobodura and Port Moresby were without a tactical offensive mission and were waiting to move closer to the fighting. The 380th Bomb Group was in the Darwin area, from where it would be able to support the left flank of the advance.

So Hollandia lay just outside the range of Allied fighter planes; Fifth Air Force P-38s could normally accompany the bombers for only about three hundred and fifty miles, and though Kenney had received fifty-eight P-38s during February with extra wing tanks which gave them the range to get to Hollandia from Gusap, with an hour over the target, he needed more. Envisaging another Wewak, he ordered extra wing tanks made up for seventy-five of the older P-38s and these planes were promised for March 25. Kenney told Whitehead not to let any of the new P-38s fly farther than Tadji or remain longer than fifteen minutes over the target under any circumstances. He did not want the aircraft at Hollandia dispersed by anybody but the Fifth Air Force.

Cancellation of the planned, but no longer necessary, Kavieng invasion released vital shipping for the Hollandia operation, and MacArthur's suggested postponement of the landing from April 15 to April 22 helped further. Whitehead still had doubts about the carrier cover of the operation and proposed that Hollandia be preceded by a landing at Aitape fifteen days before. He hoped that his land-based fighters could be there, ready, four days before the Hollandia landing. However, it was decided that simultaneous landings would be made at Humboldt Bay, Tanahmerah Bay, and Aitape, rather than sacrifice surprise.

Beginning on the first day of April the Pacific Fleet would attack Palau, Yap, and Woleai with their fast carriers and battleships, then six days later they would strike Truk and Satawan. Admiral Nimitz wanted Southwest Pacific to establish long-range search sectors to cloak the movement of his fleet, and to intensify bombardment of the enemy bases along the New Guinea coast while his fleet struck Palau, as well as neutralizing Woleai for him during the attacks on Truk and Satawan. MacArthur then asked for strikes by the fast carriers against Hollandia and Wakde, a hundred miles farther to the west, from the day before until the day after the Hollandia landing, as well as the loan of six escort carriers for the close support of his operation.

A conference among the representatives of the three theaters in Brisbane produced an over-all plan for the air operations: the Allied Air Forces were to provide reconnaissance and photography and neutralize enemy air bases on the New Guinea coast as far west as Wakde, attack enemy bases in the Arafura Sea between northwest Australia and western New Guinea, neutralize enemy ground forces, and continue their normal missions. Land-based air forces were split this way: Advon would support the Hollandia and Aitape movements while the RAAF would protect the left flank and the Thirteenth Air Force would guard the right flank.

When advised of the plans for Hollandia in March, Whitehead regrouped his forces. Confident that Nadzab was the best base for long-range attacks against the new target, he wanted to move the 8th and 475th Fighter Groups there; the P-38s could reach Hollandia if they staged through Gusap on their way back. The two Lightning groups moved into Nadzab during March as space became available and by April Kenney had over one hundred long-range P-38s, adequate for the job that lay ahead.

More than one hundred B-24s from nine squadrons were available for Hollandia

Two Green Dragons head out in the gloom. On the left is *Tokio Sleeper*, a group original aircraft, with one hundred and thirty-six missions to her credit by the end of March 1944. The 38th had four old stagers in all, veterans of the battles all the way back to Buna: *Stinky*, which had well over a hundred missions when she crashed at Dobodura in February 1944; the *Grasscutter* with one hundred and seven; *Ole Gappy* with one hundred and sixteen; and *Tokio Sleeper*, queen of the 38th. (Larry Tanberg)

Liberators from the 64th Squadron parade over Hollandia as bombs erupt among the Japanese aircraft below.

attacks and light and medium bombers were no problem, the 38th and 345th Groups at Nadzab having over one hundred and fifty B-25s. Although many were old, most were operational. The 3rd Attack at Nadzab, the 312th at Gusap, and the 417th at Dobodura had an over-all strength of about one hundred and seventy A-20s. When the 417th moved to Saidor in the second week of April the entire twin-engined bomber force was within range of Hollandia.

So Hollandia's fate was sealed—intelligence estimated that at the end of March the Japanese had around three hundred and fifty planes there. Small night raids begun on March 4 had not done a great deal of damage, and these attacks had ceased five days after March 22 while Allied submarines were off Humboldt and Tanahmerah bays gathering hydrographic information. During the last three days of the month the Fifth continued their night attacks, and on March 28 ten Liberators were staged through Saidor. Only four got through the weather, and found the target so obscured that they could not bomb. The bad weather continued the next night but seven Liberators dumped their loads in the airdrome area.

After a long discussion between Kenney, Crabb, Cooper, and Whitehead, it was resolved that every available B-24 would be put over Hollandia loaded with frag bombs. On the first day the target would be the antiaircraft machine gun positions and fuel dumps. The next day the Liberators would again go over but this time to hit the airplanes on the ground. The third strike would be the cleanup—the B-24s would open the attack, followed by the strafers. All three operations would be covered by every available fighter plane.

On the morning of March 30, before dawn, seven Liberators began the first major strike on Hollandia. Then sixty-one more B-24s from eleven squadrons, with P-38 escort, attacked with frag bombs and frag clusters. The Japanese resistance was weak; the Headhunters shot down seven planes.

The next day Hollandia took it again from a similar force. The dispersals at the three airdromes were shattered and the pictures showed that nearly two hundred aircraft had been destroyed over the two days. Twenty-five Japanese fighters intercepted the Headhunters, who shot down six, along with a Dinah bomber they came upon. The 431st Squadron met a similar Japanese force and got seven, for the loss of one. After March 31 the Japanese began flying their planes out of the area.

Yankee Doodle Dandy managed to chalk up one hundred missions with the Jolly Rogers, destroying seven fighters along the way. They got her on her one hundred and first, over Hollandia. The old Liberator straggled and three Zekes methodically shot her down. (Art Rogers)

Cyclops airdrome, Hollandia, disappearing under a shroud of smoke and dust as the B-25s roar over. (Larry Tanberg)

Clear weather on April 3 allowed the Fifth to make their largest strike of the war to that point. Sixty-three B-24s, carrying heavy bombs, began the attack, dropping their loads on the antiaircraft positions. Thirty fighters tried to stop the lumbering B-24s as they paraded over the target, but the escorting Headhunters shot down ten, three of them falling to Lieutenant Cy Homer, and the bomber gunners got two more. Then ninety-six A-20s rolled in over the low hills and strafed and bombed the three airstrips, leaving piles of burning wreckage scattered in their wake. The covering 432nd Fighter Squadron shot down twelve of the twenty enemy fighters they met, losing one of their own. The B-25s of the third wave, striking at noon, blanketed the area with parafrags and parademos as they strafed. Two squadrons of the 475th dispatched the three fighters they encountered and Hollandia was no longer a major Japanese air base.

There was only one brief attempt at retaliation. On April 11 a small enemy fighter force staged to Wewak and shot down three P-47s from the newly arrived 58th Fighter Group. It seemed they had pulled back from Wewak to Hollandia again the next day because about twenty Japanese fighters caught a straggling B-24 there and destroyed it. The Liberator gunners got one of the fighters and the Headhunters got eight more. Captain Richard Bong of Fifth Fighter Command scored his twenty-sixth and twenty-seventh victories flying with them and topped the World War I score of Eddie Rickenbacker. That day Kenney promoted him to major, took him out of combat, and sent him to the United States, where he was to take a course in gunnery. He was never the best shot in the Fifth Air Force, scoring most of his victories by his skill and daring. Bong thought he missed too often with long-range shots and when asked by another pilot the secret of his success he answered simply, "I fly right up their ass."

Black Sunday

Co-ordinated strikes continued during the first two weeks of April, although on April 8 only the heavies succeeded in penetrating the weather. These were mostly ordinary missions which simply added to the destruction. One exception was April 16, a day that would become known in the Fifth as Black Sunday. The previous night a 63rd Squadron B-24 had been reporting weather in the target area every fifteen minutes, and the reports were not good, but with time running out Whitehead decided to get in another Hollandia strike.

Over the target area the B-24s, B-25s, and A-20s were successful, virtually wiping out the fixed defenses in the Humboldt Bay area, but on the way back the planes met a weather front which had quickly moved in over the Markham Valley, cloaking Nadzab and other fields with cloud and rain.

Lieutenant Carroll Anderson was flying with the 433rd Squadron that day. Anderson reflects, "No fighter opposition had developed, so as the planes left Hollandia behind, Captain Dick Kimball led the P-38s into a 'rat race' in and around the bombers. With each pass the tail gunners and waist gunners could be seen smiling and waving to the fighter pilots as they sped by. Later, external belly tanks began to run dry, and here and there a P-38 would lag momentarily as an engine stopped

Lieutenant Carroll Anderson, 475th Fighter Group. (Anderson)

and windmilled until the pilot could direct new fuel into it. The innocent 'rat race' had caused excessive fuel consumption in the planes of the rear flights as each pilot had attempted to hold his position.

"As the fighters of the 433rd, low on fuel, neared the narrow mouth of the Markham Valley, the radio began to foretell the danger which lay ahead."

Anderson could hear two P-38 pilots who had turned back earlier talking back and forth, and the conversations between B-24 pilots.

"These conversations were the tipoff to trouble," he says. "The ever dangerous New Guinea weather had socked in the mouth of the Markham Valley, sealing it as neatly as a black and white block of cement. Nowhere was there an opening through it. Already various planes were breaking away from their squadrons and striking out for the coast. Still other pilots were making the first calls to Gusap for directional homing.

"As they flew closer to the weather front, every pilot knew he was effectively sealed off from home. Fighters and bombers were flying in and out of the black stratus hunting for a passageway into the Markham Valley. The radio waves gradually filled with urgent commands.

"The front towered up into the sunshine to thirty thousand feet. It was white and silver and fascinating to see, but at the base of it where it wisped into the heavy foliage of the jungle it was black and mean-looking. It stretched from the mountains to the south and to the north as far as we could see. Within minutes every pilot of the 433rd knew he would have to fly on instruments to reach home. Carefully, Dick Kimball led the fourteen fighters into an apparent opening in the weather. Just as carefully, he turned and led the squadron back out.

"The squadron was tucked so tightly it was difficult to avoid collisions but somehow the turns were made without the flights coming together. The precision formation flying which our squadron had constantly practiced was paying off. Another gradual turn into the weather and the first serious trouble developed. Captain Robert Tomberg's flight became separated from the rest of the aircraft and, wishing to avoid the possibility of midair collision, he made his choice and led his flight away from the possible course of the squadron. The four P-38s of Blue flight, including mine, were now on their own.

"Gradually the flight began a steadily steepening spiral to the left. Unknown to the rest of us, Tomberg's radio and instruments had failed. I radioed, 'Hello, Tomberg. This is Anderson. You are in a spiral to the left. Pick up your left wing.'

"No answer. As the airspeed moved up to close to three hundred miles per hour, the balance of the flight stayed in formation. Suddenly we swept out into the open in a deep canyon which was completely enshrouded with cloud cover. Lieutenant Pierre Schoener grinned wryly, waved his hand in a goodbye gesture and peeled off to try it alone. Tomberg looked back at me and my wingman, Lieutenant Joe Price, shrugged his shoulders and started back into the weather again.

"Tomberg really had little choice. The jungle below was impassable. In addition it very probably was enemy occupied. His choice was either to try to fly by the seat of his pants or die in the jungle below. Obviously, we could only fly on. Price and I followed Tomberg with grim confidence in his ability as a seasoned pilot, but completely unaware of the true circumstances of his so-called instrument flying.

"A few minutes later in a tight climbing turn, Joe Price's P-38 stalled out and he spiralled away. As he did so, I began calling Tomberg. 'Hello, Tommy. This is Andy. You are stalling me out, you are turning to the left and stalling me.'

"No answer. Just before a complete stall Tomberg's aircraft levelled, then nosed downward into another spiral to the left. The airspeed built up to three hundred and seventy-five miles an hour and was still going up when the green jungle flashed into view. Instinctively both pilots pulled back on the yoke. Still in tight formation, the P-38s zoomed away from the side of the mountain down which they were flying and zoomed back up into the overcast leaving dozens of stunned parrots and cockatoos in their wakes.

"At this point, I stalled completely and fell away into a spiral. Carefully I brought the plane under control. Gradually I began the delicate operation of flying a fighter plane on instruments. At the very moment I stalled away, Tomberg released his canopy and bailed out. Japanese or no Japanese, jungle or no jungle, he decided it would be better to get out and walk than risk the presence of another cool, green mountain. As he swayed downward through the rain and fog, he could hear the steady droning of the lost aircraft above him. He did not return to base until a week later.

"In the meantime the other pilots were finding it increasingly difficult to listen to their radios. Every second was crowded with sometimes firm, sometimes panicky calls for homing from either Nadzab, Gusap or Saidor.

"As the pilots of the 433rd Squadron slipped away from each other to try to get through alone, three rolled away in tight spirals never to be seen again.

"Joe Price was in trouble on the northern coast of New Guinea and asking for homing. After an hour of instrument flying he was being guided into a strip at Saidor. He lined up on the runway, dropped his gear and cracked his flaps. Half way down the final approach, an engine ran dry and stopped. At that instant the Saidor tower frantically called to advise him that an A-20 was on final approach immediately beneath the staggering P-38.

"With one engine dead, and the other ready to die at any moment, gear down and full flaps, Joe knew he couldn't go around. He yanked the gear and gave his remaining engine everything it could take. The landing gear was still retracting as the P-38 started to roll over on its back, but Joe chopped the throttle, rolled the plane out, and with a crash of flying mud, sticks, stones and miscellaneous debris, bellied in next to the flight strip. An excited officer ran up to the wreck and advised Price to evacuate the premises before the plane exploded but Joe was beyond advice. Proceeding deliberately, he removed his canteen and maps from the plane. He stood on the wing very calmly, then fell on his face in the mud unconscious.

"Although the weather continued bad, some form of order was appearing as more planes were able to get on the ground. Less planes in the air at Saidor meant more control over traffic. Pierre Schoener had successfully made it to his home base.

"Meanwhile, I was descending at five hundred feet per minute. The outer wing tanks of my ship were empty. The mains were empty. The reserve tanks were half gone. I had decided to let down to ten thousand feet. If no hole had appeared by then I was going to bail out. The break in the weather occurred between Lae and Nadzab. I dove on through it and flew into homebase. On the peeloff a belly tank, which I presumed had dropped clear earlier, flew off and exploded near the tower with a resounding roar."

As the afternoon waned, and remnants of the Fifth's mission to Hollandia straggled in, the 433rd Squadron had four pilots unaccounted for and seven airplanes wrecked or missing. That night searchlights burned up into the overcast at Nadzab as landing beacons for any aircraft still in the air or for any crewmen down in the jungle. Seventy planes were missing on the night of Black Sunday.

As the aircraft straggled back, Saidor was the most hectic place in New Guinea. Aircraft with only enough gas for direct approaches ignored flight patterns. A P-38 coming in from one end of the runway met a Liberator coming in from the opposite way and leaped over it. An F-5 and a Mitchell collided in the middle of the strip; the fiery remains were scraped away to clear a path for the next arrivals.

When the final tally was clear, thirty-one aircraft failed to return and thirty-two pilots and crewmen were lost. Kenney said, "It was the worst blow I took in the whole war."

Even as the last lonely stragglers found refuge on that April Sunday, the troops who would invade Hollandia were aboard the ships of the task force, and despite the weather's cruel interference, the Fifth had won its victory at Hollandia. A Japanese air division was so shattered it would soon be inactivated, and when the area was captured examination revealed three hundred and forty wrecked aircraft on the fields. Another sixty planes were shot out of the sky. In exchange the Fifth's battle losses were two P-38s, a B-24, and an F-7.

Other Fifth planes helped tighten the blockade around Hollandia, which took a toll of 65 per cent of the shipping bound there in March, according to enemy reports. On April 12 the 3rd Group had attacked Humboldt Bay and sunk the *Narita Maru,* and the 17th Recon and 63rd Squadron scored three confirmed sinkings of sea trucks, while other planes destroyed luggers and barges to the south.

The major effort of the Fifth had been focused on the forward targets, but the enemy at Hansa Bay, Wewak, and Aitape had suffered from strikes by the shorter-range aircraft, and all aircraft whenever the weather blocked off Hollandia. Aitape village, the Tadji airstrips, and the offshore islands had rocked under more than a thousand tons of bombs by April 20. Wewak and Hansa Bay were priority targets throughout the month, partly to lead the Japanese to believe that the next landing would be in that area. Enemy airfields in Geelvink Bay, on the Vogelkop, and all their bases along the west flank of the main line of advance were handled by the Australian command, which included the Flying Circus and its B-24s. After a temporary stay in New Guinea, the 380th returned to Long and Fenton fields in northern Australia and on March 15 the group carried out the first of two missions which involved seventeen-hour flights to the Japanese naval base at Soerabaja in Java. Smaller missions were sent to Babo airdrome and to photograph the Halmaheras, and generally to scrutinize the Geelvink and Vogelkop area.

On the morning of April 22 the landings at Humboldt and Tanahmerah bays were carried out unopposed, and there was equal success at Aitape, where Australian engineers immediately began repairing the north strip at Tadji. On April 24 RAAF P-40s were brought in and they began patrols to Hollandia the next morning. The airstrip had to be closed for three days of repair on April 26, but a second Australian fighter squadron, followed by the 65th Troop Carrier Squadron, flew into the Tadji strip as soon as it was ready again.

At Tanahmerah Bay there were problems other than the enemy. Both landing beaches were likely to become severe bottlenecks because routes inland were as bad as aerial recon had suggested they might be. General Eichelberger decided to move his main thrust through Humboldt Bay and on April 26 Hollandia airdrome was captured after troops had slithered along a bog track which even jeeps could not negotiate. The infantry moving inland was running short of food and ammunition and had to call for air supply. Drenching rain and cloud kept the planes away for two days, but on April 26 twelve 17th Recon Squadron B-25s were able to drop food and ammunition and the following day B-25s and B-24s dropped rations on Hollandia airdrome. With some captured equipment and some machinery brought by road from Pim, the engineers cleared and smoothed Cyclops strip enough to declare it usable on April 28.

When the field was ready to receive two squadrons of 49th Group P-40s on May 3, the escort carriers were relieved of their duty as a floating fighter base; to help supply the small fighter force, the 41st Troop Carrier Squadron was transferred to Hollandia the next day.

The enemy sent only six small night raids against Hollandia during the critical period. The first, on April 23, was the most effective. A single bomber crossed the main landing beach at Humboldt Bay and one of its bombs set fire to a Japanese bomb dump on the beach. Twenty-four soldiers were killed and before it could be controlled the blaze spread and destroyed much of the Allied supplies landed on

The first plane to land at Hollandia was a C-47 named *Texas Honey,* flown by the Fifth's Assistant A-3, Colonel A. J. Beck. Whitehead had called Beck into his office soon after Hollandia had been captured and said that certain information and documents had to be delivered to General Eichelberger immediately. There was a discussion about how it should be done, terminated characteristically by Whitehead: "Beck, I don't care how you get in there, but do it now." The answer was the old reliable C-47, and Captain Chuck Beck of the 433rd Troop Carrier Group agreed to go as co-pilot. When they arrived over Hollandia the strips were even worse than photos had indicated, and in addition to the bomb damage, the troops had dug trenches and gun emplacements across the strips. Beck remembers: "It came to a choice between Cyclops, Sentani, or a deliberate crash landing. Cyclops was the best bet, but it would have to be a shorter landing than either of us had ever made. We buckled in, with our crew chief and two passengers assuming the crash landing position. We made our approach power on and nose up, just skimming the treetops. The aircraft hit and hit hard short of the runway but on the overrun. I thought the gear would come up through the wings, but didn't have time to worry about it. The column was pulled all the way back with Chuck holding it while I applied more throttle to hold the tail down as I clamped the brakes on. The old gooney bird skidded straight ahead but slowed rapidly. We missed a couple of bomb craters in the runway and stopped just short of a trench." Next day *Texas Honey* made a bumpy, short takeoff on the quickly "improved" Cyclops field, and returned to Nadzab carrying twenty-three stretcher cases.

As the airstrips were patched up, the aircraft began moving in to Hollandia. This 501st Squadron strafer, identified by a white tail band and orange cowl rings, flew over one hundred and twenty-five missions. Sharing a corner of Cyclops field are an Avenger from one of the carriers and the 433rd Group's C-47s. (Army)

A veteran of the 64th Bomb Squadron, this B-17F crashed at Tadji on May 2, 1944, while flying with the 375th Troop Carrier Group's 57th Squadron. These old Fortresses were able to go where the C-47s could not, and performed valiantly as armed transports. This aircraft has been fitted with the nose piece from a B-17E. (Army)

Lieutenant Joe Dally, whose gunners got four fighters in one mission to Noemfoor. The 380th fought a long, lonely war, and the only time Dally recalls seeing friendly fighters was when B-24s returned early and Australian Spitfires came up to look them over. (Dally)

the beach. The problems of inadequate air warning facilities led Wurtsmith to ask for amphibious vessels which could be fitted with radar and radio equipment, but the shortage of shipping prevented this. Again the old all-purpose C-47 came to mind; three were transferred to Fifth Fighter Command for the installation of equipment that would provide a complete fighter control center, and this "flying circus" would be ready for emergency use at Biak.

A closer look at the fields showed that the huge base envisaged at Hollandia could never become a reality. There was no suitable anchorage and the area was so swampy that it would be impossible to develop major installations. Whitehead, concerned, requested Eichelberger to get the Tami strip, on the coastal flat of Humboldt Bay, ready for troop carriers, as he intended to shuttle supplies and troops in. Work began on the strip, little more than a cratered grassy ridge in the center of a swamp, and it was handling C-47s by May 3. During the critical days nearly five hundred planeloads of supplies were flown inland from Tami. Meanwhile, Whitehead was using the 54th Troop Carrier Wing and the Directorate of Air Transport to ferry four thousand C-47 loads into Hollandia from Aitape, Nadzab, and Finschhafen.

                              *   *   *

From northern Australia the Flying Circus had been carrying out its lonely part in the operations, assigned to strike airfields in Geelvink Bay to draw enemy fighters farther up the coast from Hollandia. The group had flown a string of daily missions against Noemfoor Island, in Geelvink Bay, until April 23, and Lieutenant Joe Dally says simply, "They used us for bait." On April 23 he was flying *Dally's Dilly,* one of five B-24s over Kamiri airdrome on Noemfoor. As the Liberators crossed the target they were intercepted by twenty Japanese fighters, the beginning of a savage air battle which lasted for nearly an hour.

Lieutenant Robert Dunseth's crew fought off twelve Zeros which pounced on his plane, but both right engines were shot out, a waist gunner was hit in the legs by three bullets, and the co-pilot was badly wounded. Dunseth was unable to keep pace with the other four planes and the Japanese were determined to destroy the B-24 before the others could drop back to cover it. The Liberator staggered under the hail of gunfire but Dunseth finally got a third engine going and flew his crippled plane into a new formation which gave him protection. His gunners had shot down four of the attackers.

Dally's plane then took the brunt of the attack—one of his engines was shot out, the aileron and right rudder cables were severed, and the plane had to be controlled by the automatic pilot. A waist gunner was shot in the buttock and fell under his gun and two other crewmen were wounded during the unrelenting attacks. Dally's gunners shot down another four enemy fighters but he was worrying about fuel as the fight dragged on over the Arafura Sea and *Dally's Dilly* limped along on three engines.

When the fighters finally turned away Dally went back, crushed some sulfa pills, and wrapped the waist gunner's gaping wound in an undershirt, the only "bandage" they had. Securing the dressing with his pilot's wings, *Dally* decided not to tell the wounded man how serious was the aircraft's situation—not realizing that he was lying beside one of the larger holes in the B-24, with a perfect view of the dead engine all the way back.

The five battered B-24s made it home, and only Dunseth had further problems, when only one landing gear dropped, but he swished across the treetops and skidded the length of the runway without overturning. The crews in the 380th Group often needed more than their share of luck.

* * *

Kenney and Whitehead had foreseen the possible problems of Hollandia, and as early as March Kenney had advised MacArthur that it might be wiser to divert a part of the airfield program to the Wakde and Sarmi area if it could be taken right after Hollandia. He had argued, but without success, for limiting the Tanahmerah Bay operation to a small party while the troops left over would seize Wakde and Sarmi. So for better or worse, Hollandia had to be developed as a forward air base quickly. In spite of a tight schedule the engineers had dry-weather facilities ready at Hollandia and Cyclops strips on May 15, and as dispersals were completed the aircraft moved in. The last squadron of the 49th, the 9th flying P-38s again, began arriving on May 13, with the 475th Fighter Group coming in over the next two days. The red dust was so bad that Colonel Donald Hutchinson of the 310th Wing decided to bring up only one squadron of A-20s, and instead of the rest of the 3rd Attack, he borrowed the two squadrons of Australian P-40s from Aitape.

The Law of Probability

With Hollandia secure, Major Dick Bong was able to increase his score to twenty-eight in a rather unusual way. Many fighter pilots claimed "probable" victories, but usually they remained that way. With General Kenney's help, Bong's probable of April 12 became a certainty.

Bong had seen the airplane go into Tanahmerah Bay but had no other pilot to verify the claim. He had identified it as an Oscar, was able to pinpoint the position on an aerial photo of the bay, and he had seen his hits on the left wing, the engine, and the cockpit, but there had been no fire. Kenney arranged for a diver to go down and have a look, and sure enough, there was an Oscar. It was hauled up out of the water, which trickled out through eleven bullet holes in the left wing. The pilot was shot in the head and neck, and two cylinders had been blown out of the engine. There was no argument.

Japanese resistance hardened southeast of Aitape early in May, and Whitehead, aggravated by this temporary reverse, asked the Army what the Fifth could do about it. The coastal trails from But were being used by Japanese troops, so during May they dropped two and a half thousand tons of bombs on the Wewak area. The 312th Bomb Group and 110th Recon Squadron from Gusap, the 417th Bomb Group and the fighters concentrated on the bypassed area.

The movement forward to new bases during June lowered the weight of bombs dropped in the Wewak area by the Fifth, and captured documents revealed the enemy was planning to launch an attack in the Aitape area with a total of over thirty thousand men. This attack was to begin during the second week of July, so Aitape was reinforced with infantry and Whitehead bolstered the air forces there

The ground echelons of the groups coming into Hollandia set up their camps among the mangled wrecks of Japanese planes littering the area. Ambitious ground crews from the 8th Fighter Squadron rebuilt an entire Japanese Oscar in their spare time, as did the 41st Troop Carrier Squadron, and the Grim Reapers restored this Dinah and flew it on June 29, 1944. (Adrian Bottge)

with the 110th Recon Squadron and RAAF Beaufighters and Beauforts. The Japanese attack came as intelligence had predicted, and although beaten back twice, a force of regimental strength succeeded in breaking through southeast of Aitape, but after three days of savage fighting they were driven back. The Navy shelled the coastal trails, and missions from Tadji and Saidor helped isolate the attacking force until on the last day of July an Allied offensive began. By August 10 it had crushed all organized resistance and the Japanese had lost nearly nine thousand men. They were defeated, and pilots of the 110th Squadron reported that the enemy troops had adopted a strange attitude, gathering daily on the beaches, waiting to be cut down by the guns of the Airacobras.

The twin operations, Hollandia and Aitape, were successfully completed.

* * *

The New Guinea campaign had to be completed by early August or Nimitz's Central Pacific forces, progressing on schedule, would lead the liberation of the Philippines—if that invasion was carried out at all. MacArthur was not going to let this happen, and remarked to Kenney that he would enter the Philippines on schedule even if he was "down to one canoe paddled by Douglas MacArthur and supported by one Taylor Cub."

Lying off the New Guinea coast nearly one hundred miles west of Hollandia were the two Wakde islands. The larger is flat, about nine thousand feet long and three thousand feet wide, and commonly called Wakde. The Japanese had built a fine coral runway there and late in 1943 they began to build up the garrison on the adjacent mainland. Along the twenty-five miles of coast between Sarmi and Toem villages they had built an airfield at Sawar, and cleared another strip at Maffin, but only the Sawar strip was operational in the spring of 1944.

The Allies estimated that the Japanese would have about two hundred and eighty fighters and two hundred and fifty bombers to oppose a landing at Wakde and Sarmi, but this included planes in the Philippines and Palaus which probably would not be risked. However, low-level recon photos showed that the Sarmi area was not suitable for airfield development and Whitehead, reporting to Kenney on May 3, had told him that the "Sarmi area is fuller of Nips and supplies than a mangy dog is with fleas."

Two days later, reflecting on the disappointments of developing satisfactory airfields on Cape Gloucester, Saidor, and Hollandia, Whitehead warned that the entire Maffin and Sawar area was a "mudhole." He felt strongly that the operation should be aimed purely at the capture of the mainland immediately opposite Wakde, and the island itself. He would move in the 348th Fighter Group and stage two B-24 groups through Wakde to beat down Biak enough to allow its capture in early June. The way Japanese work was proceeding there made Whitehead sure that Biak was the most promising airfield site in the whole area between Nadzab and Mindanao in the Philippines. MacArthur tentatively accepted the recommendations and sent representatives to Finschhafen to talk over the changed maneuver. On May 9 it was agreed that it would be feasible to capture Wakde on May 17, and Biak ten days later.

Biak is in the center of Geelvink Bay, and the position justified its capture. It promised to be a hard campaign because Biak is little more than an outcrop in the shallow seas, and a narrow coastal shelf along the southern two thirds of the island is broken by rugged limestone ridges and cliffs which rise to an inland plateau. In these cliffs and ridges were caves, many interconnected by fissures and tunnels, and access to Biak from the sea was complicated by cliffs and coral reefs along most of the coastline. Specific information was scarce, and the first good photos of Biak were not taken until April 17.

The aerial operations would be mostly the responsibility of Advon, and they brought the 3rd Attack, the 345th, and the 49th and 475th Fighter Groups forward to Hollandia. Under the 310th Bombardment Wing, they would provide local defense, fighter cover to forward missions, and direct support and cover to the beachheads and convoys. Fifth Bomber Command would use three B-24 groups in attacks on the Wakde and Biak areas from May 12 onward, and the 63rd Squadron's Liberators were to knock out ground defenses on the coast at Toem just after dawn on D-Day, the day of the Wakde landing. On Z-Day, the Biak landing, the B-24s would strike the Japanese airfields at Manokwari, Moemi, Ransiki in the Vogelkop, and on Noemfoor; after Z-Day they would support the ground operation. On May 25, the 38th Group would stage to Merauke and for the next three days would neutralize the enemy airfields at Nabire. Aitape and Wewak would also be kept under attack.

The Thirteenth Air Task Force, with its two Liberator groups, would harass Woleai and Truk to disrupt repair and reinforcement, and would take part in strikes of Wakde, Sarmi, and Biak. The Thirteenth would also search the north coast of New Guinea daily and hit the ground defenses at Biak just before the landing.

Biak was to become a major air base, but the immediate problem would be to get the tactical units there as quickly as facilities could be put into use again. The 308th Bomb Wing, commanded by Colonel David W. Hutchison, was to be the air task force headquarters for both operations. After sending an advanced echelon to Wakde, it would bring forward the 348th and 8th Fighter Groups, a flight of the 418th Night Fighter Squadron, and a Navy Liberator squadron. The main body of the 308th Wing would go to Biak with the 49th and 35th Fighter Groups, the 421st Night Fighter Squadron, the 25th Photo Recon Squadron, the 17th, 82nd, and 110th Tactical Recon Squadrons, and the 43rd Bomb Group. When the 308th left Wakde, command there would pass on to the 310th Bomb Wing.

Wakde, Sarmi, and Biak had been attacked before, but the first large daylight strikes began on April 28 when Jolly Rogers and Ken's Men B-24s flew from Nadzab to bomb Mokmer strip on Biak. The Jolly Rogers met twelve fighters, shot three of them down, and destroyed ten more planes on the ground. Ken's Men only saw one fighter and got three more grounded aircraft. Before dawn, twelve 63rd Squadron Liberators had attacked Wakde, and while the Liberators struck Mokmer 38th Group B-25s bombed and strafed Wakde, destroying five planes, and the Air Apaches hit Sawar airstrip, getting another four aircraft. Ten minutes later, the Red Raiders bombed the Japanese headquarters at Sarmi, and twelve B-25s of the 17th Recon were shooting up coastal targets between Sarmi and Sawar. The fighters met no opposition during the day, and no planes were lost. That night Liberators of both the Fifth's and Thirteenth's "Snooper" squadrons bombed Wakde.

The weather closed in along the north coast of New Guinea at the end of April and frustrated most missions into the Wakde and Sarmi area until May 13. Although the elements kept the Fifth's B-24s out, it did not interfere with the plans of the two Thirteenth Air Force Liberator groups based in the Admiralties, and on May 4 they took over the neutralization of Biak. Their first three missions met hot opposition, but after that the Japanese did not try to stop the bombers, although eighteen fighters tried to shoot down an F-7 cruising over Biak on May 24. They lost seven aircraft to the 7th Fighter Squadron's P-40s in the attempt.

With improving weather, the Fifth went back to work. Wakde was heavily attacked on May 11 and the B-24s bombed Wakde and Sawar heavily after May 13. On May 17, D-Day at Wakde, they turned their attention to Biak.

The 310th Bomb Wing had its forces ready at Hollandia on May 16, and the next day fighter cover from Hollandia arrived just as the naval bombardment lifted, and an unopposed landing began at Arara, on the coast opposite Wakde. The following morning the troops landed on Wakde, where they were greeted by a hail of rifle and machine gun fire. Eight hundred Japanese troops were dug in so well that they could only be killed by direct bomb hits or hand-to-hand combat

Lieutenant Ray Pannell's *Pannell Job* over Wakde on May 11, 1944. Once named *Red Wrath,* this was an original 345th Group aircraft and carries the blue and white tail insignia of the Rough Raiders, the 500th Bomb Squadron. Pannell was killed when the aircraft crashed a month after this mission. (Maury Eppstein)

and throughout the day A-20s were sent against the bunkers and strongpoints. After a quick, bloody fight, all Japanese resistance ended in the late afternoon of May 18.

A C-47 was able to land on Wakde on May 21 but preparation of the desired facilities was a problem. Kenney had to flatten Biak and initiate heavy bomber strikes on the Palaus in support of Central Pacific operations, so he needed provision at Wakde for a fighter group and a Navy Liberator squadron, and staging facilities for the 17th Recon's B-25s, another fighter group, and a couple of Liberator groups. The aim was to fulfill the requirements by July 27, and it was agreed the only answer was to build a bomber strip and large undispersed parking areas.

The aircraft would have to be cramped together, a tempting target for night raiders, but Whitehead agreed the risk was necessary.

Work was rushed on Wakde, and on May 26 the 348th Group's P-47s flew in. The 17th Recon's B-25s, without ground crews, had arrived the day before. Seven Navy Liberators from the VB-115 Squadron flew to Wakde and on May 27 made the first regular reconnaissance flight to southern Mindanao since early 1942. A flight of P-70s from the 421st Night Fighter Squadron completed the Wakde garrison.

Wakde was cluttered, unpleasant, and dangerous. Fifty-six Japanese were killed in two nights of suicide charges, and the stench of enemy corpses and the swarms of flies which bred on them threatened disease until measures were taken to lessen the hazard. Also, huge and as yet undispersed quantities of gasoline and bombs made Wakde a powder keg. Under the circumstances, fighter defense was unusually important, and early in June five new P-61 Black Widows joined the 421st Squadron, replacing the P-70s, an A-20 conversion which never quite did the job. Again the Japanese missed a chance to hit the Fifth hard, leaving Wakde alone until May 27. Then only eight "listless" night attacks were made, but even these were inordinately destructive. A pair of raiders had the most success on the night of June 5, when their bombs killed five men, destroyed six planes and damaged eighty more.

While the Fifth was building up Wakde, the ground campaign over on the adjacent mainland was being supported by the 49th's P-40s from Hollandia, but after that the 348th Group Thunderbolts from Wakde were able to furnish most of the air support as the campaign dragged on. Results of the strikes were not easy to assess, but their destruction of bridges across the Orai River between Sarmi and

The smoldering wreckage of a Jolly Roger B-24, destroyed at cluttered Wakde on the night of June 5, 1944. (Army)

Sawar was believed to have sped the withdrawal of Japanese artillery from forward areas. The almost total collapse of resistance by July 20 lessened the need for air operations, although occasional strikes were flown even after the operation officially ended on September 2.

Bloody Biak

The Biak campaign followed the timetable. Whitehead used his three Liberator groups and the two Thirteenth Air Force groups to send nearly one hundred B-24s to bomb Bosnek, Sorido, and Mokmer, the three airstrips, on May 17. Every day but one until the landing, the Thirteenth's B-24s were over Biak. The Fifth's Liberators also devoted most of their time to the island, but weather and the long trip from Nadzab caused problems. The A-20s of the 8th Squadron struck Sorido, barges, and targets of opportunity west of Mokmer drome during the week before the landing. All of these missions were escorted by the 49th Fighter Group, and on May 23 9th Fighter Squadron P-38s were returning from an abortive mission when they decided to cruise over Biak and clean out any enemy planes that might be there. All was quiet as they arrived high over the target area. They saw no planes on any of the airstrips but as Captain Ralph Wandrey circled lower he saw four small barges cruising about half a mile offshore. He radioed his second flight to stay above while his flight went down for a look. As the P-38s dropped down, the barges ran for shore.

Wandrey says, "I lined up the two lead barges and opened fire. What looked like a boatload of coconuts suddenly became helmets of Jap soldiers who were jammed into the barge. As my bullets and cannon shells exploded in those packed quarters, the Japs poured overside like bees from a disturbed hive. I flashed past the first barge and concentrated my fire on the second. Some brave character climbed atop the engine room where a 20 mm cannon was mounted, and aimed it in my direction. I raked him and the cannon overboard with one burst, setting fire to the engine room also.

"As I veered away from this barge I saw heavy shell bursts exploding above me. They were coming from shore batteries located on cliffs overlooking the airstrips, and I quickly observed that none of the guns could be aimed below the cliff level. I radioed my flight to keep low, and we started mopping up survivors. All four barges were disabled and burning after our first pass. The second time I came around I noticed some Japs trying to climb back into one of the barges I was shooting up. It finally dawned on me that sharks or barracuda were eating the swimmers; three of the barges sank on our second pass, and the fourth was burning on the reef.

"While my flight was cleaning up the last of the swimmers, I circled the island and sneaked up behind the cliff guns. I stretched out two members of a crew I caught loading one of the guns, and bore down on a truck which was speeding away from the airstrip. Before I could fire a shot, two Japs jumped out opposite sides of the cab and the truck crashed into a tree. One of the Japs crawled into the brush alongside the road, but the one on the other side could only find a gas drum to hide in.

"I made a wide circle, keeping an eye on the drum to make sure my man was still inside. Then I rolled the barrel along the ground for about fifteen yards with a hail of bullets. I didn't have time to see the results as I headed out to sea and rejoined the squadron."

Smashing the other Japanese airfields in Geelvink Bay and on the Vogelkop was the task of the Flying Circus. On May 19 their B-24s attacked Manokwari airdrome, escorted by 9th and 431st Squadron P-38s from Hollandia. The 380th Liberators were intercepted by six Tojos—the bombers got one and the 9th Squadron four more. The 431st Squadron ran into another four Japanese fighters and shot down one of them. The Flying Circus, carrying out a maximum effort to support the Biak operation, hit Manokwari twice more but continuing confusion over fighter cover reduced the effectiveness of the missions.

The fifteen 8th Squadron A-20s from Hollandia had more success; early in the morning of May 19 a dozen of them went over Manokwari harbor, destroying or badly damaging seven or eight vessels. Still carrying leftover ammunition, they flew on to Kamiri airstrip on Noemfoor, where they demolished at least four planes and strafed about a hundred Japanese working on the strip. The P-38s of the 475th Group were covering them and the 433rd Squadron shot down a Rufe floatplane. Two days later twelve A-20s went back to Kamiri and made four strafing and bombing passes, ignoring ground fire and destroying about eight aircraft. For two days weather forced them to attack Biak, but on May 24 they hit Namber and Kamiri, claiming ten more planes. These raids added to the reduction of the Japanese air force and disrupted shipping, but the single squadron did not have the weight to crater the Japanese airfields on Noemfoor.

Although it could not get the 345th to Hollandia, Advon staged the 38th Group's B-25s to Merauke, enabling them to attack some of the Vogelkop airfields. The group was sent to strike Babo on May 26, but they found the area socked in, and attacked Dobo in the Aroe Islands. The next day was Z-Day at Biak and the 38th got through to the Vogelkop to hit Babo and Otawiri. They found there were only a few planes at Babo, where they destroyed a Betty, and Otawiri was still under construction. It had been planned to use the B-24s against the Vogelkop and Noemfoor airfields on Z-Day, but Whitehead decided to throw them against Biak, where he expected heavy opposition to the landings.

As soon as it was light enough to identify targets on May 27, a dozen B-24s from the Snooper squadrons flew in to bomb the Bosnek defenses. The second wave of twenty-five Liberators appeared at seven o'clock and plastered the beaches, already rocked by naval fire, and the troops started ashore. Just after eleven o'clock the Fifth's Liberators bombed targets in the airdrome area.

First indications made capture of the airfields look easy, but the Japanese showed that they considered this a decisive battle. A search plane had found the Allied convoy the day before the landing and the enemy's 23rd Air Flotilla had started bringing reinforcements in from Davao. The Japanese air opposition began in the late afternoon of Z-Day when the 342nd Fighter Squadron caught eight fighters streaking low, about ten miles from Bosnek. The P-47s knocked down five, and lost one of their own. Two hours later five more Japanese planes were shot down by antiaircraft fire as they tried to attack the beachhead.

The enemy had planned to fight on the beaches until bombardment forced them to withdraw, and the Japanese commander had prepared a trap in the cliffs high over the road between Bosnek and Mokmer. His advance guard retreated before the American infantry, then a mortar barrage began as the American troops reached Mokmer village, and at the same time the road was blocked behind them. Counterattacks supported by tanks forced the infantry to fight its way back through the road block and fall halfway back to Bosnek. More troops were called for, and it became clear that capture of the airdromes would take time.

The troops on Biak needed more air support than the 310th Wing could give and Liberators hit antiaircraft positions at the east end of Mokmer on May 29 and knocked a heavy battery out. When Whitehead heard the Japanese had tanks he sent six 345th Group B-25Hs up to Wakde, hoping their nose cannon might finally pay their way. The tanks were already knocked out so the B-25Hs hit gun positions, but one was shot down when making the dangerously predictable run that had to be employed. The Fifth gave direct support as it was called for and it was a doubly dangerous business because the Allied gunners were trigger-happy and nervous. Bad weather canceled missions on May 30, also curtailing Japanese air attacks until late in the evening. Reinforced and regrouped, the infantry began its offensive on June 1 and six days later they had broken through the coral cliffs northeast of Mokmer and had a tenuous hold on the airstrip, still under sniper and artillery fire from the ridges. Forces landed to the west broke through the Japanese barrier from both sides and opened the road between Mokmer and Bosnek on June 9. The Fifth had wanted to use squadrons of Liberators daily to pave the way for the ground forces, but weather and the need to hit other targets prevented it. On June 8 the B-24s were staged to Hollandia for a mission to the Palaus, and those heavy strikes made against Biak were only partly successful, expending unwarranted effort.

The Battle of Cape Waios

As the American troops closed in on the Biak airstrips, the Japanese Combined Fleet decided to rush two thousand five hundred men to Biak. On June 2 a force of two cruisers, six destroyers, and troop transports sailed to Sorong, where it was decided to make a swifter run into Biak by using the six destroyers. Six hundred men were loaded into three of them, with the other three providing their escort. They set out for Biak early on June 8.

Both the Fifth and the Navy had been alerted, and on June 4 Whitehead had rushed aircraft to Wakde. When Liberators of the 63rd Squadron found the main body of the Japanese force heading back north that night and sank a transport, the Fifth and the Navy relaxed. However, continuing reports indicated that the Japanese were up to something, and on June 6 Flying Circus B-24s found the Japanese cruisers off Waigeo Island. Their attack was unsuccessful.

Luck seemed to favor the Japanese. The Allied Air Forces were involved in heavy bomber attacks against the Palaus before Nimitz's landing in the Marianas, and had released as much forward staging space as possible. The night raid against Wakde on June 5 had damaged many aircraft, and all the 310th Wing really had was the 17th Recon Squadron. Covered by 475th Group P-38s, ten of their B-25s

Miss Exterminator, a B-25D from the 17th Reconnaissance Squadron, with one flexible and two fixed nose guns. Package guns mounted below the cockpit gave these Mitchells only slightly less firepower than the pure strafers.

were sent to meet the Japanese destroyers thirty to forty miles north of Cape Waios on June 8.

As the B-25s closed in, the Japanese warships turned to the north and moved into battle formation. Major William Tennille, commander of the squadron, took his planes down in a steep dive, picking up speed as the element leaders chose their targets. Tennille selected one of the larger destroyers, which the B-25 crews thought were cruisers, and advised his planes of his choice.

High over the B-25s, Colonel Charles MacDonald's P-38s headed for about ten covering Zekes and Oscars. MacDonald put *Putt Putt Maru* behind a Zeke and blasted it to pieces. In minutes the 475th had shot down three of the fighters and driven off the rest. They could now watch the grim events unfolding below them as the destroyers' fire reached out for the incoming B-25s before they were close enough to get their own fire on the decks. The sea was flecked with white as spent metal fell.

Tennille and his wingman opened fire but a shell smashed the entire wing from the second B-25. It slammed into the water and disintegrated in a second. Tennille was shooting his way in, the bullets splashing a foamy trail across the water, then up the sides of the ship. As the bullets spattered over the destroyer, Tennille's plane was hit and crippled but he held his course, the B-25 trailing fire.

Lieutenant Glenn Pruitt, in *Dragon Myasz,* watched the wheels of Tennille's B-25 pop down from the blazing aircraft. Pruitt and others made urgent calls to their commander, but Tennille never answered; the B-25, sheathed in flame, crossed the destroyer, rolled, and crashed into the sea. Pruitt at this time was using the rudders to swing the nose guns of his B-25 along the decks of a destroyer. He released a bomb, it hit the bow of the warship, and a large explosion threw heat and fire into the air as his wingman took his turn to bomb.

Miss Cue, piloted by Lieutenant Wesley Strawn, was flying at a destroyer when for some reason the Japanese stopped firing and the decks of his target were bare. Strawn's bomb hit the ship above the waterline, tearing through the side and exploding. Captain Sumner Lind, pilot of *The Straggler,* had the wing of his plane shot away before he could bring his guns to bear. The plane hit the water while Lind's wingman, Lieutenant Fred Rimmer in *Little Stinker,* was listening to the wind howling through a huge hole in the nose of his B-25 and fighting for control. Rimmer's navigator was dying, his leg shot away.

Lieutenant Archie Trantham got his plane down to water level and opened the bomb bay. Strafing his way in, he and his wingman, Lieutenant Robert Beck in *Sacramento Bell,* ran the gauntlet. The tail gunners in both planes saw their target shudder and go under until only its outline was visible.

As the last B-25s left the ships, Strawn looked back and counted three. The P-38s above also saw only three destroyers—there was nothing else in sight. Pruitt had watched his target settle in the water, its entire length ablaze. An observer in the same aircraft had seen Strawn's target "blow up" and Trantham and Beck's destroyer "sink almost at once."

The seven surviving B-25s and crews started back for Wakde, where the official 17th Recon report claimed one destroyer definitely sunk and two more left in sinking condition. The mission cost nineteen men—eighteen were claimed quickly, but Rimmer's navigator died in a hospital bed. The seven B-25s which came back were so badly mauled that the squadron had to be sent to Finschhafen to reform. The 17th was officially credited with the sinking of the troop-laden *Harusame* and damage to three other destroyers. The surviving warships soon set course for Biak again, but before they could unload they were engaged by Allied destroyers and chased out of the area.

Japanese air attacks on the attacking American forces at Biak built up during this period of attempted reinforcement, and the delays in completing the ground campaign had slowed down the Fifth's operation to a corresponding degree. Once Mokmer was secure, Fifth Fighter Command's new airborne control center was flown in, and this improved warning system, aided by the arrival of 421st Night Fighter Squadron P-61s, made Japanese raids against Biak and Owi, an island a couple of miles south, more dangerous to them.

The enemy had strengthened Jefman and Samate airdromes on the northern tip of the Vogelkop near Sorong, and Babo, Sagan, and Otawiri on McCluer Gulf. These planes could hit Biak by staging through Manokwari, Noemfoor, and other strips, and Whitehead had been relying on the Flying Circus and the 38th Group to keep pressure on the Japanese in the Vogelkop. Weather turned back the Flying Circus from Jefman once, and a second strike had been canceled when their B-24s went after the Japanese cruisers. By June 7 enemy strength in the area had built up so much that it was no longer a job for unescorted Liberators. The 38th Group had been only partly successful against Babo, getting there on three days during

May, but in June weather prevented all missions. The long flights on lean gas mixtures were burning up engines, and other difficulties reduced the 38th's effectiveness, but Babo was too close to Hollandia for Allied comfort. On June 3, P-38s nearly wiped out the Japanese air strength there but lost their squadron commander, Lieutenant Colonel David A. Campbell. As soon as the situation allowed, Whitehead sent the 3rd Attack, by now calling themselves the Grim Reapers, on strikes against the Geelvink Bay fields, and from June 5 they also took over the job of pounding Babo, relieving the 38th Group.

Central Pacific forces invaded the Marianas on June 6, and the Japanese air strikes at Biak dwindled as their reinforcements began moving to the Central Pacific front. Cleaning out Japanese air power at Jefman and Samate was difficult, involving longer flights than the B-25s had ever made, but Kenney felt the area was a key link in the enemy defense, and Whitehead was planning to crush it as soon as the commitments to Nimitz were completed.

By June 14 all was ready and the Fifth staged the 38th, the 345th, and the 8th Fighter Group into Hollandia. The 8th and 475th moved their Lightnings over to Wakde early on June 16, refueled, and took off to cover forty-one B-25s from Hollandia which reached Jefman just before one o'clock. The B-25s of the 38th, followed by the Air Apaches, whipped over at treetop level, strafing and scattering parafrags on planes, dumps, and personnel. The Japanese were caught on the ground again; Oscars, Zekes, and Sonias were on the runway, some of them warming up, and ground crews scurried around them. Dust eddied from the strip as the planes tried to get airborne ahead of the first bullets of the 38th.

From the cockpits of the B-25s the pilots watched the airfield and the planes lined up on either side of it disappear in clouds of smoke and dust. Their guns and bombs blew the grounded aircraft to pieces and the planes taking off were caught in the sleet of bullets. More B-25s sped through the smoke and debris, the later wave forced to fly on instruments. Above the turmoil, the P-38 pilots were wondering if anything would be left for them.

The Mitchells roared across the four-mile channel separating Jefman Island from Samate and repeated their performance, stunned Japanese gunners shooting down only one plane. Major Thomas McGuire got two of the twenty-five planes that did fall to the Lightnings, the 38th Group shot down eleven, and the 345th one. Under the pall of dust and smoke fourteen more planes lay wrecked on the ground.

Whitehead, delighted, wanted to use the B-25s against Babo the next day, but there had been so many reports of tempting shipping targets around Sorong that he sent the Mitchells and P-38s there instead. The 345th attacked two evidently deserted airfields and the 38th claimed eight vessels sunk and others left burning. The Lightnings found four enemy planes and shot down one of them. A few Japanese fighters had survived at Sorong, because two of them pounced on a 38th Group B-25 and shot it down on June 22, but the enemy air force admitted defeat in New Guinea and the 23rd Air Flotilla headquarters withdrew from Sorong to Amboina on June 28.

On Biak, aviation engineers had begun to get Mokmer strip ready for fighters on June 10, but it was not possible to get heavy equipment over the road from Bosnek for the dug-in Japanese stopped work after three days of intensive resistance. The end of the New Guinea campaign was in sight but time was slipping away. On June

19 an attack was launched with fresh troops and Borokoe and Sorido airfields were captured the next day, helping relieve Japanese pressure on Mokmer. General Eichelberger told the Fifth they could start moving in.

Far East Air Forces

On June 15 the provisional Far East Air Forces was formed, with General Kenney commanding. It combined the Fifth and Thirteenth Air Forces, and that day Whitehead assumed command of the Fifth, opened his command post at Nadzab, and the old Advon, Fifth Air Force, and the Thirteenth Air Task Force were disbanded. The new organization was officially activated on August 5, and MacArthur, having "found that it takes an aviator to run aviators," was content to leave almost all air force matters in his theater to Kenney. Most of the Far East Air Forces personnel were from the Fifth and there was a continuation of the excellent relations between the two headquarters—Kenney and Whitehead had always worked closely together. Unfortunately, and perhaps naturally, this did not extend to the Thirteenth Air Force, although its commander, General St. Clair Streett, was encouraged to work with Whitehead on the same informal basis. Kenney would have liked to put Thirteenth Air Force people into his new headquarters, but the tiny South Pacific air force barely had enough staff for its own needs. The Fifth, because of its sheer size, would lead the way in most of the operations after June 1944 with the smaller Thirteenth playing a supporting role. This caused some "chaffing" but there was no alternative, and Kenney's Far East Air Forces would actually gain another small air force, the Seventh, before the end of the war.

Owi

The delays on Biak had been anticipated very soon after the landing, and a site for an airfield had been found on nearby Owi Island, a couple of miles off the southeastern coast of Biak. Work began on June 9 and went so well that P-38s returning from the June 17 Sorong strike had been able to land there, and the strip could handle two groups of fighters in an emergency. In order to give the engineers as much time as possible, Colonel Hutchinson did not begin bringing forward planes of the 8th Fighter Group until June 21, and a detachment of night-fighting P-61s and the 82nd Reconnaissance Squadron with their Airacobras followed a week later.

Meanwhile, on Biak, the infantry was burning and blasting the Japanese out of a maze of caves, holes, and fissures where the last of them had gathered to fight. The 49th Fighter Group began moving to Mokmer on June 21, the 17th Recon Squadron was there by early July, and Whitehead had the necessary strength for the Fifth to play its part in the invasion of Noemfoor. In July the infantry forced the last of the Japanese into a pocket north of Mokmer village and, after a heavy artil-

When the capture of Biak was delayed the Fifth's attention turned to Owi, a couple of miles south. Work went well, and Lightnings returning from the Sorong strike on June 17, 1944 were able to land there. This 431st Squadron aircraft is taking off on June 19, after minor repairs. (Army)

lery barrage and Liberator bombardment, moved in and wiped them out. The Biak campaign was officially over on August 20.

When Whitehead saw Biak he had been able to specify his requirements for coming operations and the engineers tried their best to deliver, but various factors led to delays of up to two weeks in the schedule. Deeper investigation revealed that Sorido could not be developed into a heavy bomber field economically, and after four thousand feet of runway had been patched up enough to handle C-47s, its development was abandoned and the other three airdromes were expanded proportionately. The shipping delays which held up construction also interfered with the movement of air units and supplies to Biak prior to the invasion of the Vogelkop, but the C-47s and bombers helped the Fifth bypass the shipping bottleneck and get stripped-down units into Biak and Owi. The Red Raiders and Air Apaches spent more than a week hauling cargoes from Nadzab to Owi, and the flight echelons of the 25th Photo Recon and 82d Recon Squadrons, the 475th Fighter, 43rd, 345th, and part of the 22nd Bomb Group, were moved forward during July. Australian P-40s flew up to Biak from Hollandia, where they waited to go on to Noemfoor. The Fifth Air Force transferred its command post from Nadzab to Owi on August 10.

Naturally under the circumstances, proper maintenance was impossible, and by August 3 over ninety aircraft in need of repair were grounded at Biak and Owi. On Wakde the Jolly Rogers had similar problems; the B-24s had arrived on June 22, but part of their ground echelon was at Hollandia during most of July, waiting to sail to Biak, while the rest of the ground echelon was at Nadzab, the group's official base. It was a frustrating situation which would not be resolved for weeks.

Corporal Al Merkling of the 20th Combat Mapping Squadron at work on the lavish decoration of *The Wango Wango Bird,* flown by Lieutenant Roy Hunt and demolished landing at Finschhafen at gross weight. Each crewman contributed an Australian pound note and the paintings were done between missions. (Merkling)

Little Joe was the elaborate design created for the 20th's commander, Major Joe Davis. (Frank Kujawski)

The best legs in the Southwest Pacific belonged to the girl on *Photo Queen,* Lieutenant Royce Harms's aircraft. This F-7 was lost in weather when she was within voice distance of Biak. The 20th received a message that a Catalina had picked up eleven men in two rafts, but the rescue plane was never heard from again. (E. P. Stevens)

ing's fame spread and his signature began appearing on other units' aircraft, in-
g A-20s, C-47s, and Liberators like this Jolly Roger. For the magnificent *Queen*
robe the only regal red Merkling could find or steal was a thick lacquer. Without
r it was impossible to work with, so it was laid on like plaster with a mess kit
(Al Lomer)

One of the best-known and most imaginative pieces of wartime artwork was *American
Beauty*. Al Merkling recalls that "this was a fun thing to paint . . . I usually would
rough in the entire painting so the spectators would have an idea what the finished art
would look like, but in this one I first sketched in Uncle Sam's ear, then I roughed in the
figure's breasts, then the stars . . . I jumped around, leaving the crowd puzzled and
making comments about this being one of those surrealistic jobs . . . *American Beauty*
drew the biggest crowds and was the hit of the airstrip." In 1949 this painting was still
fading in the sun at Nadzab, somewhere among a jumble of junked warplanes waiting to
be cut up and smelted. (Merkling)

Noemfoor

At one time Biak had been the only objective in Geelvink Bay, but back in May it had been decided that Noemfoor Island, about eighty miles west, was also desirable. Fighters based there would be able to cover bomber strikes on the Halmaheras, continuing neutralization of the Vogelkop airfields would be simplified, and any Japanese efforts to reinforce their then held base at Biak from Manokwari could be halted.

Noemfoor's fringing coral reef almost completely surrounds the island, and there were few possible landing beaches. The Japanese had begun building three airdromes—Kornasoren, Kamiri, and Namber—on the low, northern half of the island. The enemy had at least forty-nine operational airfields within eight hundred miles, seven staging fields within two hundred miles, and it was possible they had about five hundred and fifty aircraft, mostly fighters, within a radius of six hundred miles of the island.

MacArthur thought Noemfoor could be invaded by June 25, although most of his staff estimated the middle of July; Kenney wanted to get his fighters to Biak in time to permit an early invasion, but finally it was decided that July 2 would be the best date. By then the task force would have been able to rehearse the landing, and the engineers would have completed a parallel taxiway on Owi. MacArthur immediately approved.

The reef off Kamiri, the selected landing point, offered only a narrow path for the landing craft, and this would allow the Japanese to concentrate their fire on the boats. Naval gunfire and aerial bombing would have to shatter the enemy defenses before the landing. The total force scheduled for the operation was just under seven and a half thousand men, and Whitehead was doubtful that so few combat troops could accomplish the mission with any degree of speed. Not sure what the enemy strength really was, the 503rd Parachute Infantry Regiment was made the task force reserve.

Kenney wrote to Whitehead that except for his "having a lot of faith in the thousand pound bomb," he would be worried about the operation. Much of the preparation for Noemfoor had already been achieved as support for Biak and in June Whitehead had told Hutchinson to send the Grim Reapers to Manokwari and Noemfoor in about equal doses, to confuse the enemy about the next Allied objective. He particularly wanted continuing strikes against small vessels at Manokwari, simultaneously to deny reinforcement of Biak and Noemfoor. During June the 310th Wing destroyed more than eighty barges and luggers, as well as twenty-four freighters. It was a busy time for the Grim Reapers, who claimed the lion's share of the destruction.

The strikes against Vogelkop airfields also contributed to the success of the Noemfoor operation, and after Jefman and Samate were knocked out, the Fifth only had to blast holes in the strips to deny their use. Toward the end of June the Grim Reapers struck at Babo, Moemi, and Waren, and the Jolly Rogers raided Jefman, Samate, Ransiki, and Moemi from Wakde. The Flying Circus helped cover their sister Liberators by neutralizing Babo. The 38th Group, staging through Hollandia, attacked Manokwari and Ransiki. There were no enemy interceptions over the Vogelkop after June 22, and the fighters occupied themselves by

General Kenney and Dick Ellis of the 3rd Attack at Hollandia. Ellis was famous for his reform policy conferences: the combat crews would air their grievances and ideas, which Ellis would faithfully record in a notebook, muttering, "Something must be done about *that*." (John P. Henebry)

poking around for targets to strafe. By July 1 there seemed to be very little left of the Japanese air force in New Guinea and the Allied Air Forces estimated that there were in fact probably less than sixty planes in northwestern New Guinea, and probably only about a dozen were serviceable. Only weather and distance could interfere with the "Gloucesterizing" of Noemfoor.

Persistent air attacks began against Noemfoor when Liberators attacked Kamiri on June 20, and again the next day. Then bad weather closed in on the Markham Valley and the Red Raiders and Ken's Men were able to reach Noemfoor on only two more days in June; the Grim Reapers and dive-bombing fighters continued their attacks, although they could not deliver the amount of explosives needed to bury the beach defenses. Whitehead called in the Thirteenth Air Force's B-24s, and on June 30 the "Long Rangers" and "Bomber Barons" teamed up with the Jolly Rogers and the other aircraft to drop about one hundred and sixty tons of bombs on Noemfoor. The next day a break in the weather allowed the five B-24 groups to attack and in eleven days Noemfoor had shuddered under eight hundred tons of explosives, mostly in the Kamiri area. The Japanese chose to save their ammunition and Noemfoor was undefended as Kenney's aircraft trampled it.

Just before sunrise on July 2 the naval bombardment began, using more than twice the usual amount of ammunition for such an operation. Then sixteen Jolly Rogers droned over, and after they had unloaded dead on target, the first assault wave landed to find the beach defenses abandoned. The first Japanese troops they met were near the center of Kamiri strip, so dazed that they showed little fight—some sat by their machine guns, numb with shock—and a seemingly risky landing was completed almost unopposed.

Reports from captured Japanese led to the belief that there were several thousand Japanese troops on Noemfoor, and reinforcement by air was called for on July 3. By the next evening the Japanese force had been correctly estimated at no more than fifteen hundred, but the additional troops were still needed to expand operations. The 317th Troop Carrier Group was at Hollandia, and during the morning of July 3, and on the following day, its C-47s dropped fourteen hundred paratroopers on Kamiri airstrip. Both drops were marred by high injury rates; on July 3, when nearly 10 per cent were injured, a smoke screen laid to shield the drop zone from enemy fire drifted over the strip and many of the jumpers landed among debris and equipment on either side of it. The next day the troops jumped well and most landed in the drop area, but the engineers had begun compacting the airstrip and there were many fractures. The situation forced the cancellation of a third drop.

Kornasoren strip was occupied on July 4. The next day a Japanese counterattack was broken, ending organized enemy resistance, and on July 6 a quick shore-to-shore operation secured Namber. Reduced to cannibalism, the last Japanese were driven to the interior of the island and annihilated by the end of August.

During July Noemfoor was the most advanced Allied base, but enemy air attacks were limited to nine planes in five raids which seemed to have originated at Ceram bases. Airfield construction began as soon as the engineers got ashore but the Japanese strips were disappointing—Kamiri was poorly surfaced and Kornasoren was just a location. C-47s could use Namber, but that would involve building about seven miles of road overland from Kamiri, which was opened for transports on July 16. Plans to begin attacks on the Halmaheras required an airstrip and parking for fifty P-38s at Kornasoren, where work had not begun, but by throwing everybody into the job this was achieved by the deadline, July 25.

If the shipping situation was bad at Biak, at Noemfoor it was worse. The conditions were the worst so far encountered and only about five thousand tons of shipping could be unloaded in the first two weeks. Demolition parties blasted a slot through the reef off Kamiri and a jetty was built, but it was still unlikely that the shipping backlog could be cleared before the end of August. Naturally this affected the air strength there, and although Australian P-40s flew to Kamiri on July 21, the RAAF Bostons and Beaufighters could not be moved in before the middle of August. The American units were running even later, and when an advanced detachment of the 309th Bomb Wing reached Kornasoren on July 28 it found only a night-fighter detachment there.

Over-all plans had been made on the assumption that it would be necessary to have an air base between Geelvink Bay and the Halmaheras, either on Waigeo Is-

July 22, 1944, and this 387th Squadron A-20 has just crossed the tin roofs of Kokas when antiaircraft fire finds its mark. The pilot, Lieutenant James Knarr, never had a chance. His wingman, Lieutenant Mel Kapson, races away from the flying wreckage. The photos were taken from *Shu Shu Baby*, which brought back over one hundred machine-gun and shrapnel holes. (Tom Jones)

land or the Vogelkop. This would assist in knocking out the Halmaheras, then covering the convoy and the invasion beaches there, and protecting the Allies' left flank. The invasion of the Halmaheras was tentatively set for September 15, so the Vogelkop operation would have to begin around August 1.

Finding a suitable site had been difficult. A recon party sent out by submarine found that Cape Sansapor had a good beach but no really promising airstrip site. However, Whitehead's air engineer had looked over the area closely from a B-25 and found two potential sites on the mainland. Offshore, Middelburg Island seemed a likely place for a fighter strip. The area was just west of the Cape of Good Hope, the most northern point in New Guinea, and the Japanese were thought to have only small detachments at Sansapor and Mar villages. They could bring in reinforcements from other points but it was doubtful that they would risk the ships needed to transport them. They did have a total of more than eight hundred aircraft within probable range of Sansapor but the Allies did not expect the Japanese to fight too hard. The target date was set for July 30. The Fifth would provide the major air effort, with the Thirteenth in reserve, and the Thirteenth would supply the air garrison to be established in the Sansapor region.

The over-all transport and construction situation hindered the movement of many Fifth Air Force bomb groups, and during July the total tonnage of bombs dropped by the Fifth was less than half the amount dropped in April. Most of the effort was expended against Japanese airfields on the Vogelkop. Early in July small forces of heavies raided Sorong, and the Babo area was kept under pressure. The A-20s and B-25s attacked barge shipping and raided the Japanese supply center and barge construction yards at Kokas village on the McCluer Gulf. The 418th Night Fighter Squadron, using B-25s, flew night intruder missions over the Vogelkop fields. Other attacks hit Manokwari and the fighters swept over the area. Most of the missions were uneventful, although occasionally antiaircraft fire claimed planes.

The Halmaheras promised a more lively target. Recon photos showed nearly one hundred and thirty planes dispersed at Galela, Lolobata, and Miti airfields on July 22, and the Japanese were attempting to build three more fields, obviously intending to bring in more aircraft. By July 24 the bases at Biak, Owi, and Noemfoor were ready to receive the aircraft needed for raids on the Halmaheras, and Whitehead ordered the attack to begin.

The weather delayed the first mission until July 27, but on that day the Fifth sent out one of its biggest forces. From Wakde and Owi came the Jolly Rogers, the Red Raiders, and Ken's Men. Four squadrons of P-38s joined them and the B-24s droned toward the Halmaheras. There they split up to hit the airdromes, two groups bombing Lolobata while the Red Raiders attended to Miti. A couple of Liberators were damaged by ground fire but they left seventeen Japanese planes destroyed on the airfields.

Meanwhile, the strafers of the Air Apaches and 38th Group had attacked Galela airdrome from low level and caught the Japanese yet again. They added ten more planes to the score, and the Lightnings from the 475th and 8th Groups had some success. The 36th Squadron, watching over the bombing at Miti, shot down three Oscars, and a fourth evidently flew into the ocean because the inexperienced pilot had looked over his shoulder too long. The unique victory belonged to Colonel

Colonel Richard Robinson's 22nd Group converted to Liberators in January 1944 and called themselves the Red Raiders. Their squadron markings were a colored rectangle on the fin, with blue for the 2nd, white for the 19th, yellow for the 33rd, and green for the 408th. This aircraft is one of the eighty Liberators attacking the Halmahera airfields on July 27, 1944. (Bill Miller)

A. J. Beck, still Assistant A-3, Fifth Air Force, and flying from Owi with the 36th. Flying just above the waves he saw a Japanese fighter heading for the cover of the antiaircraft guns in the harbor. The enemy plane turned left to take evasive action, Beck following him. Then the Oscar turned right sharply, dug his wingtip in the water, and simply went under. Captain Kenny Giroux had witnessed the destruction of the plane from above and Beck got the credit, the write-up of which said the enemy fighter became "disorganized." The Headhunters got three Oscars and a Lily over Lolobata, and the 431st Squadron disposed of three more. At Galela the 35th Squadron casually picked off four fighters as they made their landing approach. One P-38 went down with mechanical trouble but a Catalina pulled the pilot out.

Adding up the score was made difficult because the Japanese had dispersed their aircraft in woods, but it seemed that in all the mission had destroyed sixty planes on the ground and in the air. Whitehead was now sure the Japanese bases in the Halmaheras were defensive so he aimed the Fifth at the Amboina, Ceram, and Boeroe area, where there were about one hundred and fifty aircraft spread over eight airstrips. The Boela oil fields were another worthwhile target on Ceram, and Whitehead had used the Flying Circus for fourteen attacks on these targets but

The 312th Group's *Eloise* at Hollandia. This group's individual squadrons were uniquely identified by a playing card symbol behind the American insignia—a club for the 386th, diamond for the 387th, heart for the 388th, and spade for the 389th.

weather had interfered with the missions. Grim Reaper and 312th Group A-20s hit the Boela oil wells, storage tanks, and airfield on July 14 and although they lost an A-20 to antiaircraft fire they were able to burn up a lot of precious Japanese oil.

Mister Lindbergh

Early in July the arrival of Charles A. Lindbergh, who had flown *The Spirit of St. Louis* from New York to Paris, caused a ripple in the 475th Fighter Group at Hollandia, particularly when he told expert pilots they could extend the range of their P-38s from around four hundred miles to eight hundred, or even a thousand. To prove his point Lindbergh began flying with the 475th, and brought back nearly enough fuel to fly the missions over again. General Kenney had felt that "if anyone could fly a little monoplane all the way from New York to Paris and have gas left over, he ought to be able to teach my P-38 pilots how to get more range out of their airplanes," and Lindbergh believed he could increase the radius of action of the Lightnings by 50 per cent. Kenney did not want the famous civilian in combat, but Lindbergh felt it would be hard to check results unless he went along and watched; Kenney knew the Japanese weren't flying over New Guinea any more, so he agreed to let him fly with the P-38s escorting the bombers and strafers anywhere except Halmahera, where a fight was certain.

On July 28, 1944, Lindbergh was flying as number three in Colonel Charles Mac-Donald's flight. The 475th Group P-38s arrived over Ceram Island at about ten

Colonel Charles MacDonald's P-38 over the Markham Valley—the drop tanks and Mr. Lindbergh's "cruise control" gave the Lightning long legs. (Ben Millis)

thousand feet, saw nothing on the Boela airstrips, then dashed over Amahai and again found nothing. The airstrips on the west coast were empty too and the interior of the island was covered by solid cloud.

The 475th circled and was ready to return home when the radio was filled with chatter which revealed that 8th Group P-38s were in a fight. The battle was taking place near Amahai airstrip and there were two enemy planes. Charles Lindbergh wrote in his diary: "We jettison our drop tanks, switch on our guns, and nose down to the attack. One Jap plane banks sharply toward the airstrip and the protection of the antiaircraft guns. The second heads off into the haze and clouds. Colonel MacDonald gets a full deflection shot on the first, starts him smoking, and forces him to reverse his bank.

"We are spaced one thousand feet apart. Captain Miller gets in a short deflection burst with no noticeable effect. I start firing as the plane is completing its turn in my direction. I see the tracers and the 20's find their mark, a hail of shells directly on the target. But he straightens out and flies directly toward me.

"I hold the trigger down and my sight on his engine as we approach head on. My tracers and my 20's spatter on his plane. We are close—too close—hurtling at each other at more than five hundred miles an hour. I pull back on the controls. His plane suddenly zooms upward with extraordinary sharpness.

"I pull back with all the strength I have. Will we hit? His plane, before a slender toy in my sight, looms huge in size. A second passes—two—three—I can see the finning on his engine cylinders. There is a rough jolt of air as he shoots past behind me.

"By how much did we miss? Ten feet? Probably less than that. There is no time to consider or feel afraid. I am climbing steeply. I bank to the left. No, that will

The taciturn Colonel Charles MacDonald, commander of the 475th Fighter Group, with Charles Lindbergh. MacDonald was the third highest-scoring ace in the Fifth, with twenty-seven victories. Lindbergh's combat victory, a Sonia, does not appear in the 475th's official total, but members of the group mentally add one. (Dennis Glen Cooper)

take me into the ack-ack fire above Amahai strip. I reverse to the right. It has all taken seconds.

"My eyes sweep the sky for aircraft. There are only P-38s and the plane I have just shot down. He is starting down in a wing over—out of control. The nose goes down. The plane turns slightly as it picks up speed—down—down toward the sea. A fountain of spray—white foam on the water—waves circling outwards as from a stone tossed in a pool—the waves merge into those of the sea—the foam disappears—the surface is as it was before."

On another mission four days later Lindbergh was nearly shot down in a meeting with Japanese fighters and although Kenney had chosen to overlook the fact that his instructions had been circumvented, this was a little too much. Colonel MacDonald was called to Wurtsmith's headquarters and grounded for sixty days. He was advised to use this time for a trip to the United States to see his baby son for the first time.

In July 1944 the 345th Group elected to call themselves the Air Apaches and this black, red, and white symbol began appearing on the tails of their B-25s.

Three Liberator strikes at the end of July were not intercepted as they struck Boela targets, and a fighter sweep over Amboina found nothing. Whitehead was puzzled, but decided to continue attacking until he found out if the Japanese had gone for good.

Attacks on shipping filled the week leading up to the Sansapor landing, and after July 27 the Air Apaches' 498th Squadron sent twice-daily missions to look for targets around the Halmaheras. The 63rd Squadron B-24s, which had been watching over the Palaus, started flying night missions to the area on July 25. A P-38 sweep over Amboina set fire to a cargo vessel and a small steamer on July 29, while other planes shot up barges from Cape Sansapor to Sorong. In all, the week led to the damage or destruction of six freighters, fifteen luggers, thirteen barges, and dozens of sailboats, canoes, and fishing boats.

The invasion convoy arrived off the beach early in the morning of July 30, and although there was no opposition, five Air Apaches shot up the main beachhead for good measure. Nor was there any opposition at Middelburg, or nearby Amsterdam Island. An infantry battalion landed and took Sansapor village the next day and there were only small fights during the whole operation. When it was over on August 31, the force had lost only ten men and killed less than four hundred Japanese.

Patched Up Piece from the 20th Combat Mapping Squadron was the first aircraft to land on Middelburg Island, after losing power in two engines during a mission on August 14, 1944. These Liberators had yellow tails with a black winged camera, and later a diving hawk.

At Middelburg, work on the strip went very well and the 20th Combat Mapping Squadron's *Patched Up Piece* was able to make an emergency landing there on August 14. It was ready for more conventional use three days later, and the Thirteenth began moving in.

With the New Guinea campaign at an end Kenney could look proudly at the record of the Fifth Air Force. The early days when their few aircraft fought an enemy who had hardly known defeat seemed long ago, and the Fifth was now a strong and victorious air force poised to return to the Philippines.

VI

Return to
the Philippines

DURING the continuing debate over objectives, all that had really been decided was that Nimitz would invade Formosa or MacArthur would occupy Luzon, depending on the situation prevailing in February 1945. In June 1944 MacArthur's staff in Brisbane had drawn up their own plans: after the successful Wakde and Biak operations, their estimate of the situation advocated the establishment of a base in the Vogelkop, another in the northern Moluccas, with another operation involving the Kai and Tanimbar islands if Japanese strength in the west of New Guinea necessitated additional protection for the left flank. They planned to accomplish this between July and October 1944, with the target date for the invasion of Morotai, north of Halmahera, to coincide with Nimitz's entry into the Palau Islands. The last months of 1944 would be taken up with the establishment of bases on Mindanao to support air operations against Luzon and north Borneo. It was planned to seize Sarangani Bay, on the southern coast of Mindanao, in October and establish airfields to support the principal effort in November against northern Mindanao, Leyte, and parts of Samar. Southern and northeastern Luzon would then be invaded between January and March 1945; Mindoro, southwest of Luzon, would be occupied by an airborne invasion in February. A major landing would be made on Luzon between April and June 1945.

The plans would change, as often before. Washington questioned the invasion of Mindanao, but neither Nimitz nor MacArthur felt they could speed up their campaign enough to justify a direct invasion of Formosa. Nimitz felt MacArthur's timing might be optimistic, but that the over-all plan was basically good, and he looked forward to support from MacArthur's aircraft on Mindanao and Leyte before he went into Formosa. Leyte Island was the key, and MacArthur had told Kenney that he would have Manila six weeks after a landing at Lingayen Gulf, and all of the Philippines within eight months. However, it would be a major task to move landing forces from New Guinea to southern Mindanao, and the build-up of Japanese air strength in the Philippines added to the problem. The island of Morotai would place the Allies three hundred miles closer, but even then they would still be three hundred and fifty miles from Mindanao.

Kenney discussed the alternatives with Whitehead and the Thirteenth Air Force's General St. Clair Streett. Kenney believed that the carriers could not provide the kind of support needed for the capture of Morotai and Mindanao or Leyte. While the proposed invasion of the northern Moluccas could be covered by his heavy bombers from Biak, Japanese airfields threatening Sarangani and Leyte would be outside the range of fighters escorting B-24s from Morotai or Biak. The distances involved were too great for mutual air support and the Japanese could choose one of Kenney's bases and knock it out before he could protect it. His answer was to scale down the invasions and move forward methodically, building an air base every twenty to thirty days, and his opinions led to a modification of the plans. Toward the end of July MacArthur advised Washington that his revised schedule would be to take Morotai on September 15, the Talaud Islands on October 15, Sarangani on November 15, and Leyte on December 20. This schedule, of course, was still tentative.

The Joint Chiefs in Washington were anxious to get into Formosa, the planned final springboard to Japan, early in March 1945, and in order to allow three months for the preparation of an air base and the neutralization of Luzon, it was imperative that Leyte be under American control by December. They asked both MacArthur and Nimitz if they could eliminate the attack on the Palaus and instead make smaller attacks on Woleai, Yap, and Ulithi, and if the invasion of the Talauds or Sarangani Bay or both could be replaced by a direct movement into northern Mindanao and Leyte. They also asked what specific operations MacArthur contemplated in northern Mindanao.

MacArthur was furious with the questions, which indicated that his entry into the Philippines was mainly to provide air bases to support the operations against Formosa. With the capture of Luzon he felt the hazardous operation against Formosa would be unnecessary and he answered that the Palaus were essential, that Sarangani Bay and the Talauds could not be eliminated, and that operations in northern Mindanao would follow Leyte as soon as possible to relieve the civilian population there. To patch up the argument, Washington sent representatives to MacArthur's headquarters in Brisbane in August. There MacArthur again insisted that the Palaus would be vital flank protection for the invasion of the southern Philippines. Both MacArthur and Kenney doubted Luzon could be neutralized from Leyte, and MacArthur repeated his belief in the seizure of Luzon, taking a few eloquent swipes at the weakness of the Formosa plans. One of the representatives at the meeting later reported that it was "very hard to keep from getting 'localitis' after having talked to MacArthur for five hours," and MacArthur had, for the time at least, won.

When it was decided that the Fifth should have two of the new P-51 "air commando" groups—completely airborne units with their own transport and liaison squadrons—Kenney's staff outlined a new airborne invasion plan for western Mindanao. Fighter fields could be prepared in an area controlled by guerrillas to cover air operations into the Visayas and southern Luzon, and on this basis, Kenney was agreeable to bypassing either the Talauds or Sarangani Bay. He believed that the Japanese air force was really a past threat, and that one fighter group could defend Leyte if they had adequate airfield and radar support.

Nimitz was willing to cover the planned operations with the Pacific Fleet but he was anxious to receive definite instructions about Formosa. Naval planners evidently hoped that part of the required forces might be pried loose from MacArthur, and they feared that unless both Leyte and Formosa were coupled in one directive MacArthur would plan the Leyte operation so as to make Formosa impossible. However, Washington's viewpoint was turning toward MacArthur's; with possibly half a million men required for the Formosa invasion, they were simply not prepared to make a definite decision at this point. Once again the Pacific Theater was reminded of its secondary importance to the war against Germany. MacArthur was to proceed with the planning to invade Leyte and establish bases to support either the Formosa or Luzon operations, Nimitz's forces were to support the Leyte operation and submit plans for the invasion of Formosa and Amoy, and be prepared for any Luzon operation.

As the discussions went on, the Fifth Air Force was moving forward into Netherlands New Guinea, taking up position to support the invasion of the northern Moluccas, the Palaus, and the southern Philippines. The Fifth and the other arms of the Far East Air Forces outnumbered the enemy, but that superiority was theoretical because Allied aircraft were based all the way back from Biak and Noemfoor to Guadalcanal and Australia, with the center of gravity still around Nadzab and the Admiralties, over a thousand miles from Morotai and farther from

Lieutenant Carroll Anderson's *Virginia Marie* fires up on Biak. (Anderson)

the Palaus. Naturally the plans presumed that the Fifth would be the assault air force in the initial Philippines operations.

At the beginning of August the most advanced Allied airfields were on Noemfoor. Three strips for fighters, bombers, and transports were being built up on Biak and a heavy bomber base was being developed nearby on Owi Island. The 49th and 475th Fighter Groups, the Air Apaches, the 17th and 82nd Recon Squadrons were among the units at Mokmer on Biak by August. The Lightnings of the 8th Fighter Group, the 43rd Bomb Group, and the 421st Night Fighter Squadron were at Owi. At Wakde the 348th Fighter Group, the 418th Night Fighter Squadron, and part of the Jolly Rogers cluttered the island. Still farther back, at Hollandia, were the Grim Reapers and 312th Groups with their A-20s. With shipping limited, there were tremendous difficulties to be overcome, particularly at Noemfoor, Owi, and Biak, but during August and September the air forces were able gradually to build up their planned strength.

The 35th Fighter Group moved into Kornasoren strip on Noemfoor on August 7, followed by the 348th, which left one squadron behind to cover Wakde and Hollandia. On September 3 the 348th was joined by the new 460th Fighter Squadron, making it the only four-squadron fighter group in the theater. Another Thunderbolt outfit, the 58th, arrived in September. The A-20s of the 417th Bomb Group moved in from Saidor. Fifth Air Force headquarters began moving to Owi in August and Whitehead brought forward the Jolly Rogers and Red Raiders from Nadzab, moving them in squadron by squadron as hardstands became available. By the end of the month the 38th Bomb Group was operating from Borokoe strip on Biak and by the middle of September the 6th Photo Group and the 71st Recon

This 340th Squadron Thunderbolt ditched off Noemfoor after engine trouble forced the pilot to turn back from his mission. The engine failed completely within sight of the strip but the crash boat quickly rescued the pilot.

Group were on Biak. As the Fifth left Wakde the Thirteenth Air Force moved in; the P-47s of the 342nd Fighter Squadron continued flying cover until September 21, when it went to join the rest of the 348th on Noemfoor, and the 418th Night Fighter Squadron retired to Hollandia to train with the P-61 Black Widow.

* * *

Although the Fifth was always somewhere below the top on the list of priorities, increased production and training programs in the United States were permitting it to grow. However, in spring 1944 replacement of combat crews was still giving Kenney "some bad headaches." He had been sending crewmen back to the States entirely on the basis of combat fatigue but had noticed most fighter and bomber crewmen began looking "a little foggy" after three hundred combat hours. With the maximum of 15 per cent monthly rotation, which also had to cover casualties, the average B-24 crew had to fly six hundred and fifty hours in a period of twenty months, P-38 pilots five hundred and sixty hours, and A-20, B-25, and P-47 crews a total of over three hundred hours before they could hope for relief. Kenney asked Washington to double his monthly replacement rates for B-24 crews and P-38 pilots before they were worn down beyond endurance; in April he got a promise of increased fighter pilot allocations, beginning in May, but heavy bomber crew replacements would have to remain at 15 per cent until November.

This meant little immediate relief. Kenney's C-47 crewmen could hope for only 7.5 per cent monthly replacements, and that rate was not met often. By March 1944, Brigadier General Paul H. Prentiss, commanding the 54th Troop Carrier Wing, observed that many of his fliers regarded surgeons' certificates of combat fatigue as the only way to get home alive. At the end of June the 342nd Fighter Squadron's older P-47 pilots had over five hundred combat hours. The accelerated operations during April and May had affected the B-25 crews more than any of the other types. By June the Air Apaches had only twenty-four out of seventy-six crews ready for combat, while the 38th had only twenty-three of sixty-seven. The rest had been grounded due to combat fatigue, and Kenney, feeling that "a half strength squadron of willing boys is better than a full strength squadron of worn out ones," sent nearly six hundred of them home during July.

The actual flow of replacements during the second half of 1944 failed to fulfill the allocations of the Fifth and it would remain short of combat crews while the Philippines operations brought increased casualties, particularly among A-20 and B-25 crews. In January 1945 alone, the 417th Bomb Group would lose its group commander, two squadron commanders, and so many of its experienced fliers that there were no pilots in the group suitable to replace the leaders.

A standard for rotation was drawn up and announced in September 1944; two hundred combat hours for A-20s, two hundred and fifty for B-25s, three hundred for photo aircraft and recon B-25s, three hundred to three hundred and fifty for fighters, four hundred for B-24s, and one thousand for transport crews. These were in fact minimum combat flight times, and rotation still hinged upon the arrival of replacements. The ground crews were even worse off, but it was a difficulty which could not be overcome. Shortages of skilled men were so bad that the 65th Bomb Squadron was turning truck drivers into mechanics in September 1944. In April it had been announced that ground personnel who had been overseas for at least eighteen months might be able to return home, but although many qualified the monthly quotas were very small—for the 54th Troop Carrier Wing, in the three months between June and August, it was just one officer and five enlisted men. This badly affected morale but there was no way around the situation.

General Kenney wanted his aircrews trained as completely as possible before they reached the theater, preferably by his own people who had returned to the States. Heavy bomber crews arriving during 1944 were considered inadequately trained in formation flying, evasive action under fire, and indentification of targets from aerial photographs. The Combat Replacement Training Center was established at Nadzab in the middle of 1944 and could teach the basic skills, but this cut down the time available to impart its specialized instruction on the type of war in the theater. Other factors, including the sometimes critical needs of combat units, caused sharp reductions in the routine five-week B-24 course and the four-week A-20, B-25, and fighter courses. Commanded by Colonel Carl Brandt until January 1945, and later by Colonel Jock Henebry, the CRTC provided ground and flight training in all types of aircraft. The fighter unit taught combat formations, dive-bombing, and strafing, and tactics that had been proved against Japanese aircraft. The bomber crews were given transition, formation, instrument, and bombing instruction. As part of the training, crews were taken on missions to Wewak as a typical jungle target, to Rabaul to face antiaircraft fire and study a town and airfield complex, and after April 1945 they flew a long-range mission against Vogelkop targets. This arrangement was a rewarding way to introduce new crews to combat as well as keeping bypassed Japanese under constant attack.

As the Philippines campaign loomed the Fifth began replacing many of its obsolete planes. The P-39s in the recon squadrons were nearly worn out as early as April 1944 and Whitehead wanted to change over to the Mustang, but it was so successful in Europe that there were none available yet. A couple of months later Whitehead reminded Kenney that the 7th and 8th Fighter Squadrons needed new aircraft as their P-40s were "on their last legs." Kenney tried to get more P-40s without success and since these squadrons had to have new aircraft Whitehead suggested making the 49th a full Lightning group. During September and October enough P-38s arrived to equip the two squadrons, and their P-40s then passed to the 82nd and 110th recon squadrons until the reconnaissance version of the Mustang became available. The Fifth never threw anything away. The 82nd on Morotai would get the first F-6Ds during November and become the first Mustang unit in the theater, followed later by the 110th Recon and the 348th and 35th Fighter Groups. A lot of the pilots were actually reluctant to part with the Jug, particularly in view of the tactical work they did, and Whitehead thought it was "the best fighter which our country possesses."

The B-25s were the oldest tactical aircraft in the Fifth. Up to September 1944 the 405th Squadron, the "Green Dragons," had received no new Mitchells in more than a year, and one of its planes, the *Tokio Sleeper,* had over one hundred and sixty combat missions. The situation with the A-20s was better and the new A-20Hs, which arrived in September, were good aircraft. Kenney would have seen the war right through with B-25s and A-20s, believing they were equal to any Japanese threat, but manufacture of both types was to end in 1944. Their intended replacement was the new A-26 Invader, a Douglas design developed from the A-20;

when four of the new planes were tried out by the Grim Reapers in July 1944 the pilots found that the long, broad nose, and the placement of the engines in particular, reduced visibility enough to restrict the use of the aircraft at low levels. Based on that expert opinion, Kenney said that he did "not want the A-26 under any circumstance as a replacement for anything," and sent Jock Henebry home to tell Douglas why. As groups in Europe changed to the Invader, enough A-20s were released to allow Kenney to keep his groups up to strength until July 1945, when he would be satisfied with the modified version of the A-26.

Many of the C-47s were also showing their age and the 54th Wing believed it had the tenth C-47 purchased by the air force, a veteran of over two thousand missions.

Work continued on getting more range from the Fifth's aircraft as well as modification of armament. The B-24 offered little scope for further changes, but the B-25Gs had their cannons removed and replaced by two .50-caliber guns fitted in the cannon hatch. Package guns were also added, but these changes were never really satisfactory, the blast damaging the skin of the aircraft. In February 1944 the B-25H had begun arriving and these had an improved, lighter 75-mm. cannon, four machine guns across the nose, package guns, a top turret, tail turret, and flexible waist guns. However, the crews in the Fifth still could not fire more than four rounds during a pass with the cannon, and the aiming requirements made it too vulnerable to ground fire. The Air Apaches' 498th Squadron was given the plane, but it was abandoned in August. When the first B-25Js arrived in the spring they had Plexiglas noses with a flexible gun and two fixed .50s; this was unsuitable for the theater and they had to be modified as strafers with eight-gun nose kits sent out from the United States, although some were used unmodified. By September the

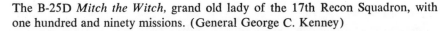

The B-25D *Mitch the Witch,* grand old lady of the 17th Recon Squadron, with one hundred and ninety missions. (General George C. Kenney)

Some modifications were less successful than others. This was one of several A-20s which arrived in the 3rd Attack Group late in 1943 armed with four 20-mm. cannon in the nose. In June 1944 it was at Hollandia rigged up to carry underwing rockets and was tried out by experienced pilots like Ellis, Howe, and Henebry. All found the rockets unsatisfacctory; Henebry says it was "a real aerodynamic abortion and a one-shot deal" which was soon abandoned.

strafer B-25Js were arriving with "solid" gun noses, but the Fifth, unused to sending anything straight into combat, added a fuel cell in the radio compartment.

Although they lacked range, the A-20s presented few problems. The Fifth was installing bomb bay tanks in the spring of 1944, but the new A-20Gs already had this feature when they arrived and the A-20Hs had improved bomb bay tanks and six .50-caliber guns in the nose. In early 1945 special wing racks for droppable fuel tanks were added, allowing longer flights or the use of napalm. At Hollandia in July 1944 there were experiments using the A-20 as a rocket-carrying plane, but the launching tubes reduced cruising speed by fifteen miles an hour and the cut in range was too great a sacrifice.

Operational range was also the main factor affecting fighters. There had been great success with the P-38s, but the P-47s had problems. The Fifth had designed its own two-hundred-and-twenty-gallon belly tank in Australia, added another sixty-five gallons to the internal capacity, and two one-hundred-and-fifty-gallon jettisonable fuel tanks. Another experiment involved a forty-two-gallon fuel cell mounted behind the pilot, and a contoured belly tank holding seventy gallons. All the methods were used but pilots who had seen crashes due to tire failure in these heavily loaded planes were unwilling to carry more than about five hundred gallons of fuel. Kenney canceled both the fuel cell and the "scab" tank and cruise control helped increase Thunderbolt range during the fall of 1944, thanks to Charles A. Lindbergh.

Springboard to the Philippines

When Admiral Halsey was relieved of the South Pacific Command on June 15, 1944, he went to Pearl Harbor to begin detailed planning for the Palaus invasion. The new plan, agreed to in July 1944, was divided into two phases: first Central Pacific forces would take Peleliu, Angaur, and possibly Ngesebus, all at the south end of the Palau chain. Fields on Peleliu would become bases for Marine fighters and a heavy bomber base would be prepared on Angaur, and these aircraft would then neutralize the twenty-seven thousand Japanese troops remaining on the other islands. Central Pacific forces would seize Ulithi atoll for a fleet anchorage, and take Yap Island for development into a fighter base to cover Ulithi. The tentative starting date was September 15.

Nimitz's order confirming fleet and carrier support for the northern Moluccas invasion was received by MacArthur on July 7. Morotai, just north of the island of Halmahera, was lightly held and the logical objective in the northern Moluccas; the Allied base should be as far north as possible and it was desirable to avoid the thirty thousand Japanese troops in these islands. There was also an abandoned airstrip on the southeastern end of Morotai. Co-ordination between the forces of the two theaters was resolved in Brisbane late in July. Vice-Admiral Marc A. Mitscher's Task Force 38 would move upon the Palaus and begin long-range fighter sweeps against Yap and the Palaus in the first week of September and hit the targets with sustained attacks. Leaving a fast carrier group and three escort carrier divisions to carry on, Task Force 38, with its other three fast carrier groups, would attack the Mindanao airfields a week before the landings and detach a fast carrier group to give support at Morotai on the day of the landing there.

It was agreed that MacArthur's air forces would support Central Pacific operations by heavily bombing the Palaus, covering the approach of Task Force 38 with attacks on southern Mindanao airfields, and stepping up attacks on enemy bases west of New Guinea to protect the fast carrier group as it approached Morotai. The Seventh Air Force, operating from the Marianas, would neutralize Truk, Yap, Ulithi, and the other islands in the Carolines, Marshalls, Marianas, and Bonins. Preliminary bombardment was up to the Allied Air Forces, which gave most of the work to its Fifth Air Force. The Thirteenth's bombers, flying from Wakde under operational control of the Fifth, would neutralize the Palaus with intensive strikes until ten days before the landing. They would also try to knock out Galela, Lolobata, and Miti airfields on Halmahera during the eight days leading up to the invasion. Navy search planes, also under Fifth control, would extend thousand-mile-long search sectors out of Owi to cover the waters between the Philippines and the Palaus. The Thirteenth Air Task Force at Sansapor and the Australian squadrons at Noemfoor would attack the northern Moluccas, neutralize remaining Japanese airfields on the Vogelkop, and provide cover for the convoys and direct support to the ground operations on Morotai. The Flying Circus and other units based in northern Australia would continue neutralization of Japanese airfields in the Ambon, Boeroe, and Ceram triangle and on other islands in the Timor and Arafura seas. It would also be ready to support the Fifth before and after the landing.

Kenney wanted a fighter strip on Morotai by two days after the landing, a bomber strip about three weeks later, with a third strip to follow. Brigadier General Donald R. Hutchinson of the 310th Bomb Wing would designate the airfield sites, a desirable procedure which had been begun at Gusap and Nadzab in the fall of 1943.

During their attacks against the northern Moluccas in support of the Cape Sansapor landing the Fifth had not generated much response from the Japanese; on August 1 four Lightnings of the 433rd Fighter Squadron destroyed two Rufes and a Val but after this the Japanese apparently chose to keep their remaining aircraft intact. As almost daily attacks continued into August even the Japanese antiaircraft crews lost interest, usually firing at the first few aircraft in the formation and then heading for cover. Only three B-25s were lost during August, one of them shot down and the other two destroyed in a collision. The Japanese were left alone only when the weather blocked out the Fifth's planes and at the beginning of September there were no Japanese aircraft operational in the Moluccas.

Since late July Whitehead had been sending missions against the airfields on Ambon, Boeroe, and Ceram, because he believed they were a dangerous threat to the line of advance. Whenever weather kept the Fifth out of the Halmaheras the planes went there, and sometimes the change in targets was made when the missions were already airborne. An intelligence officer in the 43rd Bomb Group once briefed crews on six different targets and decided that the necessary maps and target photos "looked like the first half of Cook's travel pamphlet of the Dutch East Indies." On Ceram, Boela's oil fields and storage were another secondary target.

A Sally bomber, already without her right engine, about to be blown apart by parafrags at Old Namlea on Boeroe.

Antiaircraft fire usually met these missions and Japanese fighters occasionally rose up, but the enemy did not seem willing to lose planes. On August 17 a Liberator mission raised fifteen to twenty fighters from Haroekoe airdrome—twelve Head-hunter Lightnings shot down three of them, losing a P-38 which crashed while chasing an enemy plane. About the same time, P-38s of the 35th Squadron taking Liberators to Liang on Ambon found about eleven enemy fighters, and despite the efforts of the Japanese to avoid a fight, shot down four Oscars and a Sally. Under the tons of bombs rained on the islands, the Japanese were still thought to have forty-eight operational aircraft on Ambon and Boeroe at the beginning of September, although Ceram was cleared.

Whenever the weather blocked out both sets of targets the Fifth's B-24s and B-25s pounded the airfields in the Vogelkop. These missions were part of the effort to prevent the Japanese night raiders from staging through the fields, but a few weak night attacks proved that it was almost impossible to completely stop these attacks as long as the enemy had any aircraft at all. The B-25s and night-flying B-24s maintained a tight shipping blockade in the waters of the Vogelkop, Ceram, and Halmahera triangle, and the Japanese were keeping their larger vessels out of the area.

While the Liberators of the Thirteenth softened the Palaus, the Fifth began attacks on the southern Philippines to prepare the way for the carrier strikes. Kenney had wanted to begin operations against Davao, the second largest city on Mindanao, as soon as possible and had advised Whitehead to use the Snooper B-24s of the 63rd Squadron until he could provide escort for daylight bombing. The 63rd began their night raids on August 5 with a single plane strike on an airdrome six miles north of Davao, and continued to attack the airfield and harbor area throughout the month, assisted by Navy Liberators flying reconnaissance missions. There was little resistance. On August 20 when the Air Apaches raided the Talaud Islands to cover low-level photography by the 17th Recon Squadron only two Japanese came up and they were not eager. This raid was well within fighter range of the enemy bases in southern Mindanao, but there was no reaction.

Recon Lightnings covered southern Mindanao to get the necessary target information and one hundred and sixty-three Japanese aircraft appeared in the photographs taken on August 20. Similar pictures taken two days later revealed only one hundred and eight planes, and it seemed the Japanese had interpreted the reconnaissance as an indication that the bombers would be coming soon, and they had withdrawn north. Most of their strength was concentrated at Likanan, Sasa, and Matina, three airdromes around Davao, while nine other airfields in the area varied from operational to probably abandoned.

MacArthur wanted the "big wallop" of Davao to take place as soon as possible to pave the way for the carrier strikes and to encourage Filipino guerrilla activity. Whitehead had wanted to use the two Thirteenth heavy groups for an initial raid by five Liberator groups, but had also been delaying a major attack until he could stage B-25s through Sansapor for a simultaneous strafing and photo mission against the Sarangani Bay area. As the Japanese air force melted away, Whitehead asked for permission to bomb Davao, but MacArthur had received intelligence that the Japanese would exploit attacks for propaganda. Accordingly, he limited attacks in the Philippines to airfields, hostile installations, and shipping; also, harbor facilities which might later be useful were to be spared as much as possible. Villages and cities were not to be bombed at all.

On September 1 fifty-five B-24s from the Red Raiders, Ken's Men and the Jolly Rogers hit the three main Davao airfields. Two Red Raiders went down to heavy, accurate antiaircraft fire over Matina, a pilot and gunner were killed in another plane, and ten enemy fighters intercepted Ken's Men over Likanan, shooting holes in a few of the bombers. The three groups, carrying frag bombs, were attempting to hit dispersed aircraft and the strike photos showed that they had knocked out twenty-two. Three squadrons of Lightnings, staged through Sansapor, had taken the B-24s within sixty miles of the target but had been forced back by weather. The next day the same three groups, with fighter escort, flew back to clean up stores and personnel areas around the airdromes with five-hundred-pound bombs. There was ineffective antiaircraft fire and a few phosphorous bombs were dropped near the Red Raiders, but the P-38s prevented any interception and the 35th Squadron pursued and shot down a Zeke and a Lily. A shipping strike at Davao Harbor was attempted on the night of September 2 using six volunteer crews from the Air Apaches, but only one of the B-25s managed to reach the harbor and scored a near miss on a merchant vessel.

Night Flight to Davao

Meanwhile, the 63rd Squadron was still flying its missions to Davao from Owi and on the night of September 4, at about eight o'clock, Lieutenant Roland Fisher lifted the B-24D *Miss Liberty* off the runway. Fisher and his crew had been briefed to search for shipping south of the Philippines and in Davao Gulf, with Matina airstrip as their secondary target. By midnight they had found no shipping, and Fisher decided to attack the airstrip.

It was a very bright, moonlit night, which the 63rd crews disliked intensely, but there was no apparent opposition as *Miss Liberty* began her bomb run at five thousand feet. They were approaching the coast and the bombardier, Lieutenant Howard Hammett, was taking control for the bomb run when the B-24 was caught perfectly in six or seven searchlight beams. Antiaircraft fire followed, but it was fairly inaccurate. Fisher felt the plane bounce as the bombs dropped and he turned hard to the left and dived to shake off the lights. He had just rolled out of the turn and picked up speed to about one hundred and seventy-five when he saw small flashes in the shadow of his plane, straight ahead. *Miss Liberty* was still nailed in the searchlights but they were coming from behind, and what Fisher was looking at was a Japanese plane coming in head on, shooting.

Fisher saw "the gun muzzles blinking and caught the outline of a plane. I started to call a warning to my crew when my senses told me that plane was going to take me head on. I reflexed and rolled the aircraft hard to the left and pulled back on the yoke. The fighter flashed by, clearly visible, and passed directly under my right engines. His right wingtip missed the lower right part of my fuselage by inches. I could see his aircraft very clearly in the bright lights and I saw his head, flying cap and goggles through the canopy as he went by. The plane was a Nick.

Roland Fisher, intended victim of one of the early
Japanese suicide attacks. (Fisher)

"I was still hollering on the intercom at the crew that we were under fighter attack and I rolled the plane back to horizontal and stuck the nose down hard to get
some speed. I think I was hitting about two hundred and was maybe at four thousand feet when I heard some pop-pop sounds and there was a terrific, muffled
bump and I went into an even steeper dive. I remember hearing the top turret
swivelling but nobody said anything and I was trying to sort out just what was
going on and read the instruments when the radar operator came on and said his
radar was gone. By then we were down perhaps to two thousand feet and I
remember my air speed was pretty well over two hundred and I decided to ease it
back and discovered I had no pressure on my elevators. Again reflexively I
snapped on my master cut-out switch on the auto pilot and began to feel for control over the elevators with the elevator knob. There was a brief response, I
thought, but it did not last and I was still in a steep dive, still picking up speed. I
could see the surf on the beach on the south end of Samal Island very clearly. It
felt as if I was looking straight down.

"I remember then thinking 'Jesus, we are going to hit—I should push the bail-
out bell, but nobody could make it anyway.' While I was thinking this, I started
rolling the trim tab back. The damn thing worked and we sailed out of the dive. I
don't know how much altitude we had left, but I will never forget being able to see

those damned waves in the moonlight, at any rate I left my power on and got her reasonably level using the trim tab and we sailed out of Davao Gulf and took up a heading for Owi.

"We lucked out going home. Those Pratt and Whitneys ran perfectly all the way and the weather was calm. The flight engineers assessed the damage and reported huge gaping holes, that our main elevator control cables had been cut, that we had no hydraulic pressure because of severed lines and the electrical system was erratic because of torn wires and conduit. We had three crewmen wounded, with masses of fragments of metal in their backs. From this we thought that we had been struck by a large shell causing the big holes in the bottom of the aircraft just in back of the bomb bay keel between the two waist windows, and also throwing fragments through the sides tearing out the cables, longerons and tearing a hole in the top. Actually it was cannon fire that cut the cables on the sides and blew the top out as well as wounding the men.

"It was all hard to figure out and we were more concerned with helping the wounded men than trying to repair the cables. The engineers worked hard with pliers and spare wire trying to splice the cables, but whenever I put pressure on the yoke the splices would part. We decided I should continue to fly home on the trim tab and that we would try to disturb the trim of the aircraft as little as possible by all sitting still. This is why we lucked out on the weather because I'm convinced I never could have made it if we had hit turbulence.

"When we approached Owi, control told me that they might request that I ditch because they had the entire day strike almost ready to line up for take off and they didn't want to take a chance of my crashing and blocking the runway. I reported to them that I did not have good elevator control and did not think I could ditch it, and we had wounded men aboard. So they agreed I could take a crack at landing. I swung the old lady down south of the island in a big gradual turn and got her headed north on a long slow final approach. We figured if we could get fluid back into the hydraulic system we would have enough to operate the brakes with maybe one shot if we cranked everything else down by hand. So we collected fluids in the customary manner of shot up bomber crews . . . grapefruit juice, coffee and water from canteens, urine and spit.

"On the approach we cranked the wheels down, but I did use hydraulic power to put down about twenty degrees of flap and lock them. I just kept on easy power and played the trim tab over the fence and made the best goddamn landing I ever made in my life. Right at the end of the strip I popped on the brakes. They lasted for a second or two and then went out so I ground looped it right in front of the palm stumps.

"Everybody was excited and kept looking at the plane. The two sides of the rear of the fuselage were intact but the top had a hole blown just above the waist windows and the bottom was shredded.

"Inspecting the torn condition of the bottom we found strange pieces of metal and glass sticking in it and only then realised that we had been struck by another aircraft. This was when I remembered a big orange boom I had seen off in the night and I felt satisfied that the twin engined fighter I had seen in the search lights had attacked us from the rear, collided with us and crashed. So we reported the mission as such."

On the ground at Davao a Japanese night fighter squadron was congratulating Warrant Officer Yoshimasa Nakagawa and his observer for destroying an American intruder. They had taken off to intercept *Miss Liberty* and were closing in when the cannon jammed and it seemed that the enemy bomber would escape. The Japanese pilot decided he would ram, and his propeller slashed into the bomber's fuselage. Nakagawa reported that the big American aircraft started to fall immediately. His plane, its canopy smashed, kept flying. His eye had been gashed by flying glass and the wind buffeting his face forced him to turn sideways in his seat, but he managed to control the battered plane. When the bomber started to level off again Nakagawa was about to repeat the attack, but the American plane reportedly faltered and plunged into the water. The damaged Japanese fighter landed safely back at its base.

Twenty years later Roland Fisher and Yoshimasa Nakagawa would meet, after Fisher read of the "loss" of *Miss Liberty* in a book about the Japanese suicide pilots.

* * *

The heavies and mediums hit southern Mindanao on September 6, when the B-24s bombed the Santa Ana dock area and eleven Air Apaches struck Buayan airdrome on southern Mindanao, shooting up four planes on the field and bombing buildings around the area. The Liberators' escort of 475th Group Lightnings met no interceptors, but Thirteenth Air Force P-38s with the Mitchells took part in the

Headquarters P-38s in the 475th Group, *Carrie's* spinners are painted in the three squadron colors, red, yellow, and blue. The plane was named for the pilot's wife and the yellow rose was borrowed from a Four Roses advertisement.
Major Oliver McAfee's Lightning at Middelburg, on the way to the Philippines. Like all

strafing and shot down a hapless Topsy transport as it tried to land. After this strike Whitehead suspended all missions against southern Mindanao, and although the bombing had not been as heavy as MacArthur had wanted, the Japanese abandoned their airfields.

The Fifth's attention turned toward the Celebes, an island lying between the Moluccas and Borneo, which had been given its plural designation by early explorers confused by its peculiar shape, which led them to believe there were two islands. Getting there would strain the B-24s from either Biak or Darwin, but fortunately the most worthwhile targets were located where even B-25s staging through Noemfoor could attack them. On the long northeastern peninsula, centering around Menado, the Japanese had built three airfields. Less was known about the southeastern peninsula, but the enemy had developed five new airfields there in addition to the old strips at Kendari and Pomelaa. At the beginning of September the Japanese were thought to have about one hundred and eighty planes on the island.

The Air Apaches flew the first large attack against the area on August 24, attacking shipping and strafing and bombing stores. After that only recon planes and night-flying B-24s were over the Celebes until September 2, weather conditions stopping more B-25 strikes. That day the Air Apaches again hit the shipping, but the antiaircraft crews, aided by gunners on the minelayer *Itsukushima*—which the Air Apaches had damaged on August 24—put up the most deadly flak since Rabaul. Two B-25s were shot down, two more were badly damaged, and the mission showed that Celebes was too heavily defended for the mediums. Next day the Liberators went out. Weather again interfered with the fighter cover and the Japanese intercepted the three B-24 groups; over Lembeh Strait the attacks were not closely pressed, although the Red Raiders shot down two Tonys. The Jolly Rogers were attacked persistently over Langoan by ten Zekes, Tojos, and Hamps, losing a B-24 and claiming two more fighters, as well as destroying thirteen on the ground.

After these early raids Japanese resistance ebbed. On September 4, when strikes from Biak and Owi were canceled by weather, Flying Circus B-24s from Darwin made a night attack on Kendari, and the following day heavies from Biak and Owi returned to attack Langoan, destroying or badly damaging seventeen Japanese aircraft on the ground. On September 7 the B-24s hit warehouses, factories, and the army headquarters at Menado, and a day later bombed Langoan again. A week-long series of missions was sent to crater the airstrips with heavy bombs, and after these raids photos showed that the three runways were so wrecked that the few remaining enemy planes in the northeastern Celebes could not be flown from them. However, the Japanese were filling the craters and the airfields would require continuing attention if Morotai was to be secure.

While the long-range aircraft had been working over the Palaus, southern Mindanao, and Celebes, other units had been trying to obliterate the Japanese airfields in the Vogelkop and along the left flank of MacArthur's advance. Over three hundred tons of bombs rained on the Ambon, Boeroe, and Ceram fields, and the importance of the campaign was underlined by the enemy's ability to slip night raiders into Netherlands New Guinea to harass Biak and Owi.

During the first two weeks of September the Allies stepped up their attacks. The Thirteenth's B-24 concentrated on the Japanese airstrips while the Fifth threw everything into softening the northern Moluccas and isolating Morotai. Fighters dive-bombed villages, supply dumps, and airfields, the Mitchells and A-20s strafed airfields and targets of opportunity. Altogether the Fifth dropped over three hundred and sixty tons of bombs into the Moluccas leading up to the invasion, although Morotai got off lightly, partly to avoid revealing the Allied objective and partly because there were no really worthwhile targets there. The 38th Group had flown a couple of treetop missions against the island and strafed and bombed a supposed radar installation on September 12; they swept the invasion area the next day and on D-Day two B-25s finished the job neatly by spraying the landing area with insecticide.

The stunning success of the carrier planes in the Palaus and Moluccas, combined with a report from a rescued Navy pilot that there were very few Japanese on Leyte, caused Halsey to suggest to Nimitz that he cancel all the Palaus operations except the capture of Ulithi as a fleet anchorage. MacArthur could then use the spare forces to go into Leyte immediately, with the carrier planes providing cover until the airfields could be restored or built ashore. This daring proposition was based on a cursory estimate of damage and incorrect information from Leyte, but might have succeeded. Nimitz, MacArthur, and the Joint Chiefs in Washington were all unwilling to eliminate the Palaus but they did favor releasing the forces required for Yap and using them to occupy Leyte, with a target date of October 20 instead of two months later. MacArthur's planned operations between Morotai and Leyte would also have to be canceled.

Truly the queen of the skies. This stripped-down B-17F flew combat with the 43rd Group as *Talisman* and carried General MacArthur over Nadzab in September 1943. When this photo was taken she had become *War Horse,* personal transport for Major General J. L. Frink, Services of Supply commander in the Southwest Pacific. (Frank Smith)

The Palau landings began on September 15 and Angaur was easily taken in five days, but Peleliu became a slow and savage battle as the Japanese fell back to fortifications honeycombing the ridge which formed the backbone of the island. Ulithi was occupied on September 23, Ngesebus two days later, and even Peleliu was considered secure on October 13. The long-range bomber force scheduled for Angaur was the Seventh Air Force's 494th Bomb Group, "Kelly's Cobras," but its field would not be ready to operate in full strength until late November. So the Palaus were of no value in the aerial preparation for Leyte, and operations in support of the landings in Leyte Gulf would depend on Morotai, where unopposed landings also began in the morning of September 15. Patrols scattered small bands of enemy troops, and offshore islands needed for radar sites were seized. The ground campaign on Morotai was over by October 4, and direct support had not been needed.

Morotai had to be prepared fast if the Leyte operations were to begin on October 20. The abandoned Japanese airfield was not as promising as a good site at Wama, where four thousand feet of steel mat were down by October 4. A second site, later called Pitoe, was selected for a bomber strip. At Kenney's request Wama was extended and nearly complete by October 20, although it had been open to fighters for over two weeks and Hutchinson had immediately brought in the 8th Fighter Group's P-38s. The 418th Night Fighter Squadron with its new P-61s arrived the next day, two flights of the 2nd Emergency Rescue Squadron moved in, and on October 17 the 38th Bomb Group and two squadrons of 35th Group P-47s were there. The 82nd Recon Squadron flew to Wama and Navy Venturas and Liberators were at Pitoe. These were the air forces at Morotai for the invasion of Leyte Gulf.

Japanese resistance had been slight, although they had anticipated both the Palaus and Moluccas attacks. It seemed that they simply wrote off both and drew a new line at the Philippines. Night attacks against Morotai were aggressive but never seriously threatened the operation or use of the base. The island, mountainous in the north and surrounded by land masses in the south, frustrated the use of radar and attacking planes could bomb the packed airfield area with little warning. Between the day of the landing and the end of January 1945, the Japanese sent eighty-two raids, mostly on moonlit nights. Many of the one- and two-plane intrusions caused no damage at all, but the worst, on November 22, killed two men and destroyed fifteen planes. Morotai was a difficult base to defend, but fulfilled its purpose.

The Balikpapan Missions

After the Flying Circus strikes on Balikpapan and Soerabaja in 1943, Kenney had observed that within two weeks "the Japs were short of aviation fuel at all of their fields from Ambon to Wewak and even at Palau and Truk." Ever since then he had been wanting to strike again, and by September 1944 it was estimated that the refineries were processing about five and a quarter million barrels of crude oil annually. Although the Japanese were believed to have two years of fuel supplies in the homeland, any reduction in aviation fuel would hamper operations at their forward bases. Kenney had tried to get some B-29s to attack from the Darwin area, but his requests were refused. Unable to get the Superfortresses, Kenney, Streett, and Whitehead planned to use Liberators from Netherlands New Guinea. They were going to wait until a strip was lengthened to take B-24s at Sansapor but Streett had suggested that he could use his two Thirteenth Air Force heavy groups from Noemfoor, rather than expose the Fifth's heavies at Sansapor. Kenney agreed to this and Whitehead offered to "lend" the Fifth's three groups whenever Streett wanted them for the series of strikes.

Balikpapan lay over one thousand miles from Noemfoor, but after careful tests the thirteenth Air Force prepared strict instructions for fuel conservation which would allow the B-24s to get there and back, although their normal ammunition load was cut by 60 per cent. It was decided that the Fifth would support the first, third, and fourth raids, and they preferred to remove all excess weight from their aircraft, such as armor plate, rather than carry less ammunition. Fighter cover was not available.

As the Thirteenth prepared, the Fifth struck Celebes targets as part of an effort to cut down opposition along the way to Borneo. In the afternoon of September 29 the Jolly Rogers staged up from Biak and the three groups were ready for the first strike. Shortly after midnight the Thirteenth's Bomber Barons began taking off, with their Long Rangers and the Fifth's Jolly Rogers following ninety seconds apart until seventy-two were lumbering through the darkness. The Bomber Barons were over the Pandansari refinery nine hours later and dropped their bombs as cloud drifted over the target. The Long Rangers followed five minutes later. The Jolly Rogers' twenty-three planes were last, and when they found solid cloud cover over Balikpapan only one of the squadrons attempted to bomb the target. The crews were ready for potent antiaircraft fire but no one had guessed that the Japanese had stationed one of their finest naval air units to defend Balikpapan. The pilots were skilled and cool. Two had met the bombers at the coast of the Celebes and had stayed with them all the way, keeping just out of range, guiding the gunners on the ground. The Thirteenth lost three B-24s, the Jolly Rogers lost one, and the three groups claimed nine fighters shot down. The strike proved that missions to Balikpapan were possible and on October 3 the Thirteenth's two groups made the second attack, but the Long Rangers lost seven B-24s—intolerable losses.

For the next raid Streett borrowed the three Fifth Air Force groups to go over the target at medium altitude and draw antiaircraft fire while the Thirteenth went over high and took on the fighters. Fifty Thunderbolt pilots went to Kenney asking to be allowed to escort the B-24s to Balikpapan, fly back to a selected spot in the Celebes, jump, and rely on being picked up by the Catalinas. Happily there was no longer a need for such extreme measures, because the experiments with long-range fighter flights during the spring and summer were paying off. By hanging a three-hundred-and-ten-gallon tank on one P-47 wing, and a one-hundred-and-sixty-five-gallon tank under the other, the latest model Thunderbolts from Morotai (and the P-38s from Sansapor or Morotai) could make it to Balikpapan. It would be hard on the pilots but it could be done. The plan called for the 40th and 41st Squadrons of the old 35th Group to sweep the sky over the target just before the bombers ar-

The 35th Fighter Group moved to Morotai in late September 1944. Improvements in new P-47D-23s like *Miss Lorraine* helped enable the fat Thunderbolt to make the long flight to the Balikpapan oil targets. (RAAF)

rived, and the 9th Squadron of the 49th Group would be the escort. In addition, 63rd Squadron Snoopers would heckle the Balikpapan defenses and try to keep the Japanese pilots awake all night. Shortly before the bombers were due a Thirteenth Air Force Snooper would scatter "chaff" to confuse the Japanese radar and draw their fighters up on a false alarm.

The elaborate plan began unfolding when seven 63rd Squadron Liberators harassed Balikpapan during the night of October 8, and five more continued the work the next night. By nine o'clock on October 10 an 868th Squadron B-24 had dropped a thousand pounds of aluminum strips on a course leading to Balikpapan, and between ten-ten and ten forty-five sixteen Thunderbolts arrived over the target at about twenty thousand feet. They jumped about thirty fighters and knocked down twelve at the cost of one P-47. The two Thirteenth Air Force groups should have gone over the target just before the Fifth, and all the B-24s were supposed to have completed their bombing runs within ten minutes, but the Fifth had arrived at the rendezvous first and waited as long as their fuel permitted before proceeding. The Jolly Rogers attacked both the Pandansari and Edeleanu refineries, fighting their way through fighters. One Liberator was exploded by an aerial phosphorous bomb, but the gunners claimed sixteen enemy planes. The Red Raiders got most of their bombs on Pandansari, although the fighter attacks threw some of the bombers off the mark. One 33rd Squadron Liberator was so badly shot up that it had to crash-land on Batoedaka Island, but on the way down it destroyed six fighters. A Zeke rammed a B-24 and exploded it, and another was crippled and methodically shot down. The 19th Squadron Liberator flown by Lieutenant Roy Parker was lashed by a storm of expended .50-caliber cartridges which knocked out all the glass in the front of the aircraft and punched a couple of hundred holes in the thin skin of the aircraft; their cockpit littered with broken glass, the pilots struggled to fasten a replacement windshield in place and began the long flight home. The Red Raiders claimed nineteen fighters.

By this time the Japanese were slowing down, allowing Ken's Men to bomb the paraffin refinery and storage area without loss, although their gunners claimed thirteen enemy fighters. When the Thirteenth arrived the enemy was no longer so eager, and eleven P-38s attacked sixteen fighters and shot down six. Flying one of the P-38s was the "retired" Major Richard Bong, who scored his twenty-ninth and thirtieth victories. Under close questioning by General Kenney, Bong reported that he had been forced to fight both in self-defense, but Kenney recalls noticing that according to the combat report the first had been shot down at fifteen hundred feet . . . and the second at eighteen thousand.

The next mission was essentially the same, except for the addition of Thirteenth Air Force P-38s. On October 14 the 35th Group P-47s shot down nineteen Japanese fighters over Balikpapan, the 41st Squadron lost two aircraft over the target, one of them knocked down by Lightnings. Two 40th Squadron Thunderbolts could not get back to Morotai because of mechanical failures but both these pilots, and the pilot shot down by the P-38s, were picked up by Catalinas. The Fifth was led over the Edeleanu refinery by the Jolly Rogers, right on schedule. The gunners claimed nine fighters at the cost of one B-24, and another had been lost somewhere along the way. Escorting P-38s of the 9th, Headhunters, and 432nd Squadrons got another sixteen Japanese fighters. The Thirteenth's B-24s smothered their target without loss and this was the first really successful mission in the series—and also the last effective strike against Balikpapan. On October 18 the Thirteenth's mission was spoiled by weather and after that the B-24s of both air forces were needed elsewhere, but the operation had given invaluable experience in long-range flying which would pay off during the coming campaign. The bombing had only scratched the oil targets and the Japanese could get the refineries operating again in a short time, without a very great reduction in the annual output, but by then the Allies would hold the bases they needed to blockade the whole of the Netherlands East Indies.

Leyte: Foothold in the Philippines

Halsey's task force had met little resistance over Mindanao and moved on to the Visayas, where the carrier planes again roamed almost at will. They destroyed scores of Japanese planes on the ground in the two days of strikes, and there was no real retaliation. During September Kenney had become convinced the Japanese air force had just about had enough and thought that "the gamble was worthwhile."

Actual Japanese strength in the Philippines was far greater than Halsey had believed, and the enemy had a very accurate idea of what the Allies were planning. During September they predicted a two-pronged attack on Luzon by MacArthur from the south and Nimitz from the Pacific. They believed MacArthur would gain

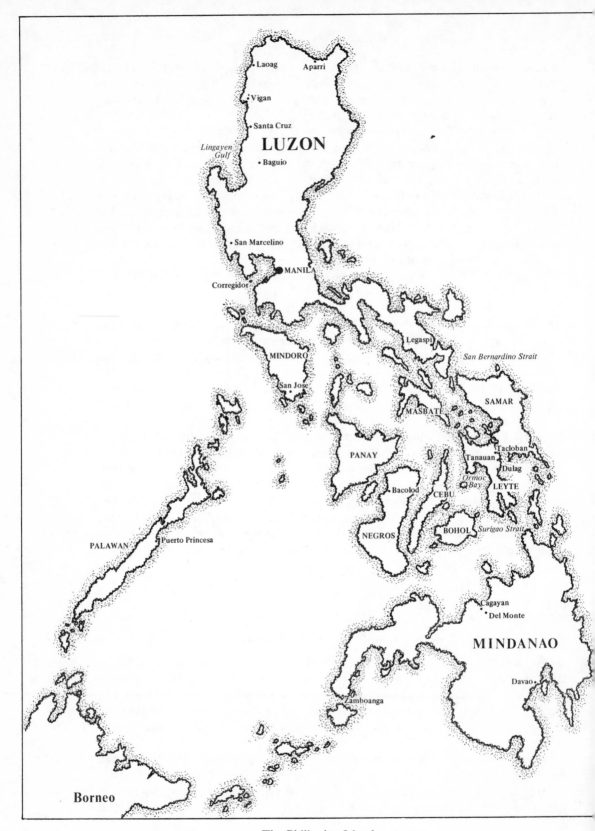

The Philippine Islands.

a foothold in Davao and Sarangani, move to Zamboanga, Leyte, or Samar, and then prepare to invade Luzon. They also knew the attack was within Allied capability in October, although they were not sure where the first invasion would be. The Morotai landing pointed to southern Mindanao, but the Palaus landings allowed a movement straight into Leyte. They planned to put five divisions on Luzon, five in the southern Philippines, with five more to be deployed from Formosa, China, and Korea after the Allies had made their landing, a scheme which required far more shipping than was actually available. When General Tomoyuki Yamashita, the "Tiger of Malaya," assumed command of the ground forces in the Philippines he tried to convince his supreme commander that the troops on Leyte and Mindanao should only fight a delaying action and that the main battle should be for Luzon. He found that the plan was not to be modified.

The Allies had little time to prepare for the operation. To Leyte's northeast lay the mountainous island of Samar, across the narrow San Juanico Strait. To the south across Surigao Strait was Mindanao, and to the west lay the rest of the Visayas. Aircraft and patrol boats had been able to keep Japanese troops from moving between the big island of Halmahera and Morotai, a distance of thirteen miles, but whether a similar blockade could be maintained between Leyte and the rest of the Visayas by the carrier planes until Kenney's aircraft moved in was questionable.

Available maps of Leyte were inadequate, but the main problem would certainly be weather, because the island lay near the path of the Philippine typhoons, and the northeast monsoon dominated conditions between November and April; this put any planned airfield construction in jeopardy. Leyte was beyond the range of Kenney's planes in New Guinea, so the Allied Air Forces were forced to play a limited part in the early preparations. They were responsible for the air garrison to be established on Leyte and undertook to provide direct support for ground operations as soon as fighters and light bombers could be based there. Co-ordination with the carrier planes was worked out at Hollandia late in September. They were to operate south of a strip along the north coast of Mindanao and were not to attack targets in waters east of the island or in the Mindanao Sea. As soon as the B-24s were ready at Morotai they would extend their operations to include the Visayas other than Leyte and Samar. The Fifth was the assault air force, with the Thirteenth backing it up as requested.

On the eve of the invasion Allied estimates were optimistic. The Navy, presuming that the Japanese aircraft carrier groups were not ready to enter combat again, felt that there was no chance of the enemy risking major portions of their fleet. Other projections pointed to their conserving what was left of their air power to protect their homeland, the Ryukyus and Formosa, rather than reinforcing the Philippines. It was believed that there would be over three hundred fighters and bombers able to attack the Leyte beachhead. The Allies were not ready for the kamikaze attacks.

Through September and into October there was little change in targets for the Fifth Air Force—it was business as usual as the Japanese moved aircraft into the Celebes to attack Morotai and desperately tried to keep their airfields operational. The Vogelkop and Ambon, Boeroe, and Ceram areas were continually hit to protect the build-up of Allied aircraft in northwestern New Guinea. The toughest fights had been during the Balikpapan missions, and Japanese aircraft within range of the bombers in other areas shunned the defensive role and seemed there solely to be used against airfields. Morotai was a magnet to these raiders.

There was limited Allied activity against the Philippines. The Red Raiders and Ken's Men hit Davao on September 18 as the Jolly Rogers bombed oil stores nearby. The returning crews reported that the Davao airfields had been repaired, but they met no interceptors and only weak antiaircraft fire. The B-24s went out to bomb oil storage tanks and warehouses at Zamboanga on October 7, escorted by 8th Fighter Group Lightnings. The P-38s found a cluster of floatplanes and destroyed six, set fire to three ships, and strafed San Roque airdrome.

On October 9 the carriers attacked Marcus Island, which Halsey thought would confuse the Japanese. Then they surprised Okinawa the following day. Sailing south they sent their fighters over southern Luzon on October 11 and the next morning Formosa was the target. But the Japanese had not been misled—they sent their Second Air Fleet south and had been able to reinforce Formosa during the Luzon strike. They had little luck reaching the American fleet on October 13, but they torpedoed a cruiser at dusk. Halsey wanted to tow the damaged ship out, and sent his fighters to Formosa on October 14 to keep the skies clear. That evening the Japanese again got through and torpedoed another cruiser. The reports in Japan were grossly exaggerated and there were joyous celebrations over the sinking of "fifty-seven American warships." The Imperial Navy Headquarters ordered a task force to go out and finish off the remnants of the American fleet.

Halsey intercepted the coded orders and deployed his cripples as bait to force a decisive engagement. He radioed MacArthur that now he needed all his carriers and their support would not be available for Leyte. Kenney was worried, and extended his aircraft's search patterns to cover the southern Philippines and ordered the Thirteenth's B-24s to Morotai. From October 18 MacArthur cleared targets in the western Visayas, and the Fifth began heavy bomber attacks on Mindanao and long-range fighter sweeps over the island from Morotai.

The Japanese on Mindanao had to be suppressed. On October 16 P-38s of the 35th Squadron and the Headhunters set fire to three vessels in Cagayan Harbor, routed a troop of mounted cavalry, shot up a Sally and a staff car at an airfield, then drove along the highway to Valencia, sweeping fifty or sixty Japanese vehicles off the road. The next day they went to Zamboanga and destroyed a floatplane and left a cargo vessel afire. Three groups of B-24s hit enemy barracks and port installations the same day, and bombed Menado in the Celebes as the fighter sweeps over Mindanao continued. On October 19 the 38th Group's B-25s flew their first mission from Morotai and bombed Malabang airfield on Mindanao; next day, the day of the Leyte landing, the Fifth's B-24s hit Japanese headquarters at Davao, while the B-25s bombed an airdrome on Negros Island. The Headhunters strafed trucks and barges in southern Mindanao and 35th Group Thunderbolts roared over the airdromes on Negros as the Fifth supported the Leyte operation from afar.

* * *

Halsey's trap, meanwhile, nearly succeeded. Enemy cruisers and destroyers ventured forth on October 15, but a scouting plane was evidently able to warn them of the true situation and they pulled back. Halsey rescued his cripples and returned to support the Leyte landing after all. The fast carriers struck Luzon for three days until October 19 and two task groups were ready to support the landings with air strikes against Cebu, Negros, Panay, and northern Mindanao, while two more stood by to the north.

On October 20 the weather was good and at ten o'clock the troops started ashore near San Jose and Dulag. The landings were not difficult and the Japanese had pulled back from their shore positions, but the naval bombardment had been spectacular rather than thorough. Looking over the beaches later that day Kenney saw concrete pillboxes which had not been touched and reflected that "if these Japs had been of the same calibre of those at Buna or around Wau and Salamaua, we would have had a casualty list that would have rivalled Tarawa."

The air opposition was vicious but scattered: a cruiser was torpedoed during the afternoon and early the next morning a suicide plane crippled another.

The first days after the landings were promising for the invading Sixth Army. Tacloban airstrip was captured on October 20, and Dulag the next day. Repairs to Tacloban, essentially a sandspit just over a mile long and three hundred yards wide, were started immediately but there were problems because it was a convenient place to land stores quickly. This caused so much interference with the operation that Kenney was forced to step in and tell the Army that at dawn on October 25 anything still obstructing the strip would be bulldozed into the sea, and this finally got things moving.

Early Japanese attacks on the beachhead were only a lead-up to what was coming, and essentially an adjunct to their main naval effort. On October 18, as soon as it was known that a landing would be made, the enemy had put their Philippines defense plan into operation. The main battleship and cruiser strength of the Japanese navy fueled at Brunei, Borneo, and sortied in two echelons on October 22. The major part of the force, under Admiral Keno Kurita, skirted the western coast of Palawan Island and headed toward San Bernardino Strait between Luzon and Samar islands. The smaller force of two battleships, a cruiser, and four destroyers under Vice-Admiral Shoji Nishimura sailed through the Sulu Sea to force an entrance at Surigao Strait between Mindanao and the southern tip of Leyte. Another force—two heavy cruisers, a light cruiser, and four destroyers under Vice-Admiral Kiyohide Shima—left Formosa on October 21 and moved south to assist Nishimura's effort. In the afternoon of October 20 four aircraft carriers with understrength and partly trained air groups, two battleships converted into carriers, three light cruisers, and eight destroyers under Vice-Admiral Jisaburo Ozawa made a general course toward Luzon to decoy American warships to the north. Enemy planes of the Second Air Fleet, supposed to cover Kurita from land bases as he moved in, began arriving at Luzon bases before October 23.

The Battle of Leyte Gulf

Kurita had been instructed to reach Tacloban at dawn on October 25, and destroy the American shipping and the troops ashore. His plan was to break through San

Bernardino Strait the night before, while Nishimura passed through Surigao for a junction with him in Leyte Gulf. The plan was audacious, but there were problems —the Japanese land-based aircraft using the island of Luzon as a vast aircraft carrier had already been drained, and co-ordination between ship and shore was far from perfect. Also there were, in effect, three independent fleet commanders.

The Allies were alerted and on October 21 Halsey warned MacArthur to get the shipping out of Leyte Gulf as quickly as he could. MacArthur tartly replied that this was the first time he was operating beyond the reach of his own air force and he expected air cover from the Navy, as had been promised. By October 23 the objective of the Japanese fleet was obvious. That morning submarines sank two Japanese cruisers, including Kurita's flagship, and another had to retire with damage. Kurita moved his command to the huge battleship *Yamato* and pressed on. In the confusion Nishimura slipped through Balabac Strait and headed for Surigao. Halsey deployed his forces: one task group was east of Luzon, another off San Bernardino Strait, one off Surigao Strait; the fourth had returned to Ulithi to refuel and resupply and would not be ready for five days.

The task group off San Bernardino located Kurita southeast of Mindoro in the morning of October 24, and the group off Surigao Strait intercepted Nishimura approaching the entrance of the Mindanao Sea shortly after. Nishimura was attacked immediately but despite damage his ships continued toward Surigao. Shima's force was not located until later in the morning but as soon as all the sightings were in Halsey ordered two task groups to concentrate toward San Bernardino, striking Kurita on the way. One group was hindered by attacks which so badly damaged the carrier USS *Princeton* that it had to be sunk, and the other group had to give some attention to Nishimura. As a result the attacks against Kurita fell to the group off San Bernardino Strait, the weakest of the three. During the afternoon all three groups sent out strikes. Kurita lost a battleship and a cruiser was badly damaged— unable to get air cover, he decided temporarily to reverse course.

All that day Halsey was concerned about the location of the Japanese carriers, until in late afternoon a plane found Ozawa's "Main Body." The reports of his pilots persuaded Halsey that Kurita had been so badly hurt he could be little danger even if he made it through, and a plan to form a battleship force to guard San Bernardino was shelved. Halsey knew MacArthur expected him to protect San Bernardino, but he considered it "childish" to do so while Japanese carriers were getting ready to attack. Although worried about the ability of the escort carriers to deal with the enemy at Surigao, he decided to leave San Bernardino unguarded and head north to attack the enemy carrier force at dawn.

Off Leyte, Admiral Thomas Kinkaid was getting ready to fight Nishimura and Shima—he presumed that San Bernardino was guarded and his forces were concentrated off Surigao. In the early morning of October 25 Nishimura was defeated and forced to retreat, and only a cruiser and destroyer escaped. Shima's ships were following half an hour behind; a cruiser and his flagship were damaged and he pulled back without pressing further. Although the American warships had not suffered any losses they were low on fuel, torpedoes, and armor-piercing ammunition, carrying shells principally intended for shore bombardment.

When the air attacks ceased on the morning of October 24, Kurita changed course and headed again for San Bernardino, boldly driving through the treach-

Tacloban was a scene of barely organized chaos as the Navy fighters sought refuge. In all, nearly seventy aircraft landed there during the naval battles, while forty more made it to Dulag, twenty miles south. Twenty-eight were destroyed landing on the unfinished airstrips.

erous strait at twenty knots. Halsey discounted the reports that Kurita had turned again, and continued north.

During the morning of October 25 Kinkaid's sixteen escort carriers were ranged off Samar and Leyte. They had sent out two air strikes and got Nishimura's last cruiser. The first indication that Kurita was near came early in the morning—the carrier aircraft attacked as the eighteen-inch guns of the Japanese opened fire from fifteen miles away. Kinkaid was in desperate danger. His battleships, out in Surigao Strait, were old and slower than the Japanese ships; his carriers were light and could not fight the kind of warships facing them. Kurita was just three hours from Leyte Gulf, and it seemed there was little to stop him. Now Kinkaid knew there was no battleship force guarding San Bernardino, and he asked Halsey for help.

Somehow, the tiny carriers held Kurita back. Tossed about by the huge Japanese shells, they stayed afloat as smaller shells tore straight through their thin plates and failed to explode. One carrier went down under close fire, destroyers and destroyer escorts rushed in and out of their own smoke screen to launch torpedoes, and three of them were sunk. Then rain temporarily hid the carriers, but they were attacked by six suicide planes and two were badly damaged. A third was torpedoed and listed, but stayed afloat. Planes could not return to the stricken ships, and many of them landed at Tacloban, where they were refueled and rearmed by air force crews. They kept up their attacks and Kurita was beginning to worry as time passed, because he had heard the calls for reinforcement. Still intending to carry out his mission, he ordered his ships to regroup and wheeled northward. He was far behind schedule and thought the shipping at Leyte might have escaped; he had lost three heavy cruisers to the planes and believed he was fighting a far stronger force and that once inside Leyte Gulf he would be trapped and destroyed. Shortly after noon he decided to return north, not realizing how close he had come to destroying the little carriers and entering Leyte Gulf, where he would have caused terrible chaos among the merchant vessels.

To the north, Halsey was closing in on Ozawa's "Main Body"; that morning three of the enemy carriers were reported dead in the water, and the opposing forces were about forty-five miles apart. Halsey ordered one task group to go back and help the escort carriers, but the rest kept on. Finally Nimitz radioed, asking where the battleship force—supposedly guarding San Bernardino—was, and a furious Halsey broke off the pursuit and returned to help the escort carriers. With two of his carrier groups and two of the fastest battleships he raced toward San Bernardino at twenty-eight knots. One carrier group and a cruiser screen remained to finish off Ozawa's carriers.

The Battle of Leyte Gulf was over except for the sinking of cripples by both sides. Carrier planes made a long-range strike on Kurita's fleet in midmorning, and some of the American planes had to ditch on the way back, while others landed at Tacloban. A second strike, like the first, claimed no more than damage and in the late afternoon the escort carrier planes made their last attack. Halsey reached San Bernardino at midnight but there was only one destroyer left, and it became the victim of a small surface battle. Kurita was heading west with his four remaining battleships, cruisers, and destroyers. Next morning Halsey's planes caught up with him and sank a cruiser and a destroyer, ending the naval action in the battle.

Participation by the Fifth had been restricted by the lack of co-ordination with the Navy, and by the fact that Morotai had been captured only about a month before and could hardly meet the requirements of even one B-24 squadron. At Biak the three groups of Liberators were briefed on a "golden opportunity" to destroy Japanese ships and two groups of B-25s were alerted on Morotai, but Kurita's shipping never came within range.

The Fifth's Liberators went out before dawn on October 25, but solid cloud prevented the planned rendezvous on the northern coast of Mindanao, and when the assembly point was changed, fifty-six B-24s lumbered in from all directions. The bomber crews lacked information about the location of the Japanese fleet and the leader by chance chose a new point in view of a Japanese light cruiser and destroyer. The Japanese warships fired among the B-24s as they milled around trying to organize themselves. Finally the Liberators tried to bomb the two ships in squadron flights or singly but they were at ten thousand feet and the Japanese were able to maneuver away from their bombs. Near misses were the best they could claim and other B-24s from the Thirteenth Air Force had no better luck. Thirty B-25s from Morotai were within sight of the ships when they had to turn back because of fuel shortage and the whole mission was a "dismal failure" which Whitehead attributed mainly to the lack of sound intelligence data. The following day the Thirteenth sent its B-24s out and the Fifth sent a strike from Biak and Owi. The Bomber Barons attacked a crippled light cruiser, the *Abukuma,* and an escorting destroyer and did more damage, setting the cruiser afire. Then three Red Raiders got two more hits and fires and explosions wracked the warship as the destroyer moved in to rescue the survivors. In the early afternoon the *Abukuma* sank.

In all the Japanese had lost three battleships, four carriers, six heavy cruisers, four light cruisers, and eleven destroyers. Kurita had escaped with a force which included four battleships and could still threaten Allied operations in the Philippines, but essentially Japan was no longer a significant naval power.

* * *

The American troops on Leyte were still in a precarious position. The escort carriers had taken a battering and with the lack of fighter cover over the beaches the Philippine-based Japanese planes were able to make twelve attacks on October 25, sinking two landing ships at Tacloban, demolishing a warehouse, and damaging a concrete dock. The next morning they struck sixteen times in less than three hours and in the early afternoon a kamikaze crippled another escort carrier. The carriers were running low on food and ammunition, but the Navy was able to keep ten off Leyte until October 29, and although two of Halsey's fast carrier groups were forced to withdraw shortly after the fleet engagement, one task group remained to provide local patrols at Leyte.

The carriers simply could not provide the kind of beach cover for an operation like Leyte, and although Kenney had responded quickly to the Navy's need for help, there were problems. On October 26 two squadrons of 49th Group P-38s staged to Morotai while their ground crews at Tacloban were helping lay steel mat on the airstrip. In the early afternoon of October 27, as the last section was laid in the center of the runway, thirty-four Lightnings buzzed the strip and came in to land. One was wrecked but the rest of the 9th Squadron's planes quickly refueled; about five o'clock in the afternoon five enemy fighters came over, and the radar on Leyte gave about ten minutes' warning. Colonel George Walker, commander of the 49th Fighter Group, took off with Bob Morrissey, Jerry Johnson, and Dick Bong, who had "attached" himself to his old squadron once again. Walker had to come back with engine trouble but the others went on. Johnson got two and Morrissey and Bong one each. The fifth Japanese fighter escaped. The next morning Bong was flying over the Tacloban area to scout for promising sites for additional airdromes. He was airborne when the radar picked up two Japanese fighters and gave him the details. He got both in two quick bursts. The fight was seen from Tacloban—that made thirty-three.

The thirty-three P-38s which were responsible for the defense of Leyte were packed together and made a choice target. In the morning of October 29 an Oscar raced along the strip, destroying one Lightning and damaging three more, and accidents further reduced the number. The P-38s had destroyed ten Japanese planes, but only twenty were flyable by the morning of October 30. That afternoon the 8th Squadron arrived, and another six Japanese were shot down in sporadic battles over the island during the day. On the last day of the month six 421st Squadron Black Widows flew to Tacloban, extended by then to four thousand feet, but a day later the situation was again critical. There were two heavy morning raids which blew holes in the airstrip, damaged a P-38, sank a destroyer, and crippled three other ships. Kenney brought one squadron from the 475th Fighter Group up to Tacloban on November 2 but could not assure total fighter cover until the ground forces provided the necessary facilities.

To help ease the pressure the Fifth also made sustained strikes against airfields in the central and southern Philippines, where the enemy planes were staging for

Lieutenant Dave Corts' *Skippy* was one of six 421st Night Fighter Squadron P-61s quickly brought forward to Tacloban to protect the strip during the hours of darkness. This squadron had scored the first Black Widow kill in the theater when one of its aircraft trailed and shot down a Dinah over Japen Island on July 7, 1944.

their attacks on Leyte. On October 28 Liberators went to Puerto Princesa on Palawan, where they blew up the strip, destroyed twenty-three aircraft on the ground, and, when they met no resistance at all, strafed the harbor at mast height. The long-range fighters and B-25s, flying from Morotai, swept the Japanese airfields. During November the Fifth lost no B-24s to fighters and only two to antiaircraft fire, but ground fire knocked down ten Mitchells. The fighters scored heavily—Lightnings from the 8th Fighter Group found Bacolod, Caroline, and Alicante airfields packed with Japanese planes on November 1. Earlier B-24 attacks had apparently exhausted the air cover and the P-38s promptly shot seven fighters out of the air, then methodically riddled about seventy-five more aircraft on the ground. Three Lightnings fell victim to antiaircraft fire but the pilot of one survived a crash landing at Leyte.

The ground personnel of the Red Raiders reached Leyte on November 15, where it was immediately obvious they could not obtain the necessary facilities. They were sent on to Angaur in the Palaus, where the Seventh Air Force's 494th Group had begun flying missions to the Philippines on November 17. By the end of the month the Red Raiders' Liberators had moved up from Owi and they were sent on a mission against Legaspi, an airfield on southern Luzon which the Japanese were using for staging. These two Liberator groups on Angaur were within easy range of Mindanao and the Visayas, and as soon as fighter cover was available they would hit Clark Field and Manila.

On Leyte, airfield development was slipping behind schedule. The rain was relentless and Whitehead summed it up by telling Kenney that "mud is still mud no matter how much you push it around with a bulldozer." The Japanese airstrips were not easily repaired and the engineers had to reconstruct them completely to meet the requirements. Tacloban was the main airstrip during the crucial times, Dulag was finally ready for fighters on November 19, and other fields were used to varying degrees. Obviously the scheduled build-up of aircraft in the Philippines was disrupted. On November 3, P-40s of the 110th Tactical Recon Squadron reached Leyte and the other two squadrons of the 475th Fighter Group began arriving on November 9. The 460th Squadron's Thunderbolts came in next day, covering attacks on a convoy on the way through. Two more squadrons of the 348th Group could not be based on Leyte until the first week of December, and while these units were hardly enough to protect Leyte itself, after December 5 the Lightnings were required to cover Allied convoys to Mindoro. Marine Corsairs were brought into Tacloban to help but there were no bombers on Leyte and even the fighters overtaxed the available facilities. The congestion reached such proportions that many damaged planes were simply pushed into the sea. The 110th Squadron P-40s and the 431st Squadron used Bayug, but by the middle of November the Lightnings were sinking into the mud and had to move to Tacloban. When steel matting was laid at Dulag the 475th Fighter Group was sent there.

Japanese air attacks on Leyte did not slow down and the preventive strikes against the staging bases were less effective than usual. During November the Japanese usually attacked at dawn, dusk, and at night. Later in the month Filipino guerrillas reported that enemy planes were being concealed in bamboo thickets five hundred yards away from the airstrip at La Carlota on Negros, and when the runway was destroyed they flew from a stretch of highway close by. These raiders were able to inflict heavy damage—on the morning of November 4 thirty-five Jap-

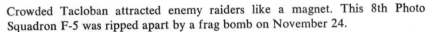

Crowded Tacloban attracted enemy raiders like a magnet. This 8th Photo Squadron F-5 was ripped apart by a frag bomb on November 24.

anese aircraft hit Tacloban from low level, killing four men, tearing up the runway, and destroying two P-38s and damaging thirty-nine other planes. Suicide planes crashed into the ships bringing in the ground echelon of the 345th Group, killing over one hundred men in the worst day of the war for the Air Apaches. On November 24 enemy bombers destroyed three Lightnings, damaged six other fighters, and sank a Liberty ship off Tacloban. In all, the enemy sent over a thousand sorties to Leyte before the end of the war. The Fifth's fighter pilots shot down more than three hundred of them, at the cost of only sixteen aircraft in combat.

The ground offensive was moving well, but the Japanese evidently thought their situation was not beyond hope. At the end of October, when the carriers withdrew and the beachhead was under heavy attack, they were able to get major reinforcements in, landing them at Ormoc on the west side of Leyte. Within two weeks of the landing they had brought in some twenty-two thousand troops, and these reinforcements cost the Army an easy victory.

The Japanese were buying time to bring in still more men. Three cargo ships, six destroyers, and four other vessels formed a convoy bringing in ten thousand troops, but this time the enemy was not able to avoid detection. Four Air Apache B-25s, at Tacloban as couriers, were loaded with bombs when the convoy was sighted late on November 9, and went out with sixteen Lightnings. The P-38s went in first, attacking the destroyers, which surrounded a transport as it off-loaded troops and supplies into barges. The B-25s came over the hills and attacked at mast height—Lieutenant Frederick Dick's B-25, its right vertical stabilizer completely shot away just before he reached the target, made a snap roll, skidded to the left, and righted itself in time to make a run on a destroyer. The crippled B-25 was last seen heading for Tacloban—but never arrived. The P-38s strafed and dive-bombed, and then P-40s bombed and shot up barges beached near Ormoc. Although none of the vessels was sunk, the deck equipment on the cargo ships was mangled; the troops could be unloaded that night, but much of their equipment could not.

Ormoc was too dangerous during daylight and the convoy pulled out before dawn on November 10, but at midday it ran into thirty B-25s from the 38th Bomb Group. They attacked at low level, each squadron dividing into two-plane elements to go after the vessels. Lieutenant Edwin Polanski's plane was leading the fourth flight of the 822nd, the first squadron to attack, through the intense antiaircraft fire. Polanski picked a destroyer that was head on to them and figured he would get it from bow to stern. The destroyer turned broadside just as he passed over so he let two bombs go. His engineer thought they hit but couldn't be sure of anything because as the B-25 passed over the warship it was jolted by a series of explosions, shook violently, and began sliding off on one wing. There had been four separate but concurrent impacts.

In the waist the radio operator, Sergeant Fred Hellman, saw the photographer on their plane crouching over, as if trying to shield himself. Hellman, right next to him, thought himself hurt. He was covered in blood and was dazed enough not to realize it was the wounded photographer's. The tail gunner had been trying to see the damage done to the shipping when he saw their wingman approaching them, weaving routinely. Just as they were hit the other B-25 erupted, breaking completely in two and falling in a cloud of black smoke.

A Mitchell from the 823rd Squadron of Colonel Ed Gavin's 38th Group makes a run on a destroyer in Ormoc Bay on November 10, 1944. Seconds later the ship's bow was blown off.

In the harbor there was chaos as the Japanese destroyers zigzagged around the transports, trying to protect themselves and at the same time keep the B-25s away from the cargo ships.

As Polanski's B-25 left the bay, the tail gunner saw more B-25s still coming in. Normally they would rendezvous with the rest of the formation, but Polanski did not know how long his B-25 would hold together, and there was a badly wounded man aboard. He headed directly for the strip. Fifteen minutes out, he was watching the badly torn underside of the left engine. Other than gradually decreasing oil pressure, his instruments told him nothing. As the plane banked toward the strip the engineer was watching the right wing, where there was a gaping tear six feet long and three feet across just behind the engine housing. The damaged left engine was smoking and one set of control cables was doing the work of two.

Polanski got the plane down and taxied off the strip to the waiting ambulance. The doctor looked at the wounded man and pulled a blanket over his face before the crew got a chance to ask how he was.

The 822nd had lost five of their eight planes. The 823rd Squadron, last over the target, lost two. The Japanese paid with two of their precious cargo vessels: the *Takatsu* exploded and sank and the *Kashi* went under a few hours later. A coast defense ship was beached and burned, and a destroyer headed back to Manila with its bow blown off. Carrier planes thwarted another attempt to land troops and supplies at Ormoc the next day.

*   *   *

Fresh American troops were brought in and the opposing armies both planned offensives, but the stalemate continued during November, although American air superiority was beginning to count. A Japanese division, which was to move by naval transports, had to be brought in by landing craft and sailboats. On November 24 Captain Rubel Archuleta led the P-40s of the 110th Recon to wipe out a small convoy which was hiding by day at Masbate Island, and guerrillas reported that fifteen hundred enemy troops had been killed. Four days later supplies and equipment were shipped from Manila during bad weather, but Navy patrol boats destroyed two small escort vessels and a cargo submarine. The survivors were not able to unload completely before dawn, and the P-40s sank two ships and a subchaser.

On November 30 it was decided to postpone the Mindoro invasion, originally scheduled for December 5, releasing shipping for an amphibious landing near Ormoc on December 7. The date of the Allied landing coincided with the arrival of a Japanese convoy, because the American and Japanese armies had selected almost the same dates for their offensives, and both air forces were out in strength. The Allied landing was accomplished without real difficulty and the P-38s of the 49th and 475th Groups furnished what the Navy considered was the finest fighter support seen in the theater. Nearly every ship commander reported the P-38s pursued Japanese planes through the antiaircraft fire with extraordinary skill and daring.

Colonel Charles MacDonald, leading the 475th Fighter Group, was over Ormoc that morning when he spotted three Jacks heading for the American shipping and climbed toward them. As they turned left MacDonald and his executive officer,

Meryl Smith, raced after them. The enemy fighters split up and MacDonald selected the one going straight ahead. It disappeared into the cloud with *Putt Putt Maru* behind, and a dangerous game began. MacDonald next glimpsed the Jack on his right, out of the clouds, and banked and followed. The Japanese pilot ducked back into the gray clouds, MacDonald turned hard left. The chase continued. The Jack pilot tried to sneak out again but MacDonald caught him and was gaining ground all the time—the Japanese fighter turned to the left and MacDonald was able to cut him off even more. The Jack again flew into the cloud, again came out. *Putt Putt Maru* streaked into the sunshine after him, slightly below and right behind. From five hundred feet MacDonald opened fire and the shells lashed the enemy plane. It didn't burn, but the propeller was slowing down. The P-38 shot past the Japanese fighter and as MacDonald looked back he saw the pilot bail out.

Meryl Smith had set another of the Jacks on fire, but the third had maneuvered behind MacDonald, who saw him in time and hauled the Lightning into a tight turn. The enemy pilot was good and MacDonald couldn't reverse the situation— whenever he tried the Jack outturned him. Caught in this dogfight, he was relieved to see Smith coming to help. The second P-38 caught the Jack unawares and shot it to pieces. It hit the water and disappeared.

Twenty minutes later MacDonald was landing at Dulag to refuel. For their third mission of the day the 475th could scrape up only four planes, but these took off about 1:30 P.M., with MacDonald leading and Smith as element leader. The Lightnings leveled off at four thousand feet over Ormoc Bay; they had already seen Japanese ships a few miles to the north, and MacDonald decided to have a look at the enemy shipping because everything looked quiet over the American landing. Just as the ships came into view he heard a warning call and looked back to see eight enemy fighters almost on top of his P-38. MacDonald stood his aircraft on its left wing, but too late—the Jacks and Zekes opened fire and MacDonald could not complete his turn before the enemy fighters were among them. He and his wingman turned toward a Jack, which broke away. Then MacDonald cut in on one of the last enemy planes from a forty-five-degree angle, off to the rear. Lining up the Japanese plane in his sight, he fired a quick burst. The shells hit the Zeke and chunks flew off before it dived straight into the water below. Ahead of him Mac-Donald saw a Lightning streaking away from one of the Zekes, but the enemy pilot was right behind. MacDonald went after him. The P-38 appeared to be Smith's, about three to four thousand feet ahead. MacDonald overhauled the Zeke rapidly and lined up on him, losing sight of the other Lightning as he opened fire. Smoke poured from the Japanese fighter as its wing slowly lifted. Still closing in, MacDonald blasted away until the tail section and part of the fuselage drifted slowly to the right while the rest of the Zeke tumbled forward.

MacDonald called Smith on his radio but there was no answer and he wondered if he had got the Zeke in time. He joined his other two Lightnings and the three took off after a lone Zeke. MacDonald got there first. The Zero turned sharply and he tried to follow but on completion of the turn the P-38 was farther behind. Mac-Donald closed again, the other two P-38s with him. He was about to fire when the Zeke zoomed up and around to the left. MacDonald followed and saw the Zeke pull slightly away as he rolled out again. MacDonald rolled out with him, a little out of range again, with the other two P-38s at his sides. Just as MacDonald had the enemy growing larger in the orange gunsight ring the Zeke tried another turn, unaware of the other two P-38s. It turned into the path of Lieutenant Leo Blakeley's aircraft, he opened fire, and the Zeke zoomed down into the sea.

MacDonald was anxious about Smith as he headed back toward the American convoy. He went after three Zekes making for the ships and they broke up, two turning hard left and heading for the clouds, the third continuing down. Mac-Donald went after the lone Zeke but saw another P-38 closer to it. The ships opened fire at the Japanese plane and MacDonald called the other P-38 off, but it kept on, already at two thousand feet, and both aircraft were flying through heavy antiaircraft fire. MacDonald watched the Zeke smash straight into a ship as the P-38 pulled up and streaked past it. MacDonald called the fighter control, found out that Smith was missing, and went back to the area where he shot the Zeke off Smith's tail. The three P-38s searched the water below and continued until their tanks were almost dry. MacDonald headed back to Dulag and immediately ordered his Lightning to be refueled. Tired and drawn, he took off with another three P-38s to continue the search, but as the daylight faded he had to accept that Smith was lost.

On December 7, effusive little Jerry Johnson of the 49th Fighter Group also had a big day. Leading the group into a formation of Japanese fighters, he shot one down in flames and then, "The other two near him tried to turn. I pulled up after them. The second one went up—puff in a ball of flame—and then the other guy tried to turn. I got him too. It only took a minute and a half and I saw the last two hit the water two hundred feet apart. Then I saw some Nip bombers and I went after them. I got a twin-engined Helen and that went down."

Major Bill Dunham, leading ten P-47s of his 460th Fighter Squadron, finished bombing a merchant vessel in the morning and found sixteen enemy fighters coming in to attack. Fourteen of them were shot down, four of them by Dunham.

Dick Bong, flying with the 475th Fighter Group, got two, taking him to thirty-eight. During the day the P-38s claimed fifty-three of the seventy-five enemy aircraft they fought. The Japanese were still able to sink a destroyer, a transport, and a landing craft with their suicide attacks, but losses could have been far greater.

The enemy began their landing about thirty-five miles north of Ormoc under constant attack by a large force of Thunderbolts, P-40s, and Marine Corsairs. All their cargo vessels and transports were either sunk or beached and burned, but most of the Japanese managed to swim ashore although they lost almost all their equipment.

On December 11 the Japanese tried again. This time they lost two cargo ships to fighter attacks, and two destroyers and a transport made it into Ormoc Bay that night to lose one destroyer and have the other badly damaged by Allied warships. Artillery fire damaged the enemy transport and the fighters finished it off the next day, along with the destroyer. The troops who made it were the last to come in from Manila. The Japanese fighters escorting the convoy lost thirty-two planes and this was also the last large formation of enemy aircraft used over Leyte. As the Japanese were being forced into a tighter and tighter area some were evacuated to Cebu, but when the Leyte campaign finally ended on May 8, 1945, over eighty thousand had been killed.

Fifth Fighter Command lost over two hundred airplanes in November and December but there had been very high operational losses due to enemy bombing. The performance of air-sea rescue by both Fifth Air Force and Navy Catalinas was superb, and Fifth Fighter Command suffered only nineteen casualties in November and forty in December. During the two months the 3rd Emergency Rescue Squadron, operating partly from Leyte, picked up one hundred and five men. One of their most spectacular rescues was back on November 12, when they picked up a crew shot down over Ormoc Bay on November 10. The pilot of the 38th Group B-25, Major Ed McLean, got through with the help of Filipino guerrillas to bring back a Catalina for the rest of his men. Escorted by P-38s, Lieutenant Edward Garich's Catalina set out for Ponson Island, five miles offshore in Ormoc Bay.

The bay was dotted with boats as the Catalina approached and touched down about four hundred yards from the island's shoreline. Garich was cautious. He lowered the landing gear into the water to slow the Catalina down, and reduced power to idling speed while cruising until he could tell where the B-25 crew was. His crewmen stationed themselves throughout the plane.

Sergeant William Hampton was in the aft gun blister. A small boat, paddled by Filipinos, slowly gained on the taxiing plane, until Hampton tossed them a line and pulled them alongside. Climbing aboard, a Filipino pointed to three barges in the clutter of boats in the bay and said they were filled with Japanese. The B-25 crew was ready to come aboard, but was hiding because of the Japanese. While the native was pointing out the boats to Garich, Hampton went back to his gun blister, and the navigator was manning the two machine guns in the nose. The flight engineer grabbed a Thompson machine gun and climbed onto the broad, flat wing to join in. They all opened up and the Japanese began tumbling into the water. The Catalina circled the barges six times, chugging along as the crew virtually wiped out about sixty Japanese.

As soon as the shooting was over, the natives rowed the B-25 crewmen out but it was necessary to stop the engines before they could be taken aboard. When it was time to go the batteries were too low to turn the engines over, so two of the crew went up to start the energizers rolling with manual cranks as the P-38s circled about, keeping the remaining Japanese away. The hull of the Catalina had been punctured by small arms fire and most of the Plexiglas had been shot away, but the engines started and the Catalina lifted off, turned southward, and landed at Tacloban after picking up the survivors of another B-25 crew along the way—in all they brought home nine men. Garich got a Silver Star.

Keeping operational at Leyte put a heavy drain on the Fifth's strength. The 8th Fighter Group at Morotai was down to thirty-eight P-38s by the end of November and lack of facilities at Leyte limited operations. The available strength was committed largely to flying continuous air patrols. The P-40s flew the first support mission for ground troops on November 26, when they strafed hill positions, and on December 23 five Thunderbolts dropped napalm tanks in preparation for an amphibious landing at Palompon, and the pilots reported that a section of the town was gutted by fire. Before the end of the year Fifth Fighter Command flew over three hundred and sixty bombing or strafing sorties against the ground targets on Leyte, and some of them were highly successful: a dozen 49th Group P-38s blew up an ammunition dump at Ormoc on October 28, and the explosion leveled a waterfront block.

The 25th Liaison Squadron reached the Fifth in November 1943. Their tiny L-5s, flown by enlisted pilots, performed gallantly rescuing downed pilots.

The congestion on the airfields limited the amount of supplies which could be flown to the ground troops, and eight C-47s of the 317th Troop Carrier Group had to fulfill this role. Although they lost two aircraft to ground fire, the C-47s dropped three hundred tons of varied equipment to the front lines. The 25th Liaison Squadron dropped an entire three hundred bed field hospital with cots, tents, instruments, and personnel in what they called "the most audacious, outstanding and sensational light plane mission in the history of the SWPA." However, the troops fighting on Leyte did not get the kind of air support which Kenney wanted to provide and usually could. The accelerated movements into Leyte had led to errors and the lack of facilities for aircraft on the island raised the price of victory. One early report had described Tacloban as "sandy surface, all weather," which the 8th Fighter Squadron pilots thought was "the supreme overstatement of 1944." The rain played its part and when the available strips failed to measure up to expectations a new one was begun parallel to the coast at Tanauan, where there was good drainage and a coral foundation. By early January, a six-thousand-foot runway was completed, and across Leyte Gulf at Guiuan on Samar, work was begun on a seven-thousand-foot strip.

Although the Leyte garrison was limited to fighters and a few troop carriers, the Fifth kept to their shipping schedules and moved ground echelons in according to the timetable. This produced the undesirable situation of having men with little to do waiting on Leyte, while combat effectiveness of the aircraft dwindled as the rest of the groups waited at other bases. Leyte was a disappointment—it had, in a negative way, underlined the real effectiveness of the Fifth's usual pattern of attack.

Mindoro: Dangerous December

Although there was still an element of doubt regarding objectives, it was decided that MacArthur, supported by Nimitz, would invade Luzon in December, and would then support Central Pacific forces in the assault on Okinawa. Mindoro lies on the southern flank of Luzon, separated from it by a passage eight miles wide. The seventh biggest island in the Philippines, its southwestern end offered good local roads and a narrow-gauge railway, and the coastal cane fields looked like better future airfields than the rice paddies of Leyte. Also, not more than a thousand Japanese troops were scattered over the island, and it was desirable as the advanced base of the movement to Luzon.

The fighter bombers from Leyte and the Thirteenth Air Force B-24s wore away the Japanese air strength in the Visayas, and Allied estimates of Japanese planes there on December 2 had been nearly halved in two weeks. From the rear bases the Fifth's bombers attacked Mindanao and Celebes, while the Red Raiders and the 494th Group flew from Angaur to bomb the Bicol Peninsula. The Japanese aircraft on Luzon, an estimated three hundred and sixty on December 9, were left for the carriers, although B-24s of the 63rd Squadron, staging through Tacloban from Angaur, harassed the airdromes nightly.

After devising new tactics for dealing with suicide attacks, Halsey and his carriers swept Luzon for three days beginning on December 14. Over the period the pilots claimed to have destroyed two hundred and seventy enemy planes, but as long as there were any Japanese aircraft there the sea route to Mindoro remained hazardous. As soon as the convoy entered the Mindanao Sea it was in danger and the Fifth had rested its long-range fighters for several days and prepared intricate plans for continuous air cover. The first attack on the convoy came in the afternoon of December 13 when a kamikaze appeared from nowhere and hurled itself into the cruiser *Nashville,* killing one hundred and seventy-five men, including Colonel John Murtha, commander of the 310th Bomb Wing. The enemy suicide attacks failed the next day, and the convoy was off Mindoro by that night. The following morning the landing began and the few Japanese defenders disappeared into the hills— only five were killed all day. About sixteen Japanese planes attacked, and although losing eight to the fighter cover, they destroyed two landing craft. Other than this the landing went well and the shipping returned to Leyte without further damage.

The carriers were to cover the establishment of Kenney's air power on Mindoro by striking Luzon, but a typhoon lashed the fleet so badly that it was forced to sail back to Ulithi for repairs. The enemy, surprised at Mindoro, grasped this opportunity to send about a hundred sorties against the beachhead on the first two days and built up their air strength on Luzon.

Major Richard Bong got his thirty-ninth victory over Mindoro on December 15 and wrote to his mother: "You know of course that General MacArthur presented the Congressional Medal of Honor to me a few days ago and you probably know I got another Nip plane on the 15th, making it thirty-nine now. Seems like one or two Nips doesn't make any difference any more. Major McGuire is doing his darndest to pass me or gain on me anyway but since I am living with him at the present why he has a hard time of it because I fly when he does and we break even. Sure is good hunting up here and it is the best place we have ever been because we are much safer than we ever have been before. Major Johnson got four a few days ago making him twenty-three so he is quite happy. I have gotten eleven since I last left home and McGuire and Johnson have both gotten ten in the same period.

"That gunnery training I got in the States sure improved my shooting about three or four hundred percent. It confirms my opinion that if I had known it before I came over the first time I could have seventy-five to a hundred now. Sounds like a lot, doesn't it? When I think of all the chances I have had and missed it doesn't sound impractical at all."

Bong had attached himself to the 431st Squadron at the time, and after December 17, 1944, he made this report: "I took off from Dulag Strip at 1450/I, as leader of Daddy Special flight on a fighter sweep to Mindoro beach-head. We climbed to 9,000 feet on course and arrived at Mindoro at 1605/I. I contacted the controller and started to patrol. At 1615/I, the controller said that the friendly beach-head was being strafed. At the same time I sighted two bogeys at 1200 o'clock high. As friendly flights were down to take care of the strafers I dropped tanks and started climbing for altitude. The Oscars made a 180° turn and headed straight north. We gave chase and I closed on the leader who had dived to the right, separating from other e/a, and shot him down at 1625/I, from an altitude of 9,000 feet. The Oscar disintegrated and then caught fire and dived straight down and crashed about twenty miles North of San Jose. I then watched Major Rittmayer, my wingman, shoot down the other Oscar. We reformed formation and patrolled over San Jose until 1715/I, and returned to home base landing at 1830/I. Lt. Fulkerson saw the Oscar crash and will confirm it."

This victory claim, Bong's fortieth and last, was approved by the commanding officer of the 431st Squadron, Major Thomas B. McGuire, Jr., who had scored his thirty-second victory the same day.

On Mindoro, a site had already been selected for a fighter strip, and on December 20 a runway and dispersals were completed. However, Hill Field, as it was named, was very dusty and susceptible to weather. Another strip, later named Elmore Field, had already been begun just west of a sugar mill near San Jose, and its runway was ready for use three days later. While Elmore could withstand moderately wet weather, both strips could only be temporary.

The 8th Fighter Group's P-38s, escorting the C-47s carrying the rest of their personnel, flew into Hill Field on December 20. The 36th Squadron began defending their new base even before they landed, being sent against nine enemy planes which endangered the unloading transports.

The P-47s of the 58th Fighter Group moved to Hill Field by squadron and the Fifth's planes were reaching Mindoro just in time. At nine o'clock on December 24 a Japanese heavy cruiser, with a light cruiser and six destroyers, began a mission to sink Allied transports and shell the Mindoro beachhead. Alerted by submarines, the Americans dispersed supplies inland, and search patterns were extended to the coast of Indo-China. The 17th Recon's B-25s and 110th Recon P-40s were flown

Mindoro was dangerous. This P-38 was tossed aside and mangled by a bomb during an enemy night attack in late December 1944.

to Elmore and Hill Fields, and then at four o'clock in the afternoon of December 26 a Navy Liberator crew reported that they had sighted what they believed was a battleship, a heavy cruiser, and six destroyers one hundred miles west of Mindoro and speeding toward the Allied positions at twenty-eight knots. Bomb stocks at Mindoro were small and carrying bomb loads off the short and rough strips at night was a risky business for fighters. Colonel Jack Wilson, the new commander of the 310th Bomb Wing, alerted all his units, ordering as many planes as possible loaded with bombs and the rest prepared for strafing. There was not time to co-ordinate the attack, virtually impossible at night anyway. At seven-forty the first planes found the Japanese warships just off shore and in the wild fight thirteen B-25s, forty-four P-38s, twenty-eight P-47s, and twenty P-40s attacked every ship at least once, one pilot summing the missions up neatly by saying, "When I saw a solid sheet of flame I knew I was over the vessel."

Captain Paul Murphey was leading the Headhunters that night, and his dozen P-38s spotted the enemy ships by following their brilliant wakes. The squadron split up to make individual attacks. To Murphey "it was spooky to start making a pass at a ship and all of a sudden see tracer bullets from another plane close by attacking the same ship. I called all my Copper flights and had them turn on their wingtip lights so they would not run into each other."

Some of the planes landed in the Mindoro darkness to rearm and made as many as three strikes against the enemy vessels. American patrol boats were also in the action, but only the destroyer *Kiyoshimo* was sunk, and the fleet continued toward the beachhead, where it fired star shells to open an ineffective forty-minute bombardment. One Liberty ship which had not hidden with the other Allied vessels was sunk, but the Japanese shelling and a simultaneous air attack caused only minor damage at Hill Field, although it was difficult for the airmen to land there. Running low on fuel, most of them made as many attacks as possible and headed for Leyte, a flight which was as dangerous as the Japanese gunfire had been. The cost of the spectacular battle was three B-25s, seven P-38s, ten P-47s, and six P-40s. It was a heavy loss, but several Japanese blamed the ineffective bombardment on the fierce aerial mauling, which had knocked out main batteries and killed most of the gun crews.

The Japanese created a lot more havoc—between December 18 and January 7 over four hundred sorties were flown into the area, concentrated on the shipping. A convoy coming into Mindoro on December 22 had lost two landing ships when about twenty Oscars and Vals dropped out of the clouds, behind the ships. Five 49th Group Lightnings which had been ordered forward of the convoy were only able to shoot down one enemy plane. A second convoy was attacked by a total of about a hundred Japanese planes, both to and from Mindoro, and lost three merchant ships, three landing ships, two destroyers, and two landing craft. The brilliant moon led to attacks around the clock and the most destructive were made on the morning of December 28, when Leyte fields were closed in by weather and the Mindoro squadrons were still recovering from attacking the warships two days earlier.

The pilots of the 418th Night Fighter Squadron had gone into combat with their P-61s in September, after flying P-70s, P-38s, and B-25s. Carroll C. Smith, their commander, looks back to late December 1944:

"We went to Mindoro when the dust settled there and had some busy days and nights, for a while. This period peaked for me on the night of December 29, when we were assigned to escort a large convoy of ships. We were careful how we did this, having found that those merchant marine gunners were very jumpy. They would start shooting if someone said boo.

"It was a moonless night with broken clouds around three to six thousand feet. We were on the seaward side of the convoy, under radar control from a ship, when they pointed us toward an unknown. My radar operator, Phil Porter, vectored me in to a visual contact on an Irving, which after a burst or two provided entertainment for the ships below, for he was a flamer. A short time later we were again in contact with an unknown, again able to close to a visual, and got him. Another Irving. The remainder of the patrol was uneventful and it appeared we had had a full night. In our business kills were not frequent or easy and here we had two on one mission and easily confirmed by people on that large number of ships down there . . . a night fighter was usually alone and someone other than your own crew had to confirm the kills.

"We returned to base and *Time's A Wastin* was hurriedly refueled, for we were needed on patrol. Only time for fuel, no ammo, but then we had shot down two already. We surely wouldn't run into any more Japs this night.

"We had been on patrol only a short time when we were vectored toward another unknown. Porter got a contact at about three miles and had me descend to five hundred feet, and we began the damnedest chase from almost sea level to five hundred feet, up and down, most of the time with flaps down for slow speed work. About the time I had become convinced Porter had lost his mind I saw the Rufe at about three hundred feet away. I fired a burst with those four 20-mm. cannon and the Rufe exploded and dove into the water. My confidence in Porter was again confirmed—when he saw something on his radar, you best believe him. His range and position information was also reliable. The most frustrating thing was to try and see something of a bogey when Porter kept saying, 'he is at eleven o'clock

Lieutenant Phil Porter and Major Carroll C. Smith, commander of the 418th Night Fighter Squadron. Smith brought the squadron to Port Moresby in November 1943 to be told by General Wurtsmith that the 418th was "a luxury I can ill afford." By January of the following year they were flying P-70s, P-38s, and, later, B-25s which proved very effective against small shipping at night. (Smith)

Carroll Smith's glistening black P-61B, *Time's A Wastin,* adorned with the white moon and star markings of his 418th Squadron. (Smith)

slightly above at one thousand . . . open your eyes, he's there.' Try to find an exhaust pattern, get closer, stay below so you can see his exhaust, hope he doesn't see yours, try to get a silhouette against the stars, anything. You can tell you are close by the pitch of Porter's voice on the intercom. It goes up in direct relation to range. Finally a star is momentarily blacked out and you can see why—an aircraft. Now to be sure it is an enemy. Remember that time not long ago at Morotai when you were vectored in and while you were trying to identify the type of aircraft the tail gunner blasted at you and thank God you saw those big double rudders in time. It was a very damaged B-24 trying to get home. He did.

"Forty-five minutes later we were again vectored toward a bogey. Porter had him at six miles, and at five thousand feet I saw him. It was about seven o'clock, and almost full daylight. As I got closer I recognised it as a Frank, the first one I had seen. I was keenly aware that I had already shot down three aircraft with one load of ammo, and although I thought I had quite a few rounds left I could not be sure. Since it was now daylight I could not run off and hide if I just made this Frank mad. I stayed below and closed to seventy-five feet. I opened fire and saw the awesome results of four 20-mm. cannon hitting an aircraft. The Frank simply disintegrated and the pieces flew into the sea with me trying to avoid the debris.

"The sun was almost up, it was seven minutes after seven, so we returned to base. After landing we first checked our ammo to see how close we had come to being out. Three hundred and eighty-two rounds used, over two hundred left. Our laughter I'm sure bordered on the hysterical . . . I remembered all too well a Dinah I had shot down over Morotai in a wide-ranging duel. I finally got the dude with my last burst of ammo. Six hundred rounds of ammo for one Dinah and now three hundred and eighty-two for two Irvings, a Rufe and a Frank. My first love of the skies will always be the P-61 . . . that ungainly looking, sweet flying Black Widow."

Smith was the top-scoring ace in the Fifth's night fighters, with seven victories in all.

* * *

The sinking of two tankers and the destruction of the storage tank at Hill Field made it unlikely that the Fifth's planes could operate from Mindoro for much longer. On December 30 Colonel Wilson told Whitehead that he was cutting his operations down to minimum fighter cover, because until tankers arrived he had little choice. The situation with ammunition was becoming equally serious—on December 28 a kamikaze had blown up a ship loaded with bombs and a week later another suicide attack exploded the ship's replacement just off San Jose.

On December 29 all but three hundred tons of steel runway planking was lost when the vessel it was being unloaded from was sunk in sixty feet of water, but the Fifth was committed and continued to move planes forward as soon as there was space for them on Mindoro. By January 9 most of the 49th Fighter and 417th Bomb Groups, as well as the 82nd Tactical Recon, 547th Night Fighter, 25th Photo, and 3rd Emergency Rescue Squadrons were on the island. The Grim Reapers were moving forward although not all the A-20s could be handled immediately. These units were not up to full strength and the 17th Squadron was suffering such a serious crew shortage that on January 1 Whitehead had urgently requested sixteen complete crews, trained or untrained. As the New Year began, the 8th Fighter Group was short seventeen P-38s and a Japanese night raid on January 2 destroyed or damaged fifteen more Lightnings and seven A-20s. However, Mindoro held a more powerful force than Kenney had specified for protection of a Lingayen landing, and with enough fuel and no heavy rain it was strong enough to extend support to the initial ground operations on Luzon.

Luzon

The geography of Luzon decided that the major landings would be made in Lingayen Gulf. Allied forces could move quickly toward Manila along the highway network, and on the way they would overrun the old American installations around Clark Field. There were other routes for subsidiary and supporting attacks: a secondary drive from southwestern Luzon would allow early capture of Nichols and Nielson fields, the other major Japanese air centers, southeast of Manila. The possible avenues of attack complicated Japanese defense planning and the Mindoro landing confused them further. They accepted that Leyte was lost by the middle of December and turned their attention to preparing to fight for Luzon.

In plans perfected during a conference at Hollandia in November it was agreed that Kenney's air forces would neutralize central Luzon for three days leading up to the landing. Seventh Air Force B-24s from Angaur were to strike the Bicol provinces, the Fourteenth Air Force in China agreed to attack Hong Kong, and the Twentieth was to provide reconnaissance on call and strike Formosa, directing all possible strength against harbors and airfields during the week surrounding the Lingayen landing.

In addition to their usual lead-up work, the Fifth was expected to begin operating from Lingayen bases as soon as possible, getting their maximum strength there during the first week to supply the greatest possible support in the early and critical phases. At that time too they should be ready to relieve the Navy's carriers. The whole air garrison, under control of the 308th Bomb Wing, was to be in place two weeks after the landing.

Assuming his B-24s would be on Leyte at the beginning of December, Whitehead had hoped to hit the Clark Field airdromes in force early in the month, but other than small night attacks from Tacloban and the unescorted raids from Angaur, heavy bomber missions had been impossible. Fighter escort finally became available, and on December 22 the Red Raiders sent twenty-three Liberators to Clark Field. The next day the 494th went to Grace Park airfield, in the northern suburbs of Manila, but the two groups were forced to strike on alternate days because they had to stage home through the traffic jam at Tacloban. Attacks against the six airdromes of Clark Field continued whenever weather permitted, and there were four more strikes during December. Japanese fighters intercepted, but were swept aside by the Fifth's fighters, which shot down ninety-four planes at a loss of only seven of their own. Bomber crews claimed seven more, but the big concentration of guns at Clark Field sent many B-24s limping home full of holes. The planes from Leyte stepped up their attacks on Luzon—the fighters had raided the

The Red Raiders head for Clark Field, December 1944. (Bill Miller)

Legaspi airdromes early in November and two 460th Squadron P-47s had made a sweep of central Luzon, the first Fifth Air Force fighters to appear over Manila, Bataan, and Corregidor. The fighters had flown fifty sweeps by the end of the year.

Lightnings over Luzon

Thomas McGuire stood about five feet and seven inches tall, gaunt and with steely gray eyes. He was a magnificent pilot, supremely confident and absolutely without fear. Once, over Wewak, a burning Japanese fighter had been closing him head on. Neither pilot gave way. There was a jarring bang and the Japanese continued on to be shot down by another pilot, and back at Dobodura they used steel wool to scrape the broad smear of Japanese paint from under the wing of McGuire's Lightning.

Major Thomas B. McGuire, wearing his five-hundred-hour hat. It was the duty of one of the enlisted men to put it behind the armor plating of his P-38, because McGuire wanted it to be the genuine article. It wasn't always done, and McGuire got "mad as hell" when he found out. (Bob Brooks)

McGuire had arrived in the theater in the spring of 1943, and at that time Dick Bong already had eight victories, and the wiry 475th Group pilot had found it impossible to gain more than temporary ground. When Bong went home with twenty-eight, McGuire had twenty, but the lack of Japanese resistance, followed by bouts of dengue fever and malaria, prevented his taking advantage of the opportunity to close the gap. At the end of November 1944, McGuire had twenty-eight victories —but Bong had thirty-six. They got two each on December 7, McGuire gained by one on December 13, but Bong retrieved his lead of eight by shooting down an Oscar two days later. He stretched the gap to nine on December 17.

When Bong had his forty victories and was finally out of combat, it seemed simply a matter of McGuire being in the right place at the right time. There was a story that when he began quickly increasing his score in the Philippines he had the squadron painter apply miniature Japanese flags to his scoreboard which were then covered with tape; when he returned after a fight the necessary tape was removed as soon as his victories were confirmed. Kenney even grounded him until Bong had a chance to get home, feeling it would be unfair if McGuire dampened the event by eclipsing his record.

Leading his 431st Fighter Squadron as close cover for the B-24s on December 26, McGuire shot down four Japanese planes to run his score to thirty-eight—he had knocked down three Zeros celebrating Christmas the day before. Flying his elaborately painted Lightning, *Pudgy* (*V*), he spotted enemy fighters and the 431st dropped their tanks. One Zeke had just finished his pass at the Liberators and a second was racing in on a bomber—the tail gunner was not firing back. McGuire had only a slim chance of helping, but opened fire at long range, nearly four hundred yards, with a forty-five-degree deflection shot. He hit the cockpit of the Zeke, which burst into flames and dived down. It was fantastic shooting. McGuire fired quickly at the third Zeke in the string attacking the B-24s, but could not see the result. Making a diving turn to the left he got two bursts into another Zero which flamed and crashed. Then three more Zekes joined the fight. McGuire selected one and fired, shattering the cockpit and the pilot. The fighter plummeted into a dry stream bed.

McGuire had lost contact with his wingman as he turned on a diving Zero and shot it down with two bursts. *Pudgy (V)* was now right down near the ground, so McGuire headed back up to six thousand feet, where he spotted another enemy fighter. Before he could get there a flight of P-38s was after it, and that Zero became the last of four fighters shot down in five minutes by the 8th Fighter Squadron's Lieutenant Sammy Pierce.

The 8th Squadron had been flying the third position in the 49th Group, assigned as middle cover to the bombers. Over the target area there was about 50 per cent cloud cover and Pierce heard the 8th Fighter Group, flying top cover, call in the enemy fighters. He saw several flights of Japanese planes breaking through the overcast and shoved on full power as his external tanks tumbled down.

Pierce says he "pulled up into the enemy flights in an effort to break them up, and since they had both altitude and speed advantage there was actually no other course. The leader of the flight that I was heading for reached my level and seemed to kind of level off, then dropped his nose slightly. He was in range and lined up. I fired a burst which appeared to hit him between the engine and canopy and his left wing root. As we closed I pulled up to go over him since he was already nosed over, and just as we passed he exploded directly underneath me. I continued a maximum climbing turn to my right and tried to locate my wingman without success. At the same time I saw the other two flights of my squadron below me, going in the opposite direction with two of the enemy flights heading for them. With the altitude advantage I started after the enemy flights while trying to warn my two lead flights of their position, but with all the talk by all the other outfits, they didn't hear me. By the time I could reach them the number three man in the second flight was being fired on by a type of enemy plane I had not seen before, a Tojo. As I started to fire at the enemy the P-38s left engine puffed smoke, he skidded to the left, then rolled. By this time the enemy pilot was aware of me and rolled to split-S out just as I was firing. The rolling action caused him to take the hits in the wing and fuel tanks, with the wing blowing apart. I pulled around looking for the damaged P-38 and observed the enemy fighters still heading for the bombers.

"One flight of three was closing in but was attacked by the leader of one of the flights from the 475th, who shot down two of them in one pass . . . I later learned it was McGuire. I attacked the second section of enemy fighters, causing one to burn and the other four to break off. At this time I became aware that I was being chased so used full power and nosed down slightly to get maximum speed. Apparently a flight of the Headhunters had observed what was going on, passed over me, and met the Japanese head on, causing him to break off. Then I noticed that my left engine oil temperature had gone completely out of limits and the coolant temperature was right at the danger mark. I used the manual override switch to fully open the oil and coolant shutters. It caused a trim problem but the temperatures started to come down.

"Seeing an enemy fighter below me heading in the same direction, I cut power and started a standard pursuit curve which I fouled up, almost overrunning to the point that I ended up practically flying formation with him. He evidently had no experience, as he sat staring straight ahead for a considerable period of time. I slid out to the right, pulled up and slid right back in a firing pass. I again led too much and fired right by his nose. Fully expecting him to roll or break sharply I fired one more very short burst that appeared to hit between the cockpit and tail section, rather than what I expected. He managed to get into a cloud deck before I could fire again, but rather than getting down into it or through it he stayed just close enough to the top so that I could still see him. He pulled up directly in front of me, allowing me to fire one burst which caused pieces to fly off and he started smoking. He dived back into the cloud deck and I did not see what happened to him.

"Pulling back up trying to find a friendly to join, I saw several P-38s chasing a single enemy fighter, but in their efforts to get him they were all overrunning and overshooting. When it looked as if the enemy was going to escape I cut power, made a standard pass, and fired a fairly long burst, causing the plane to break up. I then joined the flight leader, who happened to be Tommy McGuire of the 475th Group."

Other P-38 pilots had added to the score: Lieutenant Nial Castle at the 8th Squadron got two Zekes, Captain Jack Fisk of the 433rd shot down a Tojo, and the 431st had destroyed three Zekes, Captain Frederic Champlin getting his ninth victory, Lieutenant "Bo" Reeves his third; and Lieutenant John Tilley became an ace when he got his fifth.

The wild battle over, McGuire had tacked onto Castle's wing, and with Pierce and two other P-38s, one from the 8th Squadron and one from the 432nd, the mixed flight began home. Their fuel supply was low and they all landed on Mindoro, where Pierce's damaged P-38 slid safely to a stop after the nosewheel collapsed—when the Tojo had exploded under him it had damaged the Lightning, and some of the enemy fighter's fuselage skin was still lodged in the left oil cooler. As the pilots talked while the P-38s were refueled, Castle thought that McGuire seemed jumpy enough to be grounded, but with only a couple more to go the excited pilot was living on his nerves . . .

* * *

After the Japanese naval raid on Mindoro the Air Apaches were quickly sent to Leyte, and on December 27 they flew a small mission against shipping off San Fernando. The next night four B-25s made low-level attacks over Clark Field, and on December 30 nine attacked the Cagayan Valley area.

When the 310th Wing at Mindoro had almost used up its store of aviation gasoline Whitehead promised aerial delivery and ordered the full offensive to continue. Curtiss C-46s of the 2nd Combat Cargo Group, flying directly from Morotai, and 317th Group C-47s from Leyte delivered about six hundred drums of gas a day for a week following January 3. Whitehead took P-38s from Leyte units to replace

310th Wing losses from the night raids, and replacement crews for the 17th Recon were sent up. On January 5 the Navy pumped off ten thousand barrels of fuel to alleviate the problem and allow the continued coastal blockade of Luzon. On December 30 the 675th Squadron teamed up with the 17th and 110th Squadrons against a Japanese supply convoy off northwest Luzon, sinking a frigate and three cargo vessels. Three days later the 417th Group's A-20s sank another frigate and four small cargo ships at San Fernando, but on this mission their commander, Colonel Howard S. Ellmore, was lost when his A-20 hit the superstructure of a ship, spun crazily into the sea, and blew up. When the Japanese stopped trying to get ships into Lingayen Gulf, the aircraft from Mindoro added their weight to the assault on communications, starting landslides in passes, destroying bridges, attacking railyards, rolling stock, vehicles, and roads in a campaign through central and southern Luzon. Although there was still not enough strength within range to completely neutralize Luzon, the B-24s were hitting Clark almost daily, and the Red Raiders, raiding Mabalacat strip on January 2, met the last Japanese fighter interception when thirteen planes were shot down by their escort. The Snoopers were setting fires nearly every night, and on January 3, four 58th Group Thunderbolts swept one of the Clark strips. Two were knocked down, one of them piloted by the group commander, Colonel Gwen Atkinson, but the other two strafed and burned eleven enemy planes, and Atkinson was rescued by guerrillas. The Air Apaches attacked Borac and Floridablanca strips the next day. However, the heavy bombers were not attacking in the usual strength—cramped by the necessity of staging through Tacloban, only one heavy group could be put over Clark each day, and nearly five hundred antiaircraft guns there made it a deadly target for minimum-altitude attack.

The fleet began to leave Leyte for Lingayen Gulf; the minesweepers went out first on January 2 and suffered damage to four ships. The task group for bombardment sailed the next day with twelve escort carriers, and one was sunk on January 4. In the afternoon of January 5, as the vessels passed Subic Bay, fifty to sixty planes broke through the fighter escort and damaged two cruisers, two carriers, and three destroyers. When minesweepers and bombardment ships deployed in Lingayen Gulf on January 6 they were vulnerable to kamikaze attacks, which damaged sixteen vessels in one day. The surrounding land masses interfered with radar, and denied the fighters the advantage of early warning. The problem had to be solved at the source of the attacks if the onslaught was to be stopped before the transports reached Lingayen.

On January 7 Major Tom McGuire was leading a flight of four P-38s on a fighter sweep over Negros Island. They eased down through several layers of cloud, breaking out ten miles from Fabrica airstrip. It was seven o'clock in the morning as they circled, looking for victims.

Finding nothing, McGuire was heading for the strips on the western coast when Captain Edward Weaver spotted an Oscar coming directly toward them, five hundred feet below and a thousand yards ahead. By the time Weaver was on the radio with the alert, McGuire had already seen the fighter, now directly below, and made a diving turn to the left. The Oscar turned too, coming around behind Lieutenant Douglas Thropp's P-38. Major Jack Rittmayer fired a burst close enough to force the Japanese to tighten his turn and release his grip on Thropp's tail, but that put him on Weaver, who tightened his turn, diving slightly. The Japanese stuck with him as McGuire, attempting to get a shot, pulled his P-38 back in a shuddering turn. The P-38 snap-rolled to the left and stopped in an inverted position, nose down. Weaver lost sight of McGuire momentarily, then saw the explosion and fire of the crash. The Oscar broke off his attack and climbed to the north, Weaver and the others chasing him. Thropp got in a burst just as the Japanese plane raced into the milky overcast.

Badly shot up, the Oscar crash-landed in the mountains; the pilot survived but was killed by Filipino guerrillas.

Moments later a Japanese fighter, which the three P-38 pilots presumed was their quarry, appeared from the clouds and headed toward them. In actual fact it was a Frank which had been about to land when the pilot saw the fight going on. When the P-38 crashed he naturally thought the Oscar pilot had shot it down. As the Oscar fled, the Frank came to join the fight.

The Japanese fired at Thropp, and smoke jetted from the Lightning's left engine. Weaver pulled up and snapped a burst from below, then followed Rittmayer in a right turn to chase the Frank, which swung around and attacked again. As the P-38s jettisoned their fuel tanks—McGuire had ordered them not to do this before the encounter with the Oscar—Weaver saw Rittmayer being hit and again whipped up the nose of his Lightning and turned for another shot. The Frank, also being closed by Thropp, made a diving turn to the right and made north. Thropp continued his right turn and started home with his shot-up engine, the Frank swinging onto his tail and firing just as the P-38 entered the clouds. Weaver was too far out of range to shoot as the Frank also soared into the overcast, breaking toward the south. Weaver circled the base of the cloud for a few minutes waiting for the enemy to show himself, then climbed through the overcast to search for a few minutes more. Thropp was safe and on his way home, but both Rittmayer and McGuire were lost. The Frank, badly damaged, flipped on its back landing at Manapurna, but the pilot survived.

McGuire had been flying a spare P-38 that day, and back on Leyte *Pudgy* (*V*), with its thirty-eight little Japanese flags, was a sad reminder of his mortality. They scraped all the elaborate paintwork off the fighter and sent it to another group.

* * *

The fast carriers had struck Formosa and the southern Ryukyus on January 3, then refueled and made ready for strikes against northern Luzon to cover the minesweeping at Lingayen. MacArthur wanted the Navy to include the Clark fields in the missions of January 6, but Halsey chose to maintain continuous air patrol over Luzon instead. That day solid cloud blocked all attempts to sweep northern Luzon, but carrier planes ranged south to Manila Bay. The Red Raiders sent twenty-two B-24s over Clark while Thirteenth Air Force B-24s from Morotai hit Nichols and Nielson fields, but neither the Navy nor the B-24s prevented the vicious attacks on the Allied ships in Lingayen Gulf. The situation was growing dangerous. Halsey had planned to spend January 7 striking Formosa, but instead he concentrated on the enemy airfields on northern Luzon and with good weather was able to cover the whole island.

These efforts were supplemented by the largest co-ordinated light and medium

Lieutenant Tom Jones, pilot of the
312th Group's *Little Joe.* (Jones)

bomber mission flown in the southwest Pacific. With the heavy concentration of antiaircraft fire protecting Clark Field, the plan of attack was daring: the Air
Apaches and part of the 312th Group were to execute a low-level strafing and
parafrag attack on the airdromes, flying from northwest to southeast in a sixty-
plane front. They were to be followed by a similar force of A-20s from the 312th
and 417th Groups, flying abreast, from northeast to southwest. Two squadrons of
P-38s were their fighter cover. Early in the morning the Air Apaches and the
312th took off from Leyte and flew to Mindoro, where they were joined by the
417th in the takeoff for Luzon. The attack began at ten twenty-five almost as
planned, although low cloud interfered with the assembly and some of the planes
were still jockeying for position as they flew over the target.

Lieutenant Tom Jones of the 389th Squadron was flying his A-20, *Little Joe,* that
day. After the briefing he found "it was difficult to sleep that night but we finally
did and awoke to a bright sky over Tanauan airstrip on Leyte. The takeoff and
joinup were uneventful and, after picking up the Air Apaches over Tacloban, we
were on our way to Mindoro to meet the other A-20 group. When we arrived over
San Jose strip we were met by the most amazing sight we had ever seen. There
below us and to the west was our invasion fleet headed for its landing at Lingayen
Gulf. It stretched for miles and miles.

"Suddenly out of nowhere there appeared two Japanese fighters and the fleet
opened up with everything it had. The Japanese planes flew straight on past, but
for us it was a nightmare. We were forced to take violent evasive action to avoid
being knocked out of the sky. The barrage stopped almost as quickly as it had
begun and we were able to complete our joinup and start on our way.

"There were one hundred and thirty-two planes in that formation and it was awesome. We were flying at only a few thousand feet as we proceeded up the coastline and soon reached our checkpoint and started our turn inland. The tension increased as we noticed that sides of the pass that we were to fly through were obscured by a low-hanging overcast. Flying abreast as we were, we could not get all our planes through. Joe Rutter and I were on the right end of the formation and we were forced to go over the overcast and then try to drop through it again after we felt we were safely through the pass. Since we had no idea how long the pass was or the exact moment when the rest of the formation would increase its speed for its run over the target, we gave it everything we had, counted to ten, and nosed down through the overcast, praying every second.

"We suddenly broke out and found that we were a good mile in front of the other aircraft and Clark Field lay directly ahead. We could see the ack-ack guns blinking at us. We could not make a pass alone so I made a tight turn and rejoined the formation as it passed underneath me. Obviously, Joe had not thought as I did. To my great surprise he had continued straight and had crossed Clark alone. He was getting hit by the Air Apache B-25s and decided the wisest course was to get away from them. The Japs never touched him but the B-25s almost knocked him down.

"Enemy aircraft circling above us were dropping phosphorous bombs in the midst of the formation. We raced across the target, made our right turn and headed down Bataan peninsula for Manila Bay. Being the first across the target, our wave was the lucky one. We lost but one aircraft over the target and three

The Air Apaches race across Clark Field on January 7, 1945. (Jerry Lahmsen)

more in the drink. The second wave came in and just as they passed over the Japanese blew up the runways with a number of partly buried bombs rigged for detonation by nearby machine gun posts. Four planes went in and one more was lost enroute home. Two more crashed preparing to land."

It was a very successful mission. There were only sporadic kamikaze attacks after January 7 and the huge invasion convoy suffered relatively little damage. The B-24s also struck airfields that day and the Navy found the enemy air attacks diminished sharply. Only after they reached Clark Field would the Americans learn of the results of these attacks—since the beginning of the campaign in October over fifteen hundred Japanese aircraft had been put out of action on the ground, mainly by the air strikes. Many of the planes required only a few spare parts and others were in need of only simple repairs. At Clark the B-24 strikes in December had created complete chaos. The Japanese had attempted dispersal but had tied themselves in knots—repair shops, dumps, and maintenance units were all over the place. Over two hundred new engines, most of them uncrated, were hidden in a village, but never more than a few in one place. Parts were even buried. One abandoned fighter was found to need only a carburetor to be ready to fly.

On January 9, 1945, the troops went ashore on the Lingayen beaches. The Air Apaches and A-20s, ready if they were needed, were dismissed forty-five minutes after the landing began and went to work over communications targets. One squadron of A-20s was called in later in the day to bomb and strafe, but it soon became obvious that the enemy had no intention of fighting on the beaches. Irregular Japanese air attacks continued against the American forces in Lingayen Gulf, but after January 12 most of them were evidently launched from Formosa.

The Flying Undertaker

On January 11 two Mustangs from the 82nd Tactical Recon Squadron left Mindoro to check over the Japanese airdromes on northern Luzon. They never got as far as their primary target, because Captain William Shomo and his wingman, Lieutenant Paul Lipscomb, spotted a Betty bomber with an escort of eleven Tonys and a Tojo about two thousand feet above them. Shomo climbed from five hundred feet, with Lipscomb on his wing.

In his first attack Shomo hit the leader and the wingman of the trailing element of fighters and both Tonys exploded. The Japanese fighters did not break up or try to fight during the first pass, evidently mistaking the F-6s for friendly fighters—the pilot of the second Tony opened his canopy and stood up, waving his arm, and other aircraft had waggled their wings.

Cutting back in, Shomo blasted another fighter and it went down in flames. Then the Japanese broke up into pairs, but seemed confused about what to do. Shomo blew up a fourth Tony and saw that the Betty was trying to dive away and escape. Shomo flew his Mustang down below it and fired up into the belly of the bomber. It began to burn and glided down toward a field, the Japanese pilot trying to line up for a belly landing. Just above the field the bomber erupted. Shomo was so close that his Mustang lurched, and bits and pieces of the Betty pelted his plane.

General Whitehead talks with Paul Lipscomb and William Shomo after the Medal of Honor presentation. Before the war Shomo was a licensed embalmer. (Al Lomer)

Shomo climbed sharply again, and the Tojo fired a deflection shot at him on the way up. Pulling the F-6 into a tight turn Shomo watched the Tojo skid under his Mustang and disappear into a cloud layer. Heading for two of the remaining fighters, Shomo shot down one from behind and the other tried to get away. Shomo dived a hundred feet and caught the last of his seven victims.

The sky was clear. There was only Lipscomb's Mustang up higher, and he had disposed of three of the Tonys in his first combat. The two pilots went down to take photographs of the burning piles of wreckage, a chore which took them nearly as long as the fight itself.

William Shomo was awarded the Medal of Honor, and when this was announced by the commander of the 71st Recon Group at their new officers' club, the fighter pilot was called upon to say a few words. The thin ace rose and said, "Gentlemen, I can think of no better speech to make at this moment than—the drinks are on me."

* * *

There was almost no enemy air strength left on Luzon, and other Allied air forces joined in to eliminate any threat of real outside interference. The Fourteenth in China had been limited in the help it could provide, but the Twentieth sent B-29s on reconnaissance as far south as Singapore and bombed Formosa and the

Okinawa airfields. Halsey's Navy planes struck the coast of French Indo-China, Hainan, Canton, and Hong Kong, and on January 22 the Fifth began a series of Formosa strikes which would not cease until the Japanese surrender.

On Luzon Fifth Air Force planes were isolating the battle area, destroying key bridges and smashing Japanese communications. By January 16 the Fifth reported it had destroyed seventy-nine locomotives and well over four hundred trucks. The Fifth's airmen enjoyed this kind of work—so much so that in the end the Army had to ask that bridges be hit only on request, and that the shooting up of railway equipment be restricted to trains in motion.

The beachhead was secure a week after the landing, and although there was stubborn resistance the troops kept moving, supported by the carrier planes. Strikes were flown on request by the 310th Wing from Mindoro, but with Army and Navy planes in the same vicinity there was always an element of risk. One mishap occurred when Navy planes attacked eight P-47s, and although the Thunderbolts refused to show any signs of fight, the Navy pilots shot down one and holed two others, explaining that they thought they were Tojos.

An airstrip on the beachhead was proceeding on schedule, although heavy seas delayed the arrival of the necessary equipment. To meet the deadline the engineers used short cuts—craters were filled with sand and the surface simply smoothed over, then palm fronds and bamboo mats were placed on top to stop erosion; five thousand feet of steel mat was laid and the whole surface sprayed with tar. With no drainage possible, it was accepted that the strip would go bad quickly when the summer rains began.

The C-47s began bringing cargo in to Lingayen strip on January 16, and P-61s of the 547th Squadron moved in from Mindoro. The following afternoon Thirteenth Air Force P-38s and the 82nd Recon Squadron arrived to bring the garrison up to requirements for cover and direct support, and the aircraft carriers were relieved by the 308th Bomb Wing. The 110th Recon Squadron reached Lingayen on January 22, followed the next day by the F-5s of the 26th Photo Squadron. A field at Mangaldan was ready for the 35th Fighter Group and 3rd Air Commandos and the 38th Bomb Group joined them in the first few days of February, the 312th Group following. This air strength gave the Army more confidence than it had had at Leyte. The Fifth's planes had already checked enemy movement along the roads during daylight and the Japanese were short of fuel. The troops pushed southward against ragged opposition and on January 21 advanced toward the Clark Field area. On January 23 the first real resistance was encountered, from enemy strongpoints in the hills, obviously designed to deny use of the easy route. After bitter fighting against cave positions which bristled with machine guns taken from wrecked planes, the troops secured the high ground and Clark was captured on January 28.

Moving steadily south along the central Luzon plain, the Army was ready to begin the drive to capture Manila. MacArthur ordered General Eichelberger to land at Subic Bay and move east to stop Japanese forces from withdrawing into Bataan. After this, Eichelberger was to land at Nasugbu on the southwest coast of Luzon and drive north and east on Manila itself.

Both the Army and Navy were concerned about the old American defenses on Grande Island at the mouth of Subic Bay; photographs had revealed activity there, and Fifth bombers and fighters dropped one hundred and seventy-five tons of

The 35th Group's *Princess Margie* lands at Mangaldan on Luzon. The yellow nose blaze and tail number identify her as a 41st Squadron aircraft.

Lieutenant Arthur Bourque's *Swing Shift Skipper,* a P-61B from the 547th Night Fighter Squadron, lands at Lingayen.

bombs on the small island during a week of uneventful missions which began on January 21. The medium and light bombers and fighters swept Bataan looking for what proved to be few military targets—they took some ground fire but found no real opposition.

On January 29 an American force landed without opposition at San Marcelino, which was in the hands of Filipino guerrillas, and the old American airfield there was opened on February 4. The 348th Fighter Group, a flight of P-61s, and a flight of the 3rd Emergency Rescue Squadron moved in over the next few days and additional hardstands were ordered for the Air Apaches—their B-25s began operations from San Marcelino on February 15—and with these units in western Luzon the 309th Bomb Wing was ready to support the ground operations and roam far out into the South China Sea.

Fifth Air Force fighters and photo planes watched over the roads south from Manila to detect troop movements and searched the bays to locate Japanese Hayabusa suicide boats, but found little activity. The Mitchells and A-20s worked with patrol boats to neutralize the suicide boat threat, searching and bombing villages along the shores of the bays and concentrating particularly on Santiago when guerrillas reported boats hidden under houses along the waterfront.

To confuse the enemy in southwest Luzon, a simulated landing was made in Tayabas Bay on the night of January 22, while troop carriers dropped dummy paratroopers east of Lake Taal in Batangas Province. The task force moved in close to the beaches at Nasugbu on January 31, and the troops went ashore. To prevent the enemy's stopping Eichelberger by defending Taygaytay Ridge, about halfway to Manila, it was decided to drop a regiment of paratroopers, and on the morning of February 3, the A-20s attacked the Japanese fields at Lipa and Kalingatan as forty-eight C-47s of the 317th Group took off from Mindoro, covered by P-38s. The troop carriers reached the drop zone without incident and the first eighteen put their paratroops exactly in the area marked by smoke pots. There was an error in a following flight and in a second drop a few hours later, meaning nearly two thirds of the men landed short of where they should have—but the accidental scattering actually made the capture of the objectives easier.

In fact, the drive toward Manila was threatened less by the Japanese than by supply shortages, and as usual the C-47s helped out. Another month of bitter fighting lay ahead and Manila would be smashed to rubble as more than sixteen thousand Japanese fought to the death, but on February 5 MacArthur could announce that the assault phase of the Luzon campaign was over. It would take time to destroy all the enemy on the island and as the American forces undertook to secure the port of Manila, Japanese troops retreated across the bay to Bataan and Corregidor. On February 11 fighters noticed a lot of barge traffic and for the next four days strafing by the 348th's Thunderbolts killed an estimated two thousand enemy troops, but other small craft were able to make the trip safely by night.

Corregidor and Bataan had to be captured before Manila's harbor could be safely used, and it was decided to land a force at Mariveles, at the tip of Bataan, and drop the 503rd Parachute Infantry on Corregidor a day later while simultaneously a force set out from Mariveles to land on the north side of the rocky island. There had been air action against Bataan as a cover for the seizure of San Marcelino and it was intensified. All visible targets in the southern section of Ba-

A Red Raider from the 33rd Squadron over Corregidor, February 1945.

taan were hit by B-24s, A-20s and fighters throughout the day on February 10, and Mariveles town, where the landing would take place, was destroyed by the heavies. Raids were continued on a similar scale through to February 15, and during the morning, after a short naval bombardment, the troops secured their objectives against only slight opposition. That same day troops following a rolling air barrage, which had begun at seven o'clock and continued for ten hours employing forty-eight B-25s and sixty fighters, found fires and Japanese bodies blown to bits and hanging from trees, attesting to the fury of the attacks. Organized resistance in Bataan was broken.

The Japanese defenses and the terrain of Corregidor made the task of the paratroopers dangerous: nobody was sure of the exact strength of the enemy force there, and the slightest miscalculation could put men in the sea or on nearby cliffs. The island had received a substantial share of Fifth Bomber Command's effort and by February 16 over three thousand tons of bombs had tumbled onto the rocky fortress. Antiaircraft fire had ceased on February 12 but two days later carefully concealed guns had scored hits on Allied ships off Mariveles before they could be silenced by gunfire and aerial strikes.

On February 16 the B-24s attacked first, followed by A-20s, then fifty-one

C-47s wheeled over the two small drop areas, depositing the paratroops from five hundred feet. All of the transports made at least three precise runs over the zones and as the paratroopers landed seventy A-20s bombed and strafed targets on Corregidor and Caballo; naval vessels opened fire on San Jose beach to pave the way for the amphibious landing on the north side of the island.

Shortly after, the C-47s were back with more troops and supplies. This drop, like the one in the morning, was marred only by a strong and tricky surface wind which blew some of the men over the cliffs or into obstacles outside the drop zones. Enemy machine gun fire caused a few casualties and damaged a few planes, but operations progressed smoothly. Air support strikes were effective and napalm penetrated some caves to a depth of thirty-five feet. By February 27 only a few small parties of Japanese remained on the island and at the beginning of March Manila Bay was again an Allied anchorage.

* * *

The original plans for Luzon envisaged little more than the tactical employment of air power and Kenney and Whitehead had asked for an exploitation which would give them heavy bomber bases as far north as possible; Fifth Air Force had moved its headquarters forward to Mindoro at the end of January and on February 20 General Kenney conferred with Generals Whitehead and Wurtsmith and Air Vice-Marshals Bostock and Isitt of the Australian and New Zealand air forces.

Kenney gave complete responsibility for all air operations south of the Philippines to Bostock, as well as operational control of the New Zealand units to assist him if he needed help, and Wurtsmith's Thirteenth Air Force would also provide support when called for. Wurtsmith's primary responsibility was the control of all operations in the Philippines, except for those on Luzon, and he would help Eichelberger in his mission to capture the Philippines south of Luzon. Landings were scheduled for Puerto Princesa on Palawan and Zamboanga on the southwestern tip of Mindanao. If necessary the Thirteenth would also add weight to the Fifth's operations in Luzon and to the north.

Kenney told Whitehead to move up to Clark Field as soon as he could and get his aircraft into Luzon as fast as airfield construction allowed. He was to assist in mopping up Luzon, to paralyze Formosa, and to blockade the China Sea.

* * *

Japanese resistance was collapsing on Luzon. In a well-planned amphibious and paratroop action, over two thousand internees at the Los Baños Agricultural College were liberated on February 23. The airborne part of the operation was carried out by ten C-47s from the 65th Troop Carrier Squadron and one hundred and twenty-five paratroopers, their jump coinciding perfectly with the arrival of infiltration parties. The paratroops landed at the edge of the college grounds and joined the others, surprising the enemy before they could get to their weapons. Fighters strafed and bombed the surrounding area and the surprise was so complete that while only two Americans were killed, nearly two hundred and fifty Japanese died.

The troops were pushing on and completed occupation of the southern shores of Manila Bay on March 2. The next stage of the plans called for the opening of Balayan and Batangas bays, followed by an advance eastward into areas held by

When the Mexican 201st Squadron reached Clark Field in April it was attached to the 58th Fighter Group and inherited many 35th and 348th Group Thunderbolts. *Me Darlin* was Captain Morgan Beamer's aircraft before the 41st Squadron received P-51s.

some ten thousand enemy troops. At the same time there was to be a landing at Legaspi about March 20 to drive northward. The attack began on March 6 and the two bays were secured by the end of the month, but reports of stiff beach defenses complicated plans for the Legaspi invasion. The Fifth, due to move its headquarters to Clark Field on March 24, gave the 310th Wing on Mindoro the job of preparing for the landing and supplying convoy cover and close support. Fifth Bomber Command was to strike the area with Liberators, particularly the port and beach defenses. However, the Navy wanted additional time to ensure neutralization of the fortifications, and the landing was postponed until April 1. Although the B-24s had problems the bombers and fighters from Mindoro dumped tons of demolition, incendiary and fragmentation bombs, and napalm on the town's defenses. While Whitehead and the Army both sought to limit attacks to specific military targets, troop movements in the town forced the Fifth to level it with a maximum effort on March 31. When the troops landed the following morning the enemy had abandoned the defenses. During April and May they worked up the Bicol Peninsula while other American troops cleared out the area southeast of Lagunade Bay. The Japanese were in scattered hill positions which they contested bitterly even in the face of frequent and devastating air attacks, but they were fighting a hopeless battle. On April 20 MacArthur announced that the entire central Philippines, the Visayas, were cleared of enemy forces.

Loaded with napalm, 58th Fighter Group P-47s head for enemy installations near Ipo Dam. Luzon had been drenched by four inches of rain before the strikes but the liquid fire sent pillars of smoke towering to three thousand feet. Japanese wing tanks captured at Clark Field made useful containers during the all-out napalm campaign.

Late in April MacArthur raised the point of the low water supply reaching Manila and recommended that the Ipo Dam be captured as soon as possible because there were dangers of disease if it was destroyed or remained in Japanese hands. Kenney was completely in favor of these missions—he invited Whitehead to his house in Manila, pointed out the empty swimming pool, and told him that if he only had water in that pool he "could invite him down for a swim before dinner sometime." He suggested that it might be a good idea if Whitehead got in touch with the Army and offered to put a couple of hundred planeloads of napalm on the Japanese positions and burn them out. If the job was done on a grand scale the enemy would not have enough time to blow up the dam.

Fifth Fighter Command quickly prepared for the largest napalm missions of the Pacific war: between May 3 and May 5, a total of nearly two hundred and fifty fighters saturated the outlying defenses of the Ipo area with napalm and bombs, turning it into a boiling sea of fire. The attacks were very destructive, and when the fire exploded near the Japanese positions the troops seemingly lost all caution and fled into the open, easy targets. The American force jumped off on May 6 and moved forward against token resistance, estimating along the way that at least six hundred and fifty Japanese had been killed by the air action alone. Many more had been cut down as they ran into the open and there were over two thousand corpses littering the area. The Ipo Dam had been rigged for demoliton but was captured intact. The troops turned the water on, and Kenney suddenly remembered that he had left the valves open in his swimming pool. He called his house and learned that there was water a foot deep all over the lawn.

*   *   *

Resistance had collapsed in southern Luzon, but in northern Luzon the Japanese were in favorable positions and fought a losing but stubborn campaign until the final surrender, giving ground slowly under continuous pressure. Working around the coastal route, a guerrilla force entered Aparri without opposition on June 21 but was too weak to hold the escape route. A paratroop attack was ordered and on three days' notice the 317th Troop Carrier Group, filled out by seven C-46s from the 433rd Group for towing cargo gliders, moved down to Lipa airstrip. On the morning of June 23 the transports dropped nearly a thousand men of the 511th Parachute Infantry on the abandoned Japanese airdrome at Camalaniugan. Three days later elements of the 511th Regiment and 37th Division met at Alcala and except for mopping-up operations the campaign for Luzon was completed.

The Fifth's close support missions were their most notable, although only part of the story. Over twenty-six thousand fighter and bomber sorties were flown between January 28 and March 10, and of these over twenty-four thousand were in support of the ground forces. More than eleven thousand tons of bombs and eight million rounds of ammunition helped clear the way for the Army, and there were few mistakes. Back on January 29 Mustangs shot up friendly troops along the Pampanga River, but Whitehead had not been able to discover which were guilty and began to suspect Japanese Tonys with American insignia might have done the strafing. So he grounded all Mustangs for ten days and sent out patrols to shoot down any they found.

There was no end to the usefulness of the C-47; Colonel John Lackey, commander of the 317th Troop Carrier Group, briefs crews on the Camalaniugan operation of June 23, 1945.

Cleo and the rest of the second flight of 317th Group C-47s drop paratroopers of the 11th Airborne Division over Camalaniugan airstrip.

From experience Kenney had cautioned his pilots against flying over friendly ships, and Whitehead demanded detailed checks and positive identification of targets before any attack. When Liberators bombed nine to ten miles off target he promptly relieved the group commander, although luckily no harm had been done.

The Fifth's role in direct support had to be judged by the men on the ground, and they called it "superb."

VII

End of an Empire

IN the spring of 1945 there was still no directive covering operations after the reduction of the Philippines. Kenney and Whitehead were anxious to get their aircraft as far forward as possible, and had hoped to put both the Fifth and Thirteenth on the northwestern coast of Luzon. Back in the middle of February Kenney had secured a commitment from headquarters defining the Luzon air garrison, and with this authority, five all-weather airdromes were secured—Clark, Porac, Floridablanca, Nichols, and Nielson. The first three were spread about twenty miles north and south of Fort Stotsensburg and were for the tactical units, Clark and Floridablanca having dual bomber runways capable of extension for B-29s. Work began on the fields early in March and they were virtually complete in May.

The five Luzon airfields were only part of what Kenney eventually wanted, but they met Far East Air Forces' immediate needs. If it was to begin missions to the China coast and sustained attacks on Formosa it needed another Luzon field as far north as possible, and when the guerrillas captured the Laoag area early in March, Colonel David Hutchison, commander of the 308th Wing, flew food up and got local natives working on the Japanese strip. On May 22 an all-weather runway became operational, and late in April the 3rd Air Commando Group moved in and took command of Gabo Field, which would become a vital link in the movement to Okinawa.

From Luzon the Fifth Air Force could look back at the large enemy forces it had bypassed in the Netherlands East Indies, Borneo, and the southern Philippines. Attacked from the air continually, these garrisons were methodically battered and were unable to interfere with Allied operations. With Luzon in Allied hands, American forces were in a position to impose even more effective interdiction of the lines of communication between these outposts and the Japanese homeland and stop any chance of reinforcement. At this stage an Allied invasion of

The 43rd Bomb Group at sprawling Clark Field. Ken's Men did not begin using tail markings until fully equipped with B-24s; the 63rd Squadron, attacking by night, developed their Seahawks insignia, and the 65th had a pair of dice on a blue circle, showing six and five for the squadron on top, with four and three for the group below. The other two squadrons used more normal markings—the 64th had a diagonal tail stripe, and the 403rd painted the tips of their fins in white on older camouflaged aircraft, in black on the newer unpainted B-24s.

Japan was considered certain, and there was a natural temptation to leave the bypassed bastions to "wither on the vine," but there were objections to this. During the planning of the Philippines operations it had been obvious that air bases in Borneo would increase effectiveness of any attempt to strangle Japanese communications in the South China Sea. The United States was by far the senior member of the alliance in the Southwest Pacific, but General MacArthur felt that Australian and Dutch interests in the bypassed area could not be ignored without violating the international agreement on which his command was built, and the forces to go back and finish these jobs were available. It had been decided not to use Australian units in the Philippines and RAAF Command and veteran Australian troops could undertake attacks on the Netherlands East Indies and Borneo. The Thirteenth Air Force could back up the Australians from its bases, and Washington's delay in deciding what would happen to MacArthur's command after the Luzon campaign was an added incentive to the planning of sidelight offensives.

The Fifth played little part in the operations, although it did step in for the invasion of Borneo on July 1. The Jolly Rogers and Flying Circus joined the Thirteenth's two heavy groups and the Australian B-24 squadrons in a sustained effort throughout June. On June 23 the Red Raiders and 38th Group moved to Thirteenth Air Force bases on Morotai and Palawan, and a Fifth Air Force night fighter squadron moved into Zamboanga to provide night cover. Antiaircraft positions were the most important targets at first, but weather often caused diversion to others. The continued onslaught had a cumulative effect, and although the antiaircraft positions were not knocked out, the minesweeping was completed on time. The bad weather had also interfered with fighter cover and it was decided to use three escort carriers for the immediate period leading up to the landing. All the other commitments were carried out thoroughly, especially accurate bombing attacks close to shore which shielded the underwater demolition work. The Fifth's share of the pre-assault bombing totals for the Balikpapan area included five hundred and sixty-three Liberator and sixty-eight Mitchell sorties.

There was the usual pattern of tactical isolation by the medium bombers, fighter sweeps of overland routes of communication with Balikpapan, barge hunts along the coastline, and heavy bomber missions against airfields within staging range of Balikpapan. On July 1, after a two-hour naval bombardment and a forty-minute precision attack by a combined force of eighty-three B-24s, the assault troops landed five minutes ahead of schedule under cover of a B-25 smoke screen. Direct air support was provided by B-24s and P-38s and in three days the town and docks of Balikpapan were secured. During the rest of the month progress was slow in eliminating enemy centers of resistance, but as the Fifth Air Force turned its attention again toward the invasion of Japan, its last operation with its Australian ally had underlined the bond cemented many months before in New Guinea.

Target: Formosa

As the Philippines campaign ground toward conclusion the Fifth, although still engaged in the tactical support of the ground and naval forces, took on new responsibilities of a more strategic nature. Formosa, lying halfway between Japan and the southern limits of her conquests, was the main outpost along the routes from Japan to the Netherlands East Indies and Malaya. It dominated vital sea lanes, was a staging and supply base for far-flung enemy garrisons, and made important contributions to Japan's economy. It was essential to protect the American forces in the Philippines and Ryukyus by neutralizing the many Formosa airfields, but the massive air attacks of 1945 served a dual purpose and were combined with efforts to strangle Japanese shipping in the South China Sea.

Formosa is nearly two hundred and fifty miles long, with a climate conducive to the production of sugar cane and its by-product, alcohol. During the war many of the sugar refineries had been converted to produce butanol, a hydrocarbon used in manufacturing aviation gasoline, and electrical power plants on Formosa helped produce about 10 per cent of Japan's aluminum. Iron, copper, salt, and oil refining were other contributions to the enemy war effort. The cities of Takao and Kiirun had extensive port facilities, and two main railway lines on either side of the mountainous backbone connected north and south. On the eastern and western coastal plains the enemy had built up an airdrome system second only to those in

Japan itself. In the spring of 1945 there were about fifty fields, the most important being Heito, Tainan, Okayama, Matsuyama, and Takao; by then Formosa was an old target, but although the island had been neutralized during the invasion of Luzon, it had to be kept under control. The job went naturally to the Fifth Air Force. Its heavy bombers had been restricted in the Philippines because of the friendly population, but Formosa was a different story.

The campaign actually began on the night of January 11, when three 63rd Squadron Liberators from Tacloban flew the first mission to Heito. One turned back with engine trouble but the other two attacked the storage, fuel dump, and administration areas, starting raging fires. The B-24s went back for the next two nights and for a week Okayama airdrome was the target. On January 16 a specially equipped B-24 flew the first of a series of anti-radar reconnaissance "ferret" missions over Formosa, and on January 21 the Fifth's fighters made a sweep from Luzon. The heavy bombers began daylight bombardment the next day, as the night bombers turned to Takao, Formosa's leading city, and its Nippon Aluminum Company. Then airfields were the primary targets for over two weeks. If the airdromes were closed in by cloud, the night bombers would make radar or elapsed-time bomb runs over sprawling Takao, where some kind of worthwhile damage was almost certain. The Formosa targets were hit repeatedly. On February 12 the 63rd Squadron was returned to its favorite target, Japanese shipping, but later its planes occasionally flew night attacks on Formosa airfields, mainly during the invasion of Okinawa. The Jolly Rogers' radar B-24s carried on the night missions against Formosa and were often used as pathfinders for daylight missions, one leading each squadron. At the end of February more of the specially equipped Liberators reached the theater and went to the 43rd, the Red Raiders, and later the Flying Circus. As well as leading the bombers through bad weather and flying night missions, these B-24s provided weather information for daylight attacks.

Day missions against Formosa had faced difficulties—Whitehead wanted to begin the attack on January 16 with two groups of B-24s, a group of B-25s, and P-38 cover, but poor weather and delays with the Mindoro airfields, coupled with the demands of the Luzon campaign, forced cancellation. A similar attack was planned for January 21, with the Red Raiders flying from their new Samar base, but the Liberator part of the mission had to be canceled when the plane carrying Colonel Richard W. Robinson, the twenty-six-year-old commanding officer of the 22nd, crashed. As the takeoff time approached that morning, the rain was pouring down, and the low spots on the Guiuan runway were full of water.

The lead B-24, piloted by Captain James Hume with Robinson in command, lined up on the runway and got the barely visible green light to go. The takeoff began normally, but then the Liberator seemed to be sliding off the center of the strip to the left. As it passed the middle of the runway the pilots were applying all the power they had. The B-24 passed close by a Marine Corsair and one of its prop blades sawed eight feet from the bomber's left wing.

Straining under full power, the Liberator tried to take off—it was too late to stop. There was a sea of mud beyond the runway where the field was being extended. Still sliding to the left, the B-24 crashed into a heavy-duty earth mover five hundred yards from the end of the strip. Everything went up in a huge ball of flame, and spiraling concussion rings rolled upward. No one survived.

"Waterhall," the code word meaning cancellation of the strike, went out, and the

8th and 49th Fighter Group Lightnings carried out a sweep of southern Formosa, meeting no opposition.

The next day the Red Raiders flew the first daylight mission to Formosa, covered by P-38s, and smothered the Heito air base with bombs. Antiaircraft fire was heavy but only one plane was damaged, and there was no fighter interception. The Formosa missions were limited by other requirements, but after the landing on Corregidor the way was clear for all-out attacks again. The weather sometimes protected the northern end of the island, but southern Formosa was pounded unmercifully.

During the campaign Japanese airfields suffered most. The Jolly Rogers flew the second daylight attack on January 29 and fifteen to twenty Japanese fighters from Takao were chased away by the P-38s before any interception was attempted. The Jolly Rogers returned to Formosa three times and when the heavies concentrated on Corregidor the 38th Group's B-25s introduced the Japanese at Kagi airdrome to minimum-altitude bombing and strafing. As soon as their work on Luzon was over, two Liberator groups were slated for Heito on February 17 but bad weather diverted them to Takao. The Flying Circus had just moved from Darwin to Mindoro, and joined in the Formosa missions on February 18, when Brigadier General Jarred V. Crabb of Fifth Bomber Command threw all four B-24 groups into a full-strength strike. Three groups had Okayama as their target, but only one bombed there and the others hit Takao. The next day clouds again protected Heito, forcing two of the three heavy groups to Koshun and Takao instead. The Formosa missions continued through February, although the main effort of the Fifth was directed to Luzon again. They returned to attack Formosa airdromes in force on March 2; while Jolly Rogers and Flying Circus B-24s hit Matsuyama, Air Apache B-25s strafed and bombed Toyohara airdrome and the 38th Group worked over Taichu. The A-20s of the 312th Group made their first visit to Formosa, but were unable to find Kagi airdrome and hit a small field at Shirakawa and other targets of opportunity including warehouses, bridges, and railway equipment. One enemy fighter intercepted but was shot down so quickly by so many people that the fighter pilots drew straws to decide who would claim him. Heavy weather interfered the next day, but the Jolly Rogers attacked Kiirun Harbor by radar and the Red Raiders bombed cloud-covered Tainan airstrip. The B-25s were also thwarted by cloud but hit Basco on Batan Island.

The bad weather and the support missions on Luzon gave Formosa respite until March 16, when eighty-six B-24s divided the job of battering the enemy's airfields. The next day the four groups sent seventy Liberators to saturate four airfields, but the cloud cover forced almost all of the bombing to be done by radar and the low-level attacks had to be called off. Forty-six Liberators followed up on March 18 at Tainan, Koshun and Toko. Cloud over other airdromes resulted in Tainan and its airdrome receiving the total tonnage from seventy-seven Liberators on March 22, and Tainan caught it again on March 28. Three days later the Red Raiders covered Matsuyama with fragmentation bombs.

The estimated number of Japanese planes on Formosa airfields dropped from six hundred on January 14 to three hundred and seventy-five at the end of March, and with the invasion of Okinawa scheduled for April 1, the Fifth continued hitting the fields day and night. Although most strikes were smaller than the big raids of March, Japanese air power continued to be the target of more than half the effort against Formosa through April. As the B-24s and B-25s hit the airdromes at every opportunity, the estimated number of enemy planes on Formosa continued to diminish, until by April 26 it was down to eighty-nine, and less than twenty were believed to be flyable at any one time. There had been few enemy raids on Luzon bases or on Allied shipping in Lingayen and Subic bays, and interception of American planes over Formosa was rare.

During the second half of April, Central Pacific forces at Okinawa were being battered by kamikazes and wanted heavy attacks on Formosa airfields, believing that this was where the suicide planes were based. The Fifth's intelligence officers insisted that Formosa's air power had been reduced to such an extent that the suicide planes must be coming from Kyushu. Later investigation proved both were right—most of the kamikaze attacks came from Kyushu, but perhaps 20 per cent were flown from Formosa, where the enemy had cleverly camouflaged and dispersed their aircraft. In February 1945, accepting the Philippines were lost and resigned to the fact that any attempt to fight for the air over Formosa would result in rapid defeat, the Japanese chose to use their planes in suicide attacks to halt an invasion of Formosa or Okinawa. They virtually discontinued flying between morning and evening, when Allied aircraft were most likely to be overhead, and although Japanese aircraft tracked bomber formations to pass on information to antiaircraft gunners, interceptions were rare. The enemy aircraft were widely dispersed, often dragged miles away from the airstrips, and in one instance ferried across a river. Some were even partly dismantled or hidden in obscure villages and towns. Dummy airplanes and airfields were built, and the regular cloud cover over northern Formosa allowed the Japanese to move planes from airfield to airfield.

A Lockheed F-5 Lightning of the 26th Photo Recon Squadron leaves Lingayen to watch over enemy activity on Formosa.

Toddy of the 380th Bomb Group was one of seven aircraft in the 531st Squadron to fly over one hundred missions. They nearly got her over Taichu on May 18, 1945, when Lieutenant Tom Cook had his nosewheel shot out, the hydraulics smashed, and his co-pilot "scratched on the fanny," but they got her home. She carries the 531st's Flying Circus motif, a seal balancing a sputtering bomb.

Allied intelligence knew of the Japanese dispersal program, but had no idea of the lengths they were going to—when they estimated only eighty-nine planes, the Japanese in fact had about seven hundred.

Headquarters agreed to the Navy's request for increased pressure on enemy airfields on Formosa, and the Fifth found reason to change its original assessment when, in May and June, photo reconnaissance revealed that planes listed as unserviceable were repaired and more dispersal fields were being prepared. While it was true that some of the kamikaze attacks came from Formosa, sending large forces against such scattered targets would be a waste of effort which could be more profitably used elsewhere. Whenever a fair concentration of aircraft was discovered on Formosa airfields the B-24s attacked in force—on June 15 eighty-four Liberators covered the Taichu airstrip with fragmentation bombs. The night-flying B-24s went out to frustrate Japanese preparations for suicide attacks, probably the most effective answer to the problem. Attacks were also begun on enemy bases on the China coast, which the Fifth believed to be another source of the suicide attacks.

While the main effort of the Liberators was being directed against airfields during the early stages of the Formosa campaign, the night bombers poked around Formosa harbors looking for shipping, or burning up docks and warehouses. The Jolly Rogers had carried out the first daylight heavy strike against harbor installations on February 27 and during March and April oil storage tanks and the large Japanese naval base at Mako, and docks and shipping installations at Kiirun and Takao were hit. Shipping sweeps by the medium bombers covered the east and west coasts of Formosa and escorting fighters often strafed along the shore before going home. In a mast-height attack in Mako Harbor on April 4, twelve Air Apaches destroyed or damaged six merchant vessels. On May 19 over a hundred Liberators bombed shore installations and shipping at Kiirun and by the end of June the damage there was so extensive that the night bombers turned their attention to Mako. All the while the B-25s, A-20s, and B-24s were littering lesser targets on Formosa with high explosive.

They also destroyed Formosa's railroad system and bridges, the heaviest damage being done by mediums and fighters strafing rolling stock. The attack on the railways peaked during the last half of May and most of the B-25 low-level sorties

Just returned from a Formosa mission, this 823rd Squadron crew is quizzed by intelligence officers while ground crewmen attend to the eight nose guns of their B-25J.

that month were directed against marshaling yards, railroad stations, and bridges. Meanwhile, Fifth Fighter Command was shooting up tracks and equipment between stations. The 49th Fighter Group got four locomotives and eight cars with an estimated two hundred passengers on May 27 and 1st Air Commando P-51s from Laoag destroyed two engines and damaged six boxcars the next day; by June the Japanese were operating their trains only by night.

Some of the most crippling attacks were the strikes against two electricity plants in the mountains—Formosa's main source of power. Four B-24 groups were supposed to make the attack on March 13, but the thick cloud forced all but sixteen Jolly Rogers to go to secondary targets; they bombed by radar without seeing anything but a promising pillar of black smoke. Ten days later, twenty-three Red Raiders hit one of the plants while fourteen Ken's Men B-24s struck the other, and direct hits on vital areas shut off 60 per cent of Formosa's power for the rest of the war. Other attacks had also disrupted lesser plants, and all but one of the principal towns and cities on Formosa were without power in the summer of 1945. Only one did not suffer loss of water supply due to damage of its water and pipe systems, and while the shortage of shipping had already seriously affected production on Formosa, the three-way blows completely crippled it. First denied materials, the plants were denied power and methodically destroyed.

The scattered sugar mills on Formosa were an important part of the enemy project for production of alcohol and butanol for aviation fuel, and air strikes against the sugar mills and alcohol plants were second in intensity only to those aimed at crushing the enemy air power. The targets were not heavily defended by antiaircraft early in the campaign as the B-25s and A-20s began the raids: the 312th Group hit an alcohol plant at Kyoshito on March 25, four days later eighteen A-20s burned out the entire area of the sugar refinery at Eiko with napalm and

Lieutenant John Boyd's *Pretty Pat,* from the Air Apaches' 499th Squadron, undergoes a thorough overhaul at Lingayen. Behind her is a 3rd Air Commando C-47.

This Air Apache was mortally hit by a concealed antiaircraft battery at the Byoritsu oil refinery on May 26, 1945, and seconds later was a heap of blazing wreckage. The minimum-altitude missions were always dangerous.

bombs, and B-25s dropped parademos throughout the oil refinery and power plant at Byoritsu. Seventeen Mitchells exploded and burned two factories at Toyohara on March 30; two locomotives and a string of freight cars were hit as the planes passed on to refineries at Kori and Tenshi, and a refinery and barracks area at Taichu. The 312th Group struck Shinei, and on April 4 the bombers fired the entire production area at Suan Tau; a sweep by thirteen 38th Group B-25s on April 11 erased another plant. The targets were so explosive that the force of planes assigned to each mission was gradually cut down. The sugar and alcohol plant at Hokko was hit on April 23 by nine Mitchells, another was knocked out by seven A-20s the next day, and five Grim Reapers smashed the Taito sugar refinery. Eighteen Mitchells plastered the Heito refinery on April 26, and the same number of Mitchells hit the Koshun alcohol plant and Koshun town two days later. The alcohol plant at Taito was hit by five Mitchells on May 5 while six others hit the sugar refinery at Shoka. Flying in two- and three-plane attacks, B-25s hit the Byoritsu alcohol plant on May 13 and five more over the next three days. Before the end of May nineteen plants had been hit.

The Japanese built up antiaircraft defenses around the plants, leading to a change in tactics in June, with the heavy and very heavy bombers taking part. Two B-32s, *Hobo Queen II* and *The Lady is Fresh,* dropped two-thousand-pound bombs through the clouds on the sugar mill at Taito on June 15. A week later a B-32 scored on the alcohol plant at Heito, and the same day Liberators hit the oil refinery and antiaircraft positions at Toshien. During the last days of June heavy strikes damaged refineries and butanol plants, and in July several single-plane strikes were flown by the heavy bombers. The final mission was run on July 12 by the Grim Reapers with nine of their new A-26s, to the Taiharo sugar refinery.

In all, about thirty known sugar refineries and alcohol and butanol plants were attacked. The onslaught on the railway system, coupled with the forced conversion from sugar cane to rice crops as the Japanese tried to make Formosa self-sufficient in food, added to the effects.

Many of the important targets on Formosa were in the cities and towns, and area bombing was often employed. The 38th and the Air Apaches teamed up to raze the town and sugar refinery at Kari on May 10 and the next day the B-25s finished off Kagi town, already partly destroyed. One Air Apache had a lucky escape. Flight Officer William Matthews' 501st Squadron B-25 was passing over Kobi town and airstrip on the approach run to Kagi when his plane took hits in the nose and right engine. The Mitchell skidded down to the right, onto the Kobi strip, but bounced back into the air. Matthews regained control and joined up with the 499th Squadron, which had just cleared the target. On one engine, he flew the battered plane back across the Formosa Strait and landed at Laoag. Four of the nose guns on the B-25 had been blasted away and there were at least one hundred and eighteen holes in the right engine nacelle.

During May the B-24s were helping burn Formosa, but commitments to support the Balikpapan landings limited heavy and medium operations against the island during June. In July the Navy's requests for airdrome strikes also cut into the tonnage available for the urban destruction, but the job had been done. Of the eleven principal cities on Formosa, five were almost completely destroyed and four were half destroyed. At Takao the city was nearly erased, and the hulks of ships sunk at

Lieutenant Harold Barrett's 403rd Squadron B-24 over sprawling Takao on June 4, 1945. (Barrett)

the entrance to the harbor blocked the channel to the point that only vessels of less than one hundred tons could use it.

Fifth Bomber Command had done most of the work, flying 87 per cent of the total sorties and dropping over 98 per cent of the bombs. The B-24s had flown over five thousand sorties and the B-25s more than fourteen hundred. The remainder, just under two hundred, was divided between the A-20s, A-26s, and B-32s. The antiaircraft defenses had been the most concentrated since Rabaul and flak damage was relatively high. The Formosa campaign was completed in July, except for a few fighter sweeps which went there in August.

Cutting the Lifeline

As the Fifth moved into Philippines bases they were able to begin strangling Japanese shipping in the South China Sea, and although other targets were higher on the list, time was found to play a major part in cutting Japan's most important lifeline.

Japanese shipping along the Asiatic coast had first been attacked by General Claire L. Chennault's Fourteenth Air Force early in the war, but when the Japanese overran the forward bases in China, Southwest Pacific planes took over the job. Although Whitehead directed most of the aerial operations it was a combined effort—Navy Liberators flew daylight search missions as far north as Shanghai and covered most of the South China Sea, and in the far southern areas they were aided by Thirteenth Air Force planes, first from Morotai and later from the Philippines. Radar-equipped B-24s of the Fifth, Thirteenth, and Fourteenth searched the seas by night, while Australian Catalinas mined the coastal waters of Formosa, Indo-China, and China.

Ten 38th Group Mitchells had good luck against a convoy on February 22 when they reported a destroyer sunk and a freighter left burning, but the claim was never officially credited. Sailing junks were presumed to be Chinese fishing vessels and left alone, but powered junks in the open seas were deemed Japanese and attacked whenever bigger shipping was scarce. Ten to fifteen of them were sunk near Hong Kong on February 27 during a B-25 sweep, and Mitchells hunting between Hong Kong and Swatow sank a fifteen-hundred-ton cargo ship on March 1.

On the night of March 27 a B-24 of the 63rd Squadron piloted by Lieutenant William Williams answered a call from an unarmed search plane which had found a large convoy. Reaching the target at about eleven o'clock in the morning, after a seven-hour flight, Williams made his bombing run at three hundred feet through heavy antiaircraft fire. Three bombs bracketed a ship he thought was a tanker, but did not explode. Williams turned his damaged plane around for a second run and got two hits which set fire to the vessel. Coming off the target the Liberator was attacked by two Oscars, and the co-pilot was killed by a cannon shell on the first pass. The radar operator was hit on the second pass, and the right inboard engine was knocked out during the third. The top turret gunner shot up one of the fighters, which trailed smoke as it disappeared into the clouds, but the B-24, with its electrical and hydraulic systems gone, became so nose-heavy that it took two

The first wave of Air Apaches pounces on one of two frigates caught off the French Indo-China coast on March 29, 1945.

men to hold the control wheels back. Finally reaching its base, the plane came in fast and crashed at the end of the strip. Williams claimed the sinking, later credited as a seven-thousand-ton cargo vessel.

Thirty-one Air Apaches hit the same convoy farther north along the Indo-China coast on March 29, and reported sinking three large merchant vessels, a smaller ship, four destroyers or frigates, and a patrol craft. The Air Apaches had decided to send their strike force in two waves; the first was to track down the convoy, while the second followed thirty minutes later and proceeded directly to the attack, guided by radio. The plan worked perfectly and two frigates were sighted. Eight planes of the 501st Squadron, led by Captain Jones, and seven from the 498th concentrated on the two vessels. Several good hits were scored and the ships burned and sank. The two frigates had been bringing up the rear of the convoy; up ahead, in foul weather, was the main body. Jones selected a merchant vessel and attacked as his wingman, out of bombs, made a strafing run. Meanwhile, Colonel Chester Coltharp, flying as co-pilot in the lead B-25, had called the squadrons of the sec-

Major George Laven of the 49th Fighter Group destroyed five enemy planes and scores of enemy locomotives. During one mission in June 1945, he and his wingman attacked a chemical plant at Shinyei on Formosa, then separated to look for targets. Seeing smoke in the distance, Laven found an engine pulling twelve flatcars and destroyed it. At Kyushu he found another train, and his strafing blew up the boilers and set fire to eight passenger coaches. Cruising north at about a thousand feet Laven found an Emily flying boat and shot it down. He wound up the day by strafing a sugar mill at Koshun. Laven's P-38L, *Itsy Bitsy II,* was maintained by the 8th Fighter Squadron, and much of the black paint covers areas where the Lightning had taken hits. (George Laven)

ond wave and given them the position of the convoy. As they approached, the burning vessels guided them in, fresh and ready for the attack. They hit the main body of the convoy and in the ensuing engagements the pilots were frequently flying on instruments going in and out of the weather. Eleven planes were damaged but only one man was grazed by a bullet, and in all the B-25s were credited with four merchant and five naval vessels.

The next night, bomber operations were extended northward to Shanghai along the Yangtze River, to search for shipping. Fifth Fighter Command was regularly covering B-25 and rescue missions, and sometimes the fighters escorted B-24s searching by day. They regularly shot down Japanese fighters and Japanese strength was pruned to such an extent that by April few enemy ships had friendly air cover. Captain Tokuma Abe, a Japanese convoy commander, said, "When we requested air cover, only American planes showed up." By that time the attacks on Formosa had forced the Japanese to withdraw most of their surviving aircraft to bases on the China coast, and ultimately their movement still farther back, to Shanghai and Kyushu.

General Crabb decided to use his heavy bombers to stop Japanese shipping hiding by day in harbors which were too heavily defended for B-25 attack, and on March 31 Liberators attacked Yulin Harbor on Hainan Island. Ken's Men and the Red Raiders hit Hong Kong on April 3, and again the next day, and twelve Air Apaches attacked the Mako naval base, where two small tankers were found on opposite sides of the fueling pier. One direct hit exploded one of the tankers, burning oil ran across the pier and set fire to the other tanker. Both were officially credited to the B-25s.

On April 5 three Grim Reapers carried out a unique strike against shipping: Colonel Richard Ellis, commanding the 3rd Attack, had rigged up extra wing tanks for his A-20s, and he asked permission to test his long-range planes against enemy shipping. Neither Whitehead nor Kenney were enthused about the idea, but unknown to them Ellis had also approached Colonel David Hutchison of the 308th Bomb Wing at Lingayen. Hutchison agreed to trying the A-20s on the next convoy, on condition that the B-25s worked it over before they went in. When enemy shipping was reported off Hong Kong on April 5 the B-25s left Lingayen, followed thirty minutes later by Colonel Ellis with his three A-20s. His two wingmen were his deputy group commander and operations officer, and the tiny force was escorted by three P-38s, flown by Colonel Jerry Johnson, Major George Laven, and Major James Watkins. While his wingmen attacked the escorts, Ellis sank a cargo ship in shallow water, and one of the escorts was dead in the water and the other was damaged before the A-20s went home. When Kenney heard the story he didn't know whether to reprimand Ellis or decorate him—so he told him no more combat flying and made him Assistant Deputy Chief of Operations of Far East Air Forces. Kenney had real problems with some of his kids.

The next day the Fifth flew one of the most savage shipping strikes of the war. It began when two dozen Air Apaches headed out to get a convoy reported off Amoy. There were two frigates and a destroyer with a jury-rigged bow, and that particular destroyer was well known to the Mitchells. It had first been seen under repair at Singapore on February 10, and during a sweep of Yulin Harbor on March 30 the same ship had shot down an Air Apache B-25. Photographs taken early in April had shown it in Hong Kong Harbor.

The 501st Squadron, leading, passed to the left of the two frigates and wheeled around and down. The nearest warship received the full weight of the attack by the squadron's six planes and went under in a few minutes. Both frigates had turned to starboard as the B-25s came in, enabling four planes to carry their attack on to the second ship. Although they got one direct hit and near misses it was the 499th's second flight, next over, which did the job. The vessel was sinking as the six planes of the 498th came in, but it was still firing and Lieutenant Charles Myers' plane was badly hit. He made it back on one engine.

Seeing the two frigates disposed of, the 500th Squadron turned south to attack the *Asashio* class destroyer with the temporary bow. It took violent evasive action and threw up intense fire, an explosive shell wounding the squadron leader, Lieutenant George Schmidt, and his co-pilot and navigator. One of the planes flying on Schmidt's wing was also hit, but both continued their run over the ship. Schmidt managed to get back to base after scoring a direct hit which caused a huge explosion, but his wingman crashed into the sea. Captain Albin Johnson, leading the

The Air Apaches found two frigates escorting the destroyer *Amatsukaze* off the coast of Amoy on April 6, 1945, and the 499th Squadron's B-25s dispatched this one quickly.

Lieutenant Francis Thompson wheels his bat-nosed B-25 over the doomed warship.

Lieutenant Louie Mikell's bombs rolled the frigate onto her side; the Air Apaches summed it up neatly when they reported that these Japanese were left "scared, shipless." (Jerry Lahmsen)

498th Squadron, swung in to attack with his five planes even though his nose guns would not fire. He dropped his two remaining bombs for a direct hit but his B-25 was crippled and on fire—he made a fair ditching about two miles farther on but only one survivor was sighted. As the last Air Apache pulled away the destroyer was burning fiercely.

A twelve-to-fifteen-ship convoy had been found on the night of April 5 and the 63rd Squadron shadowed it for three days and nights, picking off a transport and a destroyer. The 38th Group's Mitchells could not find the ships in bad weather and the convoy finally made it beyond the range of the night bombers, but by this time permission had been received to bomb targets on the Chinese mainland, so that secondary targets, usually airdromes, regularly suffered at the end of a blank sea search.

Few ships were being found in open water so the heavy and medium bombers visited harbors in China and Indo-China. Liberators hit shipping at Saigon and Yulin Harbor on Hainan, and on April 28 B-25s sweeping the Saigon River claimed four large merchant vessels probably sunk, although antiaircraft fire and enemy fighters shot down three of the Mitchells. Except for the regular searches, few shipping missions were flown in May—the night bombers made many attacks during the month but none of their claims were officially confirmed. On June 13 sixty-two Liberators loaded with napalm went after the wooden ships crammed into Hong Kong Harbor, and the bay became a sea of fire.

The Japanese tried everything, but the pressure from air and sea was strangling them. On April 9 Whitehead had reported to Kenney, "as of this date the Japanese sea lane to its captured empire from Hong Kong south is cut . . . while there is some clean-up work remaining to be done, namely small shipping around Hainan Island and along the China Coast, not many targets remain."

Out of the Night II, a black B-24M flying from Clark Field with the 63rd Squadron.

Although the Fifth had no commitment to attack the Chinese mainland, it was obvious to Whitehead that it would be hard to blockade the China Sea effectively without smashing enemy air bases along the coast. These fields sheltered the last aircraft which could be used to cover convoys, and also the heavily defended ports and harbors were being used as a refuge by shipping. Kenney wanted to begin the attack and by March 20 permission was granted to strike the Chinese mainland when other commitments had been met. The approved targets were Japanese installations and air bases in specific areas along the China and Indo-China coasts, the railroad between Saigon and Tourane, waterfront areas and supply bases at Hong Kong, Saigon, Canton, and other targets designated by Chennault. Whitehead's Liberators had hit the Canton airdromes, White Cloud and Tien-Ho, as secondary targets in March, and two groups of Liberators with fighter cover worked over Samah airdrome in Hainan Island on March 21. Attacks which were intended to cripple Japanese shipping repair facilities started on the last day of March, when B-24s hit Yulin Harbor. The Liberators were over Hong Kong for four straight days before they turned to Yulin again on April 6.

The campaign against Saigon began on April 19 when Thirteenth Air Force Liberators staged through Palawan and bombed the harbor. Three days later twenty Flying Circus B-24s hit the naval yards and shipping, and the Jolly Rogers blasted the dry docks, warehouses, and oil storage tanks the next day. The two groups joined forces against Saigon on April 25, and again on April 26. On May 3 both groups bombed the Texaco, Standard, Shell, and Socony-Vacuum oil installations. Meanwhile the radar B-24s, mediums, and fighters on shipping sweeps were finding little and turning to their secondary land targets. Japanese fighters were still on the coastal bases, and unescorted bombers might be intercepted, but the last fighter encounter occurred on April 2 over Hong Kong when P-51s claimed one destroyed and two probables.

When photo reconnaissance indicated that enemy air strength in the Hong Kong and Canton areas was increasing, it was interpreted as a Japanese decision to defend the area, and the heavy bombers went out on May 9; B-24s struck the White Cloud dispersals and revetments through cloud cover, while other planes bombed Tien-Ho airstrip. Four groups attacked the Canton airdromes the following day, and the count of enemy planes dropped again. The airdrome targets were allocated to the night bombers for random strikes.

Attacks on Indo-China's rail system began on May 7, when B-25s roared along the coastal railroad, bombing and strafing. The Liberators struck railroad bridges the next day, while Mitchells cleared the tracks. The heavy bombers attacked bridges along the same coastal stretch, and the Jolly Rogers and Flying Circus B-24s made effective strikes on marshaling yards on May 27. The next day the Jolly Rogers were again over the rail yards, and made strafing passes after expending their bombs. The two groups again combined against the railroad at Saigon on June 12.

The technique employed on these missions to the Asiatic mainland was usually mass strikes on key points, and although other commitments caused unusually long intervals between them, and while it had been anticipated that the China coast would yield targets of major importance, the Fifth was moving up to Okinawa, aimed at Japan itself.

The Shores of the Empire

The American forces now in the Philippines and on Iwo Jima and Okinawa had systematically driven the Japanese back across the Pacific to their home islands. To that point the Pacific war had been fought without a united command, but as the armadas gathered within striking distance of Japan itself, it seemed continuing division of authority could add to the cost of the final victory. Even though the war in Europe was finally over, Washington planners were uncertain about the best way to take Japan; after the Leyte operation they knew any move toward Tokyo must include provision of good bases for the preliminary air operations. There were seven different air forces engaged in the war against Japan—the Fifth, Seventh, Tenth, Eleventh, Thirteenth, Fourteenth, and Twentieth—and with the imminent movement of other units from Europe to the Pacific, reorganization became an urgent necessity. It was a difficult problem but President Roosevelt perhaps came close to solving it when he sent word to MacArthur via Kenney that he would have "a lot of work to do well to the north of the Philippines before very long."

After a great deal of argument a directive for a landing on Kyushu was spelled out on May 25, with a target date of November 1. For this landing MacArthur was assigned the "primary responsibility," which included control of the actual amphibious assault through appropriate naval commanders. He was directed to "cooperate" with Nimitz in planning the amphibious phase of the operation and in accord with the fragile relations developed over the years, the wording was careful throughout. Nimitz was instructed to "correlate" his plans with MacArthur . . . the Twentieth Air Force would "co-operate" in the execution of the operation and might be placed under the "direction" of either Nimitz or MacArthur for the support of their operations.

Kenney was the air force's most experienced and distinguished leader in the Pacific, and Far East Air Forces combined the three air forces which would carry the main burden of tactical operations in support of the invasion of Japan. As early as September 1944 Whitehead had realized the strategic importance of the Ryukyus for operations against Japan, and a study had determined which units could be based on Okinawa. Kenney and Whitehead both felt the enemy could be defeated without the use of forces from Europe if, as Whitehead put it, "we keep crowding him." Whitehead would not accept that the Japanese could be beaten solely by the B-29 raids burning out their cities, and he believed that carrier aircraft could neither blockade Japan nor adequately prepare Kyushu for invasion. Land-based air power in the Ryukyus was a necessity. "I naturally believe that the Fifth Air Force is the best equipped and best trained air force in the world to accomplish the job," he concluded.

When the capture of Okinawa began to lag shortly after the landings on April 1, the seizure of nearby Ie Shima, where there were three Japanese airstrips, was accelerated; troops were landed on April 16 and secured the small island after a six-day battle. With complete possession of Okinawa delayed until late June, the planes needed to support the ground campaign naturally had first claim to the captured air facilities. The fields on Okinawa were lightly surfaced and badly damaged, but Yontan was quickly patched up and Marine fighters were soon able to

The 35th Fighter Group switched to P-51D Mustangs in March 1945; *Mickey* is from the 41st Squadron. The best of the 35th's Thunderbolts were handed down to the 58th Fighter Group and the Mexican 201st Squadron, as the 348th Group's had been.

use it. At Kadena the situation was worse, but the strip was considered suitable for all-weather operations at the beginning of May.

Original plans called for eight airstrips on Okinawa and two on Ie Shima, and agreement reached between Nimitz and MacArthur required the Ryukyus airfields to be developed for fifty-one air groups, twenty-nine of them from the Fifth and Thirteenth Air Forces. It was a huge project, involving about twenty-five miles of paved airstrips and the movement of about five and a half million truckloads of coral and earth. Heavy rains at the end of May forced suspension of the airfield work until the middle of June but on July 11 Kenney could tell Arnold that new fields were "appearing like magic and construction was going on faster than I have ever seen it before." Marine, Navy, and Seventh Air Force units moved into the Ryukyus as soon as captured airfields could be prepared. Suspecting that Nimitz might try to monopolize space for defensive aircraft, Whitehead wanted to push his Fifth Air Force planes forward as soon as there was room for them. When Brigadier General David Hutchison opened his 308th Bomb Wing Headquarters on Okinawa on June 15 a flood of instructions alerted units in the Philippines. The 35th Fighter Group with its P-51s was at Yontan by July 2, after moving so fast that Nimitz was not aware of it until Hutchison filed intent for a second fighter sweep to Kyushu. On July 3 the P-51s swept the west coast of Kyushu, seeing only three floatplanes in the air. The Mustangs got them all, and the honor of claiming the first victory over Japan went to Captain Richard Cella.

After the initial burst of speed Whitehead insisted that aircrews not move forward until some sort of ground echelon was in place, and this slowed the northward movement. By the end of the war, four of the Fifth's fighter groups and two

Last used by Lieutenant Richard Benson, the 380th's *Embarrassed* was one of the most tenacious B-24s in the Fifth. (F. H. Nolta)

A Fortress from the 5th Emergency Rescue Group over the Philippines. Equipped with droppable lifeboats, these guardian angels would fly with strikes to within ten miles of the target, cruising at around one thousand feet and looking for aircraft in trouble. (Dennis G. Cooper)

night fighter squadrons had begun operations from the Ryukyus—the 8th, 35th, 58th, and 348th Fighter Groups and 418th and 421st Night Fighter Squadrons. They operated from improvised airfields, often flying from runways which were still under construction. By the end of July the Air Apaches and the 38th and 43rd Bomb Groups were flying from Ie Shima, with B-24s of the Red Raiders, Jolly Rogers, and Flying Circus on Okinawa.

Whitehead assumed command of Advon, Far East Air Forces, on July 16, and took over the running of the air war from Okinawa. His responsibility was broad —his planes were to strike at Japanese air power, deny the use of shipping lanes to the enemy, isolate Japan from Asia, disrupt communications in Kyushu and western Honshu, destroy or neutralize enemy concentrations and vital installations in the area, carry out aerial reconnaissance and photography, and provide air cover for naval forces on call. Whitehead had his own plan to crush enemy air power from Nagoya to the Siberian border in three phases of concentrated fighter and medium bomber operations, and after worthwhile air targets were finished, he intended to unleash his fighters and attack bombers against rail communications. However, although he kept these intentions from the Navy, he found himself ordered to concentrate on Kyushu airfields to cover carrier strikes against Japan. Whitehead's continued dependence on Fifth Air Force personnel made his headquarters basically another outpost of the Fifth, and it was run the way it always had been; one Seventh Air Force intelligence officer claimed targets were "pulled out of Whitehead's back pocket."

The 348th Fighter Group had received their Mustangs in January 1945. Lieutenant Tommy Sheets' *Doris Marie II* was one of four P-51s in Colonel William Dunham's flight over Kyushu on August 1, 1945. Sighting about twenty enemy fighters below, the Mustangs dived, and both Dunham and Sheets got two Franks on their first pass. On the fuselage is the 460th's Black Ram insignia. (Bob Stevens)

"There Are No Civilians in Japan"

When Fifth Fighter Command had been flying against Kyushu for six weeks it had destroyed only thirty-two Japanese planes in combat. Only one plane was lost to interceptors, four to flak, and fourteen more to unknown or operational causes. Finding little real opposition in the air, the fighters quickly turned their attacks to railways, bridges, shipping, and any targets of opportunity they could find. On July 21 the Fifth had decided there were no civilians in Japan and that the entire population was a proper target—intelligence had learned that all men aged between fifteen and sixty and all women from seventeen to forty were being molded into a "People's Volunteer Corps."

Fifth and Seventh Air Force bombers struck enemy airfields and railroad yards on Kyushu and in the Shanghai and Hangchow areas of China. The Fifth's fighters attacked shipping off the China coast and the Mustangs flew five sweeps to the coast of Korea. Night-flying B-24s of the 63rd Squadron went into action against Korea late in July.

On August 4, two days before the first atomic bomb was dropped on Hiroshima, Fifth Air Force pilots told of Japanese civilians waving white flags from fields and villages. The next day the Fifth and Seventh combined to strike Tarumizu, where a factory was believed to be producing suicide rocket planes. One hundred and seventy-nine B-25s and A-26s with nearly one hundred and fifty P-51s buried the town and factory under explosives and napalm.

Windy City Kitty, elaborately painted B-24 of the 65th Squadron, taxies out along Ie Shima's glaring strip. (Al Lomer)

With the rocky outcrop known as "Nellie's Tit" as a backdrop, the 17th Recon Squadron's *My Buck* comes into Ie Shima. This B-25J flew sixty-five missions and carries the squadron insignia as part of her tail marking. (Albert Gruer)

The Fifth got the Convair B-32 Dominator, which no one else seemed to want, to try out in combat. This very heavy "super Liberator" had features which suited the Fifth's airfields—the Davis wing and reversible pitch propellers. When testing ended in June 1945 the reports were hardly glowing, but Whitehead recommended the 312th Group be equipped with the aircraft. Only the 386th Squadron had converted before the end of the war and this B-32, *Hobo Queen II,* was in on their first and last battles. On August 18, 1945, she was one of the two B-32s on reconnaissance over Japan. Lieutenant John Anderson, piloting the other Dominator, dropped down to take a closer look at the atom bomb damage to Hiroshima. Fourteen Tojos and Zekes jumped Lieutenant James Klein and his crew in *Hobo Queen,* but were driven off by the heavy return fire. Down below, Anderson was in trouble with one engine shot out, a crewman dead and two more seriously wounded, but both B-32s made it back to Okinawa.

Wolf Pack B-25Js, a small part of the huge air armada gathering to strike Japan, line up for takeoff from Okinawa on August 4, 1945.

The Japanese radio announced their desire for peace on August 10, and the next day President Truman suspended B-29 operations. Far East Air Forces were allowed to carry on, and were ordered to attack on August 14, but the next day a cease-fire order came through and efforts were made to call back the planes already out. Reconnaissance had to be continued and the crews were to fight if they were attacked; on August 17 four 312th Group B-32 Dominators, flying one of their first missions from Okinawa, were attacked by fifteen enemy fighters while reconnoitering Tokyo. The huge B-32s were again attacked the next day.

Then at twelve forty-five on August 19 two white Bettys, marked with green crosses, landed at Ie Shima with Japanese envoys sent to arrange the surrender. Surveillance missions were continued without incident, except that Colonel Clay Tice, commander of the 49th Fighter Group, and another pilot, violating their orders under a plea for the need of fuel, landed at Nittagahara airdrome on Kyushu, where the Japanese greeted them with candy. The date was August 25, and the report Tice made was meticulously worded: "I called Jukebox 36 [B-17 of the 6th Air Sea Rescue Squadron], and informed him of my intentions and requested assistance. I landed at Nittagahara, four hundred and fifty miles from base, at 1205. There were no Japanese in sight after landing and I checked the gas supply in Flight Officer Hall's plane. He had dropped his external tank previous to informing me of his difficulty and, upon inspection, I found that his wing tanks were dry and I estimated his fuel at one hundred and fifty gallons in mains and reserves by visual check of fuel indicators and tanks. At 1305 we were contacted by officers and men of the Japanese Army and although conversation was difficult, we were greeted in a friendly manner. Jukebox 36 landed at approximately 1315 and with a fuel pump and hose furnished by the Japanese, we transferred approximately two hundred and sixty gallons of gas from the B-17 to the P-38. After landing at Nittagahara, I dropped my external tank on the runway still containing twenty-five to

General Whitehead tells the 475th, "The president has just announced that the Japanese have surrendered and the war is over . . . you men have done a splendid job, but our work is not yet over. We must guarantee the peace . . . we will move to Tokyo quickly, as soon as arrangements can be made. We who have spearheaded the fight to Japan all the way from Darwin and Port Moresby will be the occupational air force . . . when you get there, go in as conquerors, dress like conquerors, act like conquerors. Wear your Fifth Air Force patches—the Nips have heard of us, now let them see the kind of soldiers they were up against." (Dennis Glen Cooper)

fifty gallons. I had used but fifteen minutes of my internal gas supply at that time. Flight Officer Hall and I were airborne behind the B-17 at 1445 . . ."

It was somehow fitting that 49th Group Lightnings were the first American aircraft to land in Japan. Kenney quickly saw the report from Whitehead and "rather enjoyed" it and felt that, "reading between the lines," Whitehead did too.

The enemy surrendered while the Far East Air Forces were still building up in

On August 19, 1945, two Bettys, freshly painted white with green crosses, landed on Ie Shima in the early afternoon. The Japanese peace delegation drew a huge crowd as they left their aircraft to board two C-54s bound for Manila.

the Ryukyus. The Fifth had flown less than two thousand sorties against Kyushu, and losses to the enemy were incredibly light—only ten planes in July, and twenty-one in August.

* * *

On September 2, 1945, General George C. Kenney and other air force officers taking part in the surrender ceremony boarded a destroyer at Yokohama and went out to the battleship USS *Missouri,* anchored in the middle of Tokyo Bay. After about half an hour the eleven Japanese who were to sign the surrender came aboard and formed a little square before the table on which the documents awaited them. General Douglas MacArthur walked to the microphone on the opposite end of the table. He made a short speech and told the defeated enemy to sign. The Japanese Minister of Foreign Affairs, dressed in a frock coat and striped trousers, seemed nervous as he glanced from one paper to another, evidently confused about which he should look at first. MacArthur's icy voice broke the silence: "Sutherland . . . show him where to sign."

Appendix

Fighter Aces of the Fifth Air Force

The following list of fighter pilots with five or more victories, by group, is based on accepted records. Some pilots had achieved victories before they came to groups associated with the Fifth—"Buzz" Wagner and Jack Donaldson had scored in the Philippines, George Welch and Harry Brown at Pearl Harbor, and Andy Reynolds and George Kiser in Java. Other pilots, like Sid Woods, Joe Kruzel, and George Preddy, went on to become aces in other air forces in other theaters, and pilots like John Landers increased their tallies. Later in the war, pilots came from European air forces with victories credited to them, often under different criteria to those established in the Fifth—among them were the 3rd Air Commando pilots Walker Mahurin and Louis Curdes. Fifth Air Force pilots often flew in more than one group, or moved on to higher organizations, so in this listing they are included with the unit they were most closely associated with.

8th Fighter Group

Jay T. Robbins	22
George S. Welch	16
Edward Cragg	15
Cyril F. Homer	15
Kenneth G. Ladd	12
Richard L. West	12
Cornelius M. Smith, Jr.	11
William K. Giroux	10
Allen E. Hill	9
William A. Gardner	8
John L. Jones	8
Boyd D. Wagner	8
Burnell W. Adams	7
John S. Dunaway	7
Edwin L. DeGraffenreid	6
Lee R. Everhart	6
Donald C. McGee	6
Paul C. Murphey, Jr.	6
Lynn E. Witt, Jr.	6
Robert H. Adams	5
Jennings L. Myers	5
Kenneth R. Pool	5
C. B. Ray	5
Louis Schriber	5
Clifton H. Troxell	5
Thomas J. Lynch	20

35th Fighter Group

Kenneth C. Sparks	11
Paul M. Stanch	10
Leroy V. Grosshuesch	8
Richard E. Smith	7
William H. Strand	7
Stanley O. Andrews	6
Ellis C. Baker, Jr.	6
Hoyt A. Eason	6
Charles S. Gallup	6
John H. Lane	6
James D. Mugavero	6
Francis E. Dubisher	5
Alvaro J. Hunter	5
Curran L. Jones	5
Charles W. King	5
William F. McDonough	5
Richard C. Suehr	5
Charles P. Sullivan	5
Robert R. Yaeger, Jr.	5

49th Fighter Group

Richard I. Bong	40
Gerald R. Johnson	22
Robert M. DeHaven	14
James A. Watkins	12

49th Fighter Group (cont.)

Robert W. Aschenbrener	10
Ernest A. Harris	10
Andrew J. Reynolds	10
Grover E. Fanning	9
George C. Kiser	9
Joel B. Paris, III	9
Robert H. White	9
Fernely H. Damstrom	8
John G. O'Neill	8
Arland Stanton	8
William J. Hennon	7
James B. Morehead	7
Sammy A. Pierce	7
Elliott E. Dent, Jr.	6
William C. Drier	6
James P. Hagerstrom	6
Robert L. Howard	6
Wallace R. Jordan	6
John D. Landers	6
Donald W. Meuten	6
Ralph H. Wandrey	6
Ellis W. Wright, Jr.	6
Ernest J. Ambort	5
Nial K. Castle	5
Warren D. Curton	5
William C. Day, Jr.	5
Frederick E. Dick	5
I. B. Jack Donaldson	5
Marion E. Felts	5
Nelson D. Flack, Jr.	5
Cheatham W. Gupton	5
Alfred B. Lewelling	5
Milden E. Mathre	5
Leslie D. Nelson	5
Robert H. Vaught, Jr.	5

348th Fighter Group

Neel E. Kearby	22
William B. Dunham	16
William M. Banks	9
Walter G. Benz, Jr.	8
Edward F. Roddy	8
Robert R. Rowland	8
Samuel V. Blair	7
George A. Davis	7
Marvin E. Grant	7
John T. Moore	7
Richard H. Fleischer	6
William B. Foulis, Jr.	6

348th Fighter Group (cont.)

George Della	5
Myron M. Hnatio	5
Robert H. Knapp	5
Lawrence F. O'Neill	5
Edward S. Popek	5
Robert C. Sutcliffe	5

475th Fighter Group

Thomas B. McGuire, Jr.	38
Charles H. MacDonald	27
Daniel T. Roberts	15
Francis J. Lent	11
John S. Loisel	11
Elliot Summer	10
Frederick F. Champlin	9
Perry J. Dahl	9
Joseph M. Forester	9
Meryl M. Smith	9
David W. Allen	8
Frederick A. Harris	8
Kenneth F. Hart	8
Zach W. Dean	7
Vincent T. Elliott	7
Jack A. Fisk	7
Verl E. Jett	7
Warren R. Lewis	7
John E. Purdy	7
Calvin C. Wire	7
Edward J. Czarnecki	6
William M. Gresham	6
William C. Gronemeyer	6
James C. Ince	6
Paul W. Lucas	6
Joseph T. McKeon	6
John Pietz, Jr.	6
Horace B. Reeves	6
John C. Smith	6
Arthur E. Wenige	6
Harry W. Brown	5
Vivian A. Cloud	5
Harry L. Condon	5
Grover D. Gholson	5
Marion F. Kirby	5
Lowell C. Lutton	5
Jack C. Mankin	5
Franklin H. Monk	5
Paul V. Morriss	5
Franklin A. Nichols	5
John A. Tilley	5

82nd Tactical *Reconnaissance Squadron*		*418th Night Fighter* *Squadron*	
William A. Shomo	8	Carroll C. Smith	7

Ed Cragg, Tom Lynch, Neel Kearby, Thomas McGuire, Danny Roberts, Billy Gresham, and John Smith were killed in action. Richard Bong, Ken Sparks, Jerry Johnson, George Welch, and "Buzz" Wagner all died in aircraft accidents during and after the war.

Contributing Fifth Air Force Veterans

Loyde H. Adams, 90th Bomb Group
Carroll R. Anderson, 475th Fighter Group
Dean H. Anholt, 19th Bomb Group
Kenneth E. Ball, 3rd Attack Group
Albert D. Bartlett, Fifth Fighter Command
Roger R. Beaty, Fifth Air Force
A. J. Beck, Fifth Air Force
George Beck, 433rd Troop Carrier Group
James H. Beck, 43rd Bomb Group
Val Bohnenberger, 22nd Bomb Group
Adrian S. Bottge, 3rd Attack Group
Harry W. Brown, 49th Fighter Group, 475th Fighter Group
Richard W. Burke, 43rd Bomb Group
John E. Bush, 38th Bomb Group
Nial K. Castle, 49th Fighter Group
William H. Cather, 345th Bomb Group
Edward J. Chudoba, 3rd Attack Group
M. H. Clay, Jr., 90th Bomb Group
Dennis Glen Cooper, 475th Fighter Group
David T. Corts, 421st Night Fighter Squadron
Melton N. Crawford, 22nd Bomb Group
Joseph W. Dally, 380th Bomb Group
Anthony J. DeAngelis, 43rd Bomb Group
Robert M. DeHaven, 49th Fighter Group
Thomas H. Dunbar, 90th Bomb Group
David W. Ecoff, 20th Combat Mapping Squadron
Robert Edgar, 22nd Bomb Group
Richard H. Ellis, 3rd Attack Group
Maury Eppstein, 345th Bomb Group
Jim Fain, 380th Bomb Group
Joe Fetherston, 348th Fighter Group
Thomas C. Fetter, 90th Bomb Group

John W. Fields, 19th Bomb Group
Al Fischer, 43rd Bomb Group
Roland T. Fisher, 43rd Bomb Group
Richard H. Fleischer, 348th Fighter Group
Donald E. Fry, 22nd Bomb Group
Francis A. Gavaghan, 3rd Attack Group
Ed Gavin, 38th Bomb Group
Walter A. Gaylor, 22nd Bomb Group
James E. Graham, 380th Bomb Group
George R. Grover, 380th Bomb Group
Larry Guzick, 6th Emergency Rescue Squadron
James B. Hall, Fifth Fighter Command
Arthur E. Handel, 22nd Bomb Group
Clifford Hanna, 345th Bomb Group
John P. Henebry, 3rd Attack Group
Lawrence J. Hickey, 345th Bomb Group
Edward Hillman, 380th Bomb Group
Fred H. Hitchcock, Jr., 79th Airdrome Squadron
Fred G. Hoffman, 81st Air Depot Group
Rich Howard, 43rd Bomb Group
Charles W. Howe, 3rd Attack Group
David B. Hutchins, 475th Fighter Group
John Irick, 38th Bomb Group
Verl E. Jett, 8th Fighter Group, 475th Fighter Group
Curran L. Jones, 35th Fighter Group
Thomas H. Jones, 312th Bomb Group
John Kasper, 3rd Attack Group
George C. Kenney, Fifth Air Force
Charles W. King, 35th Fighter Group
James L. Klein, 312th Bomb Group
Sherman Kuharske, 22nd Bomb Group
Jerry Lahmsen, 345th Bomb Group
Aleron H. Larson, 22nd Bomb Group

George Laven, Jr., 49th Fighter Group
Adolph P. Leirer, 22nd Bomb Group
Allan W. Lomer, 110th Tactical Recon
Squadron
Nicholas P. Loverro, 22nd Bomb Group
Bill Lybrand, 90th Bomb Group
Oliver S. McAfee, 475th Fighter
Group
Robert J. McClurkin, 110th Tactical
Recon Squadron
Marvin L. McCrory, 22nd Bomb Group
Robert F. McMahon, 35th Fighter
Group
J. Harrison Mangan, 3rd Attack Group
Al G. Merkling, 20th Combat Mapping
Squadron
H. Ross Miller, 3rd Attack Group
William K. Miller, 22nd Bomb Group
Ben Millis, 475th Fighter Group
Foster Mitchell, 22nd Bomb Group
Robert V. Moody, 375th Troop Carrier
Group
James B. Morehead, 49th Fighter
Group
Robert C. Morrison, 22nd Bomb Group
Paul C. Murphey, Jr., 8th Fighter
Group
Charles E. Newton, 3rd Attack Group
Franklin A. Nichols, 49th Fighter
Group, 475th Fighter Group
Clarence E. O'Connor, 19th Bomb
Group, 43rd Bomb Group
Philip G. Ostrander, 380th Bomb Group
Dean S. Page, 43rd Bomb Group
Alexander Panzano, 3rd Attack Group
Roy Parker, 22nd Bomb Group
H. C. Parry, 3rd Attack Group
R. J. Peters, 22nd Bomb Group
James T. Pettus, 43rd Bomb Group
Sammy A. Pierce, 49th Fighter Group
Glenn Pruitt, 17th Recon Squadron
Jack Purdy, 475th Fighter Group
A. Bill Ritenour, 43rd Bomb Group

Arthur H. Rogers, 90th Bomb Group
Bert S. Rosenbaum, 345th Bomb Group
Robert J. Rouse, 35th Fighter Group
Yale Saffro, 8th Fighter Group
R. J. Sanderson, 90th Bomb Group
Albert W. Schinz, 35th Fighter Group,
475th Fighter Group
Charles E. Shipe, 308th Bomb Wing
Walter C. Sismilich, 43rd Bomb Group
J. C. Slaton, 49th Fighter Group
Carroll C. Smith, 418th Night Fighter
Squadron
Howard Stackpole, 22nd Bomb Group
Bob Stevens, 348th Fighter Group
E. P. Stevens, 43rd Bomb Group, 20th
Combat Mapping Squadron
Robert Stiastny, 12th Air Depot Group
J. B. Stone, 90th Bomb Group
Ralph W. Swindle, 90th Bomb Group
Larry Tanberg, 38th Bomb Group
Merrill E. Taylor, 90th Bomb Group
Clay Tice, 49th Fighter Group
John A. Tilley, 475th Fighter Group
Clinton U. True, 345th Bomb Group
William H. True, 43rd Bomb Group
Bernie Ussett, 43rd Bomb Group
Al Vacaro, 417th Bomb Group, 6th
Emergency Rescue Squadron
Roger E. Vargas, 43rd Bomb Group
Arthur C. Vogt, 3rd Attack Group
Leo Walbrum, 90th Bomb Group
J. V. Wallace, 38th Bomb Group
Ralph H. Wandrey, 49th Fighter
Group
Joseph R. Waterman, 345th Bomb
Group
Burton D. West, 38th Bomb Group
Robert P. Willis, 38th Bomb Group
Sidney S. Woods, 49th Fighter Group
Wiley O. Woods, Jr., 90th Bomb Group
William E. Wrenn, 20th Combat
Mapping Squadron

Acknowledgments

I have wanted to write this book for many years, and as time passed, much of the foundation was laid during the course of other projects. This enabled me to devote my efforts largely to areas which were new to me over the past few years. It was fascinating work and I hope that I have been able to add something worthwhile to the record.

There are gaps in the story but I have tried to ensure that the information here is accurate. It would be difficult to tell the entire story of the Fifth in one book, and there are blank spots in the available records, but knowing what General Kenney did to the last person who told him "it was about time these combat units learned how to do their paper work properly," I'm not going to complain. With or without putting every detail on paper, the Fifth wrote an indelible record. If readers of this book can add to the record, either the over-all story or fascinating sidelights like the use of B-17s as armed transports, I would be delighted to hear from them.

As I tried to collect the stories of the men and planes I was assisted by many people. When General Kenney wrote that he would "do his damnedest" to help it meant a great deal to me. The general told his own story in *General Kenney Reports,* and his words appear often in this book because I admire his writing as much as I admire the man himself.

My books would probably not exist without the co-operation of the Department of Defense, and the assistance I receive is magnificent. Once again Miss Bettie Sprigg and Mrs. Virginia Fincik have made that part of the work a pleasure for me. Other organizations helped in important ways—the Australian War Memorial has a fine historical collection which quite naturally touches often on the Fifth, and Mr. A. J. Sweeting has continually helped me with photos and information. The Memorial's collection of unofficial unit histories is excellent, and the gracious library staff helped me make full use of the brief time I had there. Dick Turner of the American Fighter Aces Association eased my entry into a sphere which was more or less new to me, at least as a writer. Royal Frey and Chuck Worman at the Air Force Museum in Ohio helped again whenever I asked, and Bruce Hoy of the Papua New Guinea Air Museum shared the valuable material he has assembled. The RAAF Directorate of Public Relations, through Mr. J. G. Sebastian, supplied several fine pictures which were not available elsewhere.

Bob Brooks joined this project in the earliest days and has worked on it continually, supplying material from his collection of records and background material, as well as helping in many other ways. His contribution to the book is hard to overestimate.

Other interested people who sent along material either on request or simply because they wanted to help were Carl Bong, Stewart Bolling, Al Clemens, Roger Freeman, Bill Hess, Michel Lavigne, Colonel Al Lynn, Greg Moreira, Lew Nalls, F. H. Nolta, Larry Reineke, Frank Smith, Jerre Vliet, and Doug Wallace.

Colonel Art Rogers of the 90th Bomb Group gave me his full support; not only did he supply photographs and material from his own souvenirs, but he also gave the project his backing through the 90th's veterans' association. The Jolly Rogers really went all out—Harry Clay called me long-distance to see if his material had arrived safely and would be useful to me, and the answers to his questions are obvious in the pages of this book. He was not the only one to assist in many ways—when I was having trouble locating photos of fighter aircraft, Tom Fetter gathered material from several people and sent it along, and Jim Stone, Mel Taylor, and Wiley Woods all helped greatly. If I could have asked anything more of the Jolly Rogers I cannot think what it might have been.

The same applied to other organizations of Fifth Air Force veterans—the 49th Fighter Group's Ralph Wandrey, Bob DeHaven, Clay Tice, and Sid Woods supplied the kind of help I could not get elsewhere. Larry Hickey, Maury Eppstein, and Cliff Hanna of the Air Apaches answered many questions about the 345th, and Larry's records of the group are obviously without equal.

From the 475th Fighter Group's veterans came Harry Brown, Verl Jett, Dave Hutchins, Oliver McAfee, John Tilley . . . and Carroll R. Anderson. Andy made a very special contribution. He is not only a fine writer who allowed me to use his published work as source material, he also offered a great deal of information from the extensive files he has built for his forthcoming history of Satan's Angels. His stories *Black Sunday, Mission to Kavieng,* and *Suicide at Cape Waios* are exemplary pieces of historical writing and, thanks to Andy's kindness, provided a sound basis for me.

Walt Gaylor's 22nd Bomb Group *Newsletter* has been fattened by my requests for information over the last couple of years, and other Red Raiders like Adolph Leirer, Bill Miller, and Roy Parker—nearly my neighbor here in Sydney—made my job easier.

Charles King patiently detailed the early story of the 39th Fighter Squadron, imparting more information than I ever expected from a single source, and Al Lomer of the 110th Recon Squadron provided similarly broad coverage of his old unit. Happily, I finally managed to meet a combat artist by the name of Al Merkling—thanks to Dave Ecoff, who supplied his serial number from old records of the 20th Combat Mapping Squadron; Royal Frey, who came up with a 1945 address; and Joseph Golden of the Philadelphia police, who checked the old neighborhood, called Al long-distance in Union, New Jersey, and asked him if it would be all right to give his current address to an Australian writer. General Jock Henebry reminisced about the minimum-altitude operations of the 3rd Attack Group both on tape and during a visit to Sydney, and his help, coupled with that of General Richard H. Ellis, then Vice-Chief of Staff of the Air Force, was invaluable. Lucky Stevens and I talked over a few cans of beer until the early hours of the morning, and he gave me an insight into the 43rd Bomb Group and their B-17s in the days of Ken McCullar.

Without the help of people who were part of the story this book would be a cold and colorless piece of history. Scores of veterans of the Fifth searched their attics, basements, and memories and sent along material for me to use as I thought best, and I have listed them together because it would be impossible to thank them all here.

War correspondents wrote much of the background material which I researched during the preparation of this book. I am bound to acknowledge International News Services' Lee Van Atta, who flew many missions with the Grim Reapers and captured their kind of war in words, and Charles Rawlings, whose sensitive stories of the Jolly Rogers in *The Saturday Evening Post* are not easily forgotten.

John Preston's paintings greatly enhance this book, and as usual it was a pleasure to work with him. John's own knowledge of the subject always helps greatly and I could not ask for a more professional fellow worker.

Harold Kuebler, my editor at Doubleday, has a deep interest in these books, which makes a great deal of difference to an author. He has taught me a lot and perhaps this book will prove easier to edit than my previous one.

My wife Sandra has typed well over one thousand pages of roughs, drafts, captions, and final manuscript. For Sandra the turning point in the Southwest Pacific war came far later than it did for the Allied forces, and I do not know how I would ever achieve anything without her.

My intention throughout this book has been to try to capture the essence of the Fifth Air Force. If the photos and stories are in some way reminders of the days that are no more, when the deafening roar of leering B-25 strafers filled the heavy, humid air, I will be satisfied. I only wish I had been able to tell it all.

STEVE BIRDSALL

Sydney, Australia

Bibliography

Birdsall, Steve, *Log of the Liberators,* New York, Doubleday, 1973
Caidin, Martin, *Fork-tailed Devil,* New York, Ballantine, 1971
Cather, William H., *Gunfight at Rabaul,* Birmingham, Cather, 1974
Craven, W. F., and Cate, J. L., *The Army Air Forces in World War II,* Vols. I, IV, V, Chicago, University of Chicago Press, 1948
Crawford, William, Jr., *Gore and Glory,* Philadelphia, David McKay, 1944
Gillison, Douglas, *Royal Australian Air Force 1939–1942,* Canberra, Australian War Memorial, 1962
Hardison, Priscilla, *The Suzy-Q,* Boston, Houghton Mifflin, 1943
Haugland, Vern, *The AAF Against Japan,* New York, Harper & Bros., 1948
Hess, William N., *The American Aces of World War II and Korea,* New York, Arco, 1968
————, *Pacific Sweep,* New York, Doubleday, 1974
Jablonski, Edward, *Flying Fortress,* New York, Doubleday, 1965
Kenney, George C., *General Kenney Reports,* New York, Duell, Sloan and Pearce, 1949
————, *The Saga of Pappy Gunn,* New York, Duell, Sloan and Pearce, 1959
————, *Dick Bong, Ace of Aces,* New York, Duell, Sloan and Pearce, 1960
Lindbergh, Charles A., *The Wartime Journals of Charles A. Lindbergh,* New York, Harcourt, Brace, Jovanovich, 1970
Maurer, Maurer, *Air Force Combat Units of World War II,* New York, Franklin Watts, 1963
————, *Combat Squadrons of the Air Forces World War II,* Washington, U. S. Government Printing Office, 1969
Odgers, George, *Air War Against Japan,* Canberra, Australian War Memorial, 1957
Robinson, Pat, *The Fight for New Guinea,* New York, Random House, 1943
Rogers, Arthur H., *Jolly Roger* (unpublished manuscript), 1944
Sims, Edward H., *American Aces,* New York, Harper & Bros., 1958
Wandrey, Ralph H., *Fighter Pilot,* Mason City, Stoyles Press, 1950

Unofficial Combat Unit Histories

Fifth Air Force, *The 5th Over the Southwest Pacific,* Los Angeles, AAF Publications, 1947
Fifth Air Force, *The Menace from Moresby,* San Angelo, Newsfoto, 1950
Fifth Fighter Command, *Pacific Sweep,* Sydney, F. H. Johnston, 1945
3rd Attack Group, *The Reaper's Harvest,* Sydney, Halstead Press, 1945
8th Photo Squadron, *The Diary of the 8th Photo Squadron,* New York, Ad Press, 1945
9th Fighter Squadron, *The Flying Knights,* Sydney, Angus and Robertson, 1944
17th Recon Squadron, *Strike,* Sydney, Jackson & O'Sullivan, 1945

22nd Bomb Group, *The Marauder,* Sydney, Halstead Press, 1944

41st Troop Carrier Squadron, *Downwind,* Philadelphia, Westbrook Publishing, 1950

43rd Bomb Group, *Down Under,* Sydney, Angus and Robertson, 1945

54th Troop Carrier Wing, *Moresby to Manila via Troop Carrier,* Sydney, Angus and Robertson, 1945

57th Troop Carrier Squadron, *Saga of the Biscuit Bomber,* Sydney, Halstead Press, 1945

67th Troop Carrier Squadron, *Sky Train,* Sydney, Angus and Robertson, 1945

71st Bomb Squadron, *The Wolf Pack,* Unknown Publisher

89th Bomb Squadron, *Altitude Minimum,* Sydney, Angus and Robertson, 1945

90th Bomb Group, *The Jolly Rogers,* Sydney, John Sands, 1944

308th Bomb Wing, *From Dobodura to Okinawa,* San Angelo, Newsfoto, 1946

319th Bomb Squadron, *Asterperious,* Sydney, Angus and Robertson, 1944

320th Bomb Squadron, *Moby Dick Heavy Bombardment Squadron,* San Francisco, Schwabacher-Frey, 1945

321st Bomb Squadron, *Bombs Away,* Sydney, John Sands, 1944

342nd Fighter Squadron, *342nd Fighter Squadron,* Jacksonville, Douglas Print, 1945

345th Bomb Group, *Warpath,* San Angelo, Newsfoto, 1946

380th Bomb Group, *The Flying Circus,* New York, Commanday-Roth, 1946

400th Bomb Squadron, *The Black Pirates,* Sydney, John Sands, 1944

417th Bomb Group, *The Sky Lancer,* Sydney, John Sands, 1946

433rd Troop Carrier Group, *Back Load,* Sydney, Halstead Press, 1945

475th Fighter Group, *Satan's Angels,* Sydney, Angus and Robertson, 1946

Index